WEBSTER'S
NEW
SPANISH-ENGLISH
ENGLISH-SPANISH
DICTIONARY

Published by
The Popular Group, LLC
1700 Broadway
New York, NY 10019

Publishing Consultant: Charles M. Levine
Design and Composition: Charlotte Staub

Published by arrangement with K DICTIONARIES LTD
http://kdictionaries.com

FOR K DICTIONARIES
Project Manager: Ilan J. Kernerman
Editor: Juan José García Pañero
Database Administrator: Vladimír Benko

ISBN: 1-59027-079-7

Printed in the United States of America

9 8 7 6 5 4 3 2 1

SPANISH-ENGLISH DICTIONARY

A

a *prep.* **1.** to **2.** into **3.** in **4.** at **5.** on **6.** with

abad *noun m.* abbot

abadesa *noun f.* abbess

abadía *noun f.* abbey

abajo *adv.* **1.** down **2.** downstairs **3.** below **4.** under **5.** beneath
—**cuesta abajo** downhill
—**hacia abajo** downward

abajo *interj.* down with!

abalanzarse *verb.* to rush forward

abandonado, -da *adj.* **1.** abandoned, deserted **2.** derelict **3.** neglected

abandonar *verb.* **1.** to abandon **2.** desert **3.** leave **4.** neglect **5.** give up **6.** renounce
—**abandonarse a** to abandon oneself to

abandono *noun m.* **1.** abandonment **2.** neglect **3.** withdrawal, resignation

abanicar *verb.* to fan

abanico *noun m.* fan

abaratar *verb.* to lower the price of

abarcar *verb.* **1.** to cover **2.** include

abarrotado, -da *adj.* **1.** packed **2.** crowded

abarrotar *verb.* to pack

abastecer *verb.* **1.** to supply **2.** provide **3.** stock

abastecimiento *noun m.* **1.** supply, provision **2.** supplying

abatido, -da *adj.* depressed

abatir *verb.* **1.** to knock down, demolish **2.** depress

abdicar *verb.* to abdicate

abdomen *noun m.* abdomen

abdominal *adj.* abdominal

abecé *noun m.* ABC

abecedario *noun m.* alphabet

abeja *noun f.* bee

abertura *noun f.* **1.** opening **2.** hole

abiertamente *adv.* openly

abierto, -ta *adj.* open

abofetear *verb.* to slap

abogado, -da *noun.* lawyer, attorney

abolición *noun f.* abolition

abolir *verb.* to abolish

abolladura *noun f.* dent

abonar *verb.* **1.** to pay **2.** fertilize
—**abonarse** to subscribe

abono *noun m.* **1.** payment, installment **2.** fertilizer, manure **3.** subscription, season ticket

abordar *verb.* **1.** to tackle **2.** deal with

aborrecer *verb.* to loathe, hate

abortar *verb.* **1.** to abort, foil, frustrate **2.** have an abortion, have a miscarriage

aborto *noun m.* **1.** abortion **2.** miscarriage

abrazadera *noun f.* brace, clamp

abrazar *verb.* **1.** to embrace, hug **2.** adopt

abrazo *noun m.* embrace, hug

abreviatura *noun f.* abbreviation

abrigar *verb.* **1.** to shelter, protect **2.** keep warm **3.** cherish, harbor
—**abrigarse 1.** to take shelter **2.** wrap oneself up

abrigo *noun m.* **1.** coat **2.** shelter

abril *noun m.* April

abrillantar *verb.* to polish

abrir *verb.* **1.** to open **2.** unlock **3.** undo

abrochar *verb.* to button, fasten
—**abrocharse** to button, tie up

abrumador, -dora *adj.* devastating, overwhelming, crushing

abrumar *verb.* **1.** to overwhelm **2.** oppress

abrupto, -ta *adj.* abrupt

absolutamente *adv.* absolutely

absoluto, -ta *adj.* absolute
—**en absoluto** not at all

absolver *verb.* **1.** to absolve **2.** acquit, clear

absorber *verb.* to absorb, soak up

absorción *noun f.* absorption

absorto, -ta *adj.* absorb

abstracto, -ta *adj.* abstract

absurdo, -da *adj.* absurd

abuela *noun f.* grandmother

abuelo *noun m.* grandfather
—**abuelos** grandparents

abultar *verb.* to bulge

abundancia *noun f.* abundance

abundante *adj.* abundant, plentiful

abundar *verb.* to abound, be plentiful

aburrido, -da *adj.* 1. boring, tedious 2. bored, fed up

aburrimiento *noun m.* boredom, tedium

aburrir *verb.* to bore
—**aburrirse** to be bored, get bored

abusar (de) *verb.* 1. to abuse 2. take advantage of

abuso *noun m.* abuse

acá *adv.* here, over here

acabado *noun m.* finish

acabado, -da *adj.* finished, done, complete, over

acabar *verb.* to finish, complete, end
—**acabarse** 1. to finish, come to an end 2. run out
—**acabar de** to just have

academia *noun f.* academy

académico, -ca *noun.* academic, academician

académico, -ca *adj.* academic

acallar *verb.* to quiet, silence

acalorado, -da *adj.* heated

acalorarse *verb.* 1. to get hot 2. get worked up, get excited

acampar *verb.* to camp

acantilado *noun m.* cliff

acariciar *verb.* to caress, stroke, pet

acarrear *verb.* 1. to carry, haul 2. bring, give rise to

acaso *adv.* perhaps
—**por si acaso** just in case

acceder *verb.* 1. to agree 2. access, gain access to

accesible *adj.* accessible, attainable

acceso *noun m.* 1. access, entry 2. admittance, entrance

accesorio *noun m.* accessory

accidentado, -da *adj.* 1. rough, uneven 2. troubled, eventful

accidental *adj.* accidental

accidente *noun m.* accident

acción *noun m.* 1. action 2. act, deed 3. share, stock

accionista *noun mf.* shareholder, stockholder

ace *noun m.* ace

acebo *noun m.* holly

aceite *noun m.* oil

aceituna *noun f.* olive

aceleración *noun f.* acceleration

acelerado, -da *adj.* intensive, accelerated

acelerar *verb.* 1. to accelerate, speed up 2. hasten 3. hurry

acento *noun m.* 1. accent 2. stress, emphasis

acentuar *verb.* 1. to accent 2. stress, emphasize

aceptable *adj.* acceptable

aceptación *noun f.* acceptance

aceptar *verb.* 1. to accept 2. approve

acera *noun f.* sidewalk

acerca de *prep.* about

acercamiento *noun m.* 1. approach 2. rapprochement

acercar *verb.* 1. to bring closer 2. take
—**acercarse** to approach, get closer

acero *noun m.* steel

acertado, -da *adj.* correct, accurate

achaque *noun m.* ailment, malady

ácido *noun m.* acid

ácido, -da *adj.* sour, acid

acierto *noun m.* 1. correct answer 2. good hit

aclamación *noun f.* acclaim, acclamation

aclamar *verb.* to acclaim, cheer

aclaración *noun f.* clarification, explanation

aclarar *verb.* 1. to clarify, explain 2. lighten 3. rinse
—**aclararse** 1. to become clear 2. clear up

acogedor, -dora *adj.* cozy, friendly

acoger *verb.* 1. to take in, receive, welcome 2. host
—**acogerse** to take refuge

acogida *noun f.* **1.** reception, welcome **2.** refuge, shelter

acolchar *verb.* to pad

acometer *verb.* **1.** to undertake, tackle **2.** attack

acomodado, -da *adj.* **1.** suitable, appropriate **2.** well-off, well-to-do

acomodar *verb.* to accommodate, make room for

　—acomodarse to adapt to

acompañamiento *noun m.* accompaniment

acompañante *noun mf.* **1.** companion **2.** accompanist

acompañar *verb.* **1.** to accompany **2.** go with

acondicionador *noun m.* conditioner

acondicionar *verb.* to arrange

aconsejable *adj.* advisable

aconsejar *verb.* to advise, counsel

acontecer *verb.* to occur, happen

acontecimiento *noun m.* event

acoplar *verb.* to connect, couple

acordar *verb.* to agree, resolve

　—acordarse to remember

acorde *noun m.* chord

acorralar *verb.* **1.** to corner **2.** corral

acortar *verb.* to shorten, reduce

　—acortarse to get shorter

acosar *verb.* to harass, hound

acoso *noun m.* harassment

acostarse *verb.* **1.** to go to bed **2.** lie down

acostumbrado, -da *adj.* **1.** accustomed **2.** usual, customary

acostumbrar *verb.* to accustom

　—acostumbrarse to get accustomed, get used

acrecentar *verb.* to increase

acreedor, -dora *noun.* creditor

acribillar *verb.* to pepper

acta *noun f.* **1.** certificate **2.** minutes **3.** proceedings

actitud *noun f.* **1.** attitude **2.** posture

activamente *adv.* actively

activar *verb.* **1.** to activate **2.** stimulate

actividad *noun f.* **1.** activity **2.** work

activo, -va *adj.* active

acto *noun m.* act, deed

actor *noun m.* actor

actriz *noun f.* actress

actuación *noun f.* performance

actual *adj.* **1.** current, present **2.** topical **3.** up-to-date

actualidad *noun f.* **1.** present time **2.** current affairs, news

　—en la actualidad nowadays, currently, at present

actualizado, -da *adj.* up-to-date

actualizar *verb.* **1.** to update, to bring up to date **2.** upgrade

actualmente *adv.* **1.** currently **2.** nowadays **3.** presently

actuar *verb.* to act, perform

acuario *noun m.* aquarium

acuartelar *verb.* to quarter

acuchillar *verb.* to knife, stab

acudir *verb.* to go, come

　—acudir a to turn to

acuerdo *noun m.* agreement, deal, understanding

　—de acuerdo OK, all right

　—de acuerdo con in accordance to

　—estar de acuerdo to agree

acumulación *noun f.* accumulation

acumular *verb.* to accumulate, amass, gather

　—acumularse to pile up

acumulativo, -va *adj.* cumulative

acunar *verb.* to cradle, rock

acuñar *verb.* to coin, mint

acusación *noun f.* **1.** accusation, charge **2.** prosecution

acusado, -da *noun.* defendant

acusado, -da *adj.* marked, pronounced

acusador, -dora *noun.* **1.** accuser **2.** prosecutor

acusar *verb.* to accuse, charge

acusica *noun mf.* sneak, tattler

acústica *noun f.* acoustics

adaptación *noun f.* adaptation

adaptar *verb.* **1.** to adapt **2.** adjust

　—adaptarse to conform, adapt

adecuadamente *adv.* appropriately

adecuado, -da *adj.* appropriate

adecuar *verb.* to adapt

adelantado, -da *adj.* **1.** advanced **2.** fast

　—por adelantado in advance

adelantar *verb.* **1.** to advance **2.** move forward **3.** pass
  —**adelantarse a** to anticipate
adelante *adv.* forward
  —**más adelante** further on, later on
adelanto *noun m.* **1.** advance, progress **2.** advance payment
adelgazar *verb.* **1.** to lose weight **2.** thin
ademán *noun m.* gesture
además *adv.* also, besides, furthermore, moreover
  —**además de** besides, as well as
adentro *adv.* inside, within
aderezar *verb.* to season, dress
adherir *verb.* to adhere, stick
  —**adherirse a** to join
adicción *noun f.* addiction
adición *noun f.* addition
adicional *adj.* additional
adicto, -ta *noun.* addict
adiós *noun m.* goodbye, farewell
¡adiós! *interj.* goodbye!
adivinanza *noun f.* riddle
adivinar *verb.* **1.** to guess **2.** foretell, predict
adjetivo *noun m.* adjective
adjudicar *verb.* to award
adjuntar *verb.* to attach, enclose
adjunto, -ta *noun.* assistant, deputy
adjunto, -ta *adj.* attached, enclosed
administración *noun f.* **1.** administration **2.** management
  —**administración pública** public administration
administrador, -dora *noun.* administrator, manager
administrar *verb.* **1.** to manage, run **2.** administer
administrativo, -va *adj.* administrative
admirable *adj.* admirable
admiración *noun f.* admiration
admirador, -dora *noun.* admirer
admirar *verb.* to admire
admisible *adj.* acceptable
admisión *noun f.* admission
admitir *verb.* **1.** to admit **2.** acknowledge, concede **3.** allow, permit
adolescente *noun mf.* adolescent, teenager

adolescente *adj.* adolescent, teenage
adonde *adv.* where
  —**adónde** where?
adondequiera *adv.* wherever, anywhere
adopción *noun f.* adoption
adoptar *verb.* **1.** to adopt **2.** take
adoptivo, -va *adj.* **1.** adopted (son) **2.** adoptive (parents)
adoquín *noun m.* paving stone, cobblestone
adoquinar *verb.* to pave, cobble
adoración *noun f.* adoration, worship
adorar *verb.* to adore, worship
adornar *verb.* **1.** to adorn, decorate **2.** trim
adorno *noun m.* ornament
adquirir *verb.* **1.** to acquire, gain **2.** purchase
adquisición *noun f.* **1.** acquisition **2.** purchase
aduana *noun f.* customs, customs office
adular *verb.* to flatter
adulterar *verb.* to adulterate
adulterio *noun m.* adultery
adulto, -ta *noun. adj.* adult
advenimiento *noun m.* advent
adverbio *noun m.* adverb
adversario, -ria *noun.* adversary, opponent
adverso, -sa *adj.* adverse, unfavorable
advertencia *noun f.* warning, caution
advertir *verb.* **1.** to warn, caution **2.** notice
adyacente *adj.* adjacent
aéreo, -rea *adj.* aerial, air
aeronáutica *noun f.* aeronautics
aeronave *noun f.* aircraft
aeropuerto *noun m.* airport
afable *adj.* affable
afán *noun m.* eagerness, desire
afectación *noun f.* affectation, pose
afectado, -da *adj.* **1.** affected **2.** afflicted
afectar *verb.* **1.** to affect **2.** feign
afecto *noun m.* affection
afectuoso, -sa *adj.* affectionate
afeitado *noun m.* shave
afeitar *verb.* to shave
  —**afeitarse** to shave, have a shave

aferrarse *verb*. to cling
afición *noun f*. **1**. fondness, liking, taste **2**. hobby, pastime
—**la afición** the fans
aficionado, -da *noun*. **1**. lover, enthusiast **2**. amateur **3**. fan, supporter
aficionado, -da *adj*. **1**. enthusiastic, keen **2**. amateur
afilado, -da *adj*. sharp
afiliación *noun f*. membership, affiliation
afiliado, -da *noun*. member
afiliarse *verb*. to join, affiliate
afinar *verb*. to tune
afinidad *noun f*. affinity, similarity
afirmación *noun f*. affirmation, assertion
afirmar *verb*. to affirm, assert
afirmativo, -va *adj*. affirmative
aflicción *noun f*. affliction, grief, sorrow
afligido, -da *adj*. grief-stricken, sorrowful
afligir *verb*. **1**. to afflict **2**. distress
aflojar *verb*. to loosen, slacken
aforo *noun m*. capacity
afortunadamente *adv*. fortunately, luckily
afortunado, -da *adj*. fortunate, lucky
África *noun f*. Africa
africano, -na *noun. adj*. African
afrontar *verb*. to confront, face up to
afuera *adv*. **1**. out **2**. outside
afueras *noun f. plural*. outskirts
agachar *verb*. to lower, bend
—**agacharse** to crouch, squat, bend down
agalla *noun f*. gill
agarrar *verb*. **1**. to hold, seize, grab, grasp **2**. catch
—**agarrarse 1**. to hold on, cling **2**. have a fight
agarre *noun m*. grip
agazaparse *verb*. **1**. to crouch **2**. hide
agencia *noun f*. agency, bureau
agenda *noun f*. **1**. agenda **2**. address book
agente *noun mf*. agent
—**agente de bolsa** stockbroker
—**agente inmobiliario** estate agent
ágil *adj*. agile, nimble
agitación *noun f*. agitation

agitado, -da *adj*. agitated, excited
agitar *verb*. **1**. to shake, agitate **2**. wave, flap
—**agitarse 1**. to stir **2**. toss
aglomeración *noun f*. **1**. agglomeration **2**. crowd
agobiante *adj*. overwhelming
agobiar *verb*. to overwhelm
agolparse *verb*. to crowd together
agonía *noun f*. agony, death throes
agosto *noun m*. August
agotado, -da *adj*. **1**. tired **2**. exhausted **3**. sold out
agotador, -dora *adj*. exhausting
agotamiento *noun m*. exhaustion
agotar *verb*. **1**. to tire out, wear out **2**. exhaust
—**agotarse 1**. to get exhausted, tire oneself out, wear oneself out **2**. sell out
agradable *adj*. agreeable, pleasant
agradar *verb*. to be pleasing, please, like
agradecer *verb*. **1**. to thank **2**. be grateful for
agradecido, -da *adj*. grateful
agradecimiento *noun m*. gratitude
agraviar *verb*. to offend, insult
agravio *noun m*. **1**. offense, insult **2**. grievance
agredir *verb*. **1**. to assault **2**. attack
agregar *verb*. to add
agresión *noun f*. **1**. aggression **2**. assault, attack
agresividad *noun f*. aggressiveness
agresivo, -va *adj*. aggressive
agresor, -sora *noun*. **1**. aggressor **2**. assailant, attacker
agreste *adj*. wild
agriar *verb*. to sour
—**agriarse** to turn sour
agrícola *adj*. agricultural
agricultor, -ora *noun*. farmer
agricultura *noun f*. agriculture, farming
agrietado, -da *adj*. cracked
agrietar *verb*. to crack
agrio, -gria *adj*. sour
agrupación *noun f*. group, association
agrupar *verb*. to group
—**agruparse** to gather together

agua *noun f.* water
—**agua corriente** running water
—**agua dulce** fresh water
—**agua mineral** mineral water
—**agua oxigenada** hydrogen peroxide
—**aguas residuales** sewage
aguado, -da *adj.* watered down, diluted
aguafiestas *noun mf.* killjoy, spoilsport
aguantar *verb.* 1. to bear, endure, withstand 2. hold
—**aguantarse** to restrain oneself
aguante *noun m.* 1. tolerance, patience 2. endurance
aguardar *verb.* to wait for, await
aguardiente *noun m.* brandy
agudeza *noun f.* 1. sharpness, acuteness 2. wit, wittiness
agudizarse *verb.* to intensify, sharpen
agudo, -da *adj.* 1. sharp, acute 2. high, high-pitched 3. clever, witty
aguijón *noun m.* 1. sting 2. goad
águila *noun f.* eagle
aguja *noun f.* needle
agujerear *verb.* to pierce, make holes in
agujero *noun m.* hole
ah *interj.* ah!, oh!
ahí *adv.* there
ahogar *verb.* 1. to drown 2. choke
ahora *adv.* 1. now 2. presently
—**ahora mismo** right now
—**hasta ahora** so far
ahorcar *verb.* to hang
ahorita *adv.* right now
ahorrador, -dora *adj.* thrifty
ahorrar *verb.* to save
ahorro *noun m.* saving
ahumado, -da *adj.* smoked
ahumar *verb.* to smoke
ahuyentar *verb.* to chase away
aire *noun m.* air
—**aire acondicionado** air conditioning
airear *verb.* to air
aislado, -da *adj.* isolated
aislamiento *noun m.* 1. isolation 2. insulation
ajardinar *verb.* to landscape
ajedrez *noun m.* chess
ajeno, -na *adj.* 1. alien 2. of another, of others

—**ajeno a** alien to, foreign to
ajo *noun m.* garlic
ajustado, -da *adj.* 1. tight, tight-fitting 2. close
ajustar *verb.* 1. to adjust 2. fit, tighten
—**ajustarse** 1. to adjust, fit 2. conform
ajuste *noun m.* adjustment
al *cont.* (See a. Contraction of a and el)
ala *noun f.* wing
alabanza *noun f.* praise
alabar *verb.* to praise
alambre *noun m.* wire
alarde *noun m.* display, show
alardear *verb.* to boast, brag
alargar *verb.* 1. to lengthen, stretch 2. prolong, extend
alarido *noun m.* howl, yell, scream
alarma *noun f.* alarm
alarmante *adj.* alarming
alarmar *verb.* to alarm
alba *noun f.* dawn
albañil *noun mf.* mason, construction worker
albedrío *noun m.* will
albergue *noun m.* 1. lodging, hostel 2. shelter, refuge
alboroto *noun m.* 1. disturbance 2. riot
álbum *noun m.* album
alcalde, -desa *noun.* mayor
alcance *noun m.* 1. reach, scope 2. range 3. extent
alcanzar *verb.* 1. to reach 2. catch up with 3. achieve, attain 4. suffice, be enough
alcoba *noun f.* bedroom
alcohol *noun m.* alcohol
alcohólico, -ca *noun. adj.* alcoholic
aldeano, -na *noun.* villager
aleatorio, -ria *adj.* random
alegación *noun f.* allegation
alegar *verb.* 1. to allege 2. plead 3. argue
alegato *noun m.* 1. plea 2. argument, dispute
alegrar *verb.* 1. to cheer up, make happy 2. liven up
—**alegrarse** to be glad, be happy
alegre *adj.* 1. glad, cheerful, happy 2. bright 3. lively 4. merry

alegremente *adv.* cheerfully, happily

alegría *noun f.* happiness, joy

alejado, -da *adj.* remote, distant

alejar *verb.* to move away

—**alejarse** to go away, move away

alemán, -mana *noun. adj.* German

Alemania *noun f.* Germany

alentador, -dora *adj.* encouraging

alentar *verb.* to encourage

alergia *noun f.* allergy

alerta *noun f.* alert

alerta *adj.* alert, watchful

alertar *verb.* to alert

aleta *noun f.* fin

alevín *noun m.* **1.** youngster, novice **2.** fry, young fish

alfabeto *noun m.* alphabet

alfarería *noun f.* pottery

alfarero, -ra *noun.* potter

alférez *noun mf.* second lieutenant

alfil *noun m.* bishop

alfiler *noun m.* **1.** pin **2.** brooch

alfombra *noun f.* carpet

alfombrilla *noun f.* rug, mat

alga *noun f.* alga

algo *adv.* somewhat, rather

algo *pron.* something, anything

—**algo de** some, a little

algodón *noun m.* cotton

alguacil *noun mf.* sheriff, constable

alguien *pron.* **1.** somebody, someone **2.** anybody, anyone

algún *adj.* (see alguno. Used before masculine singular nouns)

alguno, -na *adj.* **1.** some, any **2.** not any, not at all (in negative sentences)

—**algunas veces** sometimes

alguno, -na *pron.* someone, somebody

—**alguno que otro** a few

—**algunos, -nas** some

alhaja *noun f.* jewel

aliado, -da *noun.* ally

aliado, -da *adj.* allied

alianza *noun f.* **1.** alliance **2.** covenant

aliarse *verb.* to form an alliance, to ally oneself (with)

aliciente *noun m.* incentive

aliento *noun m.* **1.** breath **2.** courage, strength

aligerar *verb.* **1.** to lighten **2.** hurry

alimentación *noun f.* nutrition

alimentar *verb.* **1.** to feed **2.** be nutritious

—**alimentarse 1.** to eat **2.** feed

alimento *noun m.* food

alinear *verb.* to line up

aliñar *verb.* to season, dress

aliño *noun m.* seasoning, dressing

alisar *verb.* to smooth

aliviado, -da *adj.* relieved

aliviar *verb.* **1.** to relieve, ease **2.** soothe

alivio *noun m.* relief

allá *adv.* there, over there

—**más allá** farther away

—**más allá de** beyond

allí *adv.* there, over there

alma *noun f.* soul

almacén *noun m.* **1.** store **2.** warehouse

almacenamiento *noun m.* storage

almacenar *verb.* to store

almeja *noun f.* clam

almendra *noun f.* almond

almendro *noun m.* almond tree

almirante *noun mf.* admiral

almirez *noun m.* mortar

almohada *noun f.* pillow

almohadilla *noun f.* cushion

almorzar *verb.* **1.** to have lunch **2.** have for lunch

almuerzo *verb.* lunch

alocado, -da *adj.* **1.** crazy **2.** wild

alocución *noun f.* speech, address

alojamiento *noun m.* accommodation , rooms, lodgings

alojar *verb.* to accommodate

—**alojarse** to lodge, stay

alpinista *noun mf.* climber

alquilar *verb.* to let, rent

alquiler *noun m.* rent, rental

alrededor *adv.* around

—**alrededor de** around, about, approximately

alrededores *noun m. plural.* **1.** surroundings **2.** outskirts

alta *noun f.* **1.** discharge **2.** membership, entry

—**dar de alta** to discharge

—**darse de alta** to join

altanero, -ra adj. arrogant
altar noun m. altar
altavoz noun m. loudspeaker
alteración noun f. 1. alteration, change 2. disturbance
alterado, -da adj. upset
alterar verb. 1. to alter, modify 2. disturb
  —**alterarse** to get excited, get upset
altercado noun m. altercation, dispute
alternar verb. 1. to alternate 2. socialize
alternativa noun f. alternative, choice, option
alternativamente adv. alternatively
alternativo, -va adj. 1. alternative 2. alternating
alterno, -na adj. 1. alternate 2. alternating
altiplano noun m. high plateau
altitud noun f. altitude
alto noun m. 1. height 2. halt, stop
alto, -ta adj. 1. tall 2. high 3. loud
alto adv. 1. high 2. loudly
altura noun f. 1. height 2. altitude 3. level 4. loftiness
alumbramiento noun m. birth
alumbrar verb. 1. to light, give light 2. give birth
aluminio noun m. aluminum
alumno, -na noun. 1. student 2. pupil, schoolboy, schoolgirl
alusión noun f. allusion, reference
alza noun f. rise
alzamiento noun m. uprising
alzar verb. to lift, raise
  —**alzarse** to rise
ama noun f. (see amo)
amabilidad noun f. kindness
amable adj. kind, nice
amablemente adv. kindly
amado, -da noun. adj. beloved
amamantar verb. to suckle, nurse
amanecer noun m. dawn, daybreak
amanecer verb. to dawn
amante noun mf. lover
amante adj. loving, fond
amañado, -da adj. fixed
amañar verb. to fix
amar verb. to love

amargado, -da adj. bitter, embittered
amargamente adv. bitterly
amargo, -da adj. bitter
amargura noun f. bitterness
amarillear verb. to yellow, turn yellow
amarillo noun m. yellow
amarillo, -lla adj. yellow
amarrar verb. to tie up, fasten
amasar verb. 1. to amass 2. mix, prepare
amateur noun mf. adj. amateur
ámbar noun m. amber
ambición noun f. ambition
ambicioso, -sa adj. ambitious
ambiental adj. environmental
ambiente noun m. 1. atmosphere 2. environment
ambigüedad noun f. ambiguity
ambiguo, -gua adj. ambiguous
ambos, -bas adj. pron. both
ambulancia noun f. ambulance
amenaza noun f. menace, threat
amenazador, -dora adj. menacing, threatening
amenazar verb. to threaten
América noun f. America
americano, -na noun. adj. American
amigable adj. amicable, friendly
amigo, -ga noun. 1. friend 2. boyfriend or girlfriend
amigo, -ga adj. friendly
amistad noun f. friendship
amnistía noun f. amnesty
amo, -ma noun. 1. master or mistress 2. owner
  —**ama de casa** housewife
  —**ama de llaves** housekeeper
amoldar verb. to adapt, adjust
  —**amoldarse** to adapt oneself, adjust oneself
amontonar verb. 1. to pile up, heap up 2. hoard
  —**amontonarse** to pile up, accumulate
amor noun m. 1. love 2. beloved
  —**amor propio** pride, self-esteem
  —**hacer el amor** make love
amoral adj. amoral
amorío noun m. love affair, romance
amortiguador noun m. shock absorber

amortiguar *verb.* **1.** to absorb, cushion **2.** alleviate

amotinarse *verb.* to riot

amparar *verb.* to safeguard, protect
—**ampararse** to shelter

amparo *noun m.* protection, refuge, shelter

amperio *noun m.* ampère

ampliación *noun f.* **1.** extension, expansion **2.** enlargement

ampliamente *adv.* widely, extensively

ampliar *verb.* **1.** to expand, extend **2.** enlarge **3.** widen

amplio, -plia *adj.* ample, wide, spacious

amplitud *noun f.* extent, wideness, spaciousness

amueblado, -da *adj.* furnished

amueblar *verb.* furnish

amuleto *noun m.* amulet, charm

amurallar *verb.* to wall, fortify

analfabetismo *noun m.* illiteracy

analfabeto, -ta *noun. adj.* illiterate

análisis *noun m.* **1.** analysis **2.** test

analista *noun mf.* analyst

analítico, -ca *adj.* analytical

analizar *verb.* to analyze

analogía *noun f.* analogy, similarity

análogo, -ga *adj.* analogous, similar

anatomía *noun f.* anatomy

ancho *noun m.* breadth, width

ancho, -cha *adj.* **1.** broad, wide **2.** loose

anchura *noun f.* breadth, width

anciano, -na *noun.* elderly person, old person

anciano, -na *adj.* aged, elderly, old

ancla *noun f.* anchor

anclar *verb.* to anchor

andador *noun m.* **1.** walker **2.** baby walker, reins

andar *noun m.* walk

andar *verb.* **1.** to walk **2.** function, work, run
—**andar tras** to follow, go after

andén *noun m.* platform

andrajos *noun m. plural.* rags

andrajoso, -sa *adj.* ragged

anegar *verb.* to flood

anestesia *noun f.* anesthesia

anexar *verb.* to annex, attach

anexión *noun f.* annexation

anexionar *verb.* to annex

anexo *noun m.* annex

anexo, -xa *adj.* attached, enclosed

anfibio *noun m.* amphibian

anfiteatro *noun m.* amphitheater

anfitrión, -triona *noun.* host or hostess

ángel *noun m.* angel

anglicano, -na *noun. adj.* Anglican

anguila *noun f.* eel

ángulo *noun m.* angle

angustia *noun f.* **1.** anguish, distress **2.** anxiety

angustiado, -da *adj.* **1.** anguished, distressed **2.** anxious

angustiar *verb.* **1.** to anguish, distress **2.** make anxious

angustioso, -sa *adj.* **1.** anguished, distressed **2.** distressing

anhelar *verb.* to long for, yearn for

anhelo *noun m.* longing, yearning

anidar *verb.* to nest

anillo *noun m.* ring

animación *noun f.* **1.** life, activity **2.** animation

animado, -da *adj.* cheerful, alive

animal *noun m.* animal
—**animal de compañía** pet

animar *verb.* **1.** to cheer up, brighten up **2.** enliven, liven up **3.** encourage
—**animarse** *verb.* **1.** to cheer up, brighten up **2.** liven up

ánimo *noun m.* **1.** spirits **2.** encouragement **3.** intention

aniquilamiento *noun m.* annihilation

aniquilar *verb.* to annihilate

aniversario *noun m.* anniversary

anoche *adv.* last night, yesterday evening

anochecer *verb.* to get dark

anonimato *noun m.* anonymity

anónimo, -ma *adj.* anonymous

anormal *adj.* abnormal

anotación *noun f.* **1.** note, annotation **2.** scoring

anotar *verb.* **1.** to note down, write down **2.** annotate **3.** score

ansiar *verb.* to long for, yearn for

ansiedad *noun f.* anxiety

ansiosamente *adv.* anxiously

ansioso, -sa *adj.* **1.** anxious, worried **2.** eager

ante *noun m.* **1.** elk, moose **2.** suede

ante *prep.* **1.** before **2.** considering, faced with

—**ante todo** above all, first and foremost

anteanoche, antes de anoche *adv.* the night before last

anteayer, antes de ayer *adv.* the day before yesterday

antecedente *noun m.* **1.** antecedent **2.** precedent

—**antecedentes 1.** record **2.** background

—**antecedentes penales** criminal record

anteceder *verb.* to precede

antecesor, -sora *noun.* **1.** predecessor **2.** ancestor, forebear

antena *noun f.* **1.** antenna **2.** aerial

anteojos *noun m. plural.* glasses, eyeglasses

antepasado, -da *noun.* ancestor, forebear

antepenúltimo, -ma *adj.* antepenultimate, third from last

anterior *adj.* **1.** previous, former **2.** front

anteriormente *adv.* previously

antes *adv.* **1.** before, earlier **2.** rather, sooner **3.** formerly, previously

—**antes bien** on the contrary

—**antes de anoche** the night before last

—**antes de ayer** the day before yesterday

—**antes de Cristo** before Christ, BC

—**antes (de) que** before

—**cuanto antes** as soon as possible

antibiótico *noun m.* antibiotic

anticipación *noun f.* anticipation

—**con anticipación** in advance

anticipado, -da *adj.* early

—**por anticipado** in advance

anticipar *verb.* **1.** to anticipate **2.** foresee **3.** pay in advance

—**anticiparse 1.** to anticipate **2.** act in advance of **3.** be ahead of

anticipo *noun m.* **1.** advance **2.** foretaste, preview

anticuado, -da *adj.* old-fashioned, outdated

antigüedad *noun f.* **1.** antiquity **2.** seniority **3.** antique

antiguamente *adv.* formerly

antiguo, -gua *adj.* **1.** old **2.** ancient **3.** former

antillano, -na *noun. adj.* West Indian

antinatural *adj.* unnatural

antipatía *noun f.* antipathy, dislike

antipático, -ca *adj.* unpleasant

antorcha *noun f.* torch

antropología *noun f.* anthropology

anual *adj.* annual, yearly

anualmente *adv.* annually, yearly

anuario *noun m.* annual, yearbook

anudar *verb.* to knot, tie

anulación *noun f.* cancellation, annulment

anular *verb.* **1.** to cancel, annul, rescind **2.** declare null and void

anunciante *noun mf.* advertiser

anunciar *verb.* **1.** to advertise **2.** announce

anuncio *noun m.* **1.** advertisement, ad, commercial **2.** announcement

anzuelo *noun m.* **1.** fishhook **2.** bait, lure

añadir *verb.* to add

año *noun m.* **1.** year **2.** grade

—**año bisiesto** leap year

—**Año Nuevo** New Year

—**tener (cinco) años** to be (five) years old

añoranza *noun f.* longing, yearning

añorar *verb.* **1.** to long for, yearn for **2.** miss

apabullante *adj.* overwhelming

apabullar *verb.* to overwhelm

apacible *adj.* calm, gentle, mild

apaciguar *verb.* to appease, pacify

—**apaciguar** to calm down

apagado, -da *adj.* **1.** off, out **2.** dull, subdued

apagar *verb.* **1.** to turn off, switch off **2.** put out, blow out

—**apagarse 1.** to go out, blow out **2.** die away

apagón *noun m.* blackout

apalear *verb.* to beat, thrash

aparato *noun m.* **1.** machine **2.** apparatus **3.** appliance, set **4.** system

aparcamiento *noun m.* **1.** parking **2.** parking lot

aparcar *verb.* to park

aparear *verb.* to mate

aparecer *verb.* **1.** to appear, turn up **2.** come out

aparejar *verb.* **1.** to prepare, get ready **2.** saddle, harness

aparejo *noun m.* **1.** equipment, gear **2.** saddle, harness **3.** rig

aparentar *verb.* **1.** to look, seem **2.** feign, pretend

aparente *adj.* apparent

aparentemente *adv.* apparently, seemingly

aparición *noun f.* **1.** appearance **2.** publication, release

apariencia *noun f.* appearance, look
—**en apariencia** apparently, seemingly

apartado *noun m.* section
—**apartado de correos, apartado postal** Pox Office Box, P.O. Box

apartado, -da *adj.* **1.** remote, isolated **2.** solitary

apartamento *noun m.* apartment

apartar *verb.* **1.** to separate, put aside, set aside **2.** move away
—**apartarse** to move away

aparte *noun m.* aside (theater)

aparte *adj.* separate, special

aparte *adv.* **1.** aside, apart **2.** separately **3.** besides
—**aparte de** apart from, besides

apasionado, -da *adj.* passionate

apasionante *adj.* fascinating, exciting

apasionar *verb.* to excite, love
—**apasionarse** to get excited, enthuse

apeadero *noun m.* halt

apearse *verb.* **1.** to get off **2.** dismount

apedrear *verb.* to stone, throw stones at

apegado, -da *adj.* attached, close

apego *noun m.* attachment, fondness

apelación *noun f.* appeal

apelar *verb.* to appeal

apellido *noun m.* last name, surname

apenar *verb.* to sadden
—**apenarse 1.** to become sad **2.** to become embarrassed

apenas *adv.* **1.** barely **2.** hardly, scarcely

apenas *conj.* as soon as

apéndice *noun m.* appendix

apertura *noun f.* **1.** opening **2.** start, beginning

apestar *verb.* to stink

apetecer *verb.* to feel like

apetecible *adj.* desirable, attractive

apetito *noun m.* appetite

apilar *verb.* to heap up, pile up

apiñar *verb.* to pack
—**apiñarse** to crowd together

apisonar *verb.* to roll

aplanar *verb.* to level

aplastante *adj.* overwhelming, crushing, sweeping

aplastar *verb.* **1.** to crush, squash **2.** overwhelm

aplaudir *verb.* to applaud, clap

aplauso *noun m.* applause, clapping

aplazamiento *noun m.* **1.** postponement **2.** deferment

aplazar *verb.* **1.** to postpone **2.** defer

aplicable *adj.* applicable

aplicación *noun f.* **1.** application **2.** diligence, dedication

aplicar *verb.* to apply
—**aplicarse** to work harder

apodar *verb.* to dub, nickname

apoderado, -da *noun.* agent, manager

apoderar *verb.* to authorize, empower
—**apoderarse de** *verb.* seize

apodo *noun m.* nickname

apología *noun f.* defense

apogeo *noun m.* height, peak

aporrear *verb.* to beat, club

aportación *noun f.* contribution

aportar *verb.* **1.** to contribute **2.** provide

apósito *noun m.* dressing

apostar *verb.* **1.** to bet, gamble **2.** station

apoyar *verb.* **1.** to support, back **2.** rest, lean
—**apoyarse 1.** to rely on, lean on **2.** lean against

apoyo *noun m.* support

apreciación *noun f.* appreciation

apreciar *verb.* to appreciate, be fond of, value, esteem

—**apreciarse** to increase in value

aprecio *noun m.* esteem

apremiante *adj.* urgent, pressing

apremiar *verb.* 1. to urge, press 2. be urgent

aprender *verb.* to learn

aprendiz, -diza *noun.* 1. apprentice 2. trainee

aprendizaje *noun m.* apprenticeship

aprensión *noun f.* apprehension

apresamiento *noun m.* seizure, capture

apresuradamente *adv.* hastily, hurriedly

apresurado, -da *adj.* hasty, hurried

apresurar *verb.* to hurry, quicken, speed up

—**apresurarse** to hurry

apretado, -da *adj.* tight

apretar *verb.* 1. to press 2. tighten 3. squeeze 4. pinch, be too tight

apretón *noun m.* squeeze

—**apretón de manos** handshake

aprieto *noun m.* predicament

aprobación *noun f.* approval, endorsement

aprobado *noun m.* pass certificate

aprobar *verb.* 1. to approve, endorse 2. pass 3. approve of

apropiadamente *adv.* appropriately, suitably

apropiado, -da *adj.* appropriate, suitable

apropiarse de *verb.* to appropriate, take possession of

aprovechado, -da *noun.* opportunist

aprovechado, -da *adj.* opportunistic

—**bien aprovechado** well-used, well-spent, well-exploited

—**mal aprovechado** wasted, badly-exploited

aprovechar *verb.* 1. to use 2. make (good) use of

—**aprovecharse** to take advantage, exploit

aprovisionamiento *noun m.* supplies

aprovisionar *verb.* to supply

aproximación *noun f.* 1. approach, rapprochement 2. approximation

aproximadamente *adv.* approximately

aproximado, -da *adj.* approximate, rough

aproximar *verb.* to bring nearer

—**aproximarse** to approach

aptitud *noun f.* aptitude

apto, -ta *adj.* fit, suitable

apuesta *noun f.* bet

apuntador, -dora *noun.* prompter

apuntar *verb.* 1. to aim 2. point 3. note down 4. prompt 5. suggest, hint

—**apuntarse** 1. to enroll, register, join 2. score

apunte *noun m.* 1. note 2. sketch

apuñalar *verb.* to stab

apurar *verb.* 1. to exhaust, drain 2. eat up, drink up 3. hurry

—**apurarse** 1. to hurry up 2. worry

apuro *noun m.* 1. predicament 2. hurry 3. embarrassment

aquel, aquella *adj.* that

—**aquellos, aquellas** those

aquél, aquélla *pron.* 1. that, that one 2. the former

—**aquéllos, aquéllas** 1. those, those one 2. the former

aquello *pron.* that, that matter

aquí *adv.* here

—**de aquí en adelante** from now on

aquietar *verb.* to calm

árabe *noun mf.* 1. Arab 2. Arabic (language)

árabe *adj.* Arab, Arabian

Arabia *noun f.* Arabia

arábigo, -ga *adj.* Arabian

—**números arábigos** Arabic numerals

arado *noun m.* plow

arancel *noun m.* tariff, duty

araña *noun f.* spider

arañar *verb.* to scratch

arañazo *noun m.* scratch

arar *verb.* to plow

arbitraje *noun m.* 1. arbitration 2. refereeing

arbitrar *verb.* 1. to arbitrate 2. referee

arbitrario, -ria *adj.* arbitrary

árbitro, -tra *noun*. 1. arbitrator, arbiter 2. referee

árbol *noun m*. tree
—**árbol genealógico** family tree
—**árboles maderables** timber

arbusto *noun m*. bush, shrub

arca *noun f*. 1. chest, coffer 2. ark

archivar *verb*. 1. to file 2. save 3. shelve

archivo *noun m*. 1. file 2. archive 3. record

arcilla *noun f*. clay

arco *noun m*. 1. arc 2. arch 3. bow
—**arco iris** rainbow

arder *verb*. 1. to burn 2. smart, sting

ardiente *adj*. 1. ardent, passionate 2. burning

ardilla *noun f*. squirrel

ardor *noun m*. ardor

área *noun f*. area

arena *noun f*. 1. sand 2. arena

arenoso, -sa *adj*. sandy

argamasa *noun f*. mortar

Argentina *noun f*. Argentina

argentino, -na *noun. adj*. Argentinean

argüir *verb*. 1. to argue 2. claim

argolla *noun f*. ring

argumentar *verb*. to argue

argumento *noun m*. 1. argument, reasoning 2. plot

ariete *noun m*. ram

aria *noun f*. aria

aridez *noun f*. aridity, dryness

árido, -da *adj*. arid, dry

arista *noun f*. edge

aristocracia *noun f*. aristocracy

aristócrata *noun mf*. aristocrat

aristocrático, -ca *adj*. aristocratic

aritmética *noun f*. arithmetic

arma *noun f*. weapon
—**arma de fuego** firearm

armada *noun f*. fleet, navy

armado, -da *adj*. 1. armed 2. assembled

armadura *noun f*. armor

armar *verb*. 1. to arm 2. assemble, put together
—**armar un escándalo** to kick up a storm

armario *noun m*. 1. closet 2. cupboard

armazón *noun mf*. 1. frame 2. framework 3. skeleton

armisticio *noun m*. armistice

armonía *noun f*. harmony

arnés *noun m*. harness

aro *noun m*. ring, hoop

aroma *noun m*. aroma, scent

arpa *noun f*. harp

arquear *verb*. to arch, bend

arqueología *noun f*. archaeology

arqueológico, -ca *adj*. archaeological

arquitecto, -ta *noun*. architect

arquitectónico, -ca *adj*. architectural

arquitectura *noun f*. architecture

arraigar *verb*. to take root

arrancar *verb*. 1. to pull out, tear out 2. pluck 3. snatch 4. start

arranque *noun m*. 1. starting mechanism 2. outburst, fit

arrasar *verb*. 1. to level 2. raze 3. sweep the board, be a runaway success

arrastrar *verb*. 1. to drag, pull 2. sweep away 3. attract
—**arrastrarse** 1. to crawl 2. grovel

arrebatar *verb*. 1. to snatch away, take 2. captivate

arrebato *noun m*. outburst, fit

arrecife *noun m*. reef

arreglado, -da *adj*. 1. repaired, fixed 2. settled, sorted out 3. neat, tidy 4. smart, trim

arreglar *verb*. 1. to repair, fix, mend 2. settle, sort out, solve, work out 3. tidy up
—**arreglarse** to get oneself ready

arreglo *noun m*. 1. repair 2. agreement 3. arrangement

arremeter *verb*. to attack, charge

arrendador, -dora *noun*. landlord or landlady

arrendar *verb*. to rent, lease

arrendatario, -ria *noun*. tenant, renter

arreos *noun m. plural*. harness

arrepentido, -da *adj*. repentant, sorry

arrepentimiento *noun m*. 1. regret 2. repentance

arrepentirse *verb*. 1. to regret, be sorry 2. repent

arrestar *verb*. to arrest, detain

arresto *noun m.* arrest

arriate *noun m.* border

arriba *adv.* **1.** above **2.** up, upward **3.** upstairs
—**cuesta arriba** uphill
—**de arriba abajo** from head to foot, from top to bottom
—**hacia arriba** upward

arriba *interj.* long live!

arribista *noun mf.* upstart, social climber

arriesgado, -da *adj.* risky

arriesgar *verb.* to risk, venture
—**arriesgarse** to take a risk

arrinconar *verb.* **1.** to corner **2.** lay aside

arrodillarse *verb.* to kneel (down)

arrogancia *noun f.* arrogance

arrogante *adj.* arrogant

arrojar *verb.* **1.** to throw, hurl, cast **2.** produce, yield **3.** spew, vomit
—**arrojarse** to throw oneself

arrollador, -dora *adj.* sweeping

arrostrar *verb.* to brave, face up

arroyo *noun m.* brook, stream

arroz *noun m.* rice

arruga *noun f.* **1.** wrinkle, line **2.** crease

arrugado, -da *adj.* **1.** wrinkled, lined **2.** creased

arruinado, -da *adj.* broke, ruined

arruinar *verb.* **1.** to ruin **2.** wreck, destroy
—**arruinarse** to go bankrupt

arsenal *noun m.* arsenal

arte *noun mf.* **1.** art **2.** skill

arteria *noun f.* artery

artesanal *adj.* handmade

artesanía *noun f.* **1.** craftsmanship **2.** crafts, handicrafts

artesano, -na *noun.* craftsman or craftswoman , artisan

ártico, -ca *adj.* Arctic

articulación *noun f.* **1.** articulation **2.** joint

articular *verb.* **1.** to articulate **2.** join together

artículo *noun m.* **1.** article **2.** commodity **3.** item
—**artículos alimenticios** foodstuffs
—**artículos de consumo** consumer goods

—**artículos de primera necesidad** essentials

artificial *adj.* artificial

artillería *noun f.* artillery

artista *noun mf.* artist

artístico, -ca *adj.* artistic

arzobispo *noun m.* archbishop

as *noun m.* ace

asa *noun f.* handle

asado *noun m.* **1.** roast **2.** barbecue

asado, -da *adj.* roasted, broiled

asador *noun m.* spit

asalariado, -da *noun.* wage-earner

asalariado, -da *adj.* wage-earning

asaltar *verb.* **1.** to assault **2.** mug, rob **3.** storm

asalto *noun m.* **1.** assault **2.** mugging, robbery **3.** round

asamblea *noun f.* assembly

asar *verb.* to roast, broil

ascendencia *noun f.* descent, ancestry, origin

ascendente *adj.* upward

ascender *verb.* **1.** to ascend, rise **2.** promote **3.** be promoted **4.** amount, reach, total

ascensión *noun f.* ascent, rise
—**la Ascensión** the Ascension

ascenso *noun m.* **1.** ascent, rise **2.** promotion

ascensor *noun m.* elevator

asco *noun m.* disgust
—**dar asco** to disgust

aseado, -da *adj.* clean, neat, tidy, trim

asediar *verb.* to besiege

asegurador, -dora *noun.* insurer

aseguradora *noun m.* insurance company

asegurar *verb.* **1.** to assure, ensure **2.** secure **3.** insure
—**asegurarse 1.** to make sure **2.** insure oneself

asentar *verb.* **1.** to place, set up **2.** lay down
—**asentarse 1.** to stand, be situated **2.** settle

asentir *verb.* **1.** to assent, agree **2.** nod

aseo *noun m.* **1.** toilet **2.** cleanliness
—**aseos** rest room

aserción *noun f.* assertion
aserto *noun m.* assertion
asesinar *verb.* **1.** to murder **2.** assassinate
asesinato *noun m.* **1.** murder, homicide **2.** assassination
asesino, -na *noun.* **1.** killer, murderer or murderess **2.** assassin
asesor, -sora *noun.* consultant, advisor
asesor, -sora *adj.* advisory
asesorar *verb.* to advice, counsel
—**asesorarse** to take advice, consult
aseverar *verb.* to assert, state
asfaltar *verb.* to asphalt
asfalto *noun m.* asphalt
asfixia *noun f.* asphyxia, suffocation
asfixiar *verb.* to suffocate
así *adj.* such
así *adv.* **1.** like this, like that **2.** so, thus, in this way
—**así así** so-so
—**así como 1.** as well as **2.** whereas, while
—**no así** unlike
así *conj.* even if
Asia *noun f.* Asia
asiático, -ca *noun. adj.* Asian
asiento *noun m.* **1.** seat, place **2.** contract **3.** bottom
asignación *noun f.* **1.** allocation **2.** allowance
asignar *verb.* **1.** to assign **2.** allocate
asignatura *noun f.* subject
asilo *noun m.* **1.** asylum **2.** shelter
asimilar *verb.* to assimilate
asimismo *adv.* **1.** similarly, likewise **2.** also, as well
asir *verb.* to seize, grab, grasp
asistencia *noun f.* **1.** assistance, help **2.** attendance
—**asistencia médica/sanitaria** medical or health care
—**asistencia social** welfare
asistente, -ta *noun mf.* **1.** assistant **2.** orderly
—**asistenta doméstica** housemaid
—**asistente social** social worker
—**los asistentes** those present
asistir *verb.* **1.** to attend, go **2.** witness **3.** help, assist
—**asistir un parto** to deliver a baby

asma *noun f.* asthma
asno *noun m.* ass, donkey
asociación *noun f.* **1.** association **2.** society
asociado, -da *noun.* **1.** associate, partner **2.** member
asociado, -da *adj.* associate, associated
asociar *verb.* **1.** to associate **2.** connect
—**asociarse 1.** to join **2.** become partners, form a partnership
asolar *verb.* to raze, destroy
asomar *verb.* to show
—**asomarse 1.** to come out, appear **2.** lean out, look out
asombrar *verb.* to amaze, astonish
—**asombrarse** to marvel, be amazed, be astonished
asombro *noun m.* amazement, astonishment
asombroso, -sa *adj.* amazing, astonishing
asomo *noun m.* **1.** appearance **2.** sign, trace
—**ni por asomo** by no means
aspa *noun f.* blade
aspaviento *noun m.* fuss
aspecto *noun m.* **1.** aspect **2.** look
ásperamente *adv.* roughly
áspero, -ra *adj.* **1.** rough **2.** coarse **3.** harsh
aspiración *noun f.* **1.** breathing in, inhalation **2.** aspiration
aspiradora *noun f.* vacuum cleaner
aspirante *noun mf.* **1.** applicant, candidate **2.** challenger
aspirar *verb.* to breathe in, inhale
—**aspirar a** to aspire to
aspirina *noun f.* aspirin
asquear *verb.* to disgust
asqueroso, -sa *adj.* **1.** disgusting **2.** filthy
asta *noun f.* **1.** horn **2.** flagpole
astillero *noun m.* dockyard, shipyard
astrónomo, -ma *noun.* astronomer
astucia *noun f.* **1.** astuteness, shrewdness **2.** cunning, guile
astuto, -ta *adj.* **1.** astute, shrewd **2.** crafty
asumir *verb.* to assume

asunto *noun m.* affair, business, issue, matter

asustado, -da *adj.* **1.** frightened, scared, afraid **2.** scared

asustar *verb.* to frighten, scare
—**asustarse** to be frightened, get scared

atacante *noun mf.* assailant, attacker

atacar *verb.* to attack

ataque *noun m.* attack
—**ataque al corazón** heart attack
—**ataque de nervios** nervous breakdown

atar *verb.* to tie, tie up

atardecer *noun m.* evening, dusk

atasco *noun m.* **1.** traffic jam **2.** obstruction, blockage

ataúd *noun m.* coffin

atavío *noun m.* attire, dress

atemorizado, -da *adj.* frightened, scared

atemorizar *verb.* to frighten, scare

atención *noun f.* attention
—**llamar la atención** to attract somebody's attention
—**prestar atención** to pay attention

atender *verb.* **1.** to take care of, look after **2.** attend **3.** pay attention **4.** wait on

atentado *noun m.* attack, attempt

atentamente *adv.* **1.** attentively **2.** sincerely yours

atentar *verb.* **1.** to make an attempt (on somebody's life) **2.** break (the law)

atento, -ta *adj.* attentive

atenuar *verb.* **1.** to attenuate **2.** dim, tone down

ateo, -tea *noun.* atheist

ateo, -tea *adj.* atheistic

aterrador, -dora *adj.* frightening, terrifying

aterrar *verb.* to terrify

aterrizaje *noun m.* landing

aterrizar *verb.* to land

aterrorizado, -da *adj.* terrified

aterrorizar *verb.* **1.** to terrify **2.** terrorize

atesorar *verb.* **1.** to hoard **2.** treasure

atestado, -da *adj.* crowded, packed

atestar *verb.* **1.** to crowd, pack, stuff **2.** attest, testify

atestiguar *verb.* to attest, testify

atiborrar *verb.* to stuff

ático *noun m.* **1.** penthouse **2.** attic

atisbo *noun m.* indication

atizar *verb.* **1.** to poke, stir **2.** fan **3.** give

atlántico, -ca *adj.* Atlantic

atleta *noun mf.* athlete

atlético, -ca *adj.* athletic

atletismo *noun m.* athletics

atmósfera *noun f.* atmosphere

atmosférico, -ca *adj.* atmospheric

atómico, -ca *adj.* atomic

átomo *noun m.* atom

atontado, -da *adj.* stupid

atormentar *verb.* **1.** to torture **2.** torment
—**atormentarse** to torture oneself

atornillar *verb.* to screw

atracar *verb.* **1.** to dock **2.** mug, rob

atracción *noun f.* attraction
—**atracción turística** sight

atractivo *noun m.* attraction, appeal

atractivo, -va *adj.* attractive

atraer *verb.* **1.** to attract **2.** draw

atrancar *verb.* to bar, block

atrapar *verb.* **1.** to trap, capture **2.** catch

atrás *adv.* **1.** back, behind **2.** ago
—**atrás de** behind
—**hacia/para atrás** backwards

atrasado, -da *adj.* **1.** backward **2.** late **3.** overdue **4.** slow

atraso *noun m.* **1.** backwardness **2.** delay
—**atrasos** arrears

atravesar *verb.* **1.** to cross **2.** put across **3.** pierce **4.** go through

atrayente *adj.* attractive

atreverse *verb.* to dare

atrevido, -da *adj.* daring, bold

atrevimiento *noun m.* daring, boldness

atribución *noun f.* attribution

atribuir *verb.* **1.** to attribute **2.** assign **3.** confer
—**atribuirse** to claim something for oneself

atributo *noun m.* attribute

atrocidad *noun f.* atrocity

atropellar *verb.* **1.** to run over **2.** disregard, violate

atroz *adj.* atrocious
atún *noun m.* tuna fish, tuna
aturdir *verb.* to stun
audaz *adj.* bold, audacious
audiencia *noun f.* 1. audience 2. court
auditar *verb.* to audit
auditor, -tora *noun.* auditor
auditoría *noun f.* audit
auge *noun m.* 1. boom 2. height, peak
augusto, -ta *adj.* august
aullar *verb.* to howl
aullido *noun m.* howl
aumentar *verb.* 1. to increase 2. raise
aumento *noun m.* 1. increase 2. raise
aun *adv.* even
aún *adv.* still, yet
aunque *conj.* although, though, even though, even if
auricular *noun m.* receiver
auscultar *verb.* sound
ausencia *noun f.* absence
ausentarse *verb.* to absent oneself
ausente *noun mf.* absentee
ausente *adj.* absent
austero, -ra *adj.* austere
Australia *noun f.* Australia
australiano, -na *noun. adj.* Australian
Austria *noun f.* Austria
austríaco, -ca *noun. adj.* Austrian
auténticamente *adv.* genuinely
auténtico, -ca *adj.* 1. authentic 2. genuine
auto *noun m.* 1. automobile, car 2. sentence, decision
auto- *prefix* self-
autobiografía *noun f.* autobiography
autobús *noun m.* bus
autorización *noun f.* permission
automáticamente *adv.* automatically
automático, -ca *adj.* automatic
automóvil *noun m.* automobile
automovilista *noun mf.* motorist
autonomía *noun f.* autonomy
autónomo, -ma *adj.* autonomous
autopista *noun f.* highway, freeway
—**autopista de peaje** turnpike
autor, -tora *noun.* author
autoridad *noun f.* authority
autoritario, -ria *adj.* authoritarian

autorización *noun f.* authorization
autorizar *verb.* 1. to authorize, sanction 2. approve
auxiliar *noun mf.* assistant, helper
auxiliar *adj.* assistant, auxiliary
auxiliar *verb.* to aid, help, assist
auxilio *noun m.* aid, help, assistance
—**primeros auxilios** first aid
avalancha *noun f.* 1. avalanche 2. flood
avance *noun m.* 1. advance 2. preview
avanzado, -da *adj.* advanced
avanzar *verb.* 1. to advance, move forward 2. progress
avaricia *noun f.* greed, avarice
avaricioso, -sa *adj.* greedy, avaricious
ave *noun f.* bird
—**aves de corral** poultry
avellano *noun m.* hazel
avenida *noun f.* avenue
aventajar *verb.* 1. to surpass, excel 2. lead
aventura *noun f.* 1. adventure 2. risk, venture
aventurar *verb.* to risk, venture
avergonzado, -da *adj.* ashamed
avergonzar *verb.* 1. to shame, put shame 2. embarrass
—**avergonzarse** 1. to be ashamed 2. be embarrassed
avería *noun f.* 1. breakdown 2. damage
averiado, -da *adj.* 1. broken down 2. damaged
averiar *verb.* 1. to cause a breakdown 2. damage
—**averiarse** 1. to break down 2. get damaged
averiguar *verb.* to find out
aversión *noun f.* dislike
aviación *noun f.* aviation
ávido, -da *adj.* eager, avid
avión *noun m.* airplane
—**avión a reacción** jet
—**avión de combate** fighter
avisar *verb.* 1. to notify, inform 2. warn 3. call
aviso *noun m.* 1. notice 2. warning 3. advertisement
avivar *verb.* 1. to enliven, brighten 2. arouse, excite

ay *interj.* oh!, ow!
ayer *adv.* yesterday
ayuda *noun f.* help, assistance, aid
ayudante *noun mf.* assistant, helper
ayudar *verb.* to help, aid, assist
ayunar *verb.* to fast
ayuno *noun m.* fast
ayuntamiento *noun m.* **1.** city council, town council **2.** city hall, town hall
azabache *noun m. adj.* jet

azotar *verb.* to whip, lash
azote *noun m.* whip, lash
azúcar *noun mf.* sugar
azucarado, -da *adj.* sweet
azucarar *verb.* to add sugar
azucena *noun f.* lily
azufre *noun m.* sulfur
azul *noun m. adj.* blue
   —**azul marino** navy blue
azulejo *noun m.* tile

B

babor *noun m.* port
bache *noun m.* **1.** pothole **2.** bad period
bacteria *noun f.* bacteria
báculo *noun m.* **1.** stick, staff **2.** crook
bahía *noun f.* bay
bailar *verb.* to dance
bailarín, -rina *noun.* dancer
baile *noun m.* **1.** dance **2.** dancing **3.** ball
baja *noun f.* **1.** casualty **2.** fall, drop, slump **3.** discharge **4.** dismissal
   —**dar de baja** to discharge, dismiss
   —**darse de baja** to leave
   —**estar de baja** to be on sick leave
bajada *noun f.* **1.** descent **2.** fall, drop **3.** slope
bajar *verb.* **1.** to lower **2.** descend **3.** fall **4.** reduce **5.** take down
   —**bajarse (de)** to get off, get out of
bajo *noun m.* **1.** bass **2.** first floor
bajo, -ja *adj.* **1.** low **2.** short **3.** lower **4.** soft **5.** base, vile
bajo *adv.* **1.** low **2.** softly, quietly
bajo *prep.* **1.** under **2.** beneath **3.** below
bajón *noun m.* slump
bala *noun f.* **1.** bullet **2.** bale
balancear *verb.* to balance, swing, sway
   —**balancearse** to swing, rock, sway
balanceo *noun m.* sway, rocking
balanza *noun f.* **1.** balance **2.** scales
balbucir *verb.* **1.** to stammer **2.** babble
balcón *noun m.* balcony
baldear *verb.* bale

baldosa *noun f.* tile
ballena *noun f.* whale
ballet *noun m.* ballet
balón *noun m.* ball
baloncesto *noun m.* basketball
bamboleo *noun m.* sway
banal *adj.* banal, trivial
banana *noun f.* banana
banca *noun f.* **1.** banking **2.** bench
bancal *noun m.* terrace
banco *noun m.* **1.** bank **2.** bench, stool **3.** school
banda *noun f.* **1.** band **2.** gang **3.** strip
   —**banda ancha** broadband
bandada *noun f.* flock
bandeja *noun f.* tray
bandera *noun f.* flag, banner
bando *noun m.* **1.** edict **2.** side, faction
banquero, -ra *noun.* banker
banquete *noun m.* banquet, feast
banquetear *verb.* to feast
banquillo *noun m.* **1.** bench **2.** dock
bañar *verb.* **1.** to bathe, wash **2.** dip, coat
   —**bañarse 1.** to have a bathe, take a bath **2.** swim
bañera *noun f.* bathtub
baño *noun m.* **1.** bath, swim **2.** bathtub **3.** bathroom
bar *noun m.* bar
baraja *noun f.* deck
barajar *verb.* **1.** to shuffle **2.** consider
barato, -ta *adj.* cheap

barba *noun f.* beard
bárbaro, -ra *noun m.* barbarian
bárbaro, -ra *adj.* 1. barbarian, uncivilized 2. fantastic
barbilla *noun f.* chin
barca *noun f.* boat
barcaza *noun f.* barge
barco *noun m.* 1. boat 2. ship
barman *noun m.* bartender
barómetro *noun m.* barometer
barón *noun m.* baron
baronesa *noun f.* baroness
barra *noun f.* 1. bar 2. rail 3. rod
barrer *verb.* to sweep
barrera *noun f.* barrier
barricada *noun f.* barricade
barrido *noun m.* sweep
barriga *noun f.* belly
barril *noun m.* barrel
barrio *noun m.* 1. neighborhood 2. quarter
barro *noun m.* 1. clay 2. mud
barroco, -ca *adj.* baroque
barrote *noun m.* bar
bártulos *noun m. plural.* things, belongings
basar *verb.* to base
 —basarse en to be based on
base *noun f.* 1. base 2. basis
 —base de datos database
básicamente *adv.* basically
básico, -ca *adj.* basic
bastante *adj.* 1. enough, sufficient 2. quite a lot of 3. quite a few
bastante *adv.* 1. enough, sufficiently 2. quite, rather
bastante *pron.* enough
bastar *verb.* to suffice, be enough
bastardo, -da *noun. adj.* bastard
bastidor *noun m.* 1. frame 2. wings
basto, -ta *adj.* coarse
bastón *noun m.* stick, cane
basura *noun f.* 1. garbage 2. trash can
bata *noun f.* 1. bathrobe, housecoat 2. lab coat
batalla *noun f.* battle
batallón *noun m.* battalion
bate *noun m.* bat
batería *noun f.* 1. battery 2. drums

 —batería de cocina set of kitchen utensils
batida *noun f.* 1. beating 2. search
batido *noun m.* shake
batidora *noun f.* mixer, blender, whisk
batir *verb.* 1. to beat 2. mix, whisk, whip
baúl *noun m.* trunk
baya *noun f.* berry
bebé *noun m.* baby
beber *verb.* to drink
 —beber a sorbos to sip
 —beber a tragos to gulp
bebida *noun f.* drink, beverage
 —bebida no alcohólica soft drink
beca *noun f.* 1. grant 2. scholarship
becario, -ria *noun.* 1. grant holder 2. scholar holder
béisbol *noun m.* baseball
belga *noun mf. adj.* Belgian
Bélgica *noun f.* Belgium
belleza *noun f.* beauty
bello, -lla *adj.* 1. beautiful 2. lovely
bemol *noun m.* flat
bendecir *verb.* 1. to bless 2. praise
bendición *noun f.* blessing
bendito, -ta *adj.* blessed, holy
beneficiario, -ria *noun.* beneficiary
beneficiar *verb.* to benefit
 —beneficiarse to profit, benefit
beneficio *noun m.* 1. benefit 2. gain, profit
beneficioso, -sa *adj.* beneficial
benéfico, -ca *adj.* charitable
benigno, -na *adj.* benign, mild
bermejo, -ja *adj.* ginger, reddish
berrear *verb.* 1. to bellow 2. howl
besar *verb.* to kiss
beso *noun m.* kiss
bestia *noun f.* beast
besuquearse *verb.* to neck
betún *noun m.* shoe polish
Biblia *noun f.* Bible
bíblico, -ca *adj.* biblical
biblioteca *noun f.* library
bibliotecario, -ria *noun.* librarian
bicho *noun m.* bug, small animal
bicicleta *noun f.* bicycle
bidón *noun m.* drum, can
bien *noun m.* good

—**bienes** goods, property
—**bienes de consumo** consumer goods
—**bienes de equipo** capital goods
—**bienes raíces** real state
bien *adj.* well-to-do
bien *adv.* 1. well 2. correctly, properly 3. all right 4. easily
—**más bien** rather
—**si bien** although
bien *interj.* good
bienestar *noun m.* 1. comfort 2. welfare, well-being
bienvenida *noun f.* welcome
—**dar la bienvenida** to welcome
bienvenido, -da *adj.* welcome
bifurcación *noun f.* fork
bifurcarse *verb.* to fork
bigote *noun m.* moustache
bilateral *adj.* bilateral
bilis *noun f.* bile
billar *noun m.* 1. pool, billiards 2. snooker
billete *noun m.* 1. bill 2. ticket
—**billete de ida y vuelta** round-trip ticket
—**billete sencillo** one-way ticket
billón *noun m.* trillion
binario, -ria *adj.* binary
biografía *noun f.* biography
biología *noun f.* biology
biológico, -ca *adj.* biological
biombo *noun m.* screen
birlar *verb.* to pinch
Birmania *noun f.* Burma
birmano, -na *noun. adj.* Burmese
bit *noun m.* bit
bizcocho *noun m.* 1. biscuit 2. sponge cake
blanco *noun m.* 1. white 2. blank 3. target
blanco, -ca *adj.* white
blandir *verb.* to brandish, flourish
blando, -da *adj.* 1. soft, tender 2. weak
blandura *noun f.* softness, tenderness
blasfemar *verb.* 1. to blaspheme 2. curse, swear
blindado, -da *adj.* armored
blindaje *noun m.* armor
bloc *noun m.* pad

bloque *noun m.* 1. block 2. bloc
bloquear *verb.* 1. to block 2. blockade 3. jam
bloqueo *noun m.* blockade
blusa *noun f.* blouse
bobada *noun f.* nonsense
bobina *noun f.* reel
bobo, -ba *noun.* fool, simpleton
bobo, -ba *adj.* silly, stupid
boca *noun f.* mouth
—**boca abajo** face down, prone
—**boca arriba** face up
bocadillo *noun m.* sandwich
bocado *noun m.* 1. bite 2. mouthful
boceto *noun m.* sketch, outline
bocha *noun f.* bowl
bochorno *noun m.* 1. sultry weather 2. shame, embarrassment
bochornoso, -sa *adj.* 1. close 2. shameful, embarrassing
bocina *noun f.* horn
boda *noun f.* wedding, marriage
bodega *noun f.* cellar
bofetada *noun f.* slap
—**dar bofetadas a alguien** to slap somebody
bofetón *noun m.* slap
boicot *noun m.* boycott
boicotear *verb.* to boycott
bol *noun m.* bowl
bola *noun f.* 1. ball 2. lie, fib
boletín *noun m.* 1. bulletin 2. journal, review
boleto *noun m.* 1. ticket 2. coupon
—**boleto de ida y vuelta** round-trip ticket
—**boleto sencillo** one-way ticket
boliche *noun m.* bowling
bolígrafo *noun m.* ballpoint pen, pen
bollo *noun m.* bread roll, bun
bolo *noun m.* tenpin
—**bolos** bowling
bolsa *noun f.* 1. bag 2. pocket
—**la Bolsa** the Stock Exchange, the Stock Market
bolsillo *noun m.* pocket
bolso *noun m.* bag, handbag, purse
bomba *noun f.* 1. bomb 2. pump
—**bomba atómica** A-bomb

bombardear verb. 1. to bomb, shell 2. bombard

bombardeo noun m. 1. bombing, shelling 2. bombardment

bombardero noun m. bomber

bombear verb. to pump

bombilla noun f. bulb, light bulb

bombón noun m. bonbon, chocolate

bondad noun f. goodness, kindness

bondadoso, -sa adj. kind, kindly

bonito, -ta adj. nice, pretty

bono noun m. 1. voucher 2. bond

boom noun m. boom

boqueada noun f. gasp

boquilla noun f. mouthpiece

borde noun m. border, edge, brink
—**al borde de** on the brink of, on the verge of

bordear verb. 1. to border, skirt 2. border on

bordillo noun m. curb

borne noun m. terminal

borracho, -cha noun. drunk, drunkard

borracho, -cha adj. drunk

borrador noun m. 1. draft 2. sketch

borrar verb. to erase

borrascoso, -sa adj. stormy

bosque noun m. forest, wood

bota noun f. boot

botar verb. 1. to bounce 2. throw out, throw away 3. fire, sack 4. launch

bote noun m. 1. bounce 2. can, tin, jar, container 3. boat
—**bote salvavidas** lifeboat

botella noun f. bottle

botín noun m. 1. booty, loot 2. ankle boot

botón noun m. button

botones noun m. bellhop

bóveda noun f. vault, arch

boxeador, -dora noun. boxer

boxear verb. to box

boxeo noun m. boxing

boya noun f. 1. float 2. buoy

bragas noun f. plural. pants, underwear

bragueta noun f. zipper, fly

bramar verb. 1. to roar 2. howl

bramido noun m. roar

branquia noun f. gill

Brasil noun m. Brazil

brasileño, -ña noun. adj. Brazilian

bravo, -va adj. 1. ferocious, fierce 2. great, excellent 3. angry

brazada noun f. stroke

brazo noun m. arm

brea noun f. pitch

brecha noun f. 1. breach, gap 2. gash, wound

breve adj. brief, short

brevemente adv. briefly

brezo noun m. heather

brigada noun f. brigade

brillante noun m. diamond

brillante adj. bright, brilliant, shiny

brillantemente adv. brightly, brilliantly

brillar verb. 1. to shine 2. sparkle 3. glitter

brillo noun m. 1. shine 2. glitter

brincar verb. to jump around

brinco noun m. jump, leap

brindar verb. 1. to toast 2. offer

brindis noun m. toast

brisa noun f. breeze

británico, -ca noun. adj. British

brizna noun f. 1. blade 2. piece, scrap

broma noun f. joke

bromear verb. to fool, joke, kid

bromista noun mf. joker

bronca noun f. fight, quarrel, row

bronce noun m. bronze

bronceado noun m. tan, suntan

bronceado, -da adj. tanned, brown

broncearse verb. to get a suntan

brotar verb. 1. to bud, sprout 2. spring up 3. break out

brote noun m. 1. bud, sprout 2. outbreak

bruja noun f. witch

brujo noun m. wizard, sorcerer

brújula noun f. compass

brusco, -ca adj. 1. sudden, abrupt 2. brusque, rough

brutal adj. brutal

bruto, -ta noun. brute, beast

bruto, -ta adj. 1. gross, raw 2. brutish, stupid

buche noun m. crop

budín *noun m.* pudding

buen *adj.* (see bueno. Used before masculine singular nouns and infinitives used as nouns)

bueno, -na *adj.* 1. good 2. kind, nice 3. large, considerable 4. healthy, well

bufanda *noun f.* scarf

bufé *noun m.* buffet

bufete *noun m.* law firm

buhardilla *noun f.* attic

búho *noun m.* owl

bulbo *noun m.* 1. bulb 2. stir

bullir *verb.* to boil

bulto *noun m.* 1. bulge 2. pack, bundle 3. shape 4. lump

bungalow *noun m.* bungalow

búnker *noun m.* bunker

buque *noun m.* ship, vessel

burbuja *noun f.* bubble

burbujear *verb.* to bubble

burgués, -guesa *noun. adj.* bourgeois

burguesía *noun f.* bourgeoisie

burla *noun f.* mockery

burlar *verb.* to deceive

  —**burlarse** to mock

burocracia *noun f.* bureaucracy

burocrático, -ca *adj.* bureaucratic

burro, -rra *noun.* ass, donkey

busca *noun f.* 1. search 2. quest

buscar *verb.* 1. to look for, seek 2. search

búsqueda *noun f.* 1. search 2. quest

busto *noun m.* bust

butaca *noun f.* 1. armchair 2. seat

C

caballería *noun f.* 1. cavalry 2. knighthood, chivalry

caballero *noun m.* 1. gentleman 2. knight

caballeroso, -sa *adj.* 1. gentlemanly 2. chivalrous

caballete *noun m.* 1. easel 2. ridge 3. bridge (of the nose)

caballo *noun m.* 1. horse 2. knight (in chess)

cabaña *noun f.* cabin, hut

cabecear *verb.* 1. to head 2. nod 3. pitch

cabecera *noun f.* 1. top, heading, title-page 2. bedside 3. head

cabello *noun m.* hair

caber *verb.* 1. to fit 2. be possible

cabeza *noun f.* head

  —**cabeza de familia** head of the household

  —**cabeza de serie** seed

  —**cabeza de turco** scapegoat

  —**cabeza dura** stubborn person

cabezazo *noun m.* 1. butt 2. header

cabezota *noun mf.* stubborn person

cabina *noun f.* 1. booth 2. cab 3. cabin 4. cockpit

cable *noun m.* 1. cable 2. wire

cablegrafiar *verb.* to cable, wire

cablegrama *noun m.* cable

cabo *noun m.* 1. cape 2. corporal 3. thread

  —**al cabo de** after

  —**al fin y al cabo** after all

  —**llevar a cabo** to carry out

cabra *noun f.* goat

cabrito *noun m.* kid

cacao *noun m.* cacao, cocoa

cacería *noun f.* hunting

cacerola *noun f.* pan, saucepan

cacharro *noun m.* object, piece of junk

  —**cacharros de cocina** pots and pans

cachear *verb.* to search, frisk

cacheo *noun m.* searching, frisking

cachete *noun m.* cheek, slap

cachivache *noun m.* junk

cacho *noun m.* piece

cachorro *noun m.* 1. cub 2. pup

cada *adj.* 1. each 2. every

  —**cada vez más** more and more

  —**cada vez mejor** better and better

cadáver *noun m.* body, corpse

cadena *noun f.* 1. chain 2. channel 3. range

—cadena perpetua life
cadera noun f. hip
caducar verb. to expire
caduco, -ca adj. 1. out of date, expired 2. deciduous 3. outdated, outmoded
caer verb. 1. to fall 2. drop 3. hang
—caerse to fall (down)
—caer bien to like
—caer mal to dislike
café noun m. 1. coffee 2. coffee shop
cagar verb. to shit
caída noun f. 1. fall 2. drop 3. collapse 4. loss
caja noun f. 1. box 2. checkout counter 3. case
—caja de caudales safe
cajetilla noun f. pack
cajón noun m. 1. drawer 2. box, crate
cal noun f. lime
calada noun f. puff
calado noun m. 1. draft 2. openwork
calado, -da adj. soaked
calavera noun f. skull
calcar verb. 1. to trace 2. copy, imitate
calcetín noun m. sock
calcio noun m. calcium
calcomanía noun f. transfer
calculadora noun f. calculator
calcular verb. 1. to calculate 2. reckon, estimate
cálculo noun m. 1. calculation 2. reckoning, estimate 3. stone
caldera noun f. 1. boiler 2. cauldron
calderilla noun f. small change
caldo noun m. stock, broth
calefacción noun f. heating
calendario noun m. 1. calendar 2. schedule
calentador noun m. heater
calentar verb. to warm, heat
—calentarse to warm oneself, warm up, heat up
calibrador noun m. gauge
calibrar verb. 1. to calibrate 2. gage
calibre noun m. caliber
calidad noun f. 1. quality, grade 2. position, status
cálidamente adv. warmly
cálido, -da adj. 1. warm 2. hot

caliente adj. 1. hot 2. warm
calificar verb. 1. to describe 2. grade
caligrafía noun f. handwriting
caliza noun f. limestone
callado, -da adj. quiet, silent
calle noun f. street, road
callejero, -ra adj. 1. street 2. stray
callejón noun m. alley
callejuela noun f. alley
callo noun m. corn, callus
calma noun f. calm, quiet
calmado, -da adj. calm
calmar verb. to calm, soothe
—calmarse to calm down
calor noun m. 1. heat 2. warmth
caloría noun f. calorie
calumnia noun f. libel
calurosamente adv. warmly
caluroso, -sa adj. 1. hot 2. warm
calvo, -va noun. bald person
calvo, -va adj. bald
calzada noun f. road
calzado noun m. footwear
calzoncillos noun m. plural. underpants, briefs, shorts
cama noun f. bed
camada noun f. litter
cámara noun f. 1. camera 2. chamber 3. house
—cámara de video video camera
—cámara fotográfica camera
camarada noun mf. 1. comrade 2. colleague
camarero, -ra noun. 1. waiter or waitress 2. steward or stewardess
camarote noun m. cabin
cambiante adj. 1. changing 2. changeable 3. moody
cambiar verb. 1. to change 2. exchange, swap 3. move
cambio noun m. 1. change 2. alteration 3. exchange, swap
—a cambio in return, in exchange
—en cambio whereas
caminar verb. to walk
caminata noun f. hike, walk
camino noun m. 1. road, path, track 2. way 3. journey 4. course
camión noun m. truck

camioneta *noun f.* van
camisa *noun f.* shirt
camiseta *noun f.* **1.** undershirt **2.** T-shirt
campamento *noun m.* camp
campana *noun f.* bell
campanada *noun f.* stroke
campanilla *noun f.* bell
campaña *noun f.* **1.** campaign **2.** country
campeón, -peona *noun.* champion
campeonato *noun m.* championship
campesinado *noun m.* peasantry
campesino, -na *noun.* peasant, farmer
campo *noun m.* **1.** country, countryside **2.** field
campus *noun m.* campus
Canadá *noun m.* Canada
canadiense *noun mf. adj.* Canadian
canal *noun m.* **1.** canal **2.** channel
canalizar *verb.* to channel
canalla *noun mf.* swine, rat
canapé *noun m.* **1.** couch **2.** canapé
canasta *noun f.* basket
cancelación *noun f.* cancellation
cancelar *verb.* **1.** to cancel **2.** pay off
cáncer *noun m.* cancer
cancha *noun f.* court, field
canciller *noun m.* chancellor
canción *noun f.* song
candente *adj.* live
candidato, -ta *noun.* **1.** applicant **2.** candidate **3.** nominee
candidatura *noun f.* candidature, candidacy
cándido, -da *adj.* **1.** naïve, naive **2.** simple
canica *noun f.* marble
canje *noun m.* exchange, swap
cano, -na *adj.* gray
canon *noun m.* canon
canónigo *noun m.* canon
cansado, -da *adj.* **1.** tired, weary **2.** tiring
cansancio *noun m.* weariness, fatigue
cansar *verb.* **1.** to tire **2.** be tiring
cansarse *verb.* to get tired
cantante *noun mf.* singer
cantar *verb.* to sing
cantera *noun f.* quarry
cántico *noun m.* chant, canticle
cantidad *noun f.* **1.** quantity, amount **2.** sum

cantimplora *noun f.* canteen, water bottle
cantina *noun f.* canteen, cafeteria
canto *noun m.* **1.** singing **2.** song **3.** chant **4.** edge
caña *noun f.* **1.** cane **2.** reed
—**caña de pescar** fishing rod
cañería *noun f.* **1.** pipe **2.** pipes
cañón *noun m.* **1.** cannon **2.** barrel **3.** canyon
caoba *noun f.* mahogany
caos *noun m.* chaos
capa *noun f.* **1.** cape, cloak **2.** coat **3.** layer
capacidad *noun f.* **1.** capacity **2.** ability, capability
capacitado, -da *adj.* qualified
capacitar *verb.* **1.** to qualify **2.** train, prepare
capataz *noun mf.* foreman or forewoman
capaz *adj.* able, capable
capilla *noun f.* chapel
capirotazo *noun m.* flip
capital *noun f.* capital
—**capital humano** human resources
capital *adj.* **1.** main, chief, key **2.** capital
capitalismo *noun m.* capitalism
capitalista *noun mf. adj.* capitalist
capitán, -tana *noun.* captain
capitanear *verb.* **1.** to captain **2.** command
capitel *noun m.* capital
capítulo *noun m.* chapter
capó *noun m.* hood
capricho *noun m.* **1.** whim, fancy **2.** caprice
captar *verb.* **1.** to catch, grasp **2.** win, attract
captura *noun f.* **1.** capture **2.** seizure **3.** catch
capturar *verb.* **1.** to capture **2.** seize
capucha *noun f.* hood
capuchón *noun m.* cap
cara *noun f.* **1.** face **2.** side **3.** look, appearance **4.** nerve, cheek
caracol *noun m.* snail
carácter *noun m.* **1.** character **2.** nature
característica *noun f.* characteristic, feature, trait
característico, -ca *adj.* characteristic

caracterizar *verb.* to characterize
carajo *interj.* damn!
caramelo *noun m.* **1.** candy **2.** caramel
carátula *noun f.* **1.** cover **2.** mask
caravana *noun f.* **1.** convoy **2.** caravan **3.** trailer
carbohidrato *noun m.* carbohydrate
carbón *noun m.* **1.** coal **2.** charcoal
carbono *noun m.* carbon
carcajada *noun f.* laughter
cárcel *noun f.* jail, prison
cardenal *noun m.* **1.** cardinal **2.** bruise
cardinal *adj.* cardinal
carecer (de) *verb.* to lack
carencia *noun f.* **1.** lack **2.** shortage
careta *noun f.* mask
carga *noun f.* **1.** load, freight, cargo **2.** burden **3.** charge
cargado, -da *adj.* **1.** loaded **2.** charged **3.** strong
cargador *noun m.* **1.** loader, longshoreman **2.** battery charger
cargamento *noun m.* cargo, load
cargar *verb.* **1.** to load **2.** carry **3.** charge
cargo *noun m.* **1.** load, burden **2.** charge **3.** post, office
cariarse *verb.* to decay
caricatura *noun f.* **1.** caricature **2.** cartoon
caricia *noun f.* **1.** caress **2.** pat, stroke
caridad *noun f.* charity
caries *noun f.* decay
cariño *noun m.* **1.** affection, love **2.** honey, darling, sweet
cariñoso, -sa *adj.* affectionate, loving
caritativo, -va *adj.* charitable
carnada *noun f.* bait
carnaval *noun m.* carnival
carnaza *noun f.* bait
carne *noun f.* **1.** meat **2.** flesh
carnero *noun m.* **1.** ram **2.** mutton
carnicería *noun f.* **1.** butcher shop **2.** slaughter
carnicero, -ra *noun.* butcher
caro, -ra *adj.* **1.** expensive **2.** dear
carpa *noun f.* **1.** carp **2.** tent **3.** big top
carpeta *noun f.* **1.** file, folder **2.** portfolio
carrera *noun f.* **1.** run **2.** race **3.** course **4.** career

carreta *noun f.* cart
carrete *noun m.* **1.** film **2.** reel
carretera *noun f.* road, highway
carretilla *noun f.* wheelbarrow
carril *noun m.* **1.** lane **2.** rail
carrito *noun m.* cart
carro *noun m.* **1.** car **2.** cart **3.** wagon
carruaje *noun m.* carriage
carta *noun f.* **1.** letter **2.** card **3.** charter **4.** map **5.** menu
cartearse con *verb.* correspond
cartel *noun m.* cartel
cartera *noun f.* **1.** wallet, billfold **2.** portfolio
cartón *noun m.* **1.** cardboard **2.** card
cartucho *noun m.* cartridge
casa *noun f.* **1.** house **2.** home **3.** household **4.** firm, company
casado, -da *adj.* married
casamiento *noun m.* **1.** wedding **2.** marriage
casar *verb.* **1.** to marry **2.** match up
—**casarse** to get marry
—**casarse con** to marry
cascar *verb.* to crack
cáscara *noun f.* **1.** skin, peel **2.** shell
casco *noun m.* **1.** helmet **2.** hull **3.** empty bottle **4.** headphones
—**casco antiguo** old quarter
casero, -ra *noun.* landlord or landlady
casero, -ra *adj.* home, homemade
casete *noun mf.* cassette
casi *adv.* **1.** almost, nearly **2.** hardly (in negative sentences)
casino *noun m.* casino
caso *noun m.* **1.** case **2.** affair
—**hacer caso de** to notice, pay attention to
casta *noun f.* **1.** caste **2.** lineage, stock
castigar *verb.* to punish
castigo *noun m.* **1.** punishment **2.** penalty
castillo *noun m.* castle
casual *adj.* **1.** chance **2.** fortuitous
casualidad *noun f.* **1.** chance **2.** coincidence
—**por casualidad** by chance
casualmente *adv.* by chance
catalogar *verb.* to catalog, classify

catálogo noun m. catalog
catar verb. to taste
catarata noun f. 1. waterfall 2. cataract
catástrofe noun f. catastrophe
cátedra noun f. chair
catedral noun f. cathedral
catedrático, -ca noun. professor
categoría noun f. 1. category 2. grade, rank
catering noun m. catering
católico, -ca noun. adj. Catholic
catorce noun m. adj. 1. fourteen 2. fourteenth
caucho noun m. rubber
causa noun f. cause
—**por causa de** because of
causar verb. 1. to cause 2. make
cautela noun f. caution
cauteloso, -sa adj. cautious
cautivador, -dora adj. captivating
cautivar verb. to captivate
cautivo, -va noun. adj. captive
cauto, -ta adj. cautious
cavar verb. to dig
caverna noun f. cave
cavidad noun f. cavity
cayado noun m. crook
caza noun f. 1. hunting 2. game
caza noun m. fighter plane
cazador, -dora noun m. hunter
cazar verb. 1. to hunt 2. catch 3. land
cazo noun m. 1. saucepan 2. ladle
cazuela noun f. 1. pan 2. casserole
CD noun m. CD, compact disk
cebada noun f. barley
cebar verb. 1. to bait 2. fatten
cebo noun m. bait
cebolla noun f. onion
ceder verb. 1. to cede, hand over 2. give in, yield 3. diminish, abate
cegar verb. 1. to blind 2. block
ceja noun f. eyebrow
celda noun f. cell
celebración noun f. celebration
celebrar verb. 1. to celebrate 2. hold 3. perform
célebre adj. celebrated, noted
celebridad noun f. 1. celebrity 2. fame, renown

celoso, -sa adj. jealous
Celsius adj. Celsius
celta adj. Celtic
célula noun f. cell
celular adj. cellular
cementerio noun m. cemetery
cemento noun m. cement
cena noun f. dinner, supper
cenar verb. 1. to have dinner, have supper, dine 2. have for dinner, have for supper
cenicero noun m. ashtray
ceniza noun f. ash
censo noun m. census
censura noun f. 1. censorship 2. censure, criticism
censurar verb. 1. to censor 2. censure, criticize
centavo noun m. cent
centellear verb. to sparkle
centelleo noun m. sparkle
centena noun f. hundred
centenario noun m. centennial
centenario, -ria adj. centenarian
centeno noun m. rye
centígrado adj. centigrade
centímetro noun m. centimeter
céntimo noun m. cent
central noun f. 1. head office, headquarters 2. plant, station
—**central eléctrica** power station
central adj. 1. central 2. main
centrar verb. 1. to center 2. focus
—**centrarse en** to focus on, center on
céntrico, -ca adj. central
centro noun m. 1. center 2. downtown
ceño noun m. frown
cepa noun f. 1. stock 2. stump
cepillado noun m. brushing
cepillar verb. 1. to brush 2. plane
cepillo noun m. 1. brush 2. plane
cera noun f. 1. polish 2. wax
cerámica noun f. 1. ceramics 2. pottery
ceramista noun mf. potter
cerca noun f. 1. fence 2. wall
cerca adv. close, near, nearby
—**cerca de** nearly, almost
cercado noun m. enclosure
cercanía noun f. proximity

—cercanías 1. neighborhood **2.** outskirts, suburbs

cercano, -na *adj.* close, near, nearby

cercar *verb.* **1.** to enclose, fence **2.** surround

cerco *noun m.* **1.** enclosure **2.** fence **3.** siege

cerdo, -da *noun.* pig, hog

—carne de cerdo pork

cereal *noun m.* **1.** cereal **2.** grain

cerebral *adj.* cerebral

cerebro *noun m.* brain

ceremonia *noun f.* ceremony

cerilla *noun f.* match

cero *noun m.* zero

cerrado, -da *adj.* **1.** closed, shut **2.** thick **3.** reserved

cerradura *noun f.* lock

cerrar *verb.* **1.** to close, shut **2.** lock **3.** turn off **4.** seal

—cerrarse 1. to close, shut **2.** end

certamen *noun m.* contest

certeza *noun f.* certainty

certificado *noun m.* certificate

certificado, -da *adj.* registered

certificar *verb.* **1.** to certify **2.** register

cervecería *noun f.* beer hall, bar

cerveza *noun f.* beer

cesar *verb.* **1.** to cease, stop **2.** dismiss

césped *noun m.* **1.** grass **2.** lawn

cesta *noun f.* basket

chal *noun m.* shawl

chalado, -da *adj.* nutty, crazy

chaleco *noun m.* vest

chalet *noun m.* villa

champán, champaña *noun m.* champagne

champiñón *noun m.* mushroom

chanza *noun m.* joke

chaparrón *noun m.* downpour, shower

chapotear *verb.* to splash

chapoteo *noun m.* splash

chapuzón *noun m.* dip

chaqueta *noun f.* jacket

charco *noun m.* pool, puddle

charla *noun f.* chat, talk

charlar *verb.* to chat, talk

charlatán, -tana *noun.* chatterbox

chasquear *verb.* **1.** to clip **2.** crack **3.** snap

chasquido *noun m.* **1.** clip **2.** crack **3.** snap

chatarra *noun f.* scrap

chaval, -vala *noun.* kid, lad

chavo, -va *noun.* kid, lad

checo, -ca *noun. adj.* Czech

chelín *noun m.* shilling

cheque *noun m.* check

chichón *noun m.* bump

chicle *noun m.* chewing gum

chico, -ca *noun.* boy or girl

chico, -ca *adj.* **1.** little, small **2.** young

chiflado, -da *adj.* nutty, crazy

chile *noun m.* chili

Chile *noun m.* Chile

chileno, -na *noun. adj.* Chilean

chillar *verb.* to scream

chillido *noun m.* scream

chillón, -llona *adj.* **1.** shrill **2.** loud

chimenea *noun f.* **1.** chimney **2.** fireplace

China *noun f.* China

chinche *noun m.* bedbug

chino, -na *noun. adj.* Chinese

chip *noun m.* chip

Chipre *noun m.* Cyprus

chipriota *noun mf. adj.* Cypriot

chirriar *verb.* to creak, squeak

chirrido *noun m.* squeak

chisme *noun m.* **1.** gossip **2.** stuff

chismorrear *verb.* to gossip

chismorreo *noun m.* gossip

chismoso, -sa *adj.* gossiping

chispa *noun f.* spark

chispeante *adj.* sparkling

chispear *verb.* **1.** to throw out sparks **2.** sparkle

chiste *noun m.* joke

chistoso, -sa *noun.* wit

chivar *verb.* to rat, squeal

chivato, -ta *noun.* **1.** informer **2.** sneak

chivo, -va *noun.* young goat

chocar *verb.* **1.** to collide, crash **2.** clash **3.** shock **4.** shake **5.** clink

chocolate *noun m.* **1.** chocolate **2.** cocoa

choque *noun m.* **1.** collision, crash **2.** clash **3.** shock

chorrear *verb.* **1.** to drip **2.** pour

chorro *noun m.* jet, stream
chubasco *noun m.* downpour
chuchería *noun f.* candy
chuleta *noun f.* chop, cutlet
chupada *noun f.* **1.** suck **2.** puff
chupar *verb.* **1.** to suck **2.** puff on **3.** absorb
chusma *noun f.* rabble
chutar *verb.* to shoot
cicatriz *noun f.* scar
ciclo *noun m.* cycle
ciego, -ga *noun.* blind person
ciego, -ga *adj.* blind
  —**a ciegas** blindly
cielo *noun m.* **1.** sky **2.** heaven
cien *noun m.* one hundred
cien *adj.* hundred, a hundred
ciénaga *noun f.* bog, swamp
ciencia *noun f.* science
científico, -ca *noun.* scientist
científico, -ca *adj.* scientific
cierre *noun m.* **1.** closure, closing **2.** clasp, fastener
cierto, -ta *adj.* **1.** certain **2.** true **3.** one, some
  —**por cierto** by the way
ciervo, -va *noun.* deer, stag
cifra *noun f.* **1.** figure **2.** number
cifrar *verb.* **1.** to code, encode **2.** pin, place
  —**cifrarse** to calculate
cigarro *noun m.* cigarette
cilindro *noun m.* cylinder
cima *noun f.* top, height, summit
cimiento *noun m.* base, foundation
cinc *noun m.* zinc
cinco *noun m. adj.* **1.** five **2.** fifth
cincuenta *noun m. adj.* fifty
cine *noun m.* **1.** cinema **2.** movie theater
cínico, -ca *noun.* cynic
cínico, -ca *adj.* cynical
cinta *noun f.* **1.** ribbon **2.** tape
cintura *noun f.* waist
cinturón *noun m.* belt
circo *noun m.* circus
circuito *noun m.* circuit
circulación *noun f.* circulation
circular *noun f. adj.* circular
circular *verb.* **1.** to circulate **2.** run **3.** walk **4.** flow

círculo *noun m.* circle
circundar *verb.* to surround
circunscripción *noun f.* constituency
circunstancia *noun f.* circumstance
ciruela *noun f.* plum
  —**ciruela pasa** prune
cirugía *noun f.* surgery
cirujano, -na *noun.* surgeon
cisne *noun m.* swan
cisterna *noun f.* **1.** tank **2.** flush
cita *noun f.* **1.** appointment, date **2.** quotation
citación *noun f.* **1.** summons **2.** quotation
citar *verb.* **1.** to quote **2.** make an appointment **3.** summon
ciudad *noun f.* city, town
ciudadanía *noun f.* citizenship
ciudadano, -na *noun.* citizen
cívico, -ca *adj.* civic
civil *adj.* **1.** civil **2.** civilian
civilización *noun f.* civilization
clan *noun m.* clan
clara *noun f.* egg white
claramente *adv.* clearly
claridad *noun f.* clarity
claro *noun m.* clearing
  —**claro de luna** moonlight
claro, -ra *adj.* **1.** clear **2.** evident **3.** bright **4.** fair, light **5.** weak, thin **6.** frank
claro *adv.* **1.** clearly **2.** sure **3.** frankly **4.** of course
clase *noun f.* **1.** class **2.** sort, type
clásico *noun m.* classic
clásico, -ca *adj.* **1.** classic **2.** classical
clasificación *noun f.* **1.** classification **2.** rating
clasificar *verb.* **1.** to classify **2.** sort **3.** rank
  —**clasificarse** to qualify
cláusula *noun f.* clause
clavar *verb.* **1.** to hammer **2.** nail **3.** plunge **4.** fix
clave *noun f.* **1.** key **2.** code **3.** clef
clave *adj.* key
clavija *noun f.* **1.** peg **2.** plug
clavo *noun m.* **1.** nail **2.** clove
claxon *noun m.* horn
clemencia *noun f.* mercy

clerical *adj.* clerical
clérigo *noun m.* clergyman, priest
clero *noun m.* clergy
clic *noun m.* click
cliente, -ta *noun.* client, customer
clientela *noun f.* **1.** customers **2.** practice
clima *noun m.* climate
clímax *noun m.* climax
clínica *noun f.* clinic
clínico, -ca *adj.* clinical
clip *noun m.* clip
club *noun m.* club
coalición *noun f.* coalition
cobertizo *noun m.* shed
cobertor *noun m.* bedspread
cobertura *noun f.* coverage
cobrador, -dora *noun.* **1.** collector **2.** conductor
cobrar *verb.* **1.** to charge **2.** collect **3.** get, earn **4.** draw
cobre *noun m.* copper
cocaína *noun f.* cocaine
cocer *verb.* **1.** to boil **2.** cook
coche *noun m.* car
cochera *noun f.* garage
cocido *noun m.* stew
cocina *noun f.* **1.** kitchen **2.** cuisine
cocinar *verb.* to cook
cocinero, -ra *noun.* **1.** chef **2.** cook
cóctel *noun m.* cocktail
codicia *noun f.* lust, greed
codicioso, -sa *adj.* greedy
codificar *verb.* **1.** to codify **2.** code
código *noun m.* code
—**código postal** zip code
codo *noun m.* elbow
cofia *noun f.* cap
coger *verb.* **1.** to take **2.** seize **3.** catch **4.** gather **5.** pick
coherencia *noun f.* coherence
coherente *adj.* coherent
cohete *noun m.* rocket
coincidencia *noun f.* coincidence
coincidir *verb.* to coincide
cojear *verb.* to limp
cojera *noun f.* limp
cojín *noun m.* cushion
cojinete *noun m.* bearing

cola *noun f.* **1.** tail **2.** line **3.** glue
colaboración *noun f.* collaboration
colaborador, -dora *noun.* **1.** contributor **2.** collaborator
colada *noun f.* washing
colapso *noun m.* collapse
colar *verb.* to strain
colcha *noun f.* bedspread
colección *noun f.* collection
coleccionista *noun mf.* collector
colectividad *noun f.* community
colectivo *noun m.* collective
colectivo, -va *adj.* collective
colega *noun mf.* **1.** colleague **2.** counterpart
colegio *noun m.* **1.** school **2.** college
cólera *noun f.* anger
cólera *noun m.* cholera
colérico, -ca *adj.* **1.** angry **2.** irritable
colgado, -da *adj.* hanging, hanged, hung
colgar *verb.* to hang
colina *noun f.* hill
colisión *noun f.* collision, crash
colisionar *verb.* to collide, crash
collar *noun m.* **1.** necklace **2.** collar
colmar *verb.* to heap
colmo *noun m.* height, extreme
colocar *verb.* **1.** to place, put **2.** arrange
—**colocarse** **1.** to get a job **2.** position oneself
colon *noun m.* colon
colonia *noun f.* **1.** colony, settlement **2.** cologne
colonial *adj.* colonial
colonizador, -dora *noun.* colonizer, settler
colono, -na *noun.* **1.** colonizer, settler **2.** tenant farmer
color *noun m.* color
colorante *noun m.* coloring
colorear *verb.* to color
columna *noun f.* column
—**columna vertebral** spine
columnista *noun mf.* columnist
columpio *noun m.* swing
comandante *noun mf.* **1.** commander **2.** major
combate *noun m.* **1.** combat **2.** fight

combatiente *noun mf.* fighter
combatir *verb.* to combat, fight
combatividad *noun f.* fighting spirit
combinación *noun f.* combination
combinar *verb.* **1.** to combine **2.** match
 —**combinarse** to get together, join together
combustible *noun m.* fuel
comedia *noun f.* comedy
comedido, -da *adj.* restrained
comedor *noun m.* dining-room
comentar *verb.* **1.** to comment **2.** remark
comentario *noun m.* **1.** comment, remark **2.** commentary
comentarista *noun mf.* commentator
comenzar *verb.* to begin, start
comer *verb.* to eat
 —**dar de comer** to feed
comercial *adj.* commercial
comerciante *noun mf.* **1.** dealer **2.** merchant **3.** trader
 —**comerciante al por menor** retailer
comerciar *verb.* **1.** to deal, trade **2.** do business (with)
comercio *noun m.* **1.** commerce, trade **2.** store
cometa *noun f.* **1.** comet **2.** kite
cometer *verb.* **1.** to commit **2.** make
cometido *noun m.* assignment
cómic *noun m.* comic
comicidad *noun m.* humor
cómico, -ca *noun.* comedian or comedienne
cómico, -ca *adj.* comic, comical
comida *noun f.* **1.** food **2.** dinner **3.** meal
comienzo *noun m.* start, beginning
comisaría *noun f.* police station
comisario, -ria *noun.* commissioner
comisión *noun f.* **1.** commission **2.** committee
comité *noun m.* committee
como *conj.* **1.** as **2.** like **3.** if **4.** since, given that
como *prep.* as, like
cómo *adv.* how
cómo *interj.* what?
cómoda *noun f.* bureau
cómodamente *adv.* **1.** comfortably **2.** conveniently

comodidad *noun f.* **1.** comfort **2.** convenience
cómodo, -da *adj.* **1.** comfortable **2.** convenient
compacto, -ta *adj.* compact
compadecer *verb.* **1.** to feel sorry, pity **2.** sympathize with
compañerismo *noun m.* fellowship, comradeship
compañero, -ra *noun.* companion, fellow
compañía *noun f.* company
comparable *adj.* comparable
comparación *noun f.* comparison
comparar *verb.* to compare
comparativo, -va *adj.* comparative
comparecencia *noun f.* appearance
comparecer *verb.* to appear
compartimiento *noun m.* compartment
compartir *verb.* to share
compás *noun m.* **1.** compass **2.** measure **3.** rhythm
compasión *noun f.* **1.** compassion **2.** pity
compasivo, -va *adj.* compassionate
compatibilidad *noun f.* compatibility
compatible *adj.* compatible
compeler *verb.* to compel
compensar *verb.* **1.** to compensate (for) **2.** make up (for)
competencia *noun f.* **1.** competence **2.** competition
competente *adj.* able, capable, competent
competición *noun f.* **1.** competition **2.** contest
competidor, -dora *noun.* competitor
competir *verb.* to compete
competitivo, -va *adj.* competitive
compilar *verb.* to compile
complacer *verb.* **1.** to please **2.** indulge
complaciente *adj.* obliging
complejidad *noun f.* complexity
complejo *noun m.* complex
complejo, -ja *adj.* complex
complementar *verb.* to complement, supplement
 —**complementarse** to complement each other
complementario, -ria *adj.* complementary

complemento *noun m.* **1.** complement **2.** object
—**complementos** accessories
completamente *adv.* completely
completar *verb.* to complete, finish
completo, -ta *adj.* **1.** complete **2.** full
complexión *noun f.* constitution, build
complicación *noun f.* complication
complicado, -da *adj.* complicated
complicar *verb.* **1.** to complicate **2.** involve
cómplice *noun mf.* accomplice
complot *noun m.* plot
componente *noun m.* component, constituent
componer *verb.* **1.** to compose, write **2.** make up **3.** fix, repair
—**componerse de** to consist of
comportamiento *noun m.* behavior, conduct
comportar *verb.* to involve, carry
—**comportarse** to behave
composición *noun f.* composition
compositor, -tora *noun.* composer
compra *noun f.* purchase, buying
comprador, -dora *noun.* purchaser, buyer
comprar *verb.* to buy, purchase
comprender *verb.* **1.** to understand, realize **2.** comprise, cover
comprensible *adj.* understandable
comprensión *noun f.* **1.** understanding, comprehension **2.** sympathy
comprensivo, -va *adj.* understanding
compresión *noun f.* compression
comprimido *noun m.* tablet
comprimir *verb.* to compress
comprobante *noun m.* **1.** proof **2.** voucher
comprobar *verb.* **1.** to check **2.** verify, probe
comprometer *verb.* **1.** to compromise **2.** commit **3.** jeopardize
—**comprometerse** to commit oneself
—**comprometerse con** to get engaged to
comprometido, -da *adj.* **1.** committed **2.** compromising
compromiso *noun m.* **1.** commitment **2.** engagement

compuesto *noun m.* compound
compuesto, -ta *adj.* **1.** compound **2.** composed
computadora *noun f.* computer
computar *verb.* to compute
computerizar *verb.* to computerize
común *adj.* common
comunal *adj.* communal
comunicación *noun f.* communication
comunicado *noun m.* statement
—**comunicado de prensa** press release
comunicar *verb.* **1.** to announce, inform **2.** connect
—**comunicarse** to communicate
comunicativo, -va *adj.* communicative
comunidad *noun f.* community
comunión *noun f.* communion
comunismo *noun m.* communism
comunista *noun mf. adj.* communist
comunitario, -ria *adj.* communal
con *prep.* **1.** with **2.** to, towards **3.** although
—**con tal que** provided that
concebir *verb.* **1.** to conceive, devise **2.** imagine
conceder *verb.* **1.** to award, grant **2.** concede, admit
concejal, -jala *noun.* councilor, councilman or councilwoman
concentración *noun f.* concentration
concentrar *verb.* to concentrate
—**concentrarse** **1.** to focus, concentrate **2.** gather
concepción *noun f.* conception
concepto *noun m.* concept
concernir *verb.* to concern
concesión *noun f.* **1.** concession **2.** franchise, license
concha *noun f.* shell
conciencia *noun f.* **1.** conscience **2.** consciousness
concienzudo, -da *adj.* thorough
concierto *noun m.* concert
conciliar *verb.* to reconcile
concluir *verb.* **1.** to conclude **2.** end
conclusión *noun f.* conclusion, end
concluyente *adj.* conclusive
concordar *verb.* **1.** to agree **2.** bring to agreement

concreto, -ta *adj.* **1.** concrete **2.** specific

concurrido, -da *adj.* busy, crowded

concurso *noun m.* **1.** contest **2.** competition

condado *noun m.* county

conde, -desa *noun.* count or countess, earl

condecoración *noun f.* decoration, honor

condecorar *verb.* to decorate, honor

condena *noun f.* **1.** condemnation **2.** conviction

condenado, -da *noun.* convict

condenado, -da *adj.* **1.** convicted **2.** damned **3.** doomed

condenar *verb.* **1.** to condemn **2.** sentence, convict **3.** damn

condición *noun f.* **1.** condition **2.** position

condicional *adj.* conditional

condicionar *verb.* to condition

condimentar *verb.* to flavor, spice

condimento *noun m.* seasoning, flavoring

condón *noun m.* condom

conducir *verb.* **1.** to drive **2.** conduct **3.** lead

conductor, -tora *noun.* driver

conectar *verb.* **1.** to connect **2.** link

conejo, -ja *noun.* rabbit

conexión *noun f.* connection

confección *noun f.* **1.** preparation **2.** dressmaking

confeccionar *verb.* **1.** to prepare **2.** make

confederación *noun f.* confederation

conferencia *noun f.* **1.** conference **2.** lecture

conferenciante *noun mf.* lecturer

confesar *verb.* to confess

confesión *noun f.* confession

confiado, -da *adj.* **1.** confident **2.** trusting

confianza *noun f.* **1.** trust **2.** confidence

confiar *verb.* **1.** to trust **2.** confide
—**confiarse** to be over-confident

confidencial *adj.* confidential

confidencialidad *noun f.* confidentiality

confinar *verb.* to confine

confirmación *noun f.* confirmation

confirmar *verb.* to confirm

confitura *noun f.* **1.** jam **2.** preserve

conflictivo, -va *adj.* **1.** controversial **2.** troubled

conflicto *noun m.* conflict

confluir *verb.* to gather

conforme *adj.* satisfied
—**conforme a** in accordance with

conforme *conj.* as

conformidad *noun f.* agreement, consent

confort *noun m.* comfort

confundido, -da *adj.* **1.** confused **2.** mistaken, wrong

confundir *verb.* to confuse
—**confundirse** to make a mistake

confusión *noun f.* confusion

confuso, -sa *adj.* confused

congelar *verb.* to freeze

congregación *noun f.* congregation

congregar *verb.* to bring together
—**congregarse** to gather

congresista *noun mf.* congressman or congresswoman

congreso *noun m.* **1.** congress **2.** conference

conjetura *noun f.* guess

conjunción *noun f.* conjunction

conjuntamente *adv.* jointly

conjunto *noun m.* **1.** group **2.** ensemble **3.** set
—**en conjunto** as a whole, altogether

conjunto, -ta *adj.* joint

conmemorar *verb.* to commemorate

conmigo *pron.* with me

conmoción *noun f.* shock

conmocionar *verb.* to shock, shake

conmovedor, -dora *adj.* moving, touching

conmover *verb.* to move, touch
—**conmoverse** to be moved, be touched

conmutador *noun m.* switch

conocedor, -dora *noun.* connoisseur

conocer *verb.* **1.** to know **2.** meet
—**conocerse 1.** to know oneself **2.** know each other **3.** meet

conocido, -da *noun.* acquaintance

conocido, -da *adj.* **1.** familiar **2.** well-known

conocimiento *noun m.* **1.** knowledge **2.** consciousness

conquista *noun f.* conquest

conquistar *verb.* to conquer

consagración *noun f.* consecration, dedication

consagrar *verb.* **1.** to consecrate, dedicate **2.** devote

consciencia *noun f.* (see conciencia)

consciente *adj.* aware, conscious

conscientemente *adv.* consciously

consecuencia *noun f.* consequence

consecuente *adj.* consistent

consecutivo, -va *adj.* consecutive

conseguir *verb.* **1.** to achieve, attain **2.** get **3.** manage (to)

consejero, -ra *noun.* adviser, counselor

consejo *noun m.* **1.** advice, counsel **2.** council

consenso *noun m.* consensus

consentimiento *noun m.* consent

consentir *verb.* **1.** to allow, consent **2.** spoil

conservación *noun f.* **1.** conservation **2.** preservation

conservador, -dora *noun.* **1.** conservative **2.** curator

conservador, -dora *adj.* conservative

conservadurismo *noun m.* conservatism

conservar *verb.* **1.** to keep, conserve **2.** preserve

considerable *adj.* considerable

consideración *noun f.* **1.** consideration **2.** regard

considerado, -da *adj.* **1.** thoughtful **2.** respected

considerar *verb.* **1.** to consider **2.** deem

consignar *verb.* **1.** to consign **2.** assign **3.** record

consigo *adv.* with you, with him, with her, with them, with one

consistencia *noun f.* consistency

consistente *adj.* **1.** consistent **2.** strong, sound

consolación *noun f.* consolation

consolar *verb.* to console

consolidación *noun f.* consolidation

consolidar *verb.* to consolidate

consonante *noun f.* consonant

consorcio *noun m.* consortium

conspiración *noun f.* conspiracy

conspirar *verb.* to plot, conspire

constancia *noun f.* **1.** record **2.** proof **3.** perseverance

constante *adj.* constant

constar *verb.* to be clear

—constar de to consist of

constelación *noun f.* constellation

consternación *noun f.* dismay

consternar *verb.* to dismay

constitución *noun f.* constitution

constitucional *adj.* constitutional

constituir *verb.* **1.** to constitute **2.** set up

constitutivo, -va *adj.* constituent

constituyente *adj.* constituent

construcción *noun f.* **1.** building **2.** construction

constructivo, -va *adj.* constructive

constructor, -tora *noun.* builder

construir *verb.* to build, construct

consuelo *noun m.* consolation

consulta *noun f.* consultation

consultar *verb.* to consult

consultor, -tora *noun.* consultant

consultorio *noun m.* office

consumado, -da *adj.* consummate, accomplished

consumidor, -dora *noun.* consumer

consumir *verb.* to consume

consumo *noun m.* consumption

contabilidad *noun f.* **1.** accountancy **2.** accounting

contactar *verb.* to contact

contacto *noun m.* contact

contador *noun m.* meter

contagiar *verb.* **1.** to infect **2.** transmit

—contagiarse 1. to become infected **2.** be contagious

contagioso, -sa *adj.* catching, contagious

contaminación *noun f.* contamination, pollution

contaminar *verb.* to contaminate, pollute

contar *verb.* **1.** to count **2.** tell
—**contar con** to rely on, count on
contemplar *verb.* **1.** to contemplate **2.** look at
contemporáneo, -nea *noun. adj.* contemporary
contencioso, -sa *adj.* contentious
contendiente *noun mf.* contender
contenedor *noun m.* container
contener *verb.* **1.** to contain **2.** hold
—**contenerse** to restrain oneself
contenido *noun m.* content
contentar *verb.* to please
contento, -ta *adj.* glad, happy, pleased
contestación *noun f.* answer
contestador *noun m.* answering machine
contestar *verb.* to answer
contexto *noun m.* context
contigo *pron.* with you
continental *adj.* continental
continente *noun m.* continent
contingencia *noun f.* contingency
contingente *noun m.* contingent
continuación *noun f.* continuation
—**a continuación** next
continuar *verb.* to continue, go on
continuidad *noun f.* continuity
continuo, -nua *adj.* continuous, constant
contorno *noun m.* outline
contra *prep.* against
contracción *noun f.* contraction
contradicción *noun f.* contradiction
contradictorio, -ria *adj.* contradictory
contraer *verb.* **1.** to contract **2.** catch
—**contraer matrimonio** to get married
contrariar *verb.* **1.** to contradict **2.** oppose **3.** annoy
contrario, -ria *adj.* contrary, opposite
—**al contrario** on the contrary
contrastar *verb.* to contrast
contraste *noun m.* contrast
contratar *verb.* to hire
contratista *noun mf.* contractor
contrato *noun m.* contract
contribución *noun f.* contribution
contribuir *verb.* **1.** to contribute **2.** pay
contribuyente *noun mf.* taxpayer

contrincante *noun mf.* opponent, challenger
control *noun m.* **1.** control **2.** check
controlador, -dora *noun.* controller
controlar *verb.* **1.** to control **2.** monitor
controversia *noun f.* controversy
controvertido, -da *adj.* controversial
convencer *verb.* to convince, persuade
convencido, -da *adj.* **1.** sure **2.** convinced
convención *noun f.* convention
convencional *adj.* conventional
convenido, -da *adj.* appointed
conveniencia *noun f.* convenience
conveniente *adj.* **1.** appropriate **2.** convenient **3.** suitable
convenio *noun m.* **1.** agreement, pact **2.** covenant
convenir *verb.* **1.** to suit **2.** agree
convento *noun m.* convent
convergencia *noun f.* convergence
conversación *noun f.* conversation, talk
conversar *verb.* to converse, talk
conversión *noun f.* conversion
converso, -sa *noun.* convert
convertible *adj.* convertible
convertir *verb.* to convert
—**convertirse en** to turn into
convicción *noun f.* conviction
convidar *verb.* to invite
convincente *adj.* convincing
convocar *verb.* to call, convene, summon
convoy *noun m.* convoy
conyugal *adj.* conjugal, marital
coñac *noun m.* brandy
cooperación *noun f.* cooperation
cooperativa *noun f.* cooperative
cooperativo, -va *adj.* cooperative
coordinación *noun f.* coordination
coordinar *verb.* to coordinate
copa *noun f.* **1.** cup **2.** drink **3.** glass
copia *noun f.* **1.** copy **2.** imitation
copiar *verb.* to copy
coque *noun m.* coke
coraje *noun m.* courage
coral *noun f.* chorale
coral *noun m.* coral
corazón *noun m.* **1.** heart **2.** core

corbata *noun* f. tie
corchete *noun* m. bracket
corcho *noun* m. cork
cordel *noun* m. cord, string
cordero *noun* m. lamb
cordillera *noun* f. range
cordón *noun* m. 1. lace, cord 2. cordon
Corea *noun* f. Korea
coreano, -na *noun. adj.* Korean
corear *verb.* to chant, chorus
cornear *verb.* to gore
coro *noun* m. 1. choir 2. chorus
corona *noun* f. crown
coronación *noun* f. coronation
coronar *verb.* to crown
coronel *noun* mf. colonel
coronilla *noun* f. crown
corporación *noun* f. corporation
corporal *adj.* bodily, corporal
corpulento, -ta *adj.* stout
corral *noun* m. farmyard, corral
correa *noun* f. belt, strap
corrección *noun* f. correction
correcto, -ta *adj.* correct, right
corredor *noun* m. corridor
corredor, -dora *noun.* 1. runner 2. broker
corregir *verb.* 1. to correct 2. grade
correo *noun* m. mail, post
correr *verb.* 1. to run, 2. rush 3. flow
correspondencia *noun* f. 1. correspondence, mail 2. equivalence
corresponder *verb.* 1. to correspond 2.
belong 3. return
correspondiente *adj.* corresponding
corresponsal *noun* mf. correspondent
corriente *noun* f. 1. current 2. draft 3.
tendency, trend
corriente *adj.* 1. common 2. ordinary
corroborar *verb.* to corroborate
corroer *verb.* 1. to corrode 2. erode
corromper *verb.* 1. to corrupt 2. rot
corrosivo, -va *adj.* corrosive
corrupción *noun* f. corruption
corrupto, -ta *adj.* corrupt
cortante *adj.* cutting, sharp
cortar *verb.* 1. to cut 2. slice 3. chop 4.
trim 5. interrupt 6. block
—**cortarse** 1. to cut oneself 2. go off
corte *noun* f. court

corte *noun* m. cut
cortejar *verb.* to court, woo
cortés *adj.* courteous, polite
cortesía *noun* f. courtesy, politeness
corteza *noun* f. 1. bark 2. crust 3. peel
cortina *noun* f. curtain
corto, -ta *adj.* 1. short 2. shy, timid 3.
scarce
cosa *noun* f. 1. thing, object, stuff 2.
matter, affair
cosecha *noun* f. crop, harvest
cosechar *verb.* 1. to harvest 2. win, earn
coser *verb.* 1. to sew 2. stitch
cosmético *noun* m. cosmetic
cosmético, -ca *adj.* cosmetic
costa *noun* f. coast, shore
—**a toda costa** at all costs
costado *noun* m. 1. flank 2. side
costar *verb.* to cost
costero, -ra *adj.* coastal
costilla *noun* f. rib
costo *noun* m. cost, price
costoso, -sa *adj.* costly
costra *noun* f. crust
costumbre *noun* f. 1. custom 2. habit
costura *noun* f. 1. seam 2. sewing
cotidiano, -na *adj.* everyday, daily
cotilla *noun* mf. gossip
cotillear *verb.* to gossip
cotilleo *noun* m. gossip
cotización *noun* f. quotation
cotizar *verb.* 1. to value 2. pay contri-
butions
—**cotizarse** to be valued
coto *noun* m. preserve, reserve
craso, -sa *adj.* gross
creación *noun* f. creation
creador, -dora *noun.* creator
crear *verb.* 1. to create 2. originate
creatividad *noun* f. creativity
creativo, -va *adj.* creative
crecer *verb.* 1. to grow 2. expand 3.
increase
creciente *adj.* growing, increasing
crecimiento *noun* m. growth
credibilidad *noun* f. credibility
crédito *noun* m. credit
credo *noun* m. creed
creencia *noun* f. belief

creer verb. 1. to believe 2. think
creíble adj. credible, believable
crema noun f. cream
crepúsculo noun m. dusk, twilight
cresta noun f. 1. crest 2. comb
cría noun f. 1. rearing, breeding 2. baby, cub, pup, young
criado, -da noun. servant, maid
crianza noun f. upbringing, rearing
criar verb. 1. to raise, bring up 2. breed
criatura noun f. 1. creature 2. baby
crimen noun m. crime
criminal noun mf. adj. criminal
crisis noun f. crisis
  —crisis nerviosa nervous breakdown
cristal noun m. crystal
cristalino noun m. lens
cristianismo noun m. Christianity
cristiano, -tiana noun. adj. Christian
Cristo noun m. Christ
criterio noun m. criterion
crítica noun f. 1. criticism 2. review
criticar verb. to criticize
crítico noun mf. critic
crítico, -ca adj. critical
crónica noun f. chronicle
crónico, -ca adj. chronic
cronometrar verb. to clock, time
croquis noun m. sketch
cruce noun m. 1. cross, crossing 2. crossroads
crucero noun m. cruise
crucial adj. crucial
crudo, -da adj. 1. crude 2. raw
cruel adj. cruel
crueldad noun f. cruelty
crujido noun m. crunch
crujiente adj. crunchy, crisp
crujir verb. to crunch
cruz noun f. cross
cruzada noun f. crusade
cruzar verb. 1. to cross 2. exchange
  —cruzarse to intersect
cuaderno noun m. notebook
cuadragésimo, -ma noun. adj. fortieth
cuadrícula noun f. grid
cuadrilátero noun m. 1. quadrilateral 2. ring
cuadrilla noun f. gang

cuadro noun m. 1. square 2. picture, painting
cual pron. 1. which 2. who, whom
cuál pron. what (one), which (one)
cualidad noun f. quality
cualificado, -da adj. 1. qualified 2. skilled
cualquier adj. (see cualquiera. Used before nouns)
cualquiera adj. 1. any 2. everyday, ordinary
cualquiera pron. 1. anybody, anyone, whoever 2. whichever, whatever
cuán adv. how
cuando conj. 1. when 2. if
cuando prep. 1. during 2. if
cuándo adv. when
cuanto, -ta adj. as many
  —cuanto más the more
  —cuanto menos the less
cuanto adv. as much as
  —cuanto antes as soon as possible
cuanto, -ta pron. all what, everything
  —unos cuantos a few
cuánto, -ta adj. pron. how much, how many
cuánto adv. 1. how much 2. how far
cuarenta noun m. adj. forty
Cuaresma noun f. Lent
cuartear verb. to quarter
cuartel noun m. barracks
  —cuartel general headquarters
cuarteto noun m. quartet
cuarto noun m. 1. room 2. quarter, fourth
cuarto, -ta noun. adj. fourth
cuatro noun m. adj. four
cuba noun f. barrel
Cuba noun f. Cuba
cubano, -na noun. adj. Cuban
cubierta noun f. 1. cover 2. deck
cubierto noun m. 1. cover, shelter 2. utensil 3. table setting
cubo noun m. 1. bucket 2. cube
  —cubo de la basura trash can
cubrir verb. to cover
cuchara noun f. spoon
cucharada noun f. spoonful
cucharilla noun f. teaspoon
cucharón noun m. ladle
cuchichear verb. to whisper

cuchillo *noun m.* knife
cuello *noun m.* **1.** neck **2.** collar
cuenca *noun f.* basin
cuenco *noun m.* basin, bowl
cuenta *noun f.* **1.** account **2.** bill, check **3.** count
cuento *noun m.* story, tale
cuerda *noun f.* cord, rope, string
cuerno *noun m.* horn
cuero *noun m.* **1.** leather **2.** hide
cuerpo *noun m.* **1.** body **2.** corps
cuesta *noun f.* slope
cuestión *noun f.* matter
cuestionable *adj.* questionable
cuestionar *verb.* to question
cuestionario *noun m.* **1.** questionnaire **2.** quiz
cueva *noun f.* cave
cuidado *noun m.* **1.** care **2.** worry, concern
—**tener cuidado** to be careful
cuidado, -da *adj.* trim
cuidadoso, -sa *adj.* careful
cuidar *verb.* **1.** to take care of, look after **2.** pay attention to, watch
culo *noun m.* **1.** bottom **2.** ass
culpa *noun f.* blame, fault
culpabilidad *noun f.* guilt
culpable *adj.* guilty
culpar *verb.* to blame
cultivado, -da *adj.* cultivated
cultivador, -dora *noun.* cultivator
cultivar *verb.* **1.** to cultivate **2.** farm **3.** raise, grow
cultivo *noun m.* **1.** crop **2.** cultivation, farming

culto *noun m.* cult
culto, -ta *adj.* cultivated, educated
cultura *noun f.* culture
cultural *adj.* cultural
cumbre *noun f.* height, peak, summit, top
cumpleaños *noun m.* birthday
cumplido *noun m.* compliment
cumplimiento *noun m.* **1.** fulfillment **2.** performance
cumplir *verb.* **1.** to accomplish, carry out **2.** fulfill, comply with **3.** expire
—**cumplirse 1.** to be fulfilled **2.** expire
cuna *noun f.* **1.** cradle **2.** birthplace
cuña *noun f.* wedge
cuota *noun f.* **1.** share **2.** quota **3.** subscription, fee **4.** installment, payment
cupón *noun m.* coupon
cúpula *noun f.* dome
cura *noun f.* cure, treatment
cura *noun m.* priest
curar *verb.* **1.** to cure **2.** heal
curiosidad *noun f.* curiosity
curioso, -sa *adj.* **1.** curious **2.** peculiar, unusual
currículum *noun m.* curriculum
curry *noun m.* curry
curso *noun m.* **1.** course **2.** school year
curtir *verb.* to tan
curva *noun f.* curve, bend
curvar *verb.* to bend
curvo, -va *adj.* curved, bent
cúspide *noun f.* height, peak, summit
custodia *noun f.* custody
cuyo, -ya *pron.* whose

D

dado *noun m.* dice
dado, -da *adj.* given
dama *noun f.* lady
danés, -nesa *noun. adj.* Danish
danza *noun f.* **1.** dance **2.** dancing
dañar *verb.* **1.** to damage **2.** harm, hurt
dañino, -na *adj.* harmful
daño *noun m.* **1.** damage **2.** harm

dar *verb.* **1.** to give **2.** hit, strike **3.** hand over, deliver **4.** produce, yield **5.** be enough
—**dar a** to overlook
—**dar con** to find
—**dar contra** to hit
—**dar por** to consider
—**darse a** to take to

—**darse de sí** to stretch
—**dárselas de** to boast about
dardo *noun m.* dart
datar (de) *verb.* to date (from)
dátil *noun m.* date
dato *noun m.* fact, piece of information
—**datos** data
de *prep.* **1.** of **2.** from **3.** in, at **4.** than **5.** by
deambular *verb.* to wander
debajo *adv.* underneath
—**debajo de** under, beneath
—**por debajo** below
debate *noun m.* debate
debatir *verb.* to debate
deber *noun m.* duty
deber *verb.* **1.** must **2.** ought to, should **3.** to owe
debidamente *adv.* duly, properly
debido, -da *adj.* due, proper
débil *adj.* **1.** weak **2.** faint **3.** feeble
debilidad *noun f.* weakness, feebleness
debilitar *verb.* to weaken
debut *noun m.* debut
década *noun f.* decade
decadencia *noun f.* **1.** decadence **2.** decline
decaer *verb.* **1.** to decline, decay **2.** weaken
decano, -na *noun.* **1.** dean **2.** senior member
decencia *noun f.* decency
decente *adj.* decent
decepción *noun f.* disappointment
decepcionado, -da *adj.* disappointed
decepcionante *adj.* disappointing
decepcionar *verb.* to disappoint, let down
decidido, -da *adj.* **1.** decisive **2.** determined
decidir *verb.* **1.** to decide **2.** determine **3.** settle
—**decidirse** to make up one's mind
décimo, -ma *noun. adj.* tenth
decimoctavo, -va *noun. adj.* eighteenth
decimocuarto, -ta *noun. adj.* fourteenth
decimonoveno, -na *noun. adj.* nineteenth
decimoquinto, -ta *noun. adj.* fifteenth

decimoséptimo, -ma *noun. adj.* seventeenth
decimosexto, -ta *noun. adj.* sixteenth
decimotercero, -ra *noun. adj.* thirteenth
decir *verb.* **1.** to say **2.** tell **3.** speak
—**decirse** to be said
decisión *noun f.* decision, choice
decisivo, -va *adj.* decisive
declaración *noun f.* **1.** declaration, statement **2.** testimony
declarar *verb.* **1.** to declare, state **2.** testify
—**declararse** **1.** to plead **2.** confess one's love
declive *noun m.* **1.** decline **2.** slope
decoración *noun f.* decoration
decorado *noun m.* scenery, stage set
decorar *verb.* to decorate
decorativo, -va *adj.* decorative
decoro *noun m.* decorum
decretar *verb.* to decree
decreto *noun m.* decree
dedicación *noun f.* **1.** dedication **2.** devotion
dedicado, -da *adj.* **1.** dedicated **2.** devoted
dedicar *verb.* **1.** to dedicate **2.** devote
—**dedicarse a** to devote oneself to
dedicatoria *noun f.* dedication
dedo *noun m.* **1.** finger (hand) **2.** toe (foot)
deducción *noun f.* deduction
deducir *verb.* **1.** to deduce **2.** deduct
defecto *noun m.* **1.** defect **2.** flaw
defectuoso, -sa *adj.* **1.** defective **2.** faulty
defender *verb.* to defend
—**defenderse** **1.** to protect oneself, defend oneself **2.** get by
defensa *noun f.* defense
defensivo, -va *adj.* defensive
defensor, -sora *noun.* **1.** advocate **2.** champion **3.** defender
deficiencia *noun f.* deficiency
deficiente *noun mf.* handicapped person
déficit *noun m.* deficit
definición *noun f.* definition

definido, -da *adj.* definite
definir *verb.* to define
definitivo, -va *adj.* definitive
—**en definitiva** all in all
deformación *noun f.* 1. deformation 2. distortion
deformar *verb.* 1. to deform 2. distort
defraudar *verb.* 1. to disappoint 2. defraud
degustación *noun f.* tasting, sampling
degustar *verb.* to taste
dejadez *noun f.* 1. laziness 2. slovenliness
dejar *verb.* 1. to leave 2. abandon 3. give up 4. let 5. allow, permit
—**dejar de** to stop, quit
—**dejarse** 1. to leave 2. forget 3. grow 4. let oneself go
delantal *noun m.* apron
delante *adv.* ahead
—**delante de** before
delantera *noun f.* 1. front 2. forward line
delantero, -ra *noun m.* forward
delantero, -ra *adj.* 1. front, fore 2. forward
delatar *verb.* 1. to betray 2. inform against, denounce
delegación *noun f.* 1. delegation 2. mission
delegado, -da *noun.* delegate
delegar *verb.* to delegate
deleitar *verb.* to delight
deleite *noun m.* delight
deletrear *verb.* to spell
delfín *noun m.* dolphin
delgado, -da *adj.* 1. thin, skinny 2. slender, slim
deliberado, -da *adj.* deliberate
delicadeza *noun f.* 1. delicacy 2. tact, discretion
delicado, -da *adj.* 1. delicate 2. fine 3. ill 4. sensitive 5. tactful
delicioso, -sa *adj.* 1. delicious 2. delightful
delictivo, -va *adj.* criminal
delincuente *noun mf.* delinquent
delirar *verb.* 1. to rave 2. be delirious
delirio *noun m.* 1. delirium 2. nonsense, ravings

delito *noun m.* 1. crime 2. offence
delta *noun m.* delta
demacrado, -da *adj.* drawn
demanda *noun f.* 1. demand 2. lawsuit 3. request
demandado, -da *noun.* defendant
demandante *noun mf.* plaintiff
demandar *verb.* 1. to sue 2. sue, file a lawsuit 3. call for
demás *adj.* rest, remaining
—**lo demás** the rest, everything else
—**los demás, las demás** the rest, everything else, the others, everyone else
—**por lo demás** 1. otherwise 2. apart from that
—**y demás** and so on
demasiado, -da *adj.* too much, too many
demasiado *adv.* too, too much
demente *adj.* insane
democracia *noun f.* democracy
demócrata *noun mf.* democrat
demócrata *adj.* democratic
democrático, -ca *adj.* democratic
demoler *verb.* to demolish
demolición *noun f.* demolition
demonio *noun m.* demon, devil
demora *noun f.* delay
demorar *verb.* to delay
—**demorarse** to take a long time
demostración *noun f.* 1. demonstration 2. show, display
demostrar *verb.* 1. to demonstrate 2. show
denegación *noun f.* denial, refusal
denominar *verb.* to designate, name
densidad *noun f.* density, thickness
denso, -sa *adj.* dense, thick
dentadura *noun f.* teeth
—**dentadura postiza** dentures
dental *adj.* dental
dentista *noun mf.* dentist
dentro *adv.* 1. inside 2. indoors
—**dentro de** 1. in, inside 2. within
—**dentro de poco** shortly, soon
—**por dentro** inside
denuncia *noun f.* denunciation
denunciar *verb.* 1. to denounce 2. report

departamento *noun m.* department
dependencia *noun f.* dependence
depender (de) *verb.* to depend (on)
dependiente, -ta *noun m.* salesperson, clerk
dependiente *adj.* dependent
deportar *verb.* to deport
deporte *noun m.* sport
deportivo, -va *adj.* 1. sporting 2. sports
depositar *verb.* 1. to deposit, place 2. store
depósito *noun m.* 1. deposit 2. store-house, warehouse
depredador, -dora *noun.* predator
depresión *noun f.* 1. depression 2. slump, recession
deprimente *adj.* depressing
deprimido, -da *adj.* depressed, blue
deprisa *adv.* quick
derecha *noun f.* right
derecho *noun m.* 1. law 2. right
  —**derechos civiles** civil rights
  —**derechos de autor** 1. copyright 2. royalties
derecho, -cha *adj.* 1. right 2. straight 3. upright
derivación *noun f.* derivation
derivar *verb.* to drift
  —**derivar de** to come from, derive from
  —**derivar en** to result in
derramar *verb.* 1. to spill 2. pour 3. shed
derretir *verb.* to melt
derribar *verb.* 1. to demolish 2. shoot down
derrocar *verb.* to overthrow
derrota *noun f.* defeat
derrotar *verb.* to defeat
derrumbar *verb.* to topple
  —**derrumbarse** to collapse
desabrido, -da *adj.* bland, tasteless
desacato *noun m.* contempt
desacreditar *verb.* to discredit
desacuerdo *noun m.* disagreement
desafiante *adj.* defiant
desafiar *verb.* 1. to defy 2. challenge
desafilado, -da *adj.* blunt
desafinado, -da *adj.* out-of-tune
desafío *noun m.* 1. challenge 2. defiance

desafortunadamente *adv.* unfortunately
desafortunado, -da *adj.* unfortunate, unlucky
desagradable *adj.* unpleasant, disagreeable
desahogado, -da *adj.* comfortable, well-off
desalentar *verb.* to discourage
desalojar *verb.* 1. to remove, clear 2. evacuate 3. evict
desamparado, -da *adj.* helpless
desanimar *verb.* to discourage
desaparecer *verb.* to disappear, vanish
desaparecido, -da *adj.* 1. missing 2. deceased
desaparición *noun f.* disappearance
desaprobación *noun f.* disapproval
desaprovechar *verb.* to waste, misuse
desarmar *verb.* to disarm
desarrollar *verb.* to develop
  —**desarrollarse** to take place
desarrollo *noun m.* development
desastre *noun m.* disaster
desastroso, -sa *adj.* disastrous
desatar *verb.* 1. to untie, undo 2. trigger
desatender *verb.* 1. to disregard 2. neglect
desayunar *verb.* to have breakfast
desayuno *noun m.* breakfast
desbancar *verb.* to oust
descansar *verb.* to rest
descansillo *noun m.* landing
descanso *noun m.* 1. rest 2. break
descarga *noun f.* discharge
descargar *verb.* 1. to discharge 2. unload
descaro *noun m.* cheek, nerve
descartar *verb.* to rule out, reject
descendente *adj.* downward, descending
descender *verb.* 1. to descend 2. go down 3. fall, drop
  —**descender de** to be a descendant of
descenso *noun m.* 1. descent 2. drop, fall
descifrar *verb.* to decipher, decode
descomponer *verb.* 1. to rot 2. break
  —**descomponerse** 1. to break down 2. decompose
descomposición *noun f.* 1. breakdown 2. decay

descomunal *adj.* **1.** enormous, giant, huge **2.** extraordinary

desconcertado, -da *adj.* confused

desconcertar *verb.* to disconcert, confuse

desconectar *verb.* to disconnect, switch off

desconfiado, -da *adj.* suspicious, distrustful

desconfiar *verb.* to suspect, distrust

desconocido, -da *noun.* stranger

desconocido, -da *adj.* **1.** unfamiliar **2.** unknown

descontar *verb.* to discount, deduct

descontento *noun m.* discontent

descontento, -ta *adj.* discontented

descorrer *verb.* to draw

descrédito *noun m.* discredit

describir *verb.* to describe

descripción *noun f.* description

descubierto, -ta *adj.* **1.** exposed, revealed **2.** naked

descubrimiento *noun m.* discovery

descubrir *verb.* **1.** to discover, find out **2.** uncover **3.** unveil

descuento *noun m.* discount

descuidado, -da *adj.* careless

descuidar *verb.* to neglect
—**descuidarse** to drop one's guard

descuido *noun m.* **1.** carelessness **2.** negligence

desde *prep.* **1.** since **2.** from
—**desde ahora** from now on
—**desde entonces** since then
—**desde luego** of course

desdén *noun m.* disdain, contempt

desdicha *noun f.* misery

deseable *adj.* desirable

desear *verb.* **1.** to wish **2.** want **3.** desire

desechar *verb.* to discard

desecho *noun m.* waste
—**desechos** garbage

desembarcadero *noun m.* landing

desembarcar *verb.* land

desembarco *noun m.* to disembark

desembocadura *noun f.* mouth

desempeñar *verb.* **1.** to play, fulfill **2.** redeem

desempeño *noun m.* performance, fulfillment

desempleado, -da *noun.* unemployed person

desempleado, -da *adj.* unemployed

desempleo *noun m.* unemployment

desencadenar *verb.* to trigger

desentonar *verb.* **1.** to clash **2.** be out of tune

deseo *noun m.* desire, wish

deseoso, -sa *adj.* **1.** eager **2.** anxious

desertar *verb.* to defect, desert

desesperación *noun f.* despair, desperation

desesperado, -da *adj.* desperate, hopeless

desesperar *verb.* **1.** to despair **2.** exasperate

desestimar *verb.* to reject

desfasado, -da *adj.* dated

desfavorable *adj.* unfavorable, adverse

desfilar *verb.* to parade

desfile *noun m.* **1.** parade **2.** procession

desgarrar *verb.* to tear, rip

desgarrón *noun m.* tear, rip

desgastar *verb.* to wear out, wear down

desgaste *noun m.* wear

desgracia *noun f.* **1.** disgrace **2.** misfortune
—**por desgracia** unfortunately

desgraciadamente *adv.* unfortunately

desgraciado, -da *adj.* unfortunate

deshacer *verb.* **1.** to destroy **2.** dissolve, melt **3.** break
—**deshacerse** to fall apart
—**deshacerse de** to get rid of

deshecho, -cha *adj.* **1.** destroyed **2.** broken

deshonra *noun f.* dishonor, disgrace, shame

deshonrar *verb.* to dishonor, disgrace

deshuesar *verb.* **1.** to bone **2.** pit

desierto *noun m.* desert

desierto, -ta *adj.* **1.** deserted **2.** empty

designar *verb.* to designate, appoint

desigual *adj.* **1.** unequal **2.** uneven

desigualdad *noun f.* **1.** inequality **2.** unevenness

desintegrar *verb.* to disintegrate

desleal *adj.* disloyal

desliz *noun m.* **1.** mistake **2.** slip

deslizar *verb.* to slide, slip
deslumbrante *adj.* dazzling
deslumbrar *verb.* to dazzle
desmayarse *verb.* to faint
desmayo *noun m.* faint
desmentir *verb.* to deny
desmenuzar *verb.* to crumble
desmigajar *verb.* to crumble
desmontar *verb.* 1. to dismantle 2. dismount
desnudar *verb.* to undress, strip
desnudo, -da *adj.* bare, naked
desocupado, -da *adj.* 1. vacant, empty 2. free 3. unemployed
desorden *noun m.* 1. disorder, mess 2. disturbance
despachar *verb.* to dispatch
despacho *noun m.* 1. office 2. dispatch
despacio *adv.* slow, slowly
desparramar *verb.* 1. to spill 2. spread, scatter
despedazar *verb.* to cut to pieces.
despedida *noun f.* farewell, good-bye
despedir *verb.* 1. to dismiss, fire 2. give, emit 3. see out
   —**despedirse** to say good-bye
despejado, -da *adj.* clear
despejar *verb.* clear
despejar *verb.* to clear
despellejar *verb.* to skin
desperdiciar *verb.* 1. to waste 2. miss
desperdicio *noun m.* waste
despertar *verb.* 1. to arouse 2. awaken, wake
   —**despertarse** to wake up
despiadado, -da *adj.* ruthless
despido *noun m.* dismissal
despierto, -ta *adj.* 1. alert 2. awake 3. smart 4. vivid
desplazar *verb.* 1. to displace 2. move, shift
desplegar *verb.* 1. to unfold 2. deploy
desplomarse *verb.* 1. to fall 2. collapse
despojar *verb.* to strip
   —**despojarse (de)** to remove
desportilladura *noun f.* chip
desportillar *verb.* to chip
despreciable *adj.* 1. despicable 2. negligible

desprecio *noun m.* disdain, contempt
desprender *verb.* 1. to detach, loosen 2. give, emit
   —**desprenderse (de) 1.** to come off 2. get rid of
despreocupado, -da *adj.* careless
desprestigio *noun m.* discredit
después *adv.* 1. afterwards 2. next, then
   —**después de** after
   —**después de todo** after all
despuntado, -da *adj.* blunt
despuntar *verb.* 1. to blunt 2. excel, stand out
desquitarse *verb.* to retaliate
destacado, -da *adj.* outstanding, prominent
destacamento *noun m.* detachment
destacar *verb.* 1. to highlight, emphasize 2. stand out
destapar *verb.* 1. to open 2. reveal, unveil
destellar *verb.* to flash, sparkle
destello *noun m.* flash, sparkle
desteñir *verb.* to fade
destinar *verb.* 1. to appoint, assign 2. allocate, earmark
destinatario, -ria *noun.* recipient
destino *noun m.* 1. destination 2. destiny, fate 3. assignment
destitución *noun f.* dismissal
destituir *verb.* to dismiss
destreza *noun f.* skill
destrucción *noun f.* destruction
destructivo, -va *adj.* destructive
destruir *verb.* to destroy
desvalido, -da *adj.* helpless
desvalijar *verb.* to ransack, rob
desvalorizar *verb.* to devalue
desván *noun f.* attic
desvanecer *verb.* 1. to dispel 2. fade
   —**desvanecerse 1.** to vanish 2. fade 3. faint
desvanecimiento *noun m.* 1. fade 2. faint
desventaja *noun f.* 1. disadvantage 2. handicap
desventurado, -da *adj.* unfortunate
desvergonzado, -da *adj.* shameless

desviación noun f. **1.** deviation **2.** diversion, detour

desviar verb. **1.** to divert **2.** turn away
—desviarse 1. to turn aside, turn away **2.** make a detour

desvío noun m. **1.** deviation **2.** diversion, detour

detallado, -da adj. detailed

detalle noun m. detail

detallista noun mf. **1.** retailer **2.** perfectionist

detectar verb. to detect

detective noun mf. detective

detención noun f. **1.** arrest, detention **2.** stop, halt

detener verb. **1.** to arrest, detain **2.** stop, halt
—detenerse 1. to stop **2.** delay

detenidamente adv. at length

deteriorado, -da adj. **1.** damaged **2.** worn

deteriorar verb. to damage
—deteriorarse 1. to deteriorate **2.** get damaged

deterioro noun m. **1.** worsening, decline **2.** deterioration, wear

determinación noun f. determination, purpose, resolve

determinado, -da adj. **1.** determined **2.** certain, particular

determinar verb. **1.** to determine **2.** bring out
—determinarse to make up one's mind

detestar verb. to detest

detonación noun f. detonation, blast

detonar verb. to detonate, explode

detrás adv. behind
—detrás de 1. behind **2.** after

deuda noun f. debt

deudor, -dora noun. debtor

devaluación noun f. devaluation

devaluar verb. to devalue
—devaluarse to depreciate

devastador, -dora adj. devastating

devoción noun f. devotion

devolver verb. **1.** to return, give back **2.** refund **3.** vomit

día noun m. **1.** day **2.** daytime
—al día up-to-date

—día festivo holiday

diabetes noun f. diabetes

diabético, -ca noun. adj. diabetic

diablo noun m. devil, demon

diagnosticar verb. to diagnose

diagnóstico noun m. diagnosis

diagrama noun m. **1.** diagram **2.** figure

dialecto noun m. dialect

dialogar verb. to dialogue

diálogo noun m. dialogue

diamante noun m. diamond

diámetro noun m. diameter

diana noun f. target, bull's eye

diapositiva noun f. slide

diariamente adv. daily

diario noun m. **1.** diary **2.** newspaper

diario, -ria adj. daily

diarrea noun f. diarrhea

dibujar verb. **1.** to draw **2.** portray

dibujo noun m. **1.** design **2.** drawing
—dibujos animados cartoon

diccionario noun m. dictionary

dicha noun f. happiness

dicho noun m. saying

dichoso, -sa adj. happy

diciembre noun m. December

dictador, -dora noun. dictator

dictadura noun f. dictatorship

dictar verb. **1.** to dictate **2.** give

diecinueve noun m. adj. nineteen

dieciocho noun m. adj. eighteen

dieciséis noun m. adj. sixteen

diecisiete noun m. adj. seventeen

diente noun m. tooth

dieta noun f. diet

diez noun m. adj. ten

difamación noun f. libel, slander

difamar verb. to libel, slander

diferencia noun f. difference
—a diferencia de in contrast to, unlike

diferenciación noun f. differentiation

diferenciar verb. **1.** to differentiate **2.** distinguish

diferente adj. different

difícil adj. difficult, hard

difícilmente adv. hardly

dificultad noun f. difficulty

difundir verb. **1.** to broadcast **2.** spread out

difunto, -ta *noun.* deceased
difunto, -ta *adj.* 1. deceased 2. late
digerir *verb.* to digest
digestión *noun f.* digestion
digital *adj.* digital
dignidad *noun f.* dignity
dignatario, -ria *noun.* dignitary
digno, -na *adj.* worthy
dilatar *verb.* to dilate, expand
dilema *noun m.* dilemma
diligencia *noun f.* 1. diligence, industry 2. promptness, speed
diluir *verb.* to dilute
dimensión *noun f.* dimension
diminuto, -ta *adj.* minute, tiny
dimisión *noun f.* resignation
dimitir *verb.* to resign
Dinamarca *noun m.* Denmark
dinámica *noun f.* dynamics
dinámico, -ca *adj.* dynamic
dinastía *noun f.* dynasty
dinero *noun m.* money
dinosaurio *noun m.* dinosaur
diócesis *noun f.* diocese
dios, diosa *noun.* god or goddess
Dios *noun m.* God
diploma *noun m.* diploma
diplomacia *noun f.* diplomacy
diplomado, -da *noun.* graduate
diplomarse *verb.* to graduate
diplomático, -ca *noun.* diplomat
diplomático, -ca *adj.* diplomatic
diputado, -da *noun.* representative
dique *noun m.* dike
dirección *noun f.* 1. address 2. direction, way 3. management 4. steering
directiva *noun f.* directive
directivo, -va *noun.* director, executive
directivo, -va *adj.* managerial, executive
directriz *noun f.* guideline
directo, -ta *adj.* 1. direct 2. immediate
—**en directo** live
director, -tora *noun.* director, manager, head, headmaster
—**director de orquesta** conductor
dirigente *noun m.* leader, ruler
dirigente *adj.* leading, ruling
dirigir *verb.* 1. to direct, lead 2. conduct 3. address

dirigirse a *verb.* 1. to address, speak to 2. head for, go towards
discapacidad *noun f.* 1. disability 2. handicap
discapacitado, -da *adj.* 1. disabled 2. handicapped
disciplina *noun f.* discipline
disciplinar *verb.* to discipline
discjockey *noun mf.* disc jockey
disco *noun m.* 1. disc, disk 2. discus 3. record
—**disco compacto** compact disc
—**disco sencillo** single
disconformidad *noun f.* disagreement
discontinuo, -nua *adj.* discontinuous
discoteca *noun f.* disco, discotheque
discreción *noun f.* discretion
discrepar *verb.* 1. to disagree 2. dissent
discreto, -ta *adj.* discreet
discriminación *noun f.* discrimination
disculpa *noun f.* 1. apology 2. excuse
disculpar *verb.* to excuse, pardon
—**disculparse** to apologize
discurso *noun m.* 1. discourse 2. speech, address
discusión *noun f.* 1. argument 2. discussion 3. dispute
discutir *verb.* 1. to argue 2. discuss 3. dispute 4. quarrel
disecar *verb.* 1. to stuff 2. dissect
diseminar *verb.* to disseminate, disperse
disentir *verb.* to dissent, disagree
diseñador, -dora *noun.* designer
diseñar *verb.* to design
diseño *noun m.* 1. design 2. designing
disfraz *noun m.* 1. costume 2. disguise
disfrazar *verb.* 1. to disguise 2. conceal
—**disfrazarse** *verb.* to be in disguise
disfrutar *verb.* to enjoy
disidente *noun mf. adj.* dissident
disimular *verb.* to conceal
disminución *noun f.* decrease, drop, fall
disminuir *verb.* 1. to decrease 2. drop, fall
disolución *noun f.* dissolution
disolver *verb.* to dissolve
disparar *verb.* 1. to fire 2. shoot
—**dispararse** to rocket
disparatado, -da *adj.* absurd

disparate *noun m.* nonsense

disparo *noun m.* shot

dispensar *verb.* 1. to dispense 2. excuse

dispersar *verb.* to scatter, disperse

disperso, -sa *adj.* scattered, dispersed

disponer *verb.* 1. to arrange 2. set out 3. order 4. prepare

disponer a hacer algo *verb.* to be about to

disponibilidad *noun f.* availability

disponible *adj.* available

disposición *noun f.* 1. arrangement 2. disposition 3. provision 4. willingness

dispuesto, -ta *adj.* ready, prepared

disputa *noun f.* dispute

distancia *noun f.* distance

distante *adj.* distant

distinción *noun f.* 1. distinction 2. honor

distinguido, -da *adj.* distinguished

distinguir *verb.* 1. to differentiate, distinguish 2. honor

distintivo, -va *adj.* distinctive

distinto, -ta *adj.* 1. different 2. distinct

distorsión *noun f.* distortion

distorsionar *verb.* to distort

distracción *noun f.* 1. distraction 2. entertainment, amusement

distraer *verb.* 1. to distract 2. entertain

distraído, -da *adj.* 1. distracted 2. absent-minded 3. entertained, amused

distribución *noun f.* distribution

distribuir *verb.* to distribute

distrito *noun m.* district

disturbio *noun m.* disturbance

disuadir *verb.* to dissuade, deter

disuasión *noun f.* dissuasion

diversidad *noun f.* diversity

diversificar *verb.* to diversify

diversión *noun f.* amusement, diversion

diverso, -sa *adj.* diverse, various

divertido, -da *adj.* 1. amusing, funny 2. entertaining

divertir *verb.* to amuse, entertain
  —**divertirse** to have a good time, have fun

dividendo *noun m.* dividend

dividir *verb.* to divide, split

divino, -na *adj.* divine

divisar *verb.* to discern

división *noun f.* division

divisor *noun m.* divisor

divorciar *verb.* to divorce
  —**divorciarse** to get divorced

divorcio *noun m.* divorce

divulgar *verb.* 1. to divulge 2. spread 3. broadcast

doblar *verb.* 1. to double 2. fold 3. dub 4. toll 5. turn

doble *noun mf. adj.* double

doblegar *verb.* to break, vanquish
  —**doblegarse** to give in

doce *noun m. adj.* twelve

docena *noun f.* dozen

docente *noun mf.* teacher

docente *adj.* educational

doctor, -tora *noun.* doctor

doctorado *noun m.* doctorate, PhD

doctrina *noun f.* doctrine

documentación *noun f.* documentation

documental *noun m. adj.* documentary

documento *noun m.* document
  —**documentos** papers

dólar *noun m.* dollar

dolencia *noun f.* ailment

doler *verb.* 1. to hurt, ache 2. grieve
  —**dolerse** to complain

dolor *noun m.* 1. ache, pain 2. grief, sorrow

dolorido *adj.* 1. aching, painful, sore 2. hurt

dolorosamente *adv.* painfully

doloroso, -sa *adj.* 1. painful 2. distressing

doméstico, -ca *adj.* domestic

dominación *noun f.* domination

dominante *adj.* dominant

dominar *verb.* 1. to dominate 2. master 3. prevail
  —**dominarse** to control oneself

domingo *noun m.* Sunday

dominio *noun m.* 1. domain 2. dominance, domination 3. mastery

don *noun m.* gift

donación *noun f.* 1. donation 2. contribution

donante *noun mf.* 1. donor 2. contributor

donar *verb.* to donate

doncella *noun f.* maiden
donde *adv.* **1.** where **2.** wherever
dónde *adv.* where
dondequiera *adv.* wherever, anywhere
dorado *noun m.* gilt
dorado, -da *adj.* golden
dormido, -da *adj.* asleep
dormir *verb.* to sleep
—**dormirse** to fall asleep
dormitorio *noun m.* bedroom
dos *noun m. adj.* two
dosis *noun f.* **1.** dose **2.** amount
dotación *noun f.* **1.** endowment **2.** staff
dotar *verb.* **1.** to endow **2.** provide, equip
dragón *noun m.* dragon
drama *noun m.* drama
dramático, -ca *adj.* dramatic
dramaturgo, -ga *noun.* playwright, dramatist
drástico, -ca *adj.* drastic
drenaje *noun m.* drainage
drenar *verb.* to drain
droga *noun f.* drug

drogar *verb.* to drug
—**drogarse** to take drugs
ducha *noun f.* shower
ducharse *verb.* to take a shower
duda *noun f.* **1.** doubt **2.** hesitation
dudar *verb.* **1.** to doubt **2.** hesitate
dudoso, -sa *adj.* **1.** doubtful **2.** dubious **3.** questionable
duende *noun m.* elf
dueño, -ña *noun.* **1.** landlord or landlady **2.** master or mistress **3.** owner
dulce *noun m.* candy, sweet
dulce *adj.* **1.** sweet **2.** gentle
duodécimo, -ma *noun. adj.* twelfth
duplicar *verb.* **1.** to double **2.** duplicate, copy
duque, -sa *noun.* duke or duchess
duración *noun f.* duration, length
duradero, -ra *adj.* durable, lasting
durante *prep.* during, for
durar *verb.* **1.** to last **2.** endure
duro, -ra *adj.* **1.** hard **2.** harsh **3.** rough
duro *adv.* hard

E

echar *verb.* **1.** to throw, throw out **2.** fire, dismiss **3.** put forth **4.** add **5.** launch **6.** put
—**echar a perder** to spoil
—**echar de menos** to miss
—**echarse** to lie down
eclesiástico *noun m.* cleric, clergyman
eclesiástico, -ca *adj.* ecclesiastic, ecclesiastical
eco *noun m.* echo
ecografía *noun f.* scan
ecología *noun f.* ecology
ecológico, -ca *adj.* ecological
ecologista *noun mf.* ecologist, environmentalist
economía *noun f.* **1.** economy **2.** economics
económico, -ca *adj.* **1.** economic **2.** economical
economista *noun mf.* economist
economizar *verb.* to save

ecuación *noun f.* equation
edad *noun f.* age
edición *noun f.* **1.** edition **2.** publishing
edificar *verb.* **1.** to edify **2.** build, construct
edificio *noun m.* building
editar *verb.* **1.** to edit **2.** publish
editor, -tora *noun.* **1.** editor **2.** publisher
editorial *noun f.* editorial
editorial *adj.* **1.** editorial **2.** publishing
educación *noun f.* education
educado, -da *adj.* polite
educar *verb.* **1.** to educate **2.** raise, bring up **3.** train
educativo, -va *adj.* educational
efectivamente *adv.* **1.** indeed **2.** really
efectivo *noun m.* cash
efectivo, -va *adj.* **1.** effective **2.** real, actual

efecto *noun m.* effect
  —**efectos personales** goods, property
  —**en efecto** in fact, actually
efectuar *verb.* to carry out
eficacia *noun f.* **1.** efficacy **2.** efficiency
eficaz *adj.* **1.** effective **2.** efficient
eficiencia *noun f.* efficiency
eficiente *adj.* efficient
efímero, -ra *adj.* ephemeral, short-lived
egipcio, -cia *noun. adj.* Egyptian
Egipto *noun m.* Egypt
ego *noun m.* ego
egoísta *adj.* selfish
eje *noun m.* **1.** axis **2.** shaft
ejecución *noun f.* **1.** execution **2.** performance
ejecutar *verb.* **1.** to execute **2.** perform
ejecutivo, -va *noun. adj.* executive
ejemplar *noun m.* **1.** copy **2.** specimen
ejemplo *noun m.* example
  —**por ejemplo** for example
ejercer *verb.* **1.** to exercise **2.** exert **3.** practice
ejercicio *noun m.* **1.** exercise **2.** practice
ejercitar *verb.* **1.** to exercise **2.** train
ejército *noun m.* army
el *art.* the
el *pron.* the one
  —**el que** he who, whoever, the one that
él *pron.* **1.** he **2.** him, it **3.** his, its
elaboración *noun f.* **1.** production **2.** preparation
elaborar *verb.* **1.** to produce **2.** make **3.** prepare
elasticidad *noun f.* elasticity
elástico *noun m.* elastic
elástico, -ca *adj.* elastic
elección *noun f.* **1.** election **2.** choice, selection
electo, -ta *adj.* elect
elector, -tora *noun.* elector, voter
electorado *noun m.* electorate
electoral *adj.* electoral
electricidad *noun f.* electricity
eléctrico, -ca *adj.* electric, electrical
electrificar *verb.* to electrify
electrodoméstico *noun m.* appliance
electrón *noun m.* electron
electrónica *noun f.* electronics

electrónico, -ca *adj.* electronic
elefante, -ta *noun.* elephant
elegancia *noun f.* elegance
elegante *adj.* elegant, smart
elegir *verb.* **1.** to elect **2.** choose, select
elemental *adj.* **1.** basic, elementary **2.** essential
elemento *noun m.* element
elepé *noun m.* long-playing record
elevación *noun f.* elevation, height
elevado, -da *adj.* **1.** high **2.** elevated
elevador *noun m.* elevator
elevar *verb.* **1.** to raise, lift **2.** increase **3.** promote
  —**elevarse** to rise
  —**elevarse a** to amount to, total
eliminación *noun f.* **1.** elimination **2.** removal
eliminar *verb.* **1.** to eliminate **2.** remove **3.** kill
ella *pron.* **1.** she **2.** it **3.** her **4.** hers, its
ello *pron.* it
ellos, ellas *pron.* **1.** they **2.** them
  —**de ellos, de ellas** theirs
elocuente *adj.* eloquent
elogiar *verb.* to praise
elogio *noun m.* praise
emancipación *noun f.* emancipation
embajada *noun f.* embassy
embajador, -dora *noun.* ambassador
embalaje *noun m.* packing, packaging
embaldosar *verb.* to tile
embalsar *verb.* to dam
embalse *noun m.* dam, reservoir
embarazada *adj.* pregnant
embarazo *noun m.* pregnancy
embarazoso, -sa *adj.* embarrassing
embarcación *noun f.* boat, craft
embarcadero *noun m.* pier, wharf
embarcar *verb.* to embark
embargar *verb.* **1.** to seize, impound **2.** overwhelm
embargo *noun m.* **1.** embargo **2.** seizure
embarque *noun m.* shipment
embestir *verb.* to charge
embolsar *verb.* to pocket
emboscada *noun f.* ambush
embotellamiento *noun m.* traffic jam
embotellar *verb.* to bottle

embrague noun m. clutch
embrión noun m. embryo
embrionario, -ria adj. embryonic
embrujar verb. to bewitch
embutir verb. to jam, stuff
emergencia noun f. emergency
emerger verb. to emerge
emigrante noun mf. adj. emigrant
emigrar verb. 1. to emigrate 2. migrate
eminente adj. eminent
emisión noun f. 1. emission 2. broadcast 3. issue
emitir verb. 1. to emit 2. broadcast 3. issue
emoción noun f. emotion, excitement
emocionado, -da adj. excited
emocional adj. emotional
emocionante adj. exciting
emocionar verb. 1. to excite, thrill 2. move, touch
emotivo, -va adj. emotional, moving, touching
empalme noun m. 1. connection, link 2. junction
empanada noun f. pie
empañar verb. 1. to steam up 2. tarnish
empapado, -da adj. soaked
empaparse verb. to soak
empapelar verb. to wallpaper
empaquetar verb. to pack, package
emparejar verb. 1. to pair, match 2. make even
—**emparejarse** to match
emparentado, -da adj. related
empastar verb. 1. to fill 2. bind
empaste noun m. filling
empatar verb. to draw, tie
empate noun m. draw, tie
empedernido, -da adj. 1. inveterate 2. heavy
empedrar verb. to pave
empeñar verb. to pawn, pledge
—**empeñarse** 1. to insist (on) 2. get into debt
empeño noun m. 1. pledge 2. pawning 3. insistence
empeorar verb. to worsen
emperador, -dora noun. emperor or empress

empezar verb. to begin, start
empleado, -da noun. employee, employee
empleado, -da adj. employed
emplear verb. 1. to employ 2. use
empleo noun m. 1. employment 2. use, usage
empollar verb. to incubate
empolvar verb. to powder
emprendedor, -dora adj. enterprising, go-ahead
emprender verb. to undertake
empresa noun f. 1. company, corporation, firm, business 2. undertaking, venture
empresario, -ria noun. 1. businessman or businesswoman 2. impresario, manager
empréstito noun m. loan
empujar verb. 1. to push 2. shove
empuje noun m. drive, push
empujón noun m. push, shove
empuñar verb. to grasp
en prep. 1. in 2. on 3. at 4. by 5. inside 6. into
enamorado, -da noun. lover
enamorado, -da adj. in love
enano, -na noun. dwarf
enardecer verb. 1. to arouse 2. stir up
encabezamiento noun m. heading
encabezar verb. 1. to head, lead 2. put a heading
encadenar verb. 1. to chain 2. link
encajar verb. 1. to fit 2. stick 3. take
encaje noun m. lace
encaminar verb. to direct
—**encaminarse hacia** to head for
encanecer verb. to gray
encantado, -da adj. 1. delighted 2. charmed 3. haunted
encantador, -dora adj. 1. delightful 2. charming
encantar verb. 1. to delight, charm 2. enchant, bewitch 3. love
encanto noun m. 1. charm 2. spell
encarcelamiento noun m. imprisonment
encarcelar verb. to imprison, jail
encargado, -da noun. person in charge

encargar *verb.* to order
—**encargarse de** to take charge of
encargo *noun m.* **1.** order **2.** errand **3.** commission, job
encarnar *verb.* to embody
encarnizado, -da *adj.* bloody, bitter
encendedor *noun m.* lighter
encender *verb.* **1.** to light **2.** switch on **3.** start **4.** arouse
encenderse *verb.* to blush
encerar *verb.* **1.** to wax **2.** polish
encerrar *verb.* **1.** to lock up, shut up **2.** contain
enchufe *noun m.* **1.** plug, socket **2.** contact, patronage
encía *noun f.* gum
encierro *noun m.* **1.** enclosure **2.** confinement
encima *adv.* **1.** above, on top **2.** upon **3.** on top of that
—**encima de 1.** above, on top, over **2.** over **3.** as well, besides
encinta *adj.* pregnant
encoger *verb.* to shrink
—**encogerse de hombros** to shrug
encontrar *verb.* **1.** to find **2.** meet **3.** encounter
—**encontrarse 1.** to meet **2.** be, feel **3.** clash
encorvar *verb.* to bend, curve
encrucijada *noun f.* crossroads
encuadernación *noun f.* binding
encuadernar *verb.* to bind
encuadrar *verb.* **1.** to frame **2.** fit, place
encuentro *noun m.* **1.** meeting, encounter **2.** match
encuesta *noun f.* survey, poll
enderezar *verb.* to straighten
endosar *verb.* to endorse
endulzar *verb.* to sweeten
endurecer *verb.* to harden
enemigo, -ga *noun. adj.* enemy
energía *noun f.* energy
enérgico, -ca *adj.* energetic
enero *noun m.* January
enfadado, -da *adj.* angry
enfadar *verb.* to annoy, make angry
—**enfadarse** *verb.* to get annoyed, get angry

énfasis *noun m.* emphasis
enfatizar *verb.* emphasize, stress
enfermedad *noun f.* **1.** disease **2.** illness, sickness
enfermería *noun f.* infirmary
enfermero, -ra *noun.* nurse
enfermo, -ma *noun.* sick person, patient
enfermo, -ma *adj.* ill, sick
enfocar *verb.* to focus
enfrentamiento *noun m.* clash, confrontation
enfrentar *verb.* to face, confront
enfriar *verb.* to cool, chill
—**enfriarse 1.** to cool down **2.** catch a cold
enfurecer *verb.* to enrage
—**enfurecerse** to fly into a rage
enganchar *verb.* to hook
engañar *verb.* **1.** to cheat **2.** deceive
engaño *noun m.* **1.** deception **2.** trick
engañoso, -sa *adj.* **1.** misleading **2.** deceitful
engastado, -da *adj.* set
engastar *verb.* to set
engendrar *verb.* **1.** to beget, father **2.** engender
engranaje *noun m.* gear
engranar *verb.* to engage
engrasar *verb.* to grease
engullir *verb.* to gulp, swallow
enigma *noun f.* enigma
enjabonar *verb.* to soap
enjaular *verb.* to cage
enjuagar *verb.* to rinse
enjuague *noun m.* rinse
enjugar *verb.* to wipe away
enjuiciar *verb.* **1.** to prosecute **2.** try
enlace *noun m.* **1.** link, connection **2.** liaison
enlatar *verb.* to can
enlazar *verb.* to join, link, connect
enlucido *noun m.* plaster
enlucir *verb.* to plaster
enmarañar *verb.* to tangle
enmarcar *verb.* to frame
enmendar *verb.* **1.** to amend **2.** correct
ennegrecer *verb.* to blacken
enojado, -da *adj.* angry
enorgullecerse *verb.* to pride oneself

enorme *adj.* enormous
enredar *verb.* 1. to confuse 2. tangle
enredo *noun m.* 1. mess 2. tangle
enriquecerse *verb.* to get rich
enrollar *verb.* to roll up
enroscar *verb.* 1. to screw 2. coil
ensalada *noun f.* salad
ensamblaje *noun m.* assembly
ensamblar *verb.* 1. to assemble 2. join
ensanchar *verb.* 1. to widen 2. expand
ensangrentado, -da *adj.* bloody
ensartar *verb.* to thread, string
ensayo *noun m.* 1. essay 2. rehearsal 3. test 4. trial
enseña *noun f.* 1. emblem, banner 2. colors
enseñanza *noun f.* teaching
enseñar *verb.* 1. to teach 2. show
ensillar *verb.* to saddle
ensuciar *verb.* to dirty, soil
entablar *verb.* to engage, enter into
entender *verb.* 1. to understand 2. think, believe
—**entender de** to know about
entendido, -da *noun.* expert
entendimiento *noun m.* understanding
enteramente *adv.* entirely, fully
enterar *verb.* to inform
—**enterarse** to learn, find out
entero, -ra *adj.* 1. entire 2. full 3. intact 4. whole
enterrar *verb.* to bury
entierro *noun m.* burial
entonces *adv.* then
entorno *noun m.* 1. environment 2. surroundings
entrada *noun f.* 1. ticket 2. access 3. doorway 4. entrance, entry
entraña *noun f.* heart
—**entrañas** bowels, entrails
entrar *verb.* 1. to enter, go in 2. access
entre *prep.* 1. between 2. among
entrega *noun f.* 1. delivery 2. handing over 3. submission 4. dedication, devotion
entregado, -da *adj.* dedicated, devoted
entregar *verb.* 1. to deliver 2. hand over 3. present
—**entregarse** 1. to surrender 2. indulge, give in 3. devote oneself

entrelazar *verb.* to intertwine, interweave
entrenador, -dora *noun.* coach, trainer, instructor
entrenamiento *noun m.* training, practice
entrenar *verb.* 1. to train 2. practice
entretanto *adv.* meanwhile
entretener *verb.* 1. to entertain, amuse 2. distract
—**entretenerse** to dally
entretenido, -da *adj.* entertaining, amusing
entretenimiento *noun m.* amusement, entertainment
entrever *verb.* 1. to glimpse 2. make out
entrevista *noun f.* interview
entrevistador, -dora *noun.* interviewer
entrevistar *verb.* to interview
entristecer *verb.* to sadden
entrometerse *verb.* to interfere, meddle
entusiasmar *verb.* to excite
entusiasmo *noun m.* enthusiasm
entusiasta *noun mf.* enthusiast
entusiasta *adj.* enthusiastic
envasar *verb.* 1. to pack 2. bottle 3. can
envase *noun m.* 1. container 2. empty 3. can
envejecer *verb.* to age, grow old
envenenar *verb.* to poison
enviado, -da *noun.* envoy
enviar *verb.* 1. to send 2. dispatch 3. ship
envidia *noun f.* envy, jealousy
envidiar *verb.* to envy
envidioso, -sa *adj.* envious, jealous
envío *noun m.* 1. dispatch 2. shipment
enviudar *verb.* to be widowed, become a widow or widower
envoltorio *noun m.* package, bundle
envolver *verb.* 1. to wrap 2. surround
enyesar *verb.* to plaster
epidemia *noun f.* epidemic
episodio *noun m.* episode
época *noun f.* age, epoch, time, period
epopeya *noun f.* epic poem
equidad *noun f.* equity

equilibrado, -da adj. well-balanced
equilibrar verb. to balance
equilibrio noun m. balance, equilibrium
equipaje noun m. baggage, luggage
equipamiento noun m. equipment
equipar verb. to equip
equiparar verb. 1. to compare 2. put on a same level
equipo noun m. 1. crew 2. team 3. gear, equipment 4. kit
equitativo, -va adj. equitable, fair
equivalente noun m. 1. equivalent 2. counterpart
equivalente adj. equivalent
equivaler verb. 1. to be equal to, be equivalent to 2. correspond
equivocación noun f. mistake
equivocar verb. to mistake
  —equivocarse to make a mistake, be wrong
era noun f. era
erecto, -ta adj. erect
erguido, -da adj. erect
erguir verb. to raise
erigir verb. 1. to erect, build 2. establish, found
erigirse verb. to set oneself up as
erosión noun f. erosion
erosionar verb. to erode
erótico, -ca adj. erotic
errar verb. 1. to miss 2. wander 3. be mistaken
erróneo, -nea adj. erroneous, wrong
error noun m. error, mistake
erudición noun f. learning, scholarship
erudito, -ta noun. scholar
erudito, -ta adj. learned
erupción noun f. 1. eruption 2. rash
esbelto, -ta adj. slender, slim
esbozar verb. 1. to outline 2. sketch
esbozo noun m. 1. outline 2. draft 3. sketch
escabullirse verb. to slip away
escala noun f. 1. range 2. scale
escalada noun f. climb
escalador, -dora noun. climber
escalar verb. 1. to climb, scale 2. escalate
escalera noun f. 1. stairs 2. ladder
escalofrío noun m. shiver, chill

escalón noun m. echelon
escama noun f. 1. scale 2. flake
escandalizar verb. to shock, scandalize
  —escandalizarse to be shocked
escándalo noun m. scandal
escandaloso, -sa adj. 1. shocking, scandalous 2. outrageous 3. noisy
escanear verb. to scan
escáner noun m. scanner
escapar verb. to escape, run away
escape noun m. 1. escape 2. leak
escarcha noun f. frost
escarchar verb. to frost
escarlata noun f. adj. scarlet
escarpado, -da adj. steep, sheer
escasez noun f. 1. scarcity, lack, shortage 2. want
escaso, -sa adj. scarce, scant
  —escaso de short of
escatimar verb. to spare
escayola noun f. plaster, plaster cast
escena noun f. scene
escenario noun m. 1. stage 2. scene, setting
escepticismo noun m. skepticism
escéptico, -ca adj. skeptical
esclarecer verb. to clarify
esclavo, -va noun. slave
esclusa noun f. lock
escocer verb. to smart, sting
escocés noun m. Scots (language)
escocés, -cesa noun. Scot
escocés, -cesa adj. Scots, Scottish, Scotch
Escocia noun f. Scotland
escoger verb. to choose, pick, select
escolta noun mf. escort
escoltar verb. to escort
escombro noun m. debris
esconder verb. to hide, conceal
escondido, -da adj. hidden
escondite noun m. hiding place
escondrijo noun m. hiding place
escorar verb. to heel, list
escoria noun m. scum
escribir verb. to write
  —escribir a máquina to type
escrito noun m. 1. written document 2. writings

escritor, -tora *noun.* writer
escritorio *noun m.* desk
escritura *noun f.* **1.** writing, handwriting **2.** deed
escrutinio *noun m.* scrutiny
escuadrón *noun m.* squadron
escuchar *verb.* **1.** to listen (to) **2.** hear
escudo *noun m.* shield
escuela *noun f.* school
escueto, -ta *adj.* plain, simple, concise
esculpir *verb.* **1.** to sculpt **2.** carve
escultura *noun f.* sculpture
escupir *verb.* to spit
escurrir *verb.* to drain
  —**escurrirse** to slip away
ese, esa *adj.* that
  —**esos** those
ése, ésa *pron.* that one
  —**ésos** those ones
esencia *noun f.* essence
esencial *adj.* essential
esfera *noun f.* **1.** sphere **2.** dial
esforzarse *verb.* to strive, make an effort
esfuerzo *noun m.* effort
esguince *noun m.* strain
eslabón *noun m.* link
eslogan *noun m.* **1.** chant **2.** slogan
eso *pron.* that
espacio *noun m.* **1.** space **2.** room **3.** period, length
espacioso, -sa *adj.* spacious
espada *noun f.* sword
espalda *noun f.* back
espanto *noun m.* fright, fear
espantoso, -sa *adj.* **1.** frightening **2.** dreadful
España *noun f.* Spain
español, -ñola *noun. adj.* Spanish
esparadrapo *noun m.* adhesive bandage
esparcir *verb.* **1.** to scatter **2.** spread
  —**esparcirse** **1.** to spread out **2.** have fun
especia *noun f.* spice
especial *adj.* special
especialidad *noun f.* specialty
especialista *noun mf.* specialist
especializarse *verb.* to specialize
especie *noun f.* **1.** species **2.** type, kind

específicamente *adv.* specifically
especificar *verb.* to specify
específico, -ca *adj.* specific
espécimen *noun m.* specimen
espectacular *adj.* spectacular
espectáculo *noun m.* **1.** spectacle **2.** show
espectador, -dora *noun.* spectator
espectro *noun m.* spectrum
especulación *noun f.* speculation
especular *verb.* to speculate
espejo *noun m.* mirror
espera *noun f.* wait
esperanza *noun f.* hope, expectation
esperar *verb.* **1.** to wait for, await **2.** expect **3.** hope
  —**esperarse** **1.** to expect **2.** hold on, hang on
esperma *noun m.* sperm
espeso, -sa *adj.* dense, thick
espesor *noun m.* density, thickness
espía *noun mf.* spy
espiar *verb.* to spy
espiga *noun f.* ear
espina *noun f.* **1.** spine **2.** thorn **3.** fish bone
espinoso, -sa *adj.* **1.** thorny **2.** difficult
espiral *noun f. adj.* spiral
espíritu *noun m.* **1.** spirit **2.** state of mind
espiritual *adj.* spiritual
espléndido, -da *adj.* **1.** splendid, great **2.** generous
esplendor *noun m.* splendor, glory
espliego *noun m.* lavender
esponja *noun f.* sponge
espontáneo, -nea *adj.* spontaneous
esposo, -sa *noun.* husband or wife
espuma *noun f.* **1.** foam **2.** scum
esqueje *noun m.* cutting
esqueleto *noun m.* **1.** skeleton **2.** framework
esquema *noun m.* sketch
esquí *noun m.* ski
esquiar *verb.* to ski
esquina *noun f.* corner
esquivar *verb.* **1.** to dodge **2.** avoid
esquivo, -va *adj.* **1.** elusive **2.** aloof
estable *adj.* stable, steady

establecer *verb.* to establish, set up, found
—**establecerse 1.** to settle **2.** establish oneself
establecimiento *noun m.* **1.** establishment **2.** institution **3.** premises
estaca *noun f.* stake
estación *noun f.* season
estacionar *verb.* **1.** to station, place **2.** park
estado *noun m.* **1.** state **2.** status **3.** condition
Estados Unidos de América *noun m. plural.* America, United States of America
estadounidense *noun mf. adj.* American
estafa *noun f.* swindle
estafar *verb.* to swindle
estafeta *noun f.* courier
estallar *verb.* **1.** to explode **2.** burst **3.** break out
estallido *noun m.* **1.** explosion **2.** burst **3.** outbreak
estampar *verb.* **1.** to stamp **2.** print
estancia *noun f.* **1.** stay, residence **2.** farm
estandarte *noun m.* banner, standard
estanque *noun m.* pond
estante *noun m.* shelf
estaño *noun m.* tin
estar *verb.* to be
—**estar en contra** to oppose
—**estarse** to stay, remain
estatuto *noun m.* **1.** statute **2.** charter
este *noun m.* east
este *adj.* east, eastern
este, esta *adj.* this
—**estos** these
éste, ésta *pron.* **1.** this one **2.** the latter
—**éstos** these ones
estela *noun f.* **1.** trail **2.** wake
estera *noun f.* mat
estigmatizar *verb.* to stigmatize, brand
estilo *noun m.* **1.** style **2.** fashion, manner
estima *noun f.* esteem, regard
estimación *noun f.* **1.** esteem, regard **2.** estimate

estimar *verb.* **1.** to esteem **2.** estimate **3.** consider, regard
estimulación *noun f.* stimulation
estimulante *noun m.* stimulant
estimulante *adj.* stimulating
estimular *verb.* **1.** to stimulate **2.** encourage
estímulo *noun m.* **1.** stimulus **2.** encouragement
estirado, -da *adj.* **1.** stretched **2.** stiff
estiramiento *noun m.* stretching
estirar *verb.* to stretch
estirón *noun m.* tug
esto *pron.* this
—**a todo esto** meanwhile
—**en esto** at this point
estómago *noun m.* stomach
estorbar *verb.* **1.** to hinder **2.** obstruct
estorbo *noun m.* **1.** hindrance **2.** obstacle
estratagema *noun f.* stratagem, device
estrategia *noun f.* strategy
estratégico, -ca *adj.* strategic
estrechar *verb.* **1.** to narrow **2.** tighten **3.** hug
—**estrechar la mano** to shake hands (with)
estrecho *adj.* **1.** narrow, tight **2.** close
estrella *noun f.* **1.** star **2.** fate, fortune
estrellar *verb.* to smash, crash
—**estrellarse** to crash
estremecerse *verb.* to shiver
estremecimiento *noun m.* shivering
estrenar *verb.* **1.** to use for the first time **2.** inaugurate, open
estreno *noun m.* premiere
estrés *noun m.* stress
estribillo *noun m.* chorus
estricto, -ta *adj.* strict
estrofa *noun f.* stanza, verse
estropear *verb.* **1.** to spoil, ruin **2.** damage
—**estropearse** to spoil
estructura *noun f.* **1.** structure **2.** framework
estructural *adj.* structural
estructurar *verb.* to structure
estrujar *verb.* **1.** to squeeze **2.** press
estuario *noun m.* estuary

estuche *noun m.* case, kit
estudiante *noun mf.* student
estudiar *verb.* to study
estudio *noun m.* **1.** study **2.** studio **3.** den
estudioso, -sa *adj.* studious
estufa *noun f.* stove
estupendo, -da *adj.* stupendous, wonderful
estupidez *noun f.* stupidity
estúpido, -da *noun f.* idiot
estúpido, -da *adj.* stupid
etapa *noun f.* stage
eterno, -na *adj.* eternal
ética *noun f.* ethics
ético, -ca *adj.* ethical
etiqueta *noun f.* **1.** label, tag **2.** etiquette
etiquetar *verb.* to label
étnico, -ca *adj.* ethnic
euro *noun m.* euro
Europa *noun f.* Europe
europeo, -pea *noun. adj.* European
evacuar *verb.* **1.** to evacuate **2.** vacate
evaluación *noun f.* evaluation, assessment
evaluar *verb.* to evaluate, assess
evangelio *noun m.* gospel
evasiva *noun f.* excuse, pretext
evento *noun m.* event
eventual *adj.* **1.** temporary **2.** possible
evidente *adj.* evident, obvious
evitar *verb.* **1.** to avoid **2.** prevent
evocador, -dora *adj.* evocative
evocar *verb.* to evoke
evolución *noun f.* evolution
evolucionar *verb.* **1.** to evolve **2.** develop
evolutivo, -va *adj.* evolutionary
exactamente *adv.* exactly
exactitud *noun f.* accuracy, exactitude
exacto, -ta *adj.* accurate, exact
exagerar *verb.* to exaggerate
examen *noun m.* **1.** examination, exam **2.** investigation
examinar *verb.* **1.** to examine **2.** inspect
—**examinarse** *verb.* to take an exam
excavación *noun f.* excavation
excavar *verb.* to excavate

excedente *noun m. adj.* excess, surplus
exceder *verb.* to exceed, surpass
excelencia *noun f.* excellence
excelente *adj.* excellent
excéntrico, -ca *noun. adj.* eccentric
excepción *noun f.* exception
excepcional *adj.* exceptional, outstanding
excepto *prep.* except, save
exceptuar *verb.* to except
excesivo, -va *adj.* excessive
exceso *noun m.* excess
excitar *verb.* to excite
exclamar *verb.* to exclaim
excluir *verb.* to exclude, leave out
exclusión *noun f.* exclusion
exclusivamente *adv.* exclusively
exclusivo, -va *adj.* **1.** exclusive **2.** sole
excremento *noun m.* excrement
excursión *noun f.* **1.** excursion, trip **2.** hike
excursionista *noun mf.* **1.** excursionist **2.** hiker
excusa *noun f.* excuse
excusar *verb.* to excuse
—**excusarse** to apologize
exención *noun f.* exemption
exento, -ta *adj.* exempt, free
exhibición *noun f.* **1.** exhibition, show **2.** display
exhibir *verb.* **1.** to exhibit, show **2.** display
exhortar *verb.* to exhort
exigencia *noun f.* demand, requirement
exigente *adj.* demanding, exacting
exigir *verb.* **1.** to demand, require **2.** exact
exiliado, -da *noun m.* exile
exiliado, -da *adj.* exiled
exiliar *verb.* to exile
—**exiliarse** to go into exile
exilio *noun m.* exile
eximir *verb.* to exempt
existencia *noun f.* existence
—**existencias** stock
existir *verb.* to exist
éxito *noun m.* success, hit
—**tener éxito** to be successful
exitoso, -sa *adj.* successful

exótico, -ca *adj.* exotic

expansión *noun f.* expansion

expectación *noun f.* expectation, anticipation

expectativa *noun f.* **1.** expectancy **2.** expectation

expedición *noun f.* expedition

expediente *noun m.* **1.** expedient **2.** brief, file, record

experiencia *noun f.* experience

experimentado, -da *adj.* experienced

experimental *adj.* experimental

experimentar *verb.* **1.** to experiment **2.** experience

experimento *noun m.* experiment

experto, -ta *noun. adj.* expert

expirar *verb.* **1.** to expire **2.** die, pass away

explicación *noun f.* explanation

explicar *verb.* to explain

explicativo, -va *adj.* explanatory

explícitamente *adv.* explicitly

explícito, -va *adj.* explicit

exploración *noun f.* exploration

explorador, -dora *noun.* explorer, scout

explorar *verb.* to explore

explosión *noun f.* **1.** explosion **2.** outbreak, outburst

explosivo *noun m.* explosive

explosivo, -va *adj.* explosive

explotación *noun f.* exploitation, development

explotar *verb.* **1.** to exploit **2.** to run, operate

exponer *verb.* **1.** to exhibit, show **2.** display **3.** expose **4.** explain

exportación *noun f.* export

exportar *verb.* to export

exposición *noun f.* **1.** exhibition, show **2.** display **3.** exposure

expresamente *adv.* expressly

expresar *verb.* to express

expresión *noun f.* expression

expresivo, -va *adj.* expressive

expreso *noun m.* express train

expreso, -sa *adj.* express

exprimir *verb.* to squeeze

expulsar *verb.* **1.** to expel, eject **2.** dismiss

expulsión *noun f.* expulsion

exquisito, -ta *adj.* exquisite

éxtasis *noun m.* ecstasy

extender *verb.* **1.** to extend **2.** stretch **3.** spread **4.** write out

—**extenderse 1.** to stretch **2.** spread

extendido, -da *adj.* **1.** outstretched **2.** widespread

extensión *noun f.* **1.** extension **2.** length **3.** extent

extenso, -sa *adj.* **1.** extensive **2.** vast

exterior *noun m.* **1.** exterior **2.** outside

exterior *adj.* **1.** exterior **2.** foreign

externo, -na *adj.* external

extinción *noun f.* extinction

extirpación *noun f.* removal

extirpar *verb.* to extirpate, eradicate, excise

extra *noun m.* extra, bonus

extra *noun mf.* extra (in movies)

extra *adj.* **1.** extra **2.** superior

extracción *noun f.* extraction

extracto *noun m.* **1.** extract **2.** abstract, summary

extraditar *verb.* to extradite

extraer *verb.* to extract

extranjero, -ra *noun.* **1.** foreigner **2.** foreign country, abroad, overseas

extranjero, -ra *adj.* foreign, alien

extrañar *verb.* to miss

—**extrañarse** to be amazed

extraño, -ña *noun.* stranger

extraño, -ña *adj.* **1.** strange, odd **2.** alien, foreign

extraordinario, -ria *adj.* extraordinary, outstanding

extraterrestre *noun mf. adj.* alien

extraviar *verb.* **1.** to mislead **2.** lose

—**extraviarse** to get lost

extremadamente *adv.* extremely

extremado, -da *adj.* extreme

extremidad *noun f.* extremity

extremista *noun mf. adj.* extremist

extremo *noun m.* end, extreme

extremo, -ma *adj.* extreme, utmost

extrovertido, -da *adj.* outgoing

F

fábrica noun f. **1.** factory **2.** plant

fabricación noun f. **1.** making **2.** manufacture

fabricante noun mf. manufacturer, maker

fabricar verb. **1.** to make **2.** manufacture

fabuloso, -sa adj. **1.** fabulous, terrific **2.** fabled

facción noun f. **1.** faction **2.** feature

facial adj. facial

fácil adj. **1.** easy **2.** likely

facilidad noun f. ease, facility

facilitar verb. **1.** to provide **2.** facilitate

fácilmente adv. easily, readily

factibilidad noun f. feasibility

factible adj. feasible, practicable

factor noun m. factor

factual adj. factual

factura noun f. **1.** invoice, bill **2.** workmanship

facturación noun f. **1.** turnover **2.** check-in

facturar verb. **1.** to invoice, bill **2.** check in

facultad noun f. **1.** faculty **2.** authority, power **3.** school

faja noun f. **1.** strip **2.** belt **3.** girdle

falda noun f. **1.** skirt **2.** side

faldón noun m. flap

falla noun f. fault

fallar verb. **1.** to fail **2.** miss **3.** rule

fallo noun m. **1.** fault, mistake **2.** sentence, verdict

falsedad noun f. **1.** falseness **2.** lie

falsificación noun f. fake, forgery, falsification

falsificar verb. to fake, forge, falsify

falso, -sa adj. **1.** false, untrue **2.** fake

falta noun f. **1.** lack, want **2.** fault, error **3.** foul

faltar verb. **1.** to be lacking **2.** be absent **3.** be unfaithful, break **4.** remain

fama noun f. **1.** fame **2.** name

familia noun f. family

familiar adj. **1.** familiar **2.** informal

familiaridad noun f. **1.** familiarity **2.** informality

famoso, -sa noun. celebrity

famoso, -sa adj. famous, well-known

fanático, -ca noun. adj. fanatic

fanfarronear verb. to boast

fantasía noun f. **1.** fantasy **2.** fancy, imagination

fantasma noun m. ghost

fantástico, -ca adj. **1.** fantastic **2.** great, terrific

fardo noun m. **1.** bundle **2.** package

farmacéutico, -ca noun. pharmacist

farmacéutico, -ca adj. pharmaceutical

farmacia noun f. drugstore, pharmacy

fascinación noun f. fascination

fascinante adj. fascinating

fascinar verb. to fascinate

fascismo noun m. Fascism

fascista noun mf. adj. fascist

fase noun f. phase, period

fastidiar verb. to annoy, bother

fastidio noun m. annoyance, nuisance

fatal adj. fatal

fatiga noun f. fatigue

fatigado, -da adj. tired, weary

fatigar verb. to fatigue, tire

—**fatigarse** to wear oneself out

fauna noun f. fauna

favor noun m. favor

—**por favor** please

favorable adj. favorable

favorecedor, -dora adj. becoming

favorecer verb. **1.** to favor **2.** suit

favorito, -ta noun. adj. favorite

fax noun m. fax

faxear verb. to fax

fe noun f. **1.** faith **2.** belief **3.** testimony

febrero noun m. February

fecha noun f. date

—**fecha de caducidad** expiration date

—**fecha límite** deadline

fechar verb. to date

federación noun f. federation

federal adj. federal

felicidad noun f. happiness

felicitar verb. to congratulate

felino, -na noun. adj. feline

feliz adj. happy

femenino, -na *adj.* feminine
feminismo *noun m.* feminism
feminista *noun mf. adj.* feminist
fénix *noun m.* phoenix
fenómeno *noun m.* phenomenon
feo, fea *adj.* 1. ugly 2. nasty
feria *noun f.* 1. fair 2. market 3. festival
feroz *adj.* fierce, ferocious
ferretería *noun f.* 1. hardware 2. hardware store
ferrocarril *noun m.* railway, railroad
ferry *noun m.* ferry
fértil *adj.* 1. fertile 2. productive
fertilidad *noun f.* fertility
fertilizante *noun m.* fertilizer
festejar *verb.* 1. to feast 2. celebrate
festejo *noun m.* 1. feast 2. celebration
festín *noun m.* feast
festival *noun m.* festival
fétido, -da *adj.* fetid, foul
feudal *adj.* feudal
fiabilidad *noun f.* reliability
fiable *adj.* reliable
fianza *noun f.* 1. bail 2. deposit
fiar *verb.* 1. to sell on credit 2. confide
  —**fiarse de** to place trust in
fibra *noun f.* fiber
ficción *noun f.* fiction
ficha *noun f.* 1. file, record 2. chip, counter 3. token
fichar *verb.* 1. to record on a file 2. punch in or out 3. sign up
ficticio, -cia *adj.* fictitious, fictional
fidelidad *noun f.* fidelity
fideo *noun m.* noodle
fiebre *noun f.* 1. fever 2. temperature
fiel *adj.* 1. faithful 2. accurate
fieltro *noun m.* felt
fiesta *noun f.* 1. party 2. holiday
figura *noun f.* 1. figure 2. shape
figurar *verb.* 1. to figure 2. be among 3. stand out
  —**figurarse** to fancy, imagine
fijar *verb.* 1. to fix 2. establish, set up 3. appoint 4. fasten
  —**fijarse** to settle
  —**fijarse en** to notice
fijo, -ja *adj.* 1. fixed 2. firm 3. permanent
fila *noun f.* 1. file, line 2. queue 3. rank, row

filial *noun f.* subsidiary
filial *adj.* filial
filmar *verb.* to film
filo *noun m.* 1. blade 2. edge
filosofía *noun f.* philosophy
filosófico, -ca *adj.* philosophical, philosophic
filósofo, -fa *noun.* philosopher
filtración *noun f.* leaking
filtrar *verb.* 1. to filter 2. leak
filtro *noun m.* filter
fin *noun m.* 1. end 2. aim, purpose
  —**fin de semana** weekend
  —**por fin** at last
final *noun m.* end, final
final *adj.* final
finalidad *noun f.* goal, finality, end
finalización *noun f.* completion
finalizar *verb.* to finish, end
financiar *verb.* to finance
financiero, -ra *adj.* financial
finanzas *noun f. plural.* finance, finances
finca *noun f.* 1. land, real state 2. farm, ranch
fingido, -da *adj.* feigned
fingir *verb.* to feign, pretend
finito, -ta *adj.* finite
finlandés, -desa *noun. adj.* Finnish
Finlandia *noun f.* Finland
fino, -na *adj.* 1. fine 2. delicate 3. slender, slim, thin 4. refined
firma *noun f.* 1. signature 2. company, firm
firmar *verb.* to sign
firme *adj.* 1. firm 2. secure 3. steady
firmemente *adv.* firmly
física *noun f.* physics
físico *noun m.* physique
físico, -ca *noun.* physicist
físico, -ca *adj.* physical
fláccido, -da *adj.* 1. flaccid 2. limp
flaco, -ca *adj.* 1. thin, skinny 2. feeble, weak
flanco *noun m.* flank
flanquear *verb.* to flank
flaquear *verb.* to flag, weaken
flauta *noun f.* flute
flautista *noun mf.* flutist
flecha *noun f.* arrow

fleco *noun m.* fringe
fletar *verb.* to charter
flete *noun m.* freight
flexibilidad *noun f.* flexibility
flexible *adj.* flexible
flojo, -ja *adj.* **1.** loose **2.** weak **3.** limp **4.** lazy
flor *noun f.* flower
flora *noun f.* flora
floración *noun f.* flowering
florecer *verb.* **1.** to bloom, blossom, flower **2.** flourish
floreciente *adj.* **1.** flowering **2.** flourishing
florero *noun m.* vase
flota *noun f.* fleet
flotar *verb.* to float
fluctuar *verb.* to fluctuate
fluido *noun m.* fluid
fluido, -da *adj.* **1.** fluid **2.** fluent
fluir *verb.* **1.** to flow **2.** roll
flujo *noun m.* flow
foca *noun f.* seal
focal *adj.* focal
foco *noun m.* **1.** focus **2.** spotlight **3.** center
folclore *noun m.* folklore
folclórico, -ca *adj.* folk
follaje *noun m.* foliage
follar *verb.* to fuck
folleto *noun m.* leaflet, brochure
fomentar *verb.* **1.** to foster, promote **2.** foment
fomento *noun m.* promotion
fonda *noun f.* inn
fondo *noun m.* **1.** bottom **2.** back, rear **3.** background **4.** fund
foráneo, -nea *adj.* foreign
forastero, -ra *noun m.* outsider, stranger
forcejear *verb.* to struggle
forense *adj.* forensic
forja *noun f.* forge
forjar *verb.* **1.** to forge **2.** create
forma *noun f.* **1.** form, shape **2.** manner, way
    —estar en forma to be fit, be in shape
formación *noun f.* **1.** formation **2.** training
formal *adj.* **1.** formal **2.** serious **3.** reliable

formalidad *noun f.* **1.** formality **2.** seriousness **3.** reliability
formalmente *adv.* formally
formar *verb.* **1.** to form **2.** educate, train **3.** constitute
    —formarse to develop, grow
formatear *verb.* to format
formato *noun m.* format
formidable *adj.* **1.** formidable **2.** huge
fórmula *noun f.* formula
formular *verb.* to formulate
formulario *noun m.* form
foro *noun m.* forum
forrar *verb.* **1.** to line **2.** cover
forro *noun m.* **1.** lining **2.** cover
fortalecer *verb.* to fortify, strengthen
fortaleza *noun f.* **1.** fortress **2.** strength
fortuito, -ta *adj.* fortuitous
fortuna *noun f.* **1.** fortune **2.** wealth
forzar *verb.* **1.** to force, compel **2.** strain
forzoso, -sa *adj.* **1.** forced, compulsory **2.** unavoidable, inevitable
fosa *noun f.* **1.** pit, ditch **2.** grave **3.** cavity
fósforo *noun m.* **1.** match **2.** phosphorus
fósil *noun m.* fossil
foso *noun m.* pit, ditch
foto *noun f.* photo, picture
fotografía *noun f.* **1.** photograph **2.** photography
fotografiar *verb.* to photograph
fotógrafo, -fa *noun.* photographer
fracasado, -da *noun.* failure
fracasado, -da *adj.* **1.** unsuccessful, failed **2.** would-be
fracasar *verb.* **1.** to fail **2.** collapse
fracaso *noun m.* failure
fracción *noun f.* fraction
fractura *noun f.* fracture
fracturar *verb.* to fracture
fragancia *noun f.* fragrance
frágil *adj.* **1.** frail, delicate **2.** fragile
fragmentar *verb.* to fragment
fragmento *noun m.* **1.** fragment **2.** excerpt
fragor *noun m.* roar, noise
francamente *adv.* **1.** frankly **2.** really
francés, -cesa *noun. adj.* French
Francia *noun f.* France

franco, -ca adj. **1.** frank **2.** clear **3.** exempt

franja noun f. **1.** band, stripe **2.** fringe

franquear verb. **1.** to cross **2.** exempt

franquicia noun f. **1.** franchise **2.** exemption

frase noun f. **1.** phrase **2.** sentence

fraude noun m. fraud

frecuencia noun f. frequency

frecuentar verb. to frequent, haunt

frecuente adj. frequent

fregadero noun m. sink

fregado noun m. scrubbing

fregar verb. **1.** to scrub **2.** wash

freír verb. to fry

frenar verb. **1.** to brake **2.** check

frenético, -ca adj. frantic

freno noun m. **1.** brake **2.** check **3.** restraint

frente noun f. **1.** front **2.** brow, forehead

fresa noun f. strawberry

fresco noun m. coolness

fresco, -ca adj. **1.** cool **2.** fresh

frescura noun f. **1.** coolness **2.** freshness

fricción noun f. friction

frigorífico noun m. refrigerator

frío noun m. **1.** cold **2.** coldness, indifference

frío, fría adj. **1.** cold **2.** indifferent, distant

frívolo, -la adj. frivolous

frontal adj. frontal, head-on

frontera noun f. border, frontier, boundary

frotar verb. to rub

fruncir verb. to gather

—**fruncir el ceño** to frown

frustración noun f. frustration

frustrado, -da adj. **1.** frustrated, would-be **2.** failed, unsuccessful

frustrar verb. to frustrate

fruta noun f. fruit

fruto noun m. **1.** fruit **2.** product, result

fuego noun m. **1.** fire **2.** light **3.** burner

fuente noun f. **1.** fountain **2.** spring **3.** source, origin

fuera adv. **1.** outside, out **2.** away **3.** abroad

—**fuera de** besides

fuerte noun m. fort

fuerte adj. **1.** strong **2.** loud

fuerte adv. **1.** hard **2.** loudly

fuerza noun f. **1.** strength **2.** force **3.** might **4.** power

—**fuerzas armadas** armed forces

fuga noun f. **1.** flight, escape **2.** leak **3.** fugue

fugarse verb. **1.** to escape **2.** run away

fugitivo, -va noun. adj. fugitive

fumar verb. to smoke

función noun f. **1.** function **2.** duty **3.** performance

funcional adj. functional

funcionamiento noun m. functioning

—**en funcionamiento** in operation

funcionar verb. **1.** to function **2.** run, work

funcionario, -ria noun. official, civil servant

funda noun f. case, cover

fundación noun f. foundation

fundador, -dora noun. founder

fundamental adj. basic, fundamental

fundamento noun m. basis, foundation

fundar verb. **1.** to found, establish **2.** base

funeral noun m. funeral

furgoneta noun f. van

furia noun f. **1.** fury **2.** rage

furioso, -sa adj. furious

furor noun m. **1.** fury **2.** rage

furúnculo noun m. boil

fusilar verb. to shoot

fusión noun f. **1.** fusion **2.** merger

fusionar verb. to merge

fusta noun f. crop

fustigar verb. to whip

fútbol noun m. soccer

—**fútbol americano** football

futuro noun m. future

futuro, -ra adj. future

G

gabarra *noun f.* barge
gabinete *noun m.* **1.** cabinet **2.** office
gafas *noun f. plural.* glasses, spectacles
gaita *noun f.* bagpipe
galaxia *noun f.* galaxy
galería *noun f.* gallery
galés *noun m.* Welsh (language)
galés, -lesa *noun. adj.* Welsh
galleta *noun f.* biscuit, cookie
gallina *noun f.* hen
gallinero *noun m.* **1.** coop **2.** gallery
gallo *noun m.* cock
galón *noun m.* **1.** gallon **2.** stripe
gama *noun f.* range, spectrum
gana *noun f.* desire, wish
  —tener ganas de to feel like
ganadería *noun f.* cattle raising
ganadero, -ra *noun.* cattle raiser
ganado *noun m.* cattle, livestock
ganador, -dora *noun.* winner
ganador, -dora *adj.* winning
ganancia *noun f.* profit, gain
ganar *verb.* **1.** to win **2.** earn **3.** gain **4.** profit **5.** make
gancho *noun m.* hook
ganga *noun f.* bargain
ganso, -sa *noun.* goose
garaje *noun m.* garage
garantía *noun f.* **1.** guarantee **2.** security
garantizar *verb.* to guarantee, assure
garganta *noun f.* **1.** throat **2.** neck **3.** defile
garra *noun f.* **1.** claw **2.** paw
gas *noun m.* gas
gaseosa *noun f.* soda
gasolina *noun f.* gasoline, gas, petrol
gasolinera *noun f.* gas station, service station
gastar *verb.* **1.** to spend **2.** use
gasto *noun m.* expense, expenditure
gatear *verb.* to crawl
gatillo *noun m.* trigger
gato, -ta *noun.* **1.** cat **2.** jack
gay *adj.* gay
gemelo, -la *noun. adj.* twin
  —gemelos 1. cuff links **2.** binoculars

gemido *noun m.* groan, moan
gemir *verb.* to groan, moan
gen *noun m.* gene
generación *noun f.* generation
generador *noun m.* generator
general *noun mf. adj.* general
  —en general/por lo general generally, in general
generalizado, -da *adj.* widespread
generalmente *adv.* usually, generally
generar *verb.* to generate
genérico, -ca *adj.* generic
género *noun m.* **1.** gender **2.** genre **3.** kind, sort
generosidad *noun f.* generosity
generoso, -sa *adj.* generous
genética *noun f.* genetics
genético, -ca *adj.* genetic
genio *noun m.* **1.** genius **2.** temper
gente *noun f.* people
genuino, -na *adj.* genuine
geografía *noun f.* geography
geográfico, -ca *adj.* geographic, geographical
geología *noun f.* geology
geológico, -ca *adj.* geological
gerente *noun mf.* manager
gestión *noun f.* **1.** management **2.** procedure
gesto *noun m.* **1.** gesture **2.** facial expression **3.** sign
gigante, -ta *noun.* giant
gigante *adj.* giant
gigantesco, -ca *adj.* giant
gimnasia *noun f.* gymnastics
gimnasio *noun m.* gym, gymnasium
ginebra *noun f.* gin
girar *verb.* **1.** to turn around **2.** rotate **3.** swing around
giro *noun m.* **1.** turn **2.** revolution
  —giro postal postal order
gitano, -na *noun. adj.* gypsy
glacial *adj.* glacial, icy
glamour *noun m.* glamour
glándula *noun f.* gland
global *adj.* global

globo *noun m.* **1.** balloon **2.** globe
gloria *noun f.* **1.** glory **2.** fame
glorieta *noun f.* traffic circle
glorioso, -sa *adj.* glorious
glucosa *noun f.* glucose
gobernador, -dora *noun.* governor
gobernanta *noun f.* housekeeper
gobernante *noun mf.* ruler
gobernante *adj.* ruling
gobernar *verb.* to govern, rule
gobierno *noun m.* government
goce *noun m.* enjoyment
gol *noun m.* goal
golf *noun m.* golf
golfista *noun mf.* golfer
golfo *noun m.* gulf
golondrina *noun f.* swallow
golosina *noun f.* candy, sweet
golpe *noun m.* **1.** blow **2.** knock **3.** stroke
 —de golpe suddenly
 —golpe de estado coup d'etat
golpear *verb.* **1.** to beat, hit **2.** knock **3.** strike
goma *noun f.* **1.** gum **2.** rubber
gordo, -da *adj.* **1.** fat **2.** thick **3.** greasy, oily
gorra *noun f.* **1.** bonnet **2.** cap
gorro *noun m.* cap
gota *noun f.* **1.** drop **2.** gout
gotear *verb.* **1.** to drip **2.** leak
goteo *noun m.* drip, dripping
gozar *verb.* to enjoy
grabación *noun f.* recording
grabado *noun m.* engraving
grabadora *noun f.* tape recorder
grabar *verb.* **1.** to engrave **2.** tape, record
gracia *noun f.* **1.** grace **2.** humor, wit **3.** favor
 —gracias thanks, thank you
gracioso, -sa *adj.* funny, witty
grado *noun m.* **1.** degree **2.** grade **3.** extent
graduación *noun f.* **1.** graduation **2.** rank
gradual *adj.* gradual
graduar *verb.* **1.** to regulate **2.** gauge
 —graduarse to graduate
gráfica *noun f.* **1.** graph, chart **2.** graphic

gráfico *noun m.* **1.** graph, chart **2.** graphic
gráfico, -ca *adj.* graphic
gramática *noun f.* grammar
gramatical *adj.* grammatical
gran *adj.* (see grande. Used before singular nouns)
Gran Bretaña *noun f.* Great Britain
grande *adj.* **1.** big **2.** large **3.** great
grandeza *noun f.* **1.** greatness **2.** generosity **3.** magnificence
granero *noun m.* barn
granito *noun m.* granite
granizar *verb.* to hail
granizo *noun m.* hail
granja *noun f.* **1.** farm **2.** farmhouse
granjero, -ra *noun.* farmer
grano *noun m.* grain
grapa *noun f.* **1.** clamp **2.** staple
grasa *noun f.* **1.** fat **2.** grease
graso, -sa *adj.* **1.** fatty **2.** greasy
gratis *adj.* free
gratitud *noun f.* gratitude
grato, -ta *adj.* pleasant, agreeable
gratuito, -ta *adj.* free
grava *noun f.* gravel
gravar *verb.* **1.** to tax **2.** burden
grave *adj.* **1.** grave **2.** acute **3.** serious
gravedad *noun f.* **1.** gravity **2.** seriousness
Grecia *noun f.* Greece
griego, -ga *noun. adj.* Greek
grieta *noun f.* crack
grifo *noun m.* **1.** tap **2.** cock, faucet
grillo *noun m.* cricket
gripe *noun f.* flu
gris *adj.* gray
gritar *verb.* to shout, cry, scream
grito *noun m.* shout, cry, scream
grosero, -ra *adj.* **1.** coarse **2.** rude
grúa *noun f.* crane
grueso, -sa *adj.* **1.** stout **2.** thick **3.** coarse
grumo *noun m.* lump
gruñido *noun m.* growl
gruñir *verb.* to growl
grupo *noun m.* **1.** group **2.** band
 —grupo de presión lobby
guante *noun m.* glove

guapo, -pa *adj.* handsome, good-looking
guarda *noun mf.* **1.** guard **2.** keeper **3.** warden
guardaespaldas *noun mf.* bodyguard
guardar *verb.* **1.** to guard **2.** keep **3.** preserve **4.** maintain **5.** observe
—**guardarse de** to refrain from
guardarropa *noun m.* wardrobe
guardia *noun mf.* **1.** guard **2.** policeman or policewoman
guardián, -diana *noun.* **1.** guardian **2.** keeper
guarida *noun f.* den
guarnecer *verb.* **1.** to adorn, decorate **2.** garrison
guarnición *noun f.* **1.** garrison **2.** garnish
guarro, -rra *noun.* pig
gubernamental *adj.* governmental
guerra *noun f.* **1.** war **2.** warfare

guerrero, -ra *noun.* warrior, fighter
guerrero, -ra *adj.* war, fighting
gueto *noun m.* ghetto
guía *noun f.* **1.** directory, guidebook **2.** guidance
guía *noun mf.* guide
guiar *verb.* **1.** to guide **2.** conduct, lead **3.** pilot
guión *noun m.* **1.** script **2.** dash
guisante *noun m.* pea
guisar *verb.* **1.** to stew **2.** cook
guiso *noun m.* stew
guitarra *noun f.* guitar
guitarrista *noun mf.* guitarist
gula *noun f.* greed
gusano *noun m.* **1.** worm **2.** maggot
gustar *verb.* **1.** to like **2.** be pleasing
gusto *noun m.* **1.** taste **2.** liking
—**a gusto** comfortable, at ease

H

haber *verb.* to have
—**haber de** **1.** to be necessary **2.** must
—**hay** there is, there are
habichuela *noun f.* bean
hábil *adj.* **1.** clever, able, skillful **2.** working
habilidad *noun f.* ability, skill
habitación *noun f.* **1.** room **2.** bedroom **3.** habitation, dwelling
habitante *noun mf.* inhabitant, resident
habitar *verb.* **1.** to inhabit **2.** reside
hábitat *noun m.* habitat
hábito *noun m.* habit
habitual *adj.* usual, habitual
habla *noun f.* **1.** speech **2.** language, dialect
—**de habla** speaking
hablado, -da *adj.* spoken
hablador, -dora *adj.* talkative
hablar *verb.* **1.** to speak **2.** talk
hacer *verb.* **1.** to make **2.** do **3.** be
—**hace dos años** two years ago
—**hacer falta** to be neccessary
—**hacerse** **1.** to become **2.** get **3.** pretend, play

hacha *noun f.* ax, hatchet
hacia *prep.* **1.** towards, toward **2.** near, about
—**hacia abajo** downward
—**hacia adelante** forward
—**hacia arriba** upward
—**hacia atrás** backward
—**hacia dentro** inward
hacienda *noun f.* **1.** estate, ranch **2.** tax office
hacinar *verb.* to stack
hada *noun f.* fairy
halago *noun m.* flattery, compliment
halcón *noun m.* hawk
hallar *verb.* **1.** to find **2.** discover
hallazgo *noun m.* **1.** discovery **2.** find
hambre *noun f.* **1.** famine **2.** hunger
—**tener hambre** to be hungry
hambriento, -ta *adj.* hungry
hambruna *noun f.* famine
handicap *noun m.* handicap
harapiento, -ta *adj.* ragged
hardware *noun m.* hardware
harina *noun f.* flour

harto, -ta *adj.* **1.** full **2.** fed up
hasta *prep.* **1.** until, till **2.** as far as
hazaña *noun f.* exploit, feat
hebra *noun f.* strand, thread
hechizar *verb.* **1.** to bewitch **2.** charm
hechizo *noun m.* **1.** spell **2.** charm
hecho *noun m.* **1.** fact **2.** deed **3.** event
hecho, -cha *adj.* **1.** done, made **2.** finished
hectárea *noun f.* hectare
hedor *noun m.* stink
helada *noun f.* frost
helado *noun m.* ice cream
helado, -da *adj.* freezing, icy
helar *verb.* to freeze
helicóptero *noun m.* helicopter
hembra *noun f.* female
hembra *adj.* **1.** female **2.** she
hemisferio *noun m.* hemisphere
hendidura *noun f.* crack
heno *noun m.* hay
heraldo *noun m.* herald
heredar *verb.* to inherit
heredero, -ra *noun.* heir or heiress
hereditario, -ria *adj.* hereditary
herencia *noun f.* **1.** heritage **2.** inheritance **3.** legacy
herida *noun f.* injury, wound
herido, -da *noun.* injured person
herido, -da *adj.* **1.** injured, wounded **2.** hurt
herir *verb.* **1.** to injure, wound **2.** hurt
hermano, -na *noun.* sibling, brother or sister
hermoso, -sa *adj.* **1.** beautiful **2.** lovely
héroe *noun m.* hero
heroico, -ca *adj.* heroic
heroína *noun f.* **1.** heroin **2.** heroine
herradura *noun f.* horseshoe
herramienta *noun f.* tool
herrero, -ra *noun.* smith
hervir *verb.* to boil
hidrógeno *noun m.* hydrogen
hiedra *noun f.* ivy
hiel *noun f.* **1.** bile **2.** gall
hielo *noun m.* ice
hierba *noun f.* **1.** grass **2.** herb
hierro *noun m.* iron
hígado *noun m.* liver

higiene *noun f.* hygiene
higo *noun f.* fig
hijo, -ja *noun.* **1.** son or daughter **2.** child
—**hijos** children
hilar *verb.* to spin
hilera *noun f.* line, row
hilo *noun m.* **1.** thread **2.** wire **3.** linen
hincar *verb.* **1.** to sink **2.** stick
—**hincarse de rodillas** to kneel
hinchado, -da *adj.* swollen
hinchar *verb.* to inflate
—**hincharse** to swell
hinchazón *noun f.* swelling
hindú *noun mf. adj.* Hindu
hipoteca *noun f.* mortgage
hipotecar *verb.* to mortgage
hipótesis *noun f.* hypothesis
hipotético, -ca *adj.* hypothetical
hispano, -na *noun. adj.* Hispanic
historia *noun f.* **1.** history **2.** story **3.** tale
historiador, -dora *noun.* historian
historial *noun m.* **1.** record **2.** background
histórico, -ca *adj.* **1.** historic **2.** historical
hito *noun m.* landmark
hockey *noun m.* hockey
hogar *noun m.* home
hoja *noun f.* **1.** sheet, page **2.** leaf **3.** blade
hojalata *noun f.* tinplate
hola *interj.* hello!, hi!
Holanda *noun f.* Holland
holandés, -desa *noun. adj.* Dutch
holgazán, -zana *noun.* idler
holgazanear *verb.* to idle
hollar *verb.* to tread
hombre *noun m.* man
hombro *noun m.* shoulder
homenaje *noun m.* homage, tribute
homicidio *noun m.* murder
homogéneo, -nea *adj.* homogeneous
homólogo, -ga *noun.* counterpart
homólogo, -ga *adj.* homologous
homosexual *noun mf. adj.* homosexual, gay
homosexualidad *noun f.* homosexuality
hondonada *noun f.* hollow
honestidad *noun f.* honesty

honesto, -ta *adj.* honest
hongo *noun m.* **1.** mushroom **2.** fungus
honor *noun m.* honor
honorable *adj.* honorable
honorario, -ria *adj.* honorary
honorarios *noun m. plural.* fees
honorífico, -ca *adj.* honorary
honradez *noun f.* honesty
honrado, -da *adj.* honest
honrar *verb.* to honor
hora *noun f.* **1.** hour **2.** time **3.** appointment
horario *noun m.* timetable, schedule
horizontal *adj.* horizontal
horizonte *noun m.* horizon
hormiga *noun f.* ant
hormigón *noun m.* concrete
hormona *noun f.* hormone
hornada *noun f.* batch
horno *noun m.* **1.** oven **2.** kiln
horrible *adj.* horrible
horror *noun m.* horror
horrorizar *verb.* to horrify
horroroso, -sa *adj.* horrible, horrifying
hortaliza *noun f.* vegetable
hospedar *verb.* to lodge
hospital *noun m.* hospital
hospitalidad *noun f.* hospitality
hostigar *verb.* to harass
hostil *adj.* hostile
hostilidad *noun f.* hostility
hotel *noun m.* hotel
hoy *adv.* today
  —**hoy en día** nowadays, today
hoyo *noun m.* hole

hueco *noun m.* **1.** hole, hollow **2.** space
hueco, -ca *adj.* hollow
huelga *noun f.* strike
  —**hacer huelga** to strike
huelguista *noun mf.* striker
huella *noun f.* **1.** footprint **2.** fingerprint **3.** track
huerto *noun m.* **1.** garden **2.** orchard
hueso *noun m.* **1.** bone **2.** pit, stone
huésped, -peda *noun.* **1.** guest **2.** host
huevo *noun m.* egg
huida *noun f.* flight
huir *verb.* **1.** to flee **2.** fly
humanidad *noun f.* **1.** humanity **2.** mankind
humano *noun m.* human being
humano, -na *adj.* human
humedad *noun f.* **1.** humidity **2.** dampness, moistness
húmedo, -da *adj.* **1.** humid **2.** damp, moist
humilde *adj.* humble
humillación *noun f.* humiliation
humillar *verb.* to humiliate
  —**humillarse** to humble oneself
humo *noun m.* smoke
humor *noun m.* **1.** humor **2.** mood **3.** temper
hundir *verb.* to sink
húngaro, -ra *noun. adj.* Hungarian
Hungría *noun f.* Hungary
huracán *noun m.* hurricane
hurtar *verb.* to steal
hurto *noun m.* theft
husmear *verb.* to sniff out

I

ida *noun f.* **1.** going **2.** departure
idea *noun f.* **1.** idea **2.** notion
ideal *noun m. adj.* ideal
idear *verb.* to devise
idéntico, -ca *adj.* identical
identidad *noun f.* identity
identificación *noun f.* identification
identificar *verb.* to identify
idioma *noun m.* language

idiota *noun mf.* idiot
idiota *adj.* stupid, idiotic
idóneo, -nea *adj.* suitable, competent
iglesia *noun f.* church
ignorancia *noun f.* ignorance
ignorante *noun mf.* ignorant person
ignorante *adj.* ignorant
ignorar *verb.* **1.** to ignore **2.** be unaware of

igual *noun mf.* equal
igual *adj.* 1. equal 2. alike 3. same
igualado, -da *adj.* 1. even 2. close
igualar *verb.* 1. to equal 2. level 3. tie
igualdad *noun f.* equality
igualmente *adv.* 1. equally 2. likewise
ilegal *adj.* illegal
iluminación *noun f.* 1. illumination 2. lighting
iluminar *verb.* to illuminate, light
ilusión *noun f.* illusion
ilustración *noun f.* illustration
ilustrado, -da *adj.* illustrated
ilustrar *verb.* to illustrate
imagen *noun f.* image
imaginación *noun f.* imagination
imaginar *verb.* to imagine
imaginario, -ria *adj.* imaginary
imaginativo, -va *adj.* imaginative
imbécil *noun mf.* 1. imbecile 2. idiot, fool
imbécil *adj.* stupid
imitación *noun f.* imitation
imitar *verb.* to imitate, copy
impaciente *adj.* impatient
impacto *noun m.* 1. impact 2. shock
impar *adj.* odd
imparcial *adj.* impartial
imparcialidad *noun f.* impartiality
impedir *verb.* 1. to impede 2. prevent 3. block
imperante *adj.* prevailing
imperativo *noun m.* imperative
imperativo, -va *adj.* imperative
imperial *adj.* imperial
imperio *noun m.* empire
ímpetu *noun m.* 1. impetus 2. momentum
impetuoso, -sa *adj.* impetuous
implacable *adj.* relentless
implicar *verb.* 1. to involve 2. imply
implícito, -ta *adj.* implicit
imponente *adj.* imposing
imponer *verb.* 1. to impose 2. exact
—**imponerse** to prevail
impopular *adj.* unpopular
importación *noun f.* import
importancia *noun f.* importance
importante *adj.* important
importar *verb.* 1. to import 2. matter,

mind 3. be important
imposible *adj.* impossible
imposición *noun f.* 1. imposition 2. tax
imprescindible *adj.* essential, indispensable
impresión *noun f.* 1. feeling, impression 2. printing
impresionante *adj.* impressive
impresionar *verb.* to impress
impresor, -sora *noun.* printer
impresora *noun f.* printer
imprimir *verb.* to print
improbable *adj.* unlikely
imprudente *adj.* imprudent, rash
impuesto *noun m.* tax, duty
impulsar *verb.* 1. to impel 2. drive
impulso *noun m.* 1. impulse 2. drive
impuro, -ra *adj.* impure
inactivo, -va *adj.* inactive, idle
inadecuado, -da *adj.* 1. inadequate 2. inappropriate
inalterable *adj.* unalterable
inapropiado, -da *adj.* inappropriate
inauguración *noun f.* inauguration, opening
incapacidad *noun f.* 1. inability 2. disability
incapaz *adj.* 1. incapable, unable 2. incompetent
incautar *verb.* to seize
incendio *noun m.* fire
incentivo *noun m.* incentive
incidente *noun m.* incident
incierto, -ta *adj.* 1. uncertain 2. unknown
incitar *verb.* 1. to incite 2. urge, encourage
inclinación *noun f.* 1. inclination 2. slope 3. propensity
inclinar *verb.* 1. to incline 2. tilt
—**inclinarse** to lean
incluir *verb.* to include
inclusión *noun f.* inclusion
incomodidad *noun f.* 1. inconvenience, bother 2. discomfort
incómodo, -da *adj.* uncomfortable
incompatible *adj.* incompatible
incompleto, -ta *adj.* incomplete
incondicional *adj.* unconditional
inconsciente *adj.* unaware, unconscious

inconsecuente adj. inconsistent
inconsistente adj. inconsistent, weak
incontable adj. countless
incorporar verb. 1. to incorporate 2. include
—**incorporarse a** to join
incorrecto, -ta adj. incorrect, wrong
increíble adj. incredible, unbelievable
incriminar verb. to incriminate
incubar verb. 1. to incubate 2. hatch
incumplimiento noun m. nonfulfillment, breach
incurrir (en) verb. to incur
incursión noun f. incursion, raid
indagación noun f. inquiry
indagar verb. to inquire
indebido, -da adj. undue, improper
indecente adj. indecent
indecisión noun f. hesitation, indecision
indeciso, -sa adj. 1. undecided 2. hesitant
indefenso, -sa adj. defenseless, helpless
indemnización noun f. indemnification, compensation
indemnizar verb. to indemnify, compensate
independencia noun f. independence
independiente adj. independent
indeseable adj. undesirable
India noun f. India
indicación noun f. 1. indication 2. hint 3. sign, signal
indicador noun m. 1. gauge 2. indicator
indicar verb. 1. to indicate 2. point out 3. show
indicativo noun m. indicative
indicativo, -va adj. indicative
índice noun m. index
indicio noun m. 1. indication 2. evidence 3. trace
indiferencia noun f. indifference
indiferente adj. indifferent
indígena noun mf. native
indígena adj. indigenous, native
indio, -dia noun. adj. Indian
indirecta noun f. hint
—**echar indirectas** to drop hints
indirecto, -ta adj. indirect
indiscreto, -ta adj. indiscreet
individual adj. 1. individual 2. single

individuo noun m. individual, guy, person
Indonesia noun f. Indonesia
indonesio, -sia noun. adj. Indonesian
indudable adj. unquestionable, indubitable
indultar verb. to pardon
indulto noun m. pardon
industria noun f. industry
industrial adj. industrial
ineficaz adj. 1. ineffective 2. inefficient
inesperado, -da adj. unexpected
inestabilidad noun f. instability
inestable adj. unstable
inestimable adj. invaluable, inestimable
inevitable adj. inevitable, unavoidable
inexperto, -ta adj. inexperienced, unskilled
infantería noun f. infantry
infantil adj. childish, infantile
infarto noun m. heart attack
infección noun f. infection
infeccioso, -sa adj. infectious
infectar verb. to infect
infeliz adj. 1. unhappy 2. unfortunate
inferencia noun f. inference
inferior noun mf. adj. inferior
infierno noun m. hell
infinitivo noun m. infinitive
infinito, -ta adj. infinite
inflación noun f. inflation
inflar verb. to inflate
—**inflarse** to swell
infligir verb. to inflict
influencia noun f. influence
influenciar verb. 1. to influence 2. sway
influir verb. 1. to influence 2. sway
influyente adj. influential
información noun f. information
informal adj. informal, casual
informar verb. 1. to inform 2. report
informativo, -va adj. informative
informatizar verb. to computerize
informe noun m. report
infracción noun f. infraction, offence
infractor, -tora noun. offender
infringir verb. to infringe, break
infundir verb. to infuse, instill
ingeniería noun f. engineering

ingeniero, -ra *noun.* engineer
ingenio *noun m.* **1.** wit **2.** device
ingenioso, -sa *adj.* witty, clever
ingenuo, -nua *adj.* naive
Inglaterra *noun f.* England
inglés, -glesa *noun. adj.* English
ingrediente *noun m.* ingredient
ingresar *verb.* to deposit
  —**ingresar en** to join
ingreso *noun m.* entrance, entry
  —**ingresos** earnings, revenue
inhabitual *adj.* unusual
inherente *adj.* inherent
inhibición *noun f.* inhibition
inhumano, -na *adj.* inhumane, inhuman
iniciado, -da *noun.* initiate
inicial *noun f. adj.* initial
iniciar *verb.* to initiate
iniciativa *noun f.* initiative
injuriar *verb.* to insult, abuse
injusticia *noun f.* injustice
injusto, -ta *adj.* unfair, unjust
inmaculado, -da *adj.* immaculate
inmediatamente *adv.* immediately
inmediato, -ta *adj.* **1.** immediate **2.**
  adjoining, nearby
inmenso, -sa *adj.* immense, vast
inmigración *noun f.* immigration
inmigrante *noun mf. adj.* immigrant
inminente *adj.* imminent
inmobiliario, -ria *adj.* real estate
inmóvil *adj.* still
inmovilizar *verb.* to immobilize
inmune *adj.* immune
inmunidad *noun f.* immunity
innato, -ta *adj.* innate
innecesario, -ria *adj.* unnecessary
innecesario *adv.* needless
innovación *noun f.* innovation
innumerable *adj.* countless
inocencia *noun f.* innocence
inocente *adj.* innocent
inocuo, -cua *adj.* harmless
inofensivo, -va *adj.* harmless, inoffensive
inquietar *verb.* to disturb, worry, trouble
inquieto, -ta *adj.* **1.** restless **2.** troubled,
  uneasy
inquietud *noun f.* **1.** restlessness **2.** concern, uneasiness

inquilino, -na *noun.* tenant
insatisfacción *noun f.* dissatisfaction
insatisfactorio, -ria *adj.* unsatisfactory
inscribir *verb.* **1.** to inscribe **2.** register
  3. enter
inscripción *noun f.* **1.** inscription **2.** registration
insecto *noun m.* insect
inseguro, -ra *adj.* **1.** insecure **2.** unsafe
insertar *verb.* to insert
insignia *noun f.* badge, insignia
insignificante *adj.* insignificant
insinuación *noun f.* hint,insinuation
insinuar *verb.* to hint, insinuate
insípido, -da *adj.* bland, insipid
insistencia *noun f.* insistence
insistir *verb.* to insist
insolvencia *noun f.* insolvency, bankruptcy
insolvente *adj.* insolvent, bankrupt
insoportable *adj.* unbearable
inspección *noun f.* **1.** inspection **2.**
  check
inspeccionar *verb.* **1.** to inspect **2.**
  check
inspector, -tora *noun.* inspector
inspiración *noun f.* **1.** inspiration **2.**
  inhalation
inspirar *verb.* **1.** to inspire **2.** inhale
instalación *noun f.* installation
instalar *verb.* to install
  —**instalarse** to settle
instancia *noun f.* petition
instantáneo, -nea *adj.* instant
instante *noun m.* instant
  —**al instante** immediately, at once
instintivo *adj.* instinctive
instinto *noun m.* instinct
institución *noun f.* institution
institucional *adj.* institutional
instituto *noun m.* institute
instrucción *noun f.* instruction
instructor, -tora *noun.* instructor
instruir *verb.* **1.** to instruct **2.** train
instrumental *adj.* instrumental
instrumento *noun m.* **1.** instrument **2.**
  tool, implement
insuficiente *adj.* insufficient, inadequate
insulina *noun f.* insulin

insultante *adj.* offensive
insultar *verb.* to insult
insulto *noun m.* insult
intacto, -ta *adj.* intact
integración *noun f.* integration
integrar *verb.* to integrate
integridad *noun f.* integrity
íntegro, -gra *adj.* 1. whole 2. honest
intelectual *noun mf. adj.* intellectual
inteligencia *noun f.* intelligence
inteligente *adj.* intelligent
intención *noun f.* intention
intencionado, -da *adj.* deliberate
intensidad *noun f.* intensity
intensificar *verb.* to intensify
intensivo, -va *adj.* intensive
intenso, -sa *adj.* intense
intentar *verb.* to try, attempt
intento *noun m.* 1. try, attempt 2. effort
interacción *noun f.* interaction
interactivo, -va *adj.* interactive
intercambiar *verb.* to exchange
intercambio *noun m.* exchange
interés *noun m.* interest
interesado, -da *adj.* 1. interested 2. selfish
interesante *adj.* interesting
interesar *verb.* 1. to interest 2. be of interest
interferencia *noun f.* interference
interferir *verb.* to interfere
interior *noun m.* 1. inside 2. interior 3. inland
interior *adj.* 1. interior 2. inner 3. internal 4. indoor
interlocutor, -tora *noun.* speaker, interlocutor
intermediario, -ria *noun. adj.* intermediary, go-between
intermedio *noun m.* intermission
intermedio, -dia *adj.* intermediate
interminable *adj.* endless
internacional *adj.* international
internar *verb.* to confine, commit
   —internarse 1. to penetrate 2. go (into the interior)
interno, -na *noun.* inmate
interno, -na *adj.* internal
interpretación *noun f.* interpretation

interpretar *verb.* 1. to interpret 2. perform
intérprete *noun mf.* 1. interpreter 2. performer
interrogar *verb.* to question
interrogatorio *noun m.* questioning, interrogation
interrumpir *verb.* to interrupt
interrupción *noun f.* interruption
interruptor *noun m.* switch
intervalo *noun m.* interval
intervención *noun f.* 1. intervention 2. operation
intervenir *verb.* 1. to intervene 2. take part 3. operate
intestinal *adj.* intestinal
intestino *noun m.* intestine
intimidad *noun f.* 1. intimacy 2. privacy
intimidar *verb.* to intimidate
íntimo, -ma *adj.* 1. intimate 2. private
intolerable *adj.* intolerable
intrincado, -da *adj.* intricate
introducción *noun f.* introduction
introducir *verb.* 1. to introduce 2. insert 3. input, insert
introductorio, -ria *adj.* introductory
inundación *noun f.* flood
inundar *verb.* to flood, inundate
inútil *adj.* useless
invadir *verb.* to invade
invalidez *noun f.* 1. invalidity 2. disability
inválido, -da *noun. adj.* invalid
invasión *noun f.* invasion
invención *noun f.* 1. invention 2. lie
inventar *verb.* 1. to invent 2. devise
inventario *noun m.* inventory
invento *noun m.* invention
invernadero *noun m.* greenhouse
inversión *noun f.* 1. inversion, reversal 2. investment
inversor, -sora *noun.* investor
invertir *verb.* 1. to invert, reverse 2. invest
investigación *noun f.* 1. investigation, inquiry 2. research
investigador, -dora *noun.* 1. investigator 2. researcher
investigar *verb.* 1. to investigate, inquire 2. research

invierno *noun m.* winter
invisible *adj.* invisible
invitación *noun f.* invitation
invitado, -da *noun.* guest
invitar *verb.* to invite
invocar *verb.* to invoke
inyección *noun f.* injection, shot
inyectar *verb.* to inject
ir *verb.* **1.** to go **2.** get on **3.** extend
  —**ir a** to be going to
  —**ir a pie** to walk
  —**irse 1.** to go **2.** leave
ira *noun f.* wrath
Irak *noun m.* Iraq
Irán *noun m.* Iran
iraní *noun mf. adj.* Iranian
Iraq *noun m.* Iraq
iraquí *noun mf. adj.* Iraqi
iris *noun m.* iris
Irlanda *noun f.* Ireland
irlandés, -desa *noun. adj.* Irish

ironía *noun f.* irony
irrazonable *adj.* unreasonable
irregular *adj.* irregular
irrelevante *adj.* irrelevant
irresistible *adj.* irresistible
irritación *noun f.* **1.** irritation **2.** exasperation
irritar *verb.* **1.** to irritate **2.** exasperate
irrumpir *verb.* to burst into, break in
isla *noun f.* **1.** island **2.** isle
Islam *noun m.* Islam
Islámico, -ca *adj.* Islamic
islandés, -desa *noun. adj.* Icelandic
Israel *noun m.* Israel
israelí *noun mf. adj.* Israeli
Italia *noun f.* Italy
italiano, -na *noun. adj.* Italian
itinerario *noun m.* route, itinerary
izquierda *noun f.* left
izquierdista *noun mf. adj.* leftist
izquierdo, -da *adj.* left

J

jabón *noun m.* soap
jactarse *verb.* to boast
jadear *verb.* to gasp
jadeo *noun m.* gasp
jaguar *noun m.* jaguar
jalea *noun f.* jelly
Jamaica *noun f.* Jamaica
jamaicano, -na *noun. adj.* Jamaican
jamón *noun m.* ham
Japón *noun m.* Japan
japonés, -nesa *noun. adj.* Japanese
jaque *noun m.* check
jardín *noun m.* garden
jardinería *noun f.* gardening
jardinero, -ra *noun.* gardener
jarra *noun f.* **1.** jug **2.** mug
jarro *noun m.* **1.** jug **2.** mug
jarrón *noun m.* vase
jaula *noun f.* cage
jazz *noun m.* jazz
jefe, -fa *noun.* **1.** boss **2.** head **3.** chief

jengibre *noun m.* ginger
jerarquía *noun f.* hierarchy
jerárquico, -ca *adj.* hierarchical
jerez *noun m.* sherry
jerga *noun f.* jargon
jersey *noun m.* **1.** jersey **2.** sweater
jinete *noun mf.* rider, horseman or horsewoman
jira *noun f.* picnic
jirón *noun m.* shred
jockey *noun m.* jockey
joder *verb.* **1.** to fuck **2.** screw
jornada *noun f.* day's journey
jornalero, -ra *noun f.* day laborer
joven *noun mf.* **1.** young person **2.** youngster
joven *adj.* **1.** young **2.** youthful
joya *noun f.* jewel
joyería *noun f.* **1.** jewelry **2.** jewelry store
jubilación *noun f.* **1.** retirement **2.** pension
jubilado, -da *noun.* retired person

jubilado, -da *adj.* retired
jubilar *verb.* to retire
jubileo *noun m.* jubilee
júbilo *noun m.* joy
judía *noun f.* bean
judicial *adj.* judicial
judío, -día *noun.* Jew
judío, -día *adj.* Jewish
juego *noun m.* **1.** play **2.** gambling **3.** game **4.** match **5.** set
 —**Juegos Olímpicos** Olympic Games
jueves *noun m.* Thursday
juez *noun mf.* judge
jueza *noun f.* judge
jugada *noun f.* **1.** move **2.** trick
jugador, -dora *noun.* **1.** player **2.** gambler
jugar *verb.* **1.** to play **2.** gamble
jugo *noun m.* juice
juguete *noun m.* toy
juicio *noun m.* **1.** trial **2.** sense, reason **3.** opinion
juicioso, -sa *adj.* **1.** reasonable **2.** wise
julio *noun m.* July
junco *noun m.* **1.** junk **2.** reed, rush
junio *noun m.* June
junta *noun f.* **1.** board **2.** meeting, assembly **3.** joint

juntar *verb.* **1.** to unite **2.** assemble, collect **3.** gather **4.** pool
 —**juntarse** to join
 —**juntarse con** to frequent the company of
junto, -ta *adj.* **1.** united **2.** together
 —**junto a** by, next to
juntura *noun f.* joint
jurado *noun m.* jury
juramento *noun m.* oath
jurar *verb.* **1.** to swear **2.** take an oath
jurídico, -ca *adj.* legal
jurisdicción *noun f.* jurisdiction
justamente *adv.* **1.** exactly, precisely **2.** fairly
justicia *noun f.* **1.** justice **2.** fairness
justificación *noun f.* justification
justificadamente *adv.* rightly
justificar *verb.* to justify
justo, -ta *adj.* **1.** fair **2.** just **3.** exact
justo *adv.* **1.** justly **2.** exactly
juvenil *adj.* **1.** juvenile **2.** youthful
juventud *noun f.* **1.** young people **2.** youth
juzgado *noun m.* court
juzgar *verb.* **1.** to judge, try **2.** deem

K

kilogramo *noun m.* kilogram
kilómetro *noun m.* kilometer
kit *noun m.* kit

Kuwait *noun m.* Kuwait
kuwaití *noun mf. adj.* Kuwaiti

L

la *art.* the
la *pron.* **1.** her, it **2.** the one
labio *noun m.* lip
laboratorio *noun m.* laboratory
labor *noun f.* labor, work
labrador, -dora *noun.* peasant, farmer
ladear *verb.* to tilt, tip

 —**ladearse** to bend over
ladera *noun f.* hillside, slope
lado *noun m.* side
 —**al lado** next (to)
ladrar *verb.* to bark
ladrido *noun m.* bark
ladrillo *noun m.* brick

ladrón, -drona *noun.* thief, robber
lady *noun m.* lady
lagarto *noun f.* lizard
lago *noun m.* lake
lágrima *noun f.* tear
laico, -ca *adj.* lay
lamentar *verb.* **1.** to be sorry **2.** regret **3.** lament
  —lamentarse to bemoan
lamer *verb.* to lick
lámina *noun f.* plate
lámpara *noun f.* **1.** lamp **2.** light
lana *noun f.* wool
lanzadera *noun f.* shuttle
lanzamiento *noun m.* **1.** throw **2.** launch **3.** pitch
lanzar *verb.* **1.** to throw, hurl **2.** launch **3.** pitch
  —lanzarse 1. to undertake **2.** throw oneself
lápida *noun f.* tombstone
lápiz *noun m.* pencil
  —lápiz de labios lipstick
largo *noun m.* length
largo, -ga *adj.* long
  —a la larga in the long run
  —a lo largo 1. lengthwise **2.** along
largometraje *noun m.* feature film
láser *noun m.* laser
lástima *noun f.* **1.** pity **2.** shame
lastimar *verb.* **1.** to hurt, harm, injure **2.** wound
lata *noun f.* **1.** can **2.** nuisance
  —dar la lata to annoy
latente *adj.* latent
lateral *adj.* lateral
latido *noun m.* beat
latigazo *noun m.* lash
látigo *noun m.* whip, lash
latín *noun m.* Latin
latino, -na *noun. adj.* Latin
latinoamericano, -na *noun. adj.* Latin American
latir *verb.* to beat
latón *noun m.* brass
laurel *noun m.* **1.** laurel **2.** bay
lavabo *noun m.* **1.** sink **2.** lavatory, toilet
lavado *noun m.* wash, cleaning
lavanda *noun f.* lavender

lavandería *noun f.* laundry
lavar *verb.* to wash, clean
lazo *noun m.* **1.** bond **2.** link **3.** bow
le *pron.* **1.** to him, to her, to it **2.** for him, for her, for it **3.** from him, from her, from it **4.** to you, for you
leal *adj.* faithful, loyal
lealtad *noun f.* allegiance, loyalty
lección *noun f.* lesson
leche *noun f.* milk
lechería *noun f.* dairy store
lecho *noun m.* bed
lechuza *noun f.* owl
lector, -tora *noun.* **1.** reader **2.** scanner
lectura *noun f.* reading
leer *verb.* to read
legal *adj.* legal, lawful
legendario, -ria *adj.* legendary
legión *noun f.* legion
legislación *noun f.* legislation
legislativo, -va *adj.* legislative
legitimidad *noun f.* legitimacy
legítimo, -ma *adj.* legitimate
lego, -ga *adj.* lay
legua *noun f.* league
lejano, -na *adj.* distant, far, remote
lejos *adv.* distant, far away
  —lejos de far from
lema *noun m.* slogan, motto
lengua *noun f.* **1.** tongue **2.** language
lenguado *noun m.* sole
lenguaje *noun m.* **1.** language **2.** speech
lentamente *adv.* slowly
lente *noun f.* lens
lento, -ta *adj.* **1.** slow **2.** dull
leña *noun f.* firewood
leño *noun m.* log
león, -ona *noun.* lion
les *pron.* **1.** to them **2.** for them **3.** from them **4.** to you
lesión *noun f.* injury, lesion
lesionado, -da *adj.* injured
letal *adj.* lethal
letra *noun f.* **1.** letter **2.** lyrics **3.** type
letrero *noun m.* sign
leucemia *noun f.* leukemia
levantar *verb.* **1.** to lift, raise **2.** erect **3.** arouse
  —levantarse 1. to get up **2.** stand up **3.** rise

leve *adj.* light, mild

léxico *noun m.* lexicon

ley *noun f.* **1.** law **2.** purity

leyenda *noun f.* **1.** legend **2.** caption

liar *verb.* **1.** to roll **2.** tie up **3.** confuse

liberación *noun f.* **1.** liberation **2.** release

liberal *adj.* liberal

liberar *verb.* **1.** to free **2.** liberate **3.** release

libertad *noun f.* freedom, liberty
   —libertad bajo fianza bail
   —libertad provisional parole

libra *noun f.* pound

librar *verb.* **1.** to deliver **2.** wage **3.** issue
   —librarse de 1. to get rid of **2.** escape

libre *adj.* **1.** free **2.** vacant

librería *noun f.* bookstore

libreta *noun f.* notebook

libro *noun m.* book

licencia *noun f.* **1.** permission **2.** franchise **3.** license **4.** permit

licenciado, -da *noun.* graduate

licenciar *verb.* **1.** to license, permit **2.** discharge **3.** dismiss **4.** confer a university degree
   —licenciarse to graduate

licenciatura *noun f.* college degree

lícito, -ta *adj.* licit, lawful

licor *noun m.* liquor

líder *noun mf.* leader

líder *adj.* leading

liderar *verb.* to lead

liderato *noun m.* leadership

liderazgo *noun m.* leadership

lienzo *noun m.* **1.** canvas **2.** linen

liga *noun f.* league

ligeramente *adv.* **1.** slightly **2.** lightly

ligero, -ra *adj.* **1.** slight **2.** light, lightweight **3.** quick, agile

lijar *verb.* to sand

lima *noun f.* **1.** file **2.** lime

limar *verb.* to file

limitación *noun f.* **1.** limitation **2.** restriction

limitado, -da *adj.* **1.** limited **2.** restricted **3.** dull

limitar *verb.* to restrict, limit

límite *noun m.* **1.** limit **2.** border, boundary

limón *noun m.* lemon

limonada *noun f.* lemonade

limpiador, -dora *noun.* cleaner

limpiar *verb.* to clean

limpio, -pia *adj.* **1.** clean **2.** free **3.** clear
   —juego limpio fair game

linaje *noun m.* lineage

lindar (con) *verb.* to border

lindo, -da *adj.* **1.** cute **2.** lovely **3.** pretty

lindo *adv.* beautifully

línea *noun f.* line

lineal *adj.* linear

lingüística *noun f.* linguistics

lingüístico, -ca *adj.* linguistic

lino *noun m.* **1.** linen **2.** flax

linterna *noun f.* lantern

lío *noun m.* **1.** mess **2.** trouble **3.** affair, liaison

líquido *noun m.* **1.** liquid, fluid **2.** liquid assets, ready cash

líquido, -da *adj.* **1.** liquid, fluid **2.** net

lírico, -ca *adj.* lyric, lyrical

lirio *noun m.* **1.** iris **2.** lily

lisiado, -da *noun.* cripple, disabled person

lisiado, -da *adj.* cripple

liso, -sa *adj.* **1.** smooth **2.** even **3.** flat **4.** plain **5.** straight

lista *noun f.* **1.** list **2.** roll **3.** stripe

listo, -ta *adj.* **1.** ready **2.** clever, smart

literal *adj.* literal

literario, -ria *adj.* literary

literatura *noun f.* literature

litigio *noun m.* litigation

litro *noun m.* liter

llaga *noun f.* sore

llama *noun f.* **1.** flame **2.** llama

llamada *noun f.* call

llamar *verb.* **1.** to call **2.** knock **3.** name
   —llamar por teléfono to phone
   —llamarse to be called, be named

llamativo, -va *adj.* showy, striking

llamear *verb.* to blaze, throw out flames

llano *noun m.* plain

llano, -na *adj.* **1.** even, flat **2.** plain, simple

llanta *noun f.* **1.** tire **2.** rim

llanura *noun f.* plain

llave *noun f.* **1.** key **2.** switch **3.** faucet
llegada *noun f.* **1.** arrival **2.** advent
llegar *verb.* **1.** to arrive **2.** appear **3.** come **4.** suffice
—**llegar a ser** to become
llenar *verb.* **1.** to fill **2.** fulfill, please
—**llenarse** to fill up
lleno, -na *adj.* full, filled
—**de lleno** completely
llevar *verb.* **1.** to carry **2.** take, take away **3.** wear **4.** endure, bear
—**llevar a cabo** to carry out, accomplish
—**llevarse** **1.** to take away **2.** get along
llorar *verb.* to cry, weep
llover *verb.* to rain
lluvia *noun f.* **1.** rain **2.** shower
lo *art.* **1.** the **2.** how
lo *pron.* **1.** him, it **2.** you
—**lo que** what
lobo, -ba *noun.* wolf
lóbrego, -ga *adj.* gloomy
local *noun m.* premises
local *adj.* **1.** local **2.** home
localidad *noun f.* locality
localizar *verb.* **1.** to locate **2.** localize
loco, -ca *noun.* crazy person
loco, -ca *adj.* crazy, mad
—**volverse loco** to go crazy
locomotora *noun f.* locomotive
locura *noun f.* **1.** folly **2.** madness
lodo *noun m.* mud
lógica *noun f.* logic
lógico, -ca *adj.* logical
lograr *verb.* **1.** to achieve **2.** attain **3.** get **4.** succeed in
logro *noun m.* achievement
loma *noun f.* hill
lombriz *noun f.* worm
lomo *noun m.* **1.** back **2.** loin **3.** spine
lona *noun f.* canvas

longitud *noun f.* length
lord *noun m.* lord
los *pron.* **1.** them **2.** you
—**los que** those who
losa *noun f.* slab .
lote *noun m.* lot, batch
lotería *noun f.* lottery
loto *noun m.* lotus
lubina *noun f.* bass
lubricar *verb.* to lubricate, oil
lucha *noun f.* **1.** fight **2.** struggle **3.** wrestling
luchador, -dora *noun.* **1.** fighter **2.** wrestler
luchar *verb.* **1.** to fight **2.** struggle **3.** wrestle
lucir *verb.* to shine
—**lucirse** **1.** to excel **2.** wear
lucrativo, -va *adj.* lucrative, profitable
lucro *noun m.* profit
luego *adv.* **1.** later **2.** then
—**desde luego** of course
—**hasta luego** see you later
luego *conj.* therefore
lugar *noun m.* **1.** place **2.** position **3.** space
—**en lugar de** instead of
—**tener lugar** to take place
lujo *noun m.* luxury
lujoso, -sa *adj.* luxurious
lujuria *noun f.* lust
luminoso, -sa *adj.* luminous, bright
luna *noun f.* moon
—**luna de miel** honeymoon
lunar *noun m.* mole
lunes *noun m.* Monday
lustrar *verb.* to shine
lustre *noun m.* shine
lustroso, -sa *adj.* shiny
luz *noun f.* **1.** light **2.** electricity **3.** span
—**dar a luz** to give birth

M

macanudo, -da *adj.* great, fantastic
maceta *noun f.* pot
macho *noun m.* male
macho *adj.* 1. male 2. he
macizo, -za *adj.* 1. solid 2. strong
madera *noun f.* 1. wood 2. timber
madre *noun f.* mother
madriguera *noun f.* den
madrugador, -dora *noun.* early riser
madurar *verb.* 1. to mature 2. ripen
madurez *noun f.* 1. maturity 2. ripeness
maduro, -ra *adj.* 1. mature 2. ripe
maestro, -tra *noun.* 1. master 2. teacher
maestro, -tra *adj.* masterly
magia *noun f.* magic
mágico, -ca *adj.* magic, magical
magistrado, -da *noun.* magistrate, judge
magnate *noun mf.* tycoon, magnate
magnético, -ca *adj.* magnetic
magnífico, -ca *adj.* magnificent, superb
magnitud *noun f.* magnitude
magro, -gra *adj.* 1. lean 2. meager
magulladura *noun f.* bruise
magullar *verb.* to bruise
maíz *noun m.* maize, corn
majestad *noun f.* majesty
mal *noun m.* 1. evil 2. wrong 3. harm 4. misfortune 5. illness, disease
mal *adj.* (see malo. Used before masculine singular nouns)
mal *adv.* 1. badly, poorly 2. hardly 3. wrong
Malasia *noun f.* Malaysia
malayo, -ya *noun. adj.* Malaysian
maldad *noun f.* evil
maldecir *verb.* to curse, damn
maldición *noun f.* curse
maldito, -ta *adj.* cursed, damned
maleante *noun mf.* crook
maleducado, -ta *adj.* rude, ill-mannered
malentendido *noun m.* misunderstanding
malestar *noun m.* 1. discontent 2. discomfort 3. indisposition, illness
maleta *noun f.* suitcase

maletero *noun m.* 1. trunk 2. porter
malgastar *verb.* 1. to waste 2. squander
malhumorado, -da *adj.* ill-humored
malicia *noun f.* 1. malice, wickedness 2. cunning
malintencionado *adj.* malicious
malla *noun f.* 1. tights 2. mesh 3. net
malo, -la *noun.* villain, bad person
malo, -la *adj.* 1. bad 2. evil 3. harmful 4. ill 5. poor, cheap 6. rotten
maltratar *verb.* to abuse
maltrato *noun m.* abuse
malvado, -da *adj.* evil, wicked
mamá *noun f.* mamma, mama, mum, mummy
mamar *verb.* to suckle, suck
 —dar de mamar to breast-feed
mamífero *noun m.* mammal
manada *noun f.* herd, pack
manar *verb.* to flow, stream
mancha *noun f.* mark, stain, spot
manchar *verb.* to stain, soil
mandar *verb.* 1. to order 2. command 3. send
mandíbula *noun f.* jaw
mandil *noun m.* apron
mando *noun m.* 1. command 2. control
 —mando a distancia remote control
manecilla *noun f.* hand
manejar *verb.* 1. to handle 2. manage 3. manipulate
manera *noun f.* way, manner
 —de manera que so that
 —de ninguna manera by no means
 —de todas maneras anyway
manga *noun f.* sleeve
mango *noun m.* 1. handle 2. mango
manicomio *noun m.* asylum
manifestación *noun f.* 1. demonstration 2. manifestation
manifestante *noun mf.* demonstrator
manifestar *verb.* 1. to demonstrate 2. exhibit, display
 —manifestarse 1. to demonstrate 2. state one's position
manifiesto *noun m.* manifesto

manifiesto, -ta *adj.* manifest, overt

manilla *noun f.* handle

maniobra *noun f.* maneuver

maniobrar *verb.* to maneuver

manipulación *noun f.* manipulation

manipular *verb.* **1.** to manipulate **2.** handle

maniquí *noun mf.* model

mano *noun f.* **1.** hand **2.** coat
  —**de primera mano** firsthand
  —**mano de obra** manpower, workforce

manojo *noun m.* bunch

manosear *verb.* **1.** to finger **2.** touch repeatedly

mansión *noun f.* mansion

manta *noun f.* blanket

manteca *noun f.* lard, fat

mantener *verb.* **1.** to keep **2.** maintain **3.** hold **4.** support **5.** sustain

mantenimiento *noun m.* **1.** maintenance **2.** preservation

mantequilla *noun f.* butter

manual *noun m.* handbook, manual

manual *adj.* manual

manuscrito *noun m.* manuscript

manzana *noun f.* **1.** apple **2.** block

mañana *noun f.* **1.** morning **2.** tomorrow

mañoso, -sa *adj.* skillful

mapa *noun m.* map

maqueta *noun f.* model

maquillaje *noun m.* make-up

máquina *noun f.* **1.** machine **2.** engine

maquinar *verb.* to plot, scheme

maquinaria *noun f.* **1.** machinery **2.** mechanism

mar *noun mf.* sea

maraña *noun f.* tangle

maratón *noun f.* marathon

maravilla *noun f.* marvel, wonder

maravilloso, -sa *adj.* marvelous, wonderful

marca *noun f.* **1.** mark, sign **2.** brand **3.** trademark **4.** record

marcador *noun m.* **1.** marker **2.** scoreboard

marcar *verb.* **1.** to mark **2.** brand **3.** score **4.** indicate **5.** dial

marcha *noun f.* **1.** march **2.** departure **3.** speed **4.** progress, course **5.** gear

marchar *verb.* **1.** to march **2.** work **3.** go
  —**marcharse 1.** to depart **2.** leave

marcial *adj.* martial

marco *noun m.* **1.** frame, framework **2.** mark

marea *noun f.* tide

mareado, -da *adj.* **1.** dizzy **2.** sick

mareo *noun m.* **1.** faint **2.** sickness

marfil *noun m.* ivory

margarita *noun f.* daisy

margen *noun m.* **1.** margin **2.** border, edge

marginal *adj.* marginal

marido *noun m.* husband

marina *noun f.* navy

marinero *noun m.* sailor

marino *noun m.* sailor

marino, -na *adj.* marine

mariposa *noun f.* butterfly

marítimo, -ma *adj.* maritime

marketing *noun m.* marketing

mármol *noun m.* marble

marrano, -na *noun.* **1.** pig, hog **2.** Marrano

marrano, -na *adj.* filthy

marrón *noun m. adj.* brown

martes *noun m.* Tuesday

martillar *verb.* to hammer

martillo *noun m.* hammer

marzo *noun m.* March

mas *conj.* but

más *noun m.* plus sign

más *adj.* **1.** more **2.** most **3.** else

más *adv.* **1.** more **2.** most **3.** further **4.** longer **5.** rather
  —**más bien** rather
  —**más vale** better

más *prep.* plus
  —**más allá de** beyond

más *pron.* more
  —**por más que** no matter how much

masa *noun f.* **1.** mass **2.** dough

masacrar *verb.* to massacre, butcher

masacre *noun f.* massacre

masaje *noun m.* massage

masajear *verb.* to massage

mascar *verb.* to chew

máscara *noun f.* mask

mascarilla *noun f.* mask

mascota *noun f.* pet
masculino, -na *adj.* masculine
masivo, -va *adj.* mass
matadero *noun m.* abattoir, slaughterhouse
matanza *noun f.* slaughter
matar *verb.* 1. to kill 2. butcher, slaughter 3. pass, waste
mate *noun m.* 1. mate 2. smash
matemáticas *noun f. plural.* mathematics
matemático, -ca *noun.* mathematician
matemático, -ca *adj.* mathematical
materia *noun f.* 1. material 2. matter
material *noun m.* 1. material 2. stuff
material *adj.* material
maternal *adj.* maternal
maternidad *noun f.* maternity
materno, -na *adj.* maternal
matiz *noun m.* 1. hue 2. shade
matón *noun m.* bully
matrícula *noun f.* 1. registration 2. register
matricular *verb.* 1. to register 2. matriculate
matrimonio *noun m.* 1. marriage 2. married couple
máxima *noun f.* maxim
máximo *noun m.* maximum
  —**al máximo** to the utmost
  —**como máximo** at the most, at the latest
máximo, -ma *adj.* maximum
mayo *noun m.* May
mayor *noun mf.* adult
mayor *adj.* 1. main, major 2. bigger, biggest 3. larger, largest 4. greater, greatest 5. elder, oldest
  —**al por mayor** wholesale
mayoría *noun f.* majority
mayorista *noun mf.* wholesaler
mayúscula *noun f.* capital letter
me *pron.* 1. me 2. to me, for me, from me 3. myself
mecánica *noun f.* mechanics
mecánico, -ca *noun.* mechanic
mecánico, -ca *adj.* mechanical
mecanismo *noun m.* mechanism, device
mecanografía *noun f.* typing, typewriting
mecanografiar *verb.* to type
mecenas *noun mf.* patron

mecenazgo *noun m.* patronage
mecer *verb.* 1. to rock 2. sway
mechón *noun m.* lock
medalla *noun f.* medal
media *noun f.* 1. average 2. stocking
mediano, -na *adj.* medium
medianoche *noun f.* midnight
mediar *verb.* 1. to mediate 2. intervene 3. reach the middle
medicamento *noun m.* medicine, drug
medicina *noun f.* medicine
medicar *verb.* to medicate
medición *noun f.* measurement, measuring
médico *noun mf.* doctor, physician
médico, -ca *adj.* medical
medida *noun f.* 1. measure, measurement 2. step 3. extent
medieval *adj.* medieval
medio *noun m.* 1. middle 2. element 3. medium 4. means
  —**medio ambiente** environment
medio, -dia *adj.* 1. middle 2. half 3. average 4. medium
medio *adv.* 1. half 2. rather
mediocre *adj.* mediocre, ordinary
mediodía *noun m.* midday, noon
medir *verb.* 1. to measure 2. gauge 3. weigh
meditación *noun f.* meditation
meditar *verb.* 1. to meditate 2. ponder
médium *noun mf.* medium
mejilla *noun f.* cheek
mejor *adj.* 1. better 2. best
mejor *adv.* 1. better 2. best 3. rather
  —**a lo mejor** probably, maybe
mejora *noun f.* 1. improvement 2. upgrade
mejorar *verb.* 1. to improve 2. make better
melancolía *noun f.* melancholy, sadness
melancólico, -ca *adj.* melancholy, sad, blue
melocotón *noun m.* peach
melodía *noun f.* melody, tune
membrana *noun f.* membrane
memorable *adj.* memorable
memorándum *noun m.* memorandum, memo
memoria *noun f.* 1. memory 2. report
  —**memorias** memoirs
mena *noun f.* ore

mención *noun f.* mention
mencionar *verb.* to mention
menor *noun mf.* minor
menor *adj.* **1.** minor **2.** smaller, smallest **3.** lesser, least **4.** younger, youngest
 —**al por menor** retail
menos *noun m.* minus sign
menos *adj.* **1.** less, least **2.** fewer, fewest
menos *adv.* **1.** less **2.** least
 —**a menos que** unless
 —**por lo menos** at least
menos *prep.* **1.** except **2.** minus
menos *pron.* less, fewer
mensaje *noun m.* message
mensajero, -ra *noun.* messenger
mensual *adj.* monthly
menta *noun f.* mint
mental *adj.* mental
mente *noun f.* mind
mentir *verb.* to lie
mentira *noun f.* lie
mentón *noun m.* chin
menú *noun m.* menu
mercadería *noun f.* merchandise
mercado *noun m.* **1.** market **2.** fair
mercancía *noun f.* merchandise, goods
mercurio *noun m.* mercury
merecedor, -dora *adj.* worthy
merecer *verb.* to deserve, be worthy of
merecido *noun m.* due
merecido, -da *adj.* just, due
merecimiento *noun m.* merit
meridional *adj.* southern
mérito *noun m.* merit
merma *noun f.* **1.** decrease, drop **2.** loss, waste
mermelada *noun f.* marmalade, jam
mero, -ra *adj.* mere, simple, plain
mes *noun m.* month
mesa *noun f.* table
meseta *noun f.* plateau
meta *noun f.* aim, goal
metáfora *noun f.* metaphor
metal *noun m.* **1.** metal **2.** brass
metálico, -ca *adj.* metallic
meter *verb.* **1.** to put (in) **2.** insert, introduce **3.** place **4.** cause **5.** make
 —**meter prisa** to hurry
 —**meterse 1.** to enter, get into **2.** meddle

 —**meterse a** to become
 —**meterse con** to tease
método *noun m.* method
metro *noun m.* **1.** meter **2.** subway **3.** underground
metropolitano, -na *adj.* metropolitan
mexicano, -na *noun. adj.* Mexican
México *noun m.* Mexico
mezcla *noun f.* mix, mixture, blend
mezclar *verb.* **1.** to mix, blend **2.** involve
 —**mezclarse** to socialize, mingle
mezquino, -na *adj.* mean, petty
mezquita *noun f.* mosque
mi *adj.* my
mí *pron.* me
microbio *noun m.* microbe
micrófono *noun m.* microphone
microondas *noun m.* microwave
microscopio *noun m.* microscope
miedo *noun m.* fear
 —**dar miedo** to frighten
 —**tener miedo** to be afraid
miel *noun f.* honey
miembro *noun m.* **1.** member **2.** limb
mientras *conj.* **1.** while, as **2.** as long as
 —**mientras que** while, whereas
 —**mientras tanto** meanwhile, in the meantime
miércoles *noun m.* Wednesday
mierda *noun f.* shit
migración *noun f.* migration
migrar *verb.* to migrate
mil *noun m.* a thousand, one thousand
mil *adj.* thousand
milagro *noun m.* **1.** miracle **2.** wonder
mililitro *noun m.* milliliter
milímetro *noun m.* millimeter
militante *noun mf. adj.* militant, activist
militar *noun mf.* soldier
militar *adj.* military
milla *noun f.* mile
millar *noun m.* thousand
millardo *noun m.* billion
millón *noun m.* million
millonario, -ria *noun.* millionaire
millonésimo *noun m.* millionth
millonésimo, -ma *adj.* millionth
mimar *verb.* to spoil
mina *noun f.* **1.** mine **2.** lead

minar *verb*. 1. to mine 2. undermine

mineral *noun m. adj*. mineral

minería *noun f*. mining

minero, -ra *noun*. miner

minero, -ra *adj*. mining

miniatura *noun f*. miniature

minifalda *noun f*. miniskirt

minimizar *verb*. to minimize

mínimo *noun m*. minimum

mínimo, -ma *adj*. 1. least, smallest 2. minimum

ministerial *adj*. ministerial

ministerio *noun m*. department, ministry

ministro, -tra *noun*. secretary, minister

minoría *noun f*. minority

minuciosamente *adv*. thoroughly

minucioso, -sa *adj*. 1. minute 2. detailed 3. thorough

minúsculo, -la *adj*. minute, tiny

minusvalía *noun f*. disability, handicap

minusválido, -da *noun*. handicapped person

minusválido, -da *adj*. disabled, handicapped

minuto *noun m*. minute

mío, mía *adj*. my, mine

mío, mía *pron*. mine

mirada *noun f*. look, glance, glare, gaze

mirar *verb*. 1. to look, look at 2. watch 3. consider

  —mirarse 1. to look at oneself 2. look at each other

misa *noun f*. mass

miserable *adj*. 1. miserable, wretched 2. despicable

miseria *noun f*. 1. misery 2. poverty

misil *noun m*. missile

misión *noun f*. mission

misionero, -ra *noun*. missionary

mismo, -ma *adj*. 1. same 2. very 3. oneself

misterio *noun m*. mystery

misterioso, -sa *adj*. mysterious

mitad *noun f*. 1. half 2. middle

mito *noun m*. myth

mixto, -ta *adj*. mixed

mobiliario *noun m*. furniture

moción *noun f*. motion

moda *noun f*. 1. fashion 2. style

  —a la moda fashionable

modales *noun m. plural*. manners

modelar *verb*. to model, mold, shape

modelo *noun m*. example, model, pattern

modelo *noun mf*. model

módem *noun m*. modem

moderado, -da *noun. adj*. moderate

moderar *verb*. to moderate

modernizar *verb*. to modernize

moderno, -na *adj*. 1. modern 2. up-to-date

modesto, -ta *adj*. 1. modest 2. humble

modificación *noun f*. modification, alteration

modificar *verb*. to modify, alter

modo *noun m*. 1. way, manner 2. mode 3. mood

  —de cualquier modo anyway

  —de modo que so

  —de todos modos anyway

módulo *noun m*. module

mojado, -da *adj*. wet

mojar *verb*. to wet

molde *noun m*. 1. mold 2. cast

moldear *verb*. 1. to mold 2. cast

molécula *noun f*. molecule

molecular *adj*. molecular

moler *verb*. to grind

molestar *verb*. 1. to annoy, bother 2. disturb 3. trouble

  —molestarse en to take the trouble, bother

molestia *noun f*. 1. annoyance, bother, nuisance 2. trouble

molesto, -ta *adj*. 1. annoyed, bothered 2. annoying, bothersome

molinero, -ra *noun*. miller

molino *noun m*. mill

momento *noun m*. 1. moment 2. time

  —al momento immediately

momia *noun f*. mummy

monarca *noun mf*. monarch

monarquía *noun f*. monarchy

monasterio *noun m*. monastery

moneda *noun f*. 1. coin 2. currency

monedero *noun m*. purse

monetario, -ria *adj*. monetary

monitor *noun m*. 1. instructor 2. monitor

monja *noun f.* sister
monje *noun m.* monk
mono, -na *noun.* monkey
mono, -na *adj.* pretty, funny
monopolio *noun m.* monopoly
monstruo *noun m.* monster
montacargas *noun m.* elevator
montaje *noun m.* assembly
montaña *noun f.* mountain
montar *verb.* 1. to mount 2. assemble 3. establish, set up 4. stage 5. whip
—**montar a caballo** to ride a horse
—**montar en bicicleta** to ride a bicycle
monte *noun m.* mountain, mount
montículo *noun m.* mound
montón *noun m.* heap, pile
—**montones de** loads of, tons of, plenty of
montura *noun f.* 1. frame 2. setting 3. mount
monumento *noun m.* monument
morada *noun f.* dwelling
morado *noun m.* purple
morado, -da *adj.* purple
moral *noun f.* 1. morale 2. morality
moral *adj.* moral
moraleja *noun f.* moral
mordaz *adj.* sarcastic, biting
morder *verb.* to bite
mordisco *noun m.* bite
moreno, -na *adj.* dark-skinned, brown
morir *verb.* to die
mortal *noun. adj.* mortal
mortalidad *noun f.* mortality
mortero *noun m.* mortar
mosaico *noun m.* mosaic
mosca *noun f.* fly
mostaza *noun f.* mustard
mostrador *noun m.* counter
mostrar *verb.* 1. to show 2. display 3. manifest
moteado, -da *adj.* spotted
motín *noun m.* riot
motivación *noun f.* motivation
motivar *verb.* 1. to motivate 2. cause
motivo *noun m.* 1. motive 2. cause
motor *noun m.* 1. motor, engine 2. cause
mover *verb.* 1. to move 2. shift 3. shake 4. prompt 5. stir

móvil *adj.* mobile
movilidad *noun f.* mobility
movilizar *verb.* to mobilize
movimiento *noun m.* 1. movement 2. motion
mozo, -za *adj.* young
muchacha *noun f.* 1. girl 2. maid
muchacho *noun m.* boy
muchedumbre *noun f.* multitude, crowd
mucho, -cha *adj.* many, much, a lot of, plenty of
mucho *adv.* much, a lot
—**como mucho** at most
—**con mucho** by far
—**mucho tiempo** long
mucho, -cha *pron.* many, much, a lot
mudanza *noun f.* 1. move 2. change
mudar *verb.* 1. to change 2. shed
—**mudarse** 1. to move 2. change
mudo, -da *adj.* 1. dumb 2. mute
muebles *noun m. plural.* furniture
muelle *noun m.* 1. dock, wharf 2. spring
muerte *noun f.* death
muerto, -ta *noun.* dead person
muerto, -ta *adj.* dead
muesca *noun f.* nick
muestra *noun f.* 1. sample 2. show
mujer *noun f.* 1. woman 2. wife
multa *noun f.* fine
multar *verb.* to fine
múltiple *adj.* multiple
multiplicar *verb.* to multiply
múltiplo *noun m.* multiple
multitud *noun f.* multitude, crowd
mundial *adj.* world, worldwide
mundo *noun m.* world
—**todo el mundo** everyone, everybody
munición *noun f.* ammunition
municipal *adj.* municipal
municipio *noun m.* municipality
muñeca *noun f.* 1. doll 2. wrist
muñón *noun m.* stump
muralla *noun f.* wall
murciélago *noun m.* bat
murmullo *noun m.* murmur
murmurar *verb.* to murmur, mutter, whisper
muro *noun m.* wall

muscular *adj.* muscular
músculo *noun m.* muscle
musculoso, -sa *adj.* muscular
museo *noun m.* museum
musgo *noun m.* moss
música *noun f.* music

musical *noun m. adj.* musical
músico, -ca *noun.* musician
muslo *noun m.* thigh
musulmán, -mana *noun. adj.* Muslim
mutuo, -tua *adj.* 1. mutual 2. reciprocal
muy *adv.* 1. very 2. quite

N

nacer *verb.* 1. to be born 2. rise
nacimiento *noun m.* 1. birth 2. source
nación *noun f.* 1. nation 2. country
nacional *noun mf.* citizen
nacional *adj.* 1. national 2. domestic
nacionalidad *noun f.* nationality
nacionalismo *noun m.* nationalism
nacionalista *noun mf.* nationalist
nada *noun f.* 1. nothingness 2. naught
nada *adv.* not at all
  —**casi nada** very little
  —**de nada** you are welcome
nada *pron.* nothing, anything
nadar *verb.* to swim
nadie *pron.* 1. nobody 2. no one
naranja *noun f.* orange (fruit)
naranja *noun m. adj.* orange (color)
nariz *noun f.* nose
narración *noun f.* narration
narrar *verb.* to narrate, relate, tell
narrativa *noun f.* narrative
nata *noun f.* cream
natal *adj.* native
nativo, -va *noun. adj.* native
natural *adj.* 1. natural 2. native
naturaleza *noun f.* nature
naturalmente *adv.* 1. naturally 2. of course
naufragio *noun m.* shipwreck
naval *adj.* naval
nave *noun f.* 1. ship 2. nave
navegación *noun f.* navigation
navegar *verb.* to sail
Navidad *noun f.* Christmas
necesario, -ria *adj.* necessary
necesidad *noun f.* 1. need, necessity 2. poverty, want

necesitar *verb.* 1. to need 2. require
necrología *noun f.* obituary
neerlandés, -desa *noun. adj.* Dutch
negar *verb.* 1. to deny 2. refuse
negativa *noun f.* 1. denial 2. refusal
negativo *noun m.* negative
negativo, -va *adj.* negative, adverse
negligencia *noun f.* negligence
negociación *noun f.* negotiation
negociador, -dora *noun.* negotiator
negociar *verb.* 1. to negotiate 2. deal
negocio *noun m.* 1. business 2. trade
  —**hombre/mujer de negocios** businessman or businesswoman
negro, -gra *noun.* black person
negro, -gra *adj.* 1. black 2. disastrous, awful
nervio *noun m.* 1. nerve 2. vein 3. energy, vigor
nervioso, -sa *adj.* nervous
neto, -ta *adj.* 1. net 2. clean, clear
neumático *noun m.* tire
neutral *adj.* neutral
neutralidad *noun f.* neutrality
neutro, -tra *adj.* 1. neuter 2. neutral
nevar *verb.* to snow
nevera *noun f.* refrigerator
ni *conj.* neither, nor
  —**ni siquiera** not even
nido *noun m.* nest
niebla *noun f.* fog
nieto, -ta *noun.* grandson or granddaughter
  —**nietos** grandchildren
nieve *noun f.* snow
ningún *adj.* (see ninguno. Used before masculine singular nouns)
ninguno, -na *adj.* no, none

ninguno, -na *pron.* **1.** none **2.** neither **3.** no one, no other

niñero, -ra *noun.* nanny, baby-sitter

niño, -ña *noun.* child, boy or girl

nítido, -da *adj.* clear, sharp

nitrógeno *noun m.* nitrogen

nivel *noun m.* **1.** level **2.** standard **3.** grade

nivelar *verb.* to level

no *adv.* **1.** no, not **2.** non

noble *noun mf.* nobleman or noblewoman

noble *adj.* noble

nobleza *noun f.* nobility

noche *noun f.* **1.** night **2.** evening
—**esta noche** tonight

noción *noun f.* notion, conception

nocivo, -va *adj.* harmful

nombramiento *noun m.* appointment, nomination

nombrar *verb.* **1.** to appoint **2.** name

nombre *noun m.* **1.** name **2.** noun

nominación *noun f.* nomination

nominal *adj.* nominal

nono, -na *adj.* ninth

norma *noun f.* **1.** rule **2.** norm

normal *adj.* **1.** normal **2.** usual **3.** standard

normalmente *adv.* usually, normally

norte *noun m.* north

norte *adj.* northern

norteamericano, -ca *noun. adj.* **1.** North American **2.** American

norteño, -ña *adj.* northern

Noruega *noun f.* Norway

noruego, -ga *noun. adj.* Norwegian

nos *pron.* **1.** us **2.** ourselves **3.** to us, for us, from us **4.** each other

nosotros, nosotras *pron.* **1.** we **2.** us
—**nosotros mismos, nosotras mismas** ourselves

nostalgia *noun f.* nostalgia

nota *noun f.* **1.** note **2.** grade, mark **3.** announcement **4.** touch

notable *adj.* notable, remarkable

notación *noun f.* notation

notar *verb.* to notice

noticia *noun f.* piece of news
—**noticias** news

novato, -ta *noun.* novice

novedad *noun f.* novelty

novedoso, -sa *adj.* novel

novela *noun f.* novel

novelista *noun mf.* novelist

noveno, -na *noun. adj.* ninth

noventa *noun m. adj.* ninety

novicio, -cia *noun.* novice

noviembre *noun m.* November

novio, -via *noun.* **1.** boyfriend or girl-friend **2.** fiancé or bride

nube *noun f.* cloud

nublar *verb.* to cloud

nuclear *adj.* nuclear

núcleo *noun m.* **1.** core **2.** nucleus

nudo *noun m.* **1.** knot **2.** node

nuestro, nuestra *adj.* our

nuestro, nuestra *pron.* ours

nueve *noun m. adj.* nine

nuevo, -va *adj.* new
—**de nuevo** again

nuez *noun f.* nut

nulo, -la *adj.* **1.** null **2.** null and void **3.** inept

numerar *verb.* to number

numérico, -ca *adj.* numerical

número *noun m.* **1.** number **2.** issue **3.** figure **4.** size

nunca *adv.* never, ever

nutrición *noun f.* nutrition

nutriente *noun m.* nutrient

O

o *conj.* **1.** or **2.** either

obedecer *verb.* to obey

obediencia *noun f.* obedience

obispo *noun m.* bishop

obituario *noun m.* obituary

objeción *noun f.* objection

objetar *verb.* to object

objetividad *noun f.* objectivity

objetivo *noun m.* **1.** objective, aim, goal **2.** lens

objetivo, -va *adj.* objective

objeto *noun m.* **1.** object **2.** objective

obligación *noun f.* obligation, duty

obligar *verb.* to force, compel, oblige

obligatorio, -ria *adj.* compulsory

obra *noun f.* **1.** work **2.** play

—**obra maestra** masterpiece

obrero, -ra *noun.* worker, laborer

obrero, -ra *adj.* working

obsceno, -na *adj.* obscene

obsequio *noun m.* gift, present

observación *noun f.* **1.** observation **2.** remark

observador, -dora *noun.* observer

observador, -dora *adj.* observant

observar *verb.* **1.** to observe **2.** notice **3.** watch

obsesión *noun f.* obsession

obsesionar *verb.* **1.** to obsess **2.** haunt

obstáculo *noun m.* obstacle

obstrucción *noun f.* obstruction

obstruir *verb.* to obstruct, block

obtener *verb.* **1.** to obtain, get **2.** attain

obvio, -via *adj.* obvious

ocasión *noun f.* **1.** occasion **2.** chance **3.** opportunity

ocasional *adj.* **1.** occasional **2.** fortuitous

ocasionar *verb.* to cause

occidental *adj.* western, occidental

occidente *noun m.* **1.** west **2.** the West

océano *noun m.* ocean

ochenta *noun m. adj.* eighty

ocho *noun m. adj.* eight

ocio *noun m.* leisure

octavo, -va *noun. adj.* eighth

octogésimo, -ma *noun. adj.* eightieth

octubre *noun m.* October

ocultar *verb.* to conceal, hide

oculto, -ta *adj.* concealed, hidden

ocupación *noun f.* occupation

ocupado, -da *adj.* **1.** busy **2.** occupied

ocupar *verb.* **1.** to occupy **2.** employ **3.** inhabit **4.** hold

—**ocuparse de** to attend, take care of

ocurrir *verb.* to happen, occur

—**ocurrirse** to have an idea, strike

odiar *verb.* to hate

odio *noun m.* hate, hatred

odontólogo, -ga *noun.* dentist

oeste *noun m.* west

oeste *adj.* west, western

ofender *verb.* to offend

ofensa *noun f.* offence

ofensiva *noun f.* offensive

ofensivo, -va *adj.* offensive

oferta *noun f.* **1.** offer **2.** bid, bidding

—**oferta y demanda** supply and demand

oficial *noun mf.* officer

oficial *adj.* official

oficina *noun f.* office

oficio *noun m.* **1.** occupation, trade **2.** craft

ofrecer *verb.* **1.** to offer **2.** present

—**ofrecerse** to volunteer

ofrecimiento *noun m.* offer

ofrenda *noun f.* offering

oído *noun m.* **1.** ear **2.** hearing

oír *verb.* **1.** to hear **2.** listen to

ojalá *interj.* I hope, I wish, hopefully

ojeada *noun f.* glance

ojera *noun f.* shadow

ojo *noun m.* eye

ola *noun f.* wave

óleo *noun m.* **1.** oil **2.** oil painting

oleoducto *noun m.* pipeline

oler *verb.* to smell

—**olerse** to suspect

olfatear *verb.* to sniff

olfato *noun m.* sense of smell

oliva *noun f.* olive

olivo *noun m.* olive tree

olor *noun m.* odor, smell

olvidar *verb.* **1.** to forget **2.** leave behind

olvido *noun m.* oblivion

omisión *noun f.* omission

omitir *verb.* to omit

once *noun m. adj.* eleven

onda *noun f.* wave

ondear *verb.* to wave

ondular *verb.* to wave

onza *noun f.* ounce

opción *noun f.* option, choice

opcional *adj.* optional

ópera *noun f.* opera

operación *noun f.* **1.** operation **2.** transaction

operar *verb.* to operate
—**operarse** to have an operation

operario, -ria *noun.* worker

operativo, -va *adj.* operational

opinar *verb.* to think

opinión *noun f.* opinion

oponente *noun mf.* opponent

oponer *verb.* to oppose

oportunidad *noun f.* opportunity

oportuno, -na *adj.* opportune, timely

oposición *noun f.* **1.** opposition **2.** competitive exam

opresión *noun f.* oppression

oprimir *verb.* to oppress

optar (por) *verb.* to opt (for)

óptico, -ca *adj.* optical

optimismo *noun m.* optimism

optimista *noun mf.* optimist

optimista *adj.* optimistic

opuesto, -ta *adj.* **1.** opposite **2.** opposed

oración *noun f.* **1.** prayer **2.** sentence, clause

oráculo *noun m.* oracle

oral *adj.* **1.** oral **2.** spoken

orar *verb.* to pray

órbita *noun f.* orbit

orden *noun f.* order, command
—**orden judicial** warrant

orden *noun m.* order
—**orden del día** agenda

ordenado, -da *adj.* orderly

ordenador *noun m.* computer

ordenar *verb.* **1.** to order **2.** arrange

ordeñar *verb.* to milk

ordinario, -ria *adj.* **1.** ordinary **2.** common

oreja *noun f.* ear

orgánico, -ca *adj.* organic

organismo *noun m.* **1.** organism **2.** organization

organización *noun f.* organization

organizador, -dora *noun.* organizer

organizar *verb.* to organize, arrange

órgano *noun m.* organ

orgullo *noun m.* pride

orgulloso, -sa *adj.* proud

orientación *noun f.* **1.** orientation **2.** direction **3.** guidance

oriental *adj.* **1.** oriental **2.** eastern

orientar *verb.* **1.** to guide **2.** orient

oriente *adj.* **1.** east **2.** the East, the Orient
—**Oriente Medio** Middle East

origen *noun m.* **1.** origin **2.** source
—**orígenes** background

original *noun m. adj.* original

originar *verb.* to originate

originario, -ria *adj.* native

orilla *noun f.* **1.** shore **2.** bank

orina *noun f.* urine

oro *noun m.* gold

orquesta *noun f.* orchestra

ortodoxo, -xa *adj.* orthodox

ortografía *noun f.* spelling

os *pron.* **1.** you, to you **2.** each other

osadía *noun f.* daring

osar *verb.* to dare

oscurecer *verb.* **1.** to darken **2.** obscure

oscuridad *noun f.* **1.** darkness **2.** obscurity

oscuro, -ra *adj.* **1.** dark **2.** obscure

oso, -sa *noun.* bear
—**oso de peluche** teddy bear

ostentación *noun f.* display

otoño *noun m.* autumn, fall

otorgar *verb.* to award, grant

otro, otra *adj.* **1.** other **2.** another
—**otra vez** again

otro, otra *pron.* **1.** other one **2.** another one

oval *adj.* oval

ovalado, -da *adj.* oval

óvalo *noun m.* oval

oveja *noun f.* sheep

ovillo *noun m.* ball

óvulo *noun m.* egg

oxígeno *noun m.* oxygen

ozono *noun m.* ozone

P

pabellón *noun m.* pavilion
pacer *verb.* to graze
paciencia *noun f.* patience
paciente *noun mf. adj.* patient
pacto *noun m.* **1.** pact, agreement **2.** covenant
padecer *verb.* to suffer
padre *noun m.* father
　—**padres** parents
paga *noun f.* **1.** allowance **2.** pay
pagadero, -ra *adj.* payable
pagano, -na *noun. adj.* pagan
pagar *verb.* to pay
página *noun f.* page
pago *noun m.* payment
país *noun m.* **1.** country **2.** region
paisaje *noun m.* **1.** landscape **2.** scenery
Países Bajos *noun m. plural.* Netherlands
paja *noun f.* straw
pajarera *noun f.* aviary
pájaro *noun m.* bird
paje *noun m.* page
pala *noun f.* shovel
palabra *noun f.* **1.** word **2.** faith
palacio *noun m.* **1.** palace **2.** court
palanca *noun f.* lever
palangana *noun f.* basin
palco *noun m.* box
Palestina *noun f.* Palestine
palestino, -na *noun. adj.* Palestinian
palidecer *verb.* to turn pale
pálido, -da *adj.* pale
paliza *noun f.* beating
　—**dar una paliza** to thrash
palma *noun f.* palm
palmada *noun f.* **1.** slap **2.** pat, tap
palmera *noun f.* palm
palmo *noun m.* span
palo *noun m.* stick
paloma *noun f.* pigeon, dove
palpar *verb.* to touch, feel
pan *noun m.* bread
pana *noun f.* corduroy
panadería *noun f.* bakery
panadero, -ra *noun.* baker

pancarta *noun f.* placard
pandilla *noun f.* **1.** group **2.** gang
panecillo *noun m.* roll
panel *noun m.* panel
pánico *noun m.* panic, scare
panorama *noun m.* **1.** panorama **2.** prospect **3.** scene
pantalla *noun f.* **1.** screen **2.** monitor
pantalones *noun m. plural.* pants, trousers
pantano *noun m.* swamp, marsh
pantorrilla *noun f.* calf
pañal *noun m.* diaper
paño *noun m.* cloth
pañuelo *noun m.* handkerchief
　—**pañuelo de papel** tissue
papa *noun f.* potato
　—**papas fritas** french fries
Papa *noun m.* pope
papá *noun m.* dad, daddy
papal *adj.* papal
papel *noun m.* **1.** paper **2.** part, role
papelera *noun f.* bin
paquete *noun m.* **1.** package **2.** packet **3.** parcel
par *noun m.* **1.** pair, couple **2.** par **3.** peer
par *adj.* even
para *prep.* **1.** for **2.** to **3.** towards **4.** by
　—**para adelante** forwards
　—**para detrás** backwards
　—**para que** so that, in order to
paracaídas *noun m.* parachute
parachoques *noun m.* bumper
parada *noun f.* **1.** stop, halt **2.** catch, save
paradero *noun m.* whereabouts
parado, -da *noun.* unemployed person
parado, -da *adj.* **1.** motionless **2.** still **3.** unemployed
paradoja *noun f.* paradox
paraguas *noun m.* umbrella
paraíso *noun m.* **1.** paradise, heaven **2.** balcony
paralelo *noun m.* parallel
paralelo, -la *adj.* parallel

parar *verb.* **1.** to stop **2.** halt

parcela *noun f.* parcel

parche *noun m.* patch

parcial *adj.* partial

parcialidad *noun f.* bias

parecer *noun m.* **1.** opinion, view **2.** appearance

parecer *verb.* **1.** to seem **2.** look **3.** appear **4.** think
   —**parecerse** to resemble, look alike

parecido *noun m.* **1.** similarity **2.** resemblance

parecido, -da *adj.* **1.** alike **2.** similar

pared *noun f.* wall

pareja *noun f.* **1.** couple **2.** pair **3.** partner

parentesco *noun m.* kinship

paréntesis *noun m.* parenthesis

pariente *noun mf.* relative

parir *verb.* to give birth, bear

parking *noun m.* parking

parlamentario, -ria *noun.* member of parliament

parlamentario, -ria *adj.* parliamentary

parlamento *noun m.* parliament.

paro *noun m.* **1.** stoppage **2.** unemployment

parpadear *verb.* to blink

parpadeo *noun m.* blink

párpado *noun m.* eyelid

parque *noun m.* park

parra *noun f.* vine

párrafo *noun m.* paragraph

parrilla *noun f.* grill

párroco *noun m.* parson, parish priest

parroquia *noun f.* parish

parroquiano, -na *noun.* patron, customer

parte *noun f.* **1.** part **2.** share **3.** side, party **4.** place **5.** role
   —**en parte** partly
   —**parte delantera** front
   —**parte trasera** back

parte *noun m.* report, dispatch

participación *noun f.* **1.** participation **2.** share

participante *noun mf.* **1.** participant **2.** competitor

participar *verb.* **1.** to take part, participate **2.** share, have a share **3.** announce

partícula *noun f.* particle

particular *noun m.* private individual
   —**particulares** details

particular *adj.* **1.** particular **2.** private **3.** special, peculiar

particularmente *adv.* specially

partida *noun f.* **1.** departure **2.** game **3.** certificate **4.** item

partidario, -ria *noun.* supporter

partido *noun m.* **1.** party **2.** game, match **3.** play **4.** tie
   —**sacar partido** to profit

partir *verb.* **1.** to cut, halve, split **2.** break, crack **3.** divide **4.** depart, leave
   —**a partir de** from
   —**partir de** to start from

partitura *noun f.* score

parto *noun m.* birth, delivery, labor

pasada *noun f.* passing

pasado *noun m.* past

pasado, -da *adj.* **1.** past **2.** out-of-date, old-fashioned **3.** bad, spoiled

pasaje *noun m.* **1.** passage **2.** ticket

pasajero, -ra *noun.* passenger

pasajero, -ra *adj.* passing

pasaporte *noun m.* passport

pasar *verb.* **1.** to happen **2.** pass **3.** come in, enter **4.** surpass **5.** cross **6.** give **7.** undergo, suffer **8.** omit
   —**pasar de largo** to go by without stopping
   —**pasar por alto** to omit, overlook
   —**pasarlo bien** to have a good time
   —**pasarlo mal** to have a bad time
   —**pasarse** to go too far

pasatiempo *noun m.* hobby

Pascua *noun f.* **1.** Easter **2.** Passover **3.** Christmas

pase *noun m.* **1.** pass **2.** permit

paseante *noun mf.* stroller

pasear *verb.* to take a walk, stroll

paseo *noun m.* **1.** walk, stroll **2.** ride

pasillo *noun m.* corridor, aisle

pasión *noun f.* passion

pasivo, -va *adj.* passive

pasmar *verb.* to stun, amaze

paso *noun m.* **1.** passage **2.** footstep **3.** pace **4.** way

pasta *noun f.* **1.** paste **2.** pasta

pastar verb. to graze

pastel noun m. 1. cake 2. pie

pastelería noun f. pastry shop

pastilla noun f. 1. pill 2. tablet 3. cake

pasto noun m. pasture

pastor, -tora noun. 1. shepherd or shepherdess 2. minister

pastoral noun f. adj. pastoral

pastoril adj. pastoral

pata noun f. 1. paw 2. leg 3. foot

patada noun f. kick

patata noun f. potato

patentar verb. to patent

patente noun f. patent

paterno, -na adj. parental

patético, -ca adj. pathetic

patín noun m. skate

patinar verb. to skate

patio noun m. courtyard

  —**patio de recreo** playground

pato, -ta noun. duck

patoso, -sa adj. awkward

patria noun f. homeland

patrimonio noun m. patrimony

patriota noun mf. patriot

patriota adj. patriotic

patrocinador, -dora noun. sponsor

patrocinar verb. to sponsor

patrocinio noun m. 1. sponsorship 2. patronage

patrón noun m. 1. model, pattern 2. standard

patrón, -trona noun. 1. employer 2. patron saint

patrulla noun f. patrol

patrullar verb. to patrol

pausa noun f. break, pause

pausado, -da adj. deliberate, slow

pavimentar verb. to pave

pavimento noun m. pavement

pavo, -va noun. turkey

pavor noun m. terror

paz noun f. peace

peaje noun m. toll

peatón, -tona noun. pedestrian

pecado noun m. sin

pecar verb. to sin

pecho noun m. 1. chest 2. breast

pechuga noun f. breast

peculiar adj. peculiar

pedazo noun m. 1. bit 2. piece

pedestre adj. pedestrian

pedido noun m. order

pedir verb. 1. to ask for, request 2. order

pegamento noun m. glue

pegar verb. 1. to hit, strike 2. glue, stick 3. paste 4. attach

  —**pegarse** to be contagious

peinar verb. to comb

peine noun m. comb

pelado, -da adj. 1. bald 2. bare

pelaje noun m. coat, fur

pelar verb. to peel

  —**pelarse** to have a haircut

pelea noun f. 1. fight 2. quarrel 3. row

pelear verb. 1. to fight 2. quarrel

película noun f. 1. film 2. movie

peligro noun m. 1. danger 2. hazard 3. menace

peligroso, -sa adj. 1. dangerous 2. hazardous

pelirrojo, -ja adj. red-haired

pellejo noun m. hide, skin

pellizcar verb. to pinch

pellizco noun m. pinch

pelmazo, -za noun. bore

pelo noun m. 1. hair 2. fur 3. pile

pelota noun f. ball

  —**en pelotas** naked

peluca noun f. wig

pena noun f. 1. pity 2. sorrow 3. penalty, punishment 4. difficulty, trouble 5. shame

  —**valer la pena** to be worthwhile

pender verb. to hang

pendiente noun f. slope

pendiente noun m. earring

pendiente adj. pending

pene noun m. penis

penetración noun f. penetration

penetrante adj. sharp, acute

penetrar verb. 1. to penetrate 2. enter

península noun f. peninsula

pensamiento noun m. thought

pensar verb. 1. to think 2. intend

pensativo, -va adj. thoughtful

pensión noun f. 1. pension 2. boarding house

pensionista noun mf. pensioner
pentágono noun m. pentagon
peña noun f. rock
peor adj. 1. worse 2. worst
peor adv. 1. worse 2. worst
pequeño, -ña adj. 1. small 2. little 3. young 4. short
pera noun f. pear
percepción noun f. perception
percha noun f. 1. hanger 2. perch
percibir verb. 1. to perceive 2. earn
perdedor, -dora noun. loser
perder verb. 1. to lose 2. miss 3. waste
—**perderse** 1. to get lost 2. miss
pérdida noun f. 1. loss 2. waste
perdido, -da adj. 1. lost 2. inveterate
perdón noun m. pardon, forgiveness
perdón interj. sorry!, excuse me!
perdonar verb. 1. to forgive, pardon 2. excuse 3. spare
perdurar verb. 1. to last 2. linger
peregrinación noun f. pilgrimage
peregrino, -na noun. pilgrim
perejil noun m. parsley
perenne adj. perennial
pereza noun f. laziness
perezoso, -sa adj. lazy
perfección noun f. perfection
perfeccionar verb. to perfect
perfecto, -ta adj. perfect
perfil noun m. profile
—**de perfil** sideways
perfilar verb. to outline
perforar verb. 1. to perforate 2. pierce 3. drill
perfumar verb. to perfume, scent
perfume noun m. perfume, scent, fragrance
periférico, -ca adj. peripheral
periódico noun m. newspaper
periódico, -ca adj. periodic
periodismo noun m. journalism
periodista noun mf. journalist
período noun m. period
perjudicar verb. to harm
perjudicial adj. harmful
perjuicio noun m. harm, damage
perla noun f. pearl
permanecer verb. to remain

permanente adj. permanent
permiso noun m. 1. permission 2. leave 3. licence, permit 4. pass
—**con permiso** excuse me!
permitir verb. to allow, permit
—**permitirse el lujo de** to afford
pernera noun f. leg
pero noun m. fault, objection
pero conj. but, yet
perpetuo, -tua adj. perpetual
perro, -rra noun. dog
persecución noun f. 1. persecution 2. pursuit
perseguir verb. 1. to persecute 2. pursue 3. worry, torment
persiana noun f. blind
persistencia noun f. persistence
persistente adj. persistent
persistir verb. 1. to persist 2. linger
persona noun f. person
personaje noun m. 1. character 2. personage
personal noun m. staff, personnel
personal adj. personal
personalidad noun f. personality
personalmente adv. personally
personificar verb. to embody
perspectiva noun f. 1. perspective 2. prospect, outlook
persuadir verb. to persuade
persuasión noun f. persuasion
persuasivo, -va adj. persuasive
pertenecer verb. to belong
pertinencia noun f. relevance
pertinente adj. relevant
pertrechos noun m. plural. equipment
perturbar verb. to disturb
Perú noun m. Peru
peruano, -na noun. adj. Peruvian
pesa noun f. weight
pesadilla noun f. nightmare
pesado, -da noun. bore, pest
pesado, -da adj. 1. heavy 2. difficult 3. boring
pesar noun m. grief, sorrow
—**a pesar de** despite, in spite of
pesar verb. 1. to weigh 2. be important 3. grieve, cause regret
pescado noun m. fish

pescador, -dora *noun.* fisherman or fisherwoman

pescar *verb.* **1.** to fish **2.** catch

pesimismo *noun m.* pessimism

pesimista *noun mf.* pessimist

pesimista *adj.* pessimistic

pésimo, -ma *adj.* terrible, very bad

peso *noun m.* **1.** weight **2.** burden **3.** importance

pesquisa *noun f.* inquiry

pestaña *noun f.* eyelash

pestañear *verb.* to blink

pestañeo *noun m.* blink

peste *noun f.* **1.** plague **2.** stink

pesticida *noun m.* pesticide

pestillo *noun m.* bolt

petición *noun f.* petition, request

petróleo *noun m.* oil, petroleum

petrolero *noun m.* oil tanker

pez *noun m.* fish

piano *noun m.* piano

picadura *noun f.* sting, bite

picante *adj.* hot, spicy

picar *verb.* **1.** to sting, bite **2.** itch **3.** punch **4.** grind

picnic *noun m.* picnic

pico *noun m.* **1.** peak **2.** beak, bill **3.** pick

pie *noun m.* **1.** foot **2.** cue

piedra *noun f.* **1.** stone **2.** flint

piel *noun f.* **1.** skin **2.** leather, hide **3.** fur **4.** peel

pierna *noun f.* leg

pieza *noun f.* **1.** piece **2.** component, part

—**pieza de recambio/repuesto** spare part

pila *noun f.* **1.** battery **2.** pile **3.** sink

pilar *noun m.* pillar

píldora *noun f.* pill

pillar *verb.* **1.** to catch **2.** get

pilotar *verb.* to pilot, drive

piloto *noun mf.* pilot, driver

pimienta *noun f.* pepper

pimiento *noun m.* pepper

pinchadiscos *noun mf.* disc jockey

pinchar *verb.* **1.** to puncture **2.** prick

—**pincharse** to get an injection

pinchazo *noun m.* **1.** puncture **2.** prick **3.** shot

pingüino *noun m.* penguin

pino *noun m.* pine, pine tree

pinta *noun f.* **1.** aspect **2.** pint

pintar *verb.* **1.** to paint **2.** draw **3.** depict

pintor, -tora *noun.* painter

pintoresco, -ca *adj.* picturesque

pintura *noun f.* **1.** paint **2.** painting

pinza *noun f.* clothespin

pionero, -ra *noun.* pioneer

pionero, -ra *adj.* pioneering

pipa *noun f.* pipe

pirámide *noun f.* pyramid

pirata *noun mf.* pirate

pisada *noun f.* footstep

pisar *verb.* to tread, trample

piscina *noun f.* pool

piso *noun m.* **1.** floor **2.** apartment

pisotear *verb.* to tread, trample

pista *noun f.* **1.** track **2.** trail **3.** clue **4.** ring, court

—**pista de aterrizaje** runway

pistola *noun f.* pistol, gun

pistolero *noun m.* gunman

pitar *verb.* **1.** to whistle **2.** boo

pitido *noun m.* whistle

pito *noun m.* whistle

pizarra *noun f.* **1.** slate **2.** blackboard

pizca *noun f.* **1.** pinch **2.** trace

pizza *noun f.* pizza

placa *noun f.* **1.** plate **2.** plaque

placer *noun m.* pleasure, delight

placer *verb.* to please, give pleasure

plaga *noun f.* plague

plan *noun m.* **1.** plan **2.** scheme

plancha *noun f.* **1.** iron **2.** grill

planchar *verb.* to iron

planear *verb.* **1.** to plan **2.** glide

planeta *noun m.* planet

planificación *noun f.* planning

planificador, -dora *noun.* planner

planificar *verb.* to plan

plano *noun m.* **1.** plan, map **2.** flat **3.** plane

plano, -na *adj.* flat, level

planta *noun f.* **1.** plant **2.** floor **3.** sole

plantación *noun f.* plantation

plantar *verb.* **1.** to plant **2.** sow

—**plantarse** **1.** to quit **2.** stand firm

plantear *verb.* **1.** to pose **2.** raise

—**plantearse** to think about
plasma *noun m.* plasma
plástico *noun m.* plastic
plástico, -ca *adj.* plastic
plata *noun f.* 1. silver 2. money
plataforma *noun f.* 1. platform 2. shelf
—**plataforma petrolífera** oil rig
plátano *noun m.* banana
plato *noun m.* 1. dish 2. plate 3. course
plausible *adj.* plausible
playa *noun f.* 1. beach 2. shore
plaza *noun f.* 1. square 2. marketplace 3. place, seat
plazo *noun m.* 1. term, period 2. installment
—**pagar a plazos** to pay in installments
plegable *adj.* folding
plegar *verb.* to fold
—**plegarse** to give in
pleito *noun m.* lawsuit
plenamente *adv.* fully, completely
pleno, -na *adj.* full, complete
pliegue *noun m.* fold
plomo *noun m.* lead
pluma *noun f.* 1. feather 2. pen
plumón *noun m.* down
plus *noun m.* bonus
plusmarca *noun f.* record
población *noun f.* 1. population 2. city, town, village
poblado *noun m.* settlement
poblado, -da *adj.* populated
poblar *verb.* to populate, settle
pobre *adj.* 1. poor 2. weak
pobreza *noun f.* 1. poverty 2. want
poco, -ca *adj.* little, few, not much
poco *adv.* little, few
—**poco a poco** little by little
—**por poco** almost, nearly
poco, -ca *pron.* little, few
podar *verb.* to prune
poder *noun m.* 1. power 2. control 3. possession 4. strength, force
poder *verb.* 1. can 2. to be able 3. may
poderoso, -sa *adj.* 1. powerful 2. mighty
podrido, -da *adj.* rotten
poema *noun m.* poem
poesía *noun f.* 1. poetry 2. poem

poeta *noun mf.* poet
poético, -ca *adj.* poetic
polaco, -ca *noun. adj.* Polish
polar *adj.* polar
polémica *noun f.* polemics, controversy
polémico, -ca *adj.* polemical, controversial
policía *noun f.* police
policía *noun mf.* policeman or policewoman
polifacético, -ca *adj.* versatile, many-sided
politécnico *noun m.* polytechnic
política *noun f.* 1. policy 2. politics
político, -ca *noun.* politician
político, -ca *adj.* 1. political 2. in-law, by marriage
póliza *noun f.* policy
polla *noun f.* cock
pollo *noun m.* chicken
polo *noun m.* 1. pole 2. polo
Polonia *noun f.* Poland
polvera *noun f.* compact
polvo *noun m.* 1. dust 2. powder 3. fuck
pólvora *noun f.* powder
polvoriento, -ta *adj.* dusty
pomo *noun m.* handle
ponche *noun m.* punch
poner *verb.* 1. to put 2. place 3. set 4. set up, establish 5. add 6. switch on, put on 7. lay 8. install
—**poner al día** to update
—**ponerse** 1. to wear, put on 2. become 3. set (sun) 4. move
póney *noun m.* pony
popular *adj.* 1. popular 2. folk
popularidad *noun f.* popularity
por *prep.* 1. for 2. during 3. by 4. through 5. along 6. around 7. per 8. from 9. because of 10. instead of
—**¿por qué?** why?
—**por si acaso** in case
porcelana *noun f.* porcelain, china
porcentaje *noun m.* percentage
porche *noun m.* porch
porción *noun f.* 1. portion 2. serving
pormenor *noun m.* detail
pormenorizado, -da *adj.* detailed
porque *conj.* because

porqué *noun m.* reason, cause
porra *noun f.* club
porrazo *noun m.* bash, blow
portal *noun m.* 1. portal 2. doorway
portátil *noun m.* laptop
portátil *adj.* portable
portavoz *noun mf.* spokesperson, spokesman or spokeswoman
portazo *noun m.* slam
porte *noun m.* 1. bearing 2. carriage
portería *noun f.* 1. caretaker's office 2. goal
portero, -ra *noun.* 1. doorman, caretaker 2. goalkeeper
pórtico *noun m.* portico
Portugal *noun m.* Portugal
portugués, -guesa *noun. adj.* Portuguese
posada *noun f.* inn
posar *verb.* 1. to pose 2. place
—**posarse** 1. to perch 2. settle
pose *noun f.* pose
poseer *verb.* to possess, have, hold, own
posesión *noun f.* possession
posibilidad *noun f.* possibility
posible *adj.* possible
posición *noun f.* 1. position 2. attitude 3. status 4. rating
positivo, -va *adj.* positive
poso *noun m.* grounds
posponer *verb.* to postpone
postal *noun f.* postcard
postal *adj.* postal
poste *noun m.* 1. pole 2. post
póster *noun m.* poster
posterior *adj.* 1. back 2. subsequent, later
posteriormente *adv.* afterwards, subsequently
postizo, -za *adj.* false
postre *noun m.* dessert
postura *noun f.* 1. position 2. posture
pote *noun m.* pot
potencia *noun f.* 1. power 2. potency
potencial *noun m. adj.* potential
potente *adj.* 1. powerful, mighty 2. potent
pozo *noun m.* 1. well 2. pool 3. shaft

práctica *noun f.* practice
practicable *adj.* practicable
prácticamente *adv.* practically, virtually
practicar *verb.* 1. to practice 2. exercise
práctico, -ca *adj.* practical
prado *noun m.* meadow
precaución *noun f.* 1. caution 2. precaution
precedente *noun m.* precedent
precedente *adj.* preceding, previous
preceder *verb.* to precede
precio *noun m.* 1. price, value 2. cost
precioso, -sa *adj.* 1. beautiful 2. precious
precipitado, -da *adj.* 1. hasty 2. rash
precipitarse *verb.* 1. to rush 2. rash 3. throw oneself
precisamente *adv.* precisely
precisar *verb.* 1. to require, need 2. specify
precisión *noun f.* accuracy, precision
preciso, -sa *adj.* 1. necessary 2. accurate, precise 3. exact
precursor, -sora *noun.* forerunner, pioneer
predador, -dora *noun.* predator
predecesor, -sora *noun.* predecessor
predecible *adj.* predictable
predecir *verb.* to predict
predicar *verb.* to preach
predicción *noun f.* prediction
predisponer *verb.* 1. to predispose 2. bias, prejudice
predisposición *noun f.* 1. predisposition 2. bias, prejudice
predominancia *noun f.* prevalence
predominante *adj.* 1. prevailing 2. prevalent
predominar *verb.* to prevail
preestreno *noun m.* preview
prefacio *noun m.* preface, introduction
preferencia *noun f.* preference
preferible *adj.* preferable
preferido, -da *noun. adj.* favorite
preferir *verb.* to prefer
pregunta *noun f.* question
preguntar *verb.* 1. to ask, question 2. inquire
—**preguntarse** to wonder

prejuicio noun m. bias, prejudice
preliminar noun m. adj. preliminary
prematuro, -ra adj. premature
premiado, -da adj. winning
premiar verb. 1. to reward 2. award
premio noun m. 1. award 2. prize
prenda noun f. 1. garment 2. pledge
prender verb. 1. to pin 2. catch 3. seize
—**prender fuego** to catch fire
prensa noun f. 1. press 2. printing-press
prensar verb. to press
preocupación noun f. concern, preoccupation, worry
preocupado, -da adj. worried
preocupar verb. to concern, trouble, worry
preparación noun f. preparation
preparado noun m. mixture
preparado, -da adj. 1. ready, prepared 2. trained
preparar verb. 1. to prepare 2. coach, train
preparativo noun m. preparation
—**preparativos** arrangements
presa noun f. 1. catch 2. prey 3. seizure 4. dam
prescindir de verb. to do without
prescribir verb. to prescribe
prescripción verb. prescription
presencia noun f. presence
presenciar verb. to witness
presentación noun f. 1. presentation 2. debut 3. introduction
presentador, -dora noun. newscaster
presentar verb. 1. to present 2. introduce 3. submit 4. make a gift
—**presentarse** 1. to introduce oneself 2. appear
presente noun m. 1. present 2. gift
presente adj. present
presentir verb. to sense
presidencia noun f. 1. presidency 2. chairmanship
presidencial adj. presidential
presidente, -ta noun. 1. president 2. chairperson, chairman or chairwoman
presidiario, -ria noun. convict
presidir verb. to preside, chair
presión noun f. pressure

presionar verb. 1. to press, push 2. pressure
preso, -sa noun. prisoner
preso, -sa adj. imprisoned
préstamo noun m. loan
prestar verb. 1. to lend, loan 2. render
—**prestar atención** to pay attention
prestigio noun m. prestige
presumido, -da adj. vain
presumir verb. to presume
presunción noun f. presumption
presunto, -ta adj. alleged
presupuestar verb. to budget
presupuesto noun m. budget
pretender verb. 1. to attempt 2. seek 3. claim 4. intend
pretexto noun m. pretext, excuse
prevalecer verb. to prevail
prevención noun f. prevention
prevenir verb. 1. to prevent 2. warn
prever verb. anticipate, envisage, foresee
previamente adv. previously
previo, -via adj. 1. previous, prior 2. upon, after
previsible adj. predictable
previsión noun f. forecast
prima noun f. bonus
primario, -ria adj. primary
primavera noun f. spring
primer adj. (see primero. Used before masculine singular nouns)
primero, -ra noun. first
primero, -ra adj. 1. first 2. former 3. prime
primero adv. first
primicia noun f. scoop
primitivo, -va adj. primitive
primo, -ma noun. cousin
princesa noun f. princess
principal adj. 1. principal 2. main 3. foremost 4. major
príncipe noun m. prince
—**príncipe heredero** crown prince
principiante noun mf. beginner, novice
principio noun m. 1. beginning, outset 2. principle
prior, priora noun. prior or prioress
prioridad noun f. priority

prisa *noun f.* hurry, rush
—**darse prisa** to hurry
—**tener prisa** to be in a hurry
prisión *noun f.* **1.** jail, prison **2.** imprisonment
prisionero, -ra *noun.* prisoner
prismáticos *noun m. plural.* binoculars
privacidad *noun f.* privacy
privación *noun f.* **1.** deprivation **2.** hardship
privado, -da *adj.* private
privar *verb.* to deprive
privilegiado, -da *adj.* privileged
privilegio *noun m.* privilege
proa *noun f.* bow
probabilidad *noun f.* probability, likelihood
probable *adj.* probable, likely
probar *verb.* **1.** to try **2.** prove **3.** taste **4.** test **5.** demonstrate
problema *noun m.* problem
problemático, -ca *adj.* problematic
proceder *verb.* **1.** to proceed **2.** behave
—**proceder de** to come from
procedimiento *noun m.* procedure
procesado, -da *noun.* defendant
procesar *verb.* **1.** to process **2.** prosecute, try
procesión *noun f.* procession
proceso *noun m.* **1.** process **2.** prosecution, trial
proclamar *verb.* to proclaim
procurador, -dora *noun.* attorney
procurar *verb.* **1.** to try **2.** get
prodigar *verb.* to lavish
pródigo, -ga *adj.* **1.** lavish **2.** prodigal
producción *noun f.* production, output
producir *verb.* **1.** to produce, yield **2.** cause
productividad *noun f.* productivity
productivo, -va *adj.* productive
producto *noun m.* product
productor, -tora *noun.* producer
proeza *noun f.* feat
profesión *noun f.* profession
profesional *noun mf. adj.* professional
profesor, -sora *noun.* **1.** teacher **2.** professor
profundidad *noun f.* depth

profundizar *verb.* **1.** to deepen **2.** study in depth
profundo, -da *adj.* **1.** deep **2.** profound
programa *noun m.* program
—**programa de estudios** syllabus
programar *verb.* **1.** to program **2.** schedule
progresar *verb.* to progress
progresivo, -va *adj.* progressive
progreso *noun m.* progress
prohibición *noun f.* ban, prohibition
prohibido, -da *adj.* forbidden
prohibir *verb.* to ban, forbid, prohibit
proletariado *noun m.* working class
proletario, -ria *noun. adj.* proletarian
promedio *noun m.* average
promesa *noun f.* **1.** promise **2.** vow
prometedor, -dora *adj.* promising
prometer *verb.* to promise
prometido, -da *noun.* fiancé or fiancée
prometido, -da *adj.* engaged
prominencia *noun f.* prominence
prominente *adj.* prominent
promoción *noun f.* promotion
promotor, -tora *noun.* promoter
promover *verb.* **1.** to promote **2.** foster **3.** further
promulgar *verb.* to enact
pronombre *noun m.* pronoun
pronosticar *verb.* to forecast, predict
pronóstico *noun m.* **1.** forecast, prediction **2.** prognosis
pronto, -ta *adj.* **1.** quick **2.** ready
pronto *adv.* **1.** quickly **2.** soon
—**de pronto** suddenly
pronunciación *noun f.* pronunciation
pronunciado, -da *adj.* **1.** pronounced **2.** marked
pronunciar *verb.* **1.** to pronounce **2.** deliver
—**pronunciarse** to declare oneself
propaganda *noun f.* propaganda
propensión *noun f.* inclination
propenso, -sa *adj.* prone
propicio, -cia *adj.* favorable, propitious
propiedad *noun f.* **1.** property **2.** ownership
propietario, -ria *noun.* owner, proprietor
propina *noun f.* tip

propio, -pia adj. 1. own 2. typical 3. self

proponer verb. to propose, suggest
  —**proponerse** to intend

proporción noun f. 1. proportion 2. ratio
  —**proporciones** size, proportions

proporcional adj. proportional

proporcionar verb. to provide, supply

proposición noun f. proposal, proposition

propósito noun m. purpose, intention, aim
  —**a propósito** 1. by the way 2. on purpose, intentionally

propuesta noun f. proposal

prosa noun f. prose

proseguir verb. to continue, go on

prosperar verb. to prosper, thrive

prosperidad noun f. prosperity

próspero, -ra adj. prosperous, thriving

prostituto, -ta noun. prostitute

protagonista noun mf. protagonist, main character, hero or heroine

protección noun f. protection

protector, -tora noun. 1. protector 2. patron

protector, -tora adj. protective

proteger verb. 1. to protect 2. preserve

proteína noun f. protein

protesta noun f. protest

protestante noun mf. adj. Protestant

protestar verb. to protest

prototipo noun m. prototype

provecho noun m. gain, profit

proveer verb. to provide, supply
  —**proveerse de** to supply oneself with

provenir de verb. to come from

provincia noun f. province

provincial adj. provincial

provisión noun f. provision

provisional adj. provisional

provocador, -dora noun. instigator

provocar verb. to provoke

proximidad noun f. proximity

próximo, -ma adj. 1. next, forthcoming 2. near

proyección noun f. projection

proyectar verb. 1. to plan 2. project 3. screen

proyectil noun m. projectile

proyecto noun m. project, plan, scheme

prudencia noun f. prudence

prudente adj. prudent

prueba noun f. 1. proof 2. evidence 3. event 4. test, trial 5. token

psicoanálisis noun m. psychoanalysis

psicoanalista noun mf. psychoanalyst

psicología noun f. psychology

psicológico, -ca adj. psychological

psicólogo, -ga noun. psychologist

psiquiatra noun mf. psychiatrist

psiquiátrico noun m. mental hospital

psiquiátrico, -ca adj. psychiatric

publicación noun f. publication

publicar verb. 1. to publish 2. reveal

publicidad noun f. publicity

público noun m. audience

público, -ca adj. public

puchero noun m. pot

pudín noun m. pudding

pudrirse verb. to rot

pueblo noun m. 1. village, town 2. people 3. common people

puente noun m. bridge

puerco, -ca noun. pig, hog

puerco, -ca adj. filthy

puerta noun f. 1. door 2. gate

puerto noun m. 1. port, harbor 2. mountain pass

Puerto Rico noun m. Puerto Rico

puertorriqueño, -ña noun. adj. Puerto Rican

pues conj. since, because, as

pues interj. well, then

puesta noun f. setting
  —**puesta de sol** sunset

puesto noun m. 1. place 2. position 3. post 4. booth, stall
  —**puesto que** since

puja noun f. bidding

pujar verb. to bid

pulcro, -cra adj. neat

pulgada noun f. inch

pulgar noun m. thumb

pulir verb. to polish

pulmón noun m. lung

pulpa noun f. pulp, flesh

pulsar verb. 1. to press 2. beat

pulso noun m. pulse

punta noun f. **1.** point, head **2.** end, tip
puntada noun f. stitch
puntal noun m. prop
puntapié noun m. kick
puntería noun f. aim
puntiagudo, -da adj. pointed, sharp
punto noun m. **1.** point **2.** dot **3.** period **4.** stitch
　—**dos puntos** colon
　—**punto final** full stop
　—**punto y coma** semicolon
puntual adj. prompt, punctual

punzada noun f. stitch
puñado noun m. handful
puñal noun m. dagger
puñetazo noun m. punch
puño noun m. **1.** fist **2.** cuff
pupila noun f. pupil (eye)
pupilo, -la noun. **1.** ward **2.** pupil, student
pupitre noun m. desk
pureza noun f. purity
puro, -ra adj. **1.** pure **2.** sheer, simple
púrpura noun f. purple

Q

que conj. **1.** that, than **2.** let
que pron. **1.** that **2.** who **3.** which **4.** whom
qué adj. what, which
qué adv. how, what
qué pron. what
quebradizo, -za adj. breakable
quebrantar verb. to break
quebrar verb. **1.** to break **2.** go bankrupt
quedar verb. **1.** to remain **2.** fit, suit **3.** be left **4.** suit
　—**quedar en** to agree
　—**quedarse** **1.** to stay **2.** linger
queja noun f. **1.** complaint **2.** protest
quejarse verb. to complain
quemadura noun f. burn
quemar verb. to burn
querellante noun mf. plaintiff
querer verb. **1.** to want **2.** love **3.** like
　—**querer decir** to mean
querido, -da noun. dear, honey
querido, -da adj. dear, beloved
queso noun m. cheese

quiebra noun f. **1.** bankruptcy **2.** break
quien pron. **1.** who, whom **2.** whoever, whomever
quién pron. who, whom
　—**de quién** whose
quienquiera pron. whoever, whomever
quieto, -ta adj. **1.** still **2.** quiet
química noun f. chemistry
químico, -ca noun. chemist
químico, -ca adj. chemical
quince noun m. adj. fifteen
quincena noun f. fortnight
quincuagésimo, -ma noun. adj. fiftieth
quinta noun f. villa
quinto, -ta noun. adj. fifth
quirófano noun m. operating-room
quirúrgico, -ca adj. surgical
quitar verb. **1.** to remove **2.** take off **3.** clear **4.** rob
　—**quitarse** **1.** to leave **2.** take off
　—**quitarse a alguien/algo de encima** to get rid of
quizá, quizás adv. maybe, perhaps

R

rabia *noun f.* rage
rabiar *verb.* to rage
rabo *noun m.* tail
racha *noun f.* 1. run, streak 2. gust
racial *adj.* racial
racimo *noun m.* bunch, cluster
ración *noun f.* helping, portion, serving
racional *adj.* rational
racionalidad *noun f.* rationality
racismo *noun m.* racism
racista *noun mf. adj.* racist
radar *noun m.* radar
radiación *noun f.* radiation
radiador *noun m.* radiator
radical *noun mf.* radical
radical *adj.* radical, drastic
radio *noun f.* radio
radio *noun m.* 1. radium 2. radius
radioactivo, -va *adj.* radioactive
radiografía *noun f.* X-ray
radionovela *noun f.* serial
ráfaga *noun f.* blast, gust
raíl *noun m.* rail
raíz *noun f.* root
raja *noun f.* crack, split
rajar *verb.* to crack, split
ralentizar *verb.* to slow
rallar *verb.* to grate
rally *noun m.* rally
ralo, -la *adj.* thin
rama *noun f.* branch
ramificarse *verb.* to branch
ramo *noun m.* 1. branch 2. division 3. bunch
rampa *noun f.* ramp
rana *noun f.* frog
rango *noun m.* rank
ranura *noun f.* groove, slot
rapidez *noun f.* speed
rápido, -da *adj.* fast, quick, swift
rápido *adv.* quick
raptar *verb.* to kidnap
raqueta *noun f.* racket
raro, -ra *adj.* 1. rare, uncommon, unusual, funny 2. bizarre, weird 3. odd
—rara vez seldom

rasar *verb.* to level
rascar *verb.* 1. to scrape 2. scratch
rasgadura *noun f.* tear, rip
rasgar *verb.* to tear, rip
rasgo *noun m.* trait
—rasgos features
rasgón *noun m.* tear, rip
rasguño *noun m.* scratch
raspadura *noun f.* scraping, scratching
raspar *verb.* to scrape
rastrear *verb.* to track
rastro *noun m.* 1. trace 2. track, trail
rata *noun f.* rat
ratificar *verb.* to ratify
rato *noun m.* while
ratón, -tona *noun.* mouse
raya *noun f.* 1. stripe 2. skate 3. streak 4. parting
rayar *verb.* 1. to scratch 2. streak
—rayar en to verge on, border on
rayo *noun m.* 1. ray, beam 2. bolt, lightning
raza *noun f.* 1. race 2. breed, strain
razón *noun f.* 1. reason 2. reasoning 3. right
—tener razón to be right
razonable *adj.* reasonable
razonamiento *noun m.* reasoning
razonar *verb.* to reason
reacción *noun f.* reaction
reaccionar *verb.* to react, respond
reacio, -cia *adj.* reluctant
reactor *noun m.* 1. reactor 2. jet
real *adj.* 1. teal 2. true 3. royal
realeza *noun f.* royalty
realidad *noun f.* reality, fact
realismo *noun m.* realism
realista *noun mf.* 1. realist 2. royalist
realista *adj.* 1. realistic 2. royalist
realizable *adj.* practicable
realización *noun f.* realization, fulfilment
realizado, -da *adj.* fulfilled
realizar *verb.* 1. to execute, perform, carry out 2. fulfill 3. realize
—realizarse to come true
realmente *adv.* really

realzar *verb.* to enhance
reanimación *noun f.* revival
reanimar *verb.* to revive
  —reanimarse to recover
reanudar *verb.* to resume
rebaja *noun f.* **1.** reduction **2.** discount
  —rebajas sales
rebajar *verb.* to reduce, lower
  —rebajarse to humble oneself
rebaño *noun m.* **1.** flock **2.** herd
rebelarse *verb.* to rebel
rebelde *noun mf.* rebel
rebelión *noun f.* rebellion
rebotar *verb.* to bounce
recado *noun m.* message
recalcar *verb.* to stress
recatado, -da *adj.* modest
recaudación *noun f.* collection
recaudar *verb.* to collect, levy
recepción *noun f.* reception
receptor, -tora *noun.* recipient
recesión *noun f.* **1.** recession **2.** slump
receta *noun f.* **1.** recipe **2.** prescription
recetar *verb.* to prescribe
rechazar *verb.* **1.** to reject, decline **2.** refuse
rechazo *noun m.* rejection, refusal
rechoncho, -cha *adj.* plump, chubby
recibir *verb.* **1.** to receive **2.** get **3.** welcome **4.** entertain
recibo *noun m.* receipt
reciclar *verb.* to recycle
recién *adv.* newly, recently
reciente *adj.* recent
recinto *noun m.* compound
recipiente *noun m.* **1.** container **2.** vessel
reclamación *noun f.* **1.** claim **2.** complaint
reclamar *verb.* **1.** to demand **2.** claim **3.** complain
recluir *verb.* to confine
recluso, -sa *noun.* convict, inmate, prisoner
recluta *noun mf.* recruit
reclutamiento *noun m.* draft, recruitment
reclutar *verb.* to draft, recruit
recobrar *verb.* to recover, regain, retrieve
recodo *noun m.* loop, turn
recoger *verb.* to collect, gather

recogida *noun f.* collection
recolectar *verb.* **1.** to collect, gather **2.** harvest
recomendación *noun f.* recommendation
recomendar *verb.* **1.** to recommend **2.** advocate
recompensa *noun f.* reward
recompensar *verb.* to reward
reconciliación *noun f.* reconciliation
reconciliarse *verb.* to reconcile
reconfortante *adj.* comforting
reconocer *verb.* **1.** to recognize **2.** acknowledge **3.** admit **4.** examine
reconocimiento *noun m.* **1.** recognition **2.** acknowledgment **3.** admission **4.** examination
reconstrucción *noun f.* reconstruction
recopilar *verb.* to compile, collect
récord *noun m.* record
recordar *verb.* **1.** to remember, recall **2.** remind
recordatorio *noun m.* reminder
recorrer *verb.* **1.** to travel through **2.** cover
recorrido *noun m.* **1.** journey **2.** route
recortar *verb.* **1.** to cut, reduce **2.** trim
recorte *noun m.* cut, reduction
recreación *noun f.* recreation
recreativo, -va *adj.* recreational
rectangular *adj.* rectangular
recto, -ta *adj.* **1.** straight **2.** upright
recto *adv.* straight
rector, -tora *noun.* rector
recubrir *verb.* to cover
recuento *noun m.* **1.** recount **2.** scrutiny
recuerdo *noun m.* **1.** memory **2.** souvenir
  —recuerdos regards
recuperación *noun f.* **1.** recovery **2.** retrieval
recuperar *verb.* **1.** to recover **2.** retrieve
recurrencia *noun f.* recurrence
recurrente *adj.* recurrent
recurrir *verb.* to appeal
  —recurrir a 1. to resort to **2.** appeal to, turn to
recurso *noun m.* **1.** appeal **2.** resort **3.** resource
  —recursos means, resources
red *noun f.* **1.** net **2.** network

redacción *noun f.* **1.** writing, composition **2.** editorial board

redactar *verb.* **1.** to write **2.** edit

redactor, -tora *noun.* editor

redada *noun f.* haul

redención *noun f.* redemption

redil *noun m.* fold

redondo, -da *adj.* **1.** round **2.** great, excellent

reducción *noun f.* reduction

reducir *verb.* **1.** to reduce, cut **2.** decrease **3.** subdue

reelegir *verb.* to re-elect

reembolsar *verb.* to refund

reembolso *noun m.* refund

reemplazar *verb.* to replace

reestreno *noun m.* revival

referencia *noun f.* reference

referéndum *noun m.* referendum

referente (a) *prep.* concerning

referir *verb.* **1.** to refer **2.** tell, relate

  —referirse a to refer to

refinado, -da *adj.* refined

reflector *adj.* reflecting

reflejar *verb.* to reflect

reflejo *noun m.* reflection

reflexión *noun f.* reflection, thought

reflexionar *verb.* to reflect, think

reforma *noun f.* reform

reformador, -dora *noun.* reformer

reformar *verb.* **1.** to reform **2.** renovate, repair

  —reformarse to mend one's ways

reforzar *verb.* to reinforce, bolster

refrenado, -da *adj.* restrained

refrenar *verb.* to restrain, curb

refrendar *verb.* to endorse

refrescante *adj.* refreshing

refrescar *verb.* to refresh

refresco *noun m.* **1.** refreshment **2.** soft drink

refuerzo *noun m.* **1.** reinforcement **2.** brace

refugiado, -da *noun.* refugee

refugiar *verb.* to shelter

  —refugiarse to take refuge

refugio *noun m.* haven, refuge, shelter

refutar *verb.* to refute

regalar *verb.* to present, give

regalo *noun m.* **1.** gift, present **2.** comfort

regar *verb.* to water

regatear *verb.* bargain

regazo *noun m.* lap

régimen *noun m.* **1.** regime **2.** diet

regimiento *noun m.* regiment

región *noun f.* region

regional *adj.* regional

regir *verb.* **1.** to rule **2.** govern **3.** be in force

registrador, -dora *noun.* registrar

registrar *verb.* **1.** to register **2.** record **3.** search

  —registrarse **1.** to register **2.** happen

registro *noun m.* **1.** register **2.** registry **3.** record **4.** search

regla *noun f.* **1.** regulation, rule **2.** ruler **3.** menstruation

reglamentar *verb.* to regulate

reglamento *noun m.* rule, regulation, ordinance

regordete, -ta *adj.* plump, chubby

regresar *verb.* to return

regreso *noun m.* return

reguero *noun m.* trail

regulación *noun f.* regulation

regulador *noun m.* regulator

regular *adj.* **1.** regular **2.** fair

regular *verb.* to regulate

rehabilitación *noun f.* rehabilitation

rehabilitar *verb.* to rehabilitate

rehén *noun mf.* hostage

rehusar *verb.* to decline, refuse

reina *noun f.* queen

reinado *noun m.* reign

reinar *verb.* **1.** to reign **2.** prevail

reino *noun m.* kingdom, realm

reír *verb.* to laugh

reivindicación *noun f.* **1.** vindication **2.** claim

reivindicar *verb.* **1.** to vindicate **2.** claim

reja *noun f.* **1.** bar **2.** grating

rejilla *noun f.* grid, grating

relación *noun f.* **1.** relation **2.** relationship **3.** account **4.** connection **5.** liaison

  —relaciones públicas public relations

  —relación sexual sexual intercourse

relacionar *verb.* to relate

  —relacionarse to interact, socialize

relajación *noun f.* relaxation
relajado, -da *adj.* relaxed, quiet
relajar *verb.* to relax
relámpago *noun m.* lightning
relatar *verb.* to relate, report
relativo, -va *adj.* 1. relative 2. comparative
relato *noun m.* 1. account 2. narration, story, tale
relegación *noun f.* relegation
relegar *verb.* to relegate
relevancia *noun f.* relevance
relevante *adj.* relevant
relevar *verb.* to relieve
relevo *noun m.* 1. relief 2. relay
relieve *noun m.* 1. relief 2. prominence
religión *noun f.* religion
religioso, -sa *adj.* religious
rellano *noun m.* landing
rellenar *verb.* 1. to fill 2. stuff
relleno *noun m.* filling, stuffing
reloj *noun m.* 1. clock 2. watch
reluciente *adj.* 1. glittering, shining 2. shiny
relucir *verb.* to glitter, gleam, shine
  —sacar a relucir to bring up
reluctante *adj.* unwilling
remar *verb.* to row
rematar *verb.* 1. to finish off 2. end, finish 3. shoot
remediar *verb.* to remedy
remedio *noun m.* 1. remedy, cure 2. option
remendar *verb.* to patch
remiendo *noun m.* patch
remitir *verb.* 1. to dispatch, send 2. refer
remojar *verb.* to soak
remolcador *noun m.* tug
remolcar *verb.* to tow
remolque *noun m.* 1. tow 2. trailer
remontar *verb.* to soar
  —remontarse a to date from
remordimiento *noun m.* remorse
remoto, -ta *adj.* remote
remover *verb.* 1. to stir 2. remove
remuneración *noun f.* pay, remuneration
remunerar *verb.* to pay, remunerate
renacimiento *noun m.* 1. Renaissance 2. revival

rendición *noun f.* surrender, fall
rendija *noun f.* crack
rendimiento *noun m.* 1. yield 2. efficiency
rendir *verb.* 1. to yield 2. render 3. cause to surrender 4. tire
  —rendirse to surrender
renovación *noun f.* 1. renewal 2. renovation
renovar *verb.* 1. to renew 2. renovate
rentable *adj.* profitable
renuencia *noun f.* reluctance
renuente *adj.* reluctant
renuncia *noun f.* 1. renunciation 2. resignation
renunciar *verb.* 1. to renounce 2. resign
reñir *verb.* to quarrel
reorganización *noun f.* reorganization
reorganizar *verb.* to reorganize
reparación *noun f.* 1. repair 2. reparation
reparar *verb.* to repair, fix
  —reparar en to notice
repartidor, -dora *noun.* distributor
repartir *verb.* 1. to deliver 2. distribute 3. divide, share 4. deal
reparto *noun m.* 1. delivery 2. distribution 3. deal 4. cast
repentino, -na *adj.* sudden
repertorio *noun m.* repertory
repetición *noun f.* 1. repeat 2. repetition
repetidamente *adv.* repeatedly
repetido, -da *adj.* repeated
repetir *verb.* to repeat
réplica *noun f.* 1. retort, reply 2. replica
replicar *verb.* to retort, reply
repollo *noun m.* cabbage
reportaje *noun m.* report
reportar *verb.* 1. to yield, bring 2. report 3. restrain
  —reportarse to control oneself
reportero, -ra *noun.* reporter
reposar *verb.* 1. to rest 2. lie
reposo *noun m.* rest
representación *noun f.* 1. performance 2. representation
  —en representación de on behalf of
representante *noun mf.* representative

representar *verb.* **1.** to represent **2.** perform **3.** portray
—**representarse** to imagine, picture oneself
representativo, -va *adj.* representative
represión *noun f.* repression
reprimir *verb.* **1.** to repress **2.** suppress
reprochar *verb.* to reproach, blame
reproducción *noun f.* reproduction
reproducir *verb.* to reproduce
—**reproducirse** to breed, reproduce
reproductor, -tora *adj.* reproductive
reptar *verb.* to crawl, creep
república *noun f.* republic
republicano, -na *noun. adj.* republican
repugnancia *noun f.* repugnance, disgust
repugnante *adj.* repugnant, disgusting
repugnar *verb.* to disgust, hate
reputación *noun f.* reputation, name
resaltar *verb.* **1.** to stand out **2.** stress
resbalar *verb.* to slip
resbalón *noun m.* slip
rescatar *verb.* to rescue, save
rescate *noun m.* **1.** rescue **2.** ransom
resentimiento *noun m.* resentment
resentirse *verb.* **1.** to suffer **2.** be hurt
reserva *noun f.* **1.** reservation **2.** booking **3.** confidentiality **4.** reserve
reservado, -da *adj.* reserved
reservar *verb.* **1.** to reserve **2.** book
resfriado *noun m.* cold
resguardar *verb.* to protect
resguardo *noun m.* receipt, voucher
residencia *noun f.* **1.** residence **2.** boarding house
residencial *adj.* residential
residente *adj.* resident
residir *verb.* **1.** to live, reside **2.** lie
residual *adj.* residual
residuo *noun m.* residue
—**residuos** waste
resignación *noun f.* resignation
resignar *verb.* to resign
—**resignarse a** to reconcile oneself to
resistencia *noun f.* resistance
resistente *adj.* **1.** resistant **2.** tough
resistir *verb.* **1.** to resist **2.** endure **3.** hold

resolución *noun f.* **1.** resolution **2.** resolve **3.** decision
resolver *verb.* **1.** to solve **2.** resolve **3.** decision
resonar *verb.* to resound, echo, ring
respaldar *verb.* to back, support
respectivamente *adv.* respectively
respectivo, -va *adj.* respective
respecto *prep.* regard, reference
—**con respecto a** regarding, in regard to
respetable *adj.* respectable
respetar *verb.* to respect, observe
respeto *noun m.* respect
respiración *noun f.* breath
respirar *verb.* to breathe
respiratorio, -ria *adj.* respiratory
resplandecer *verb.* to shine, glow
resplandeciente *adj.* shining, glowing
resplandor *noun m.* blaze, glitter, radiance
responder *verb.* to answer, reply, respond
responsabilidad *noun f.* responsibility
responsable *adj.* responsible
respuesta *noun f.* answer, reply, response
resquebrajarse *verb.* to crack, split
resquicio *noun m.* **1.** crack, slit **2.** chance
resta *noun f.* subtraction
restablecer *verb.* to restore, reestablish
—**restablecerse** to recover
restablecimiento *noun m.* **1.** reestablishment **2.** recovery
restar *verb.* **1.** to deduct **2.** remain
—**restar importancia** to minimize, play down
restauración *noun f.* **1.** restoration **2.** catering
restaurante *noun m.* restaurant
restaurar *verb.* to restore
resto *noun m.* remainder
—**restos** remains, leftovers
restregar *verb.* **1.** to rub **2.** scrub
restricción *noun f.* restriction
restrictivo, -va *adj.* restrictive
restringido, -da *adj.* limited, restricted
restringir *verb.* to limit, restrict

resucitar *verb*. **1.** to resuscitate **2.** raise

resuelto, -ta *adj*. **1.** determined, resolved **2.** solved

resultado *noun m*. **1.** outcome, result **2.** score

resultar *verb*. **1.** to result **2.** prove **3.** work

resumen *noun m*. summary

resumir *verb*. to summarize

resurgimiento *noun m*. revival

resurgir *verb*. to revive

resurrección *noun f*. resurrection

retar *verb*. to challenge

retazo *noun m*. **1.** scrap **2.** excerpt, fragment

retención *noun f*. retention

retener *verb*. **1.** to retain, keep **2.** detain **3.** hold

retirada *noun f*. **1.** retreat **2.** withdrawal

retirar *verb*. **1.** to take away, remove **2.** withdraw
—**retirarse 1.** to retreat **2.** retire

retiro *noun m*. **1.** retreat **2.** retirement

reto *noun m*. challenge, dare

retoño *noun m*. shoot

retoque *noun m*. finishing touch

retorcer *verb*. to twist

retornar *verb*. to return

retorno *noun m*. return, comeback

retraído, -da *adj*. retiring

retransmisión *noun f*. broadcast

retransmitir *verb*. to broadcast

retrasado, -da *adj*. **1.** retarded **2.** backward **3.** behind

retrasar *verb*. **1.** to delay **2.** postpone
—**retrasarse 1.** be late **2.** lag

retraso *noun m*. **1.** delay **2.** lag

retratar *verb*. **1.** to portray **2.** photograph **3.** depict

retrato *noun m*. **1.** portrait **2.** photograph **3.** depiction

retribuir *verb*. to pay

retroceder *verb*. **1.** to move back **2.** shrink

retumbar *verb*. **1.** to resound **2.** roar **3.** roll

retumbo *noun m*. **1.** reverberation **2.** roll **3.** roar

reunión *noun f*. meeting, gathering, rally, reunion

reunir *verb*. **1.** to gather, collect **2.** raise **3.** join **4.** unite **5.** have
—**reunirse** to meet

revelación *noun f*. revelation

revelador, -dora *adj*. revealing

revelar *verb*. **1.** to reveal, disclose, unfold **2.** develop

reventar *verb*. to burst

reventón *noun m*. burst

reverencia *noun f*. bow, curtsy

reverendo, -da *noun. adj*. reverend

reverso *noun m*. **1.** back **2.** reverse

revés *noun m*. **1.** back **2.** reversal **3.** backhand
—**al revés** the other way, inside out, upside down

revestimiento *noun m*. covering, lining

revestir *verb*. **1.** to cover, line **2.** to take on

revisar *verb*. **1.** to check, inspect **2.** revise

revisión *noun f*. **1.** check, inspection **2.** revision

revista *noun f*. journal, magazine

revocar *verb*. to revoke

revolución *noun f*. revolution

revolucionario, -ria *noun. adj*. revolutionary

revolver *verb*. **1.** to stir **2.** turn upside down

revuelta *noun f*. revolt

rey *noun m*. king

rezar *verb*. to pray

rezo *noun m*. prayer

riachuelo *noun m*. brook, stream

ribera *noun f*. bank

ribetear *verb*. to edge

rico, -ca *adj*. **1.** rich **2.** wealthy **3.** delicious

ridículo, -la *adj*. ridiculous

rienda *noun f*. rein

riesgo *noun m*. risk

rifa *noun f*. raffle

rifar *verb*. to raffle

rifle *noun m*. rifle

rígido, -da *adj*. rigid, stiff

riguroso, -sa *adj*. rigorous, strict

rincón *noun m*. corner

ring *noun m*. ring

riña *noun f*. quarrel

riñón noun m. kidney
río noun m. river
riqueza noun f. wealth
risa noun f. laugh, laughter
risueño, -ña adj. cheerful
rítmico, -ca adj. rhythmic, rhythmical
ritmo noun m. 1. rhythm 2. pace
rito noun m. rite
ritual noun. adj. ritual
rival noun. adj. rival
rivalidad noun f. rivalry
rivalizar verb. to compete, rival
rizado, -da adj. curly
rizar verb. to curl
rizo noun m. curl
róbalo noun m. bass
robar verb. 1. to rob, steal 2. abduct
roble noun m. oak
robo noun m. burglary, robbery, theft
robusto, -ta adj. robust, stout, sturdy
roca noun f. rock
roce noun m. 1. brush, graze 2. friction
rock noun m. rock
rocoso, -sa adj. rocky
rodar verb. 1. to roll 2. film, shoot
rodear verb. 1. to go around 2. surround, encircle
rodilla noun f. knee
rodillo noun m. roller
rogar verb. 1. to beg 2. pray
rojo noun m. red
rojo, -ja adj. red
rollo noun m. 1. roll 2. bore
romance noun m. romance
romano, -na noun. adj. Roman
romántico, -ca adj. romantic
rompecabezas noun m. puzzle
romper verb. 1. to break 2. smash, shatter 3. rip, tear
—**romper a** to begin to
ronda noun f. 1. round 2. beat, patrol
rondar verb. 1. to patrol, police 2. haunt 3. be approximately

ronzar verb. to crunch
ropa noun f. clothing, clothes
—**ropa blanca** linen
—**ropa sucia** laundry
ropero noun m. wardrobe
rosa noun f. 1. rose 2. pink
rosa adj. pink
rosado, -da adj. pink
rosca noun f. thread
rostro noun m. face
rotación noun f. rotation
rotar verb. 1. to rotate 2. spin
roto, -ta adj. 1. broken 2. ripped, torn
rotulador noun m. marker
rotura noun f. break, tear
rozar verb. 1. to graze 2. scrape 3. touch
rubio, -bia adj. blond
rublo noun m. ruble
rubor noun m. flush, blush
ruborizarse verb. to blush
rudimentario, -ria adj. rudimentary
rudimentos noun m. plural. basics
rudo, -da adj. rough
rueda noun f. wheel
rugby noun m. rugby
rugido noun m. roar
rugir verb. to roar
ruido noun m. noise, sound
ruidoso, -sa adj. noisy
ruina noun f. 1. ruin 2. downfall, collapse
rulo noun m. roller
Rumania noun f. Romania
rumano, -na noun. adj. Romanian
rumbo noun m. course, direction, route
rumor noun m. rumor
rural adj. rural
Rusia noun f. Russia
ruso, -sa noun. adj. Russian
ruta noun f. route
rutina noun f. routine
rutinario, -ria adj. routine

S

sábado *noun m.* Saturday
sábana *noun f.* sheet
saber *noun m.* knowledge
saber *verb.* 1. to know 2. can 3. learn
—**a saber** namely
—**saber a** to taste like
sabiduría *noun f.* wisdom
sabio, -bia *noun.* wise person, learned person
sabio, -bia *adj.* wise, learned
sabor *noun m.* flavor, taste
saborear *verb.* 1. to taste, savor 2. relish
sacar *verb.* 1. to take out 2. get, obtain 3. get out 4. produce, invent 5. introduce 6. take (a photo) 7. release (a book, a disc, a film) 8. make (a copy) 9. stick out (one's tongue)
sacerdocio *noun m.* priesthood
sacerdote, -tisa *noun.* priest or priestess
saco *noun m.* 1. sack 2. coat
sacrificar *verb.* to sacrifice
sacrificio *noun m.* sacrifice
sacudida *noun f.* 1. shaking 2. jerk
sacudir *verb.* 1. to shake 2. jerk
—**sacudirse** to shake off
safari *noun m.* safari
sagrado, -da *adj.* sacred, holy
sainete *noun m.* comedy sketch
sal *noun f.* salt
sala *noun f.* 1. hall, room 2. living room
salado, -da *adj.* salty
salar *verb.* to salt
salario *noun m.* salary, wage
salchicha *noun f.* sausage
saldar *verb.* to settle
saldo *noun m.* balance
salida *noun f.* 1. exit 2. departure 3. way out 4. witty remark
—**salida del sol** sunrise
saliente *adj.* 1. outgoing 2. salient, prominent
salir *verb.* 1. to go out, get out 2. depart, leave 3. come out, appear 4. turn out 5. become, be elected
—**salir a** to resemble
saliva *noun f.* saliva

salmón *noun m.* salmon
salón *noun m.* 1. lounge 2. parlor, sitting-room 3. salon
salpicadura *noun f.* splash
salpicar *verb.* to splash
salsa *noun f.* 1. sauce 2. salsa
saltar *verb.* 1. to jump, leap 2. burst, explode 3. pop out
—**saltarse** to skip
salto *noun m.* 1. jump, leap, skip 2. gap 3. dive
salud *noun f.* health
saludable *adj.* healthy
saludar *verb.* 1. to greet 2. salute
saludo *noun m.* 1. greeting 2. salute
—**saludos** regards
salvación *noun f.* salvation
salvaguardar *verb.* to safeguard
salvaguardia *noun f.* safeguard
salvaje *noun mf.* savage
salvaje *adj.* 1. savage 2. wild
salvar *verb.* 1. to save 2. overcome 3. cover
—**salvarse** 1. to escape 2. save one's soul
salve *interj.* hail!
salvedad *noun f.* qualification, reservation
salvo, -va *adj.* safe
salvo *prep.* except, save
—**salvo que** unless
sanción *noun f.* sanction
sancionar *verb.* to sanction
sándwich *noun m.* sandwich
sangrar *verb.* to bleed
sangre *noun f.* blood
sangría *noun f.* 1. drain 2. sangria
sangriento, -ta *adj.* bloody
sano, -na *adj.* 1. healthy 2. unhurt, unharmed
santo, -ta *noun.* saint
santo, -ta *adj.* 1. holy 2. saint
santuario *noun m.* sanctuary, shrine
saque *noun m.* service
saquear *verb.* to sack, loot
sarcástico, -ca *adj.* sarcastic

sargento *noun mf.* sergeant

sarpullido *noun m.* rash

sarta *noun f.* string

sartén *noun f.* frying pan

sastre, -tra *noun.* tailor

satélite *noun m.* satellite

satisfacción *noun f.* satisfaction

satisfacer *verb.* 1. to satisfy 2. fulfill, meet 3. settle

satisfactorio, -ria *adj.* 1. satisfactory 2. satisfying

satisfecho, -cha *adj.* content, pleased, satisfied

sazonar *verb.* to season, spice

se *pron.* 1. to him, to her, to you, to them 2. himself, herself, itself, yourself, yourselves, themselves 3. each other

secar *verb.* to dry

sección *noun f.* 1. department 2. section

seco, -ca *adj.* 1. dry 2. dried 3. sharp 4. barren, arid 5. curt, brusque

secreción *noun f.* secretion

secretario, -ria *noun.* secretary

secreto *noun m.* 1. secret 2. secrecy

secreto, -ta *adj.* secret

sector *noun m.* sector

secuela *noun f.* sequel

—**secuelas** aftermath

secuencia *noun f.* sequence

secuestrar *verb.* 1. to kidnap 2. hijack

secular *adj.* secular

secundar *verb.* to second, support

secundario, -ria *adj.* secondary

sed *noun f.* thirst

—**tener sed** to be thirsty

seda *noun f.* silk

sedal *noun m.* fishing line

sede *noun f.* 1. seat 2. see

—**sede central** headquarters

sedimento *noun m.* sediment

seducir *verb.* to seduce

seglar *adj.* secular

segmento *noun m.* segment

seguido, -da *adj.* 1. consecutive 2. straight

—**en seguida** immediately

seguido *adv.* straight

seguidor, -dora *noun.* follower

seguimiento *noun m.* follow-up

seguir *verb.* 1. to follow 2. keep on 3. pursue 4. remain

según *verb.* 1. according to 2. depending on

segundo *noun m.* second

segundo, -da *noun. adj.* second

seguramente *adv.* 1. probably 2. surely

seguridad *noun f.* 1. security 2. assurance, certainty 3. confidence

seguro *noun m.* 1. insurance 2. fastener, clasp

seguro, -ra *adj.* 1. safe, secure 2. sure 3. reliable 4. self-assured, confident 5. firm, fixed

seguro *adv.* certainly

seis *noun m. adj.* six

selección *noun f.* selection

seleccionar *verb.* to select

selectivo, -va *adj.* selective

selecto, -ta *adj.* 1. exclusive 2. select

sellar *verb.* 1. to seal 2. stamp

sello *noun m.* 1. seal 2. stamp

selva *noun f.* 1. jungle 2. forest

semana *noun f.* week

semanal *adj.* weekly

semanalmente *adv.* weekly

semanario *noun m.* weekly

sembrar *verb.* to sow, plant

semejante *adj.* 1. similar 2. such

semejanza *noun f.* resemblance, similarity

semestre *noun m.* semester

semifinal *noun f.* semi-final

semilla *noun f.* seed

senado *noun m.* senate

senador, -dora *noun.* senator

sencillez *noun f.* simplicity

sencillo, -lla *adj.* 1. simple, easy 2. plain 3. single 4. straightforward

senda *noun f.* path

sendero *noun m.* path

sendos, -das *adj.* each

seno *noun m.* breast

sensación *noun f.* 1. feeling 2. sensation

sensatez *noun f.* good sense

sensato, -ta *adj.* reasonable, sensible, sound, wise

sensibilidad *noun f.* 1. feeling 2. sensitivity

sensible *adj.* sensitive
sentar *verb.* **1.** to sit, seat **2.** set, establish
—**sentar bien 1.** to suit **2.** agree with
—**sentarse** to sit down
sentencia *noun f.* sentence
sentenciar *verb.* to sentence
sentido *noun m.* **1.** sense **2.** meaning **3.** direction, way **4.** consciousness
sentimental *adj.* sentimental
sentimiento *noun m.* **1.** sentiment, emotion, feeling **2.** sorrow, grief
sentir *verb.* **1.** to feel **2.** feel sorry, regret **3.** sense
—**sentirse** to feel
seña *noun f.* sign
—**señas** domicile, address
señal *noun f.* **1.** signal **2.** sign **3.** deposit **4.** mark **5.** token
señalar *verb.* **1.** to indicate, show **2.** mark **3.** point out
señor *noun m.* **1.** gentleman **2.** sir **3.** owner, master **4.** mister **5.** lord
señora *noun f.* **1.** lady **2.** madam **3.** mistress **4.** wife
señoría *noun f.* lordship
señorita *noun f.* **1.** young woman **2.** Miss
separación *noun f.* **1.** separation **2.** division **3.** gap
separado, -da *adj.* separate
separar *verb.* **1.** to separate **2.** divide
—**separarse** to divorce
separatista *noun mf.* separatist
septiembre *noun m.* September
séptimo, -ma *noun. adj.* seventh
septuagésimo, -ma *noun. adj.* seventieth
sequía *noun f.* drought
ser *noun m.* being
ser *verb.* to be
—**ser de** to belong to
seriado, -da *adj.* serial
serie *noun f.* **1.** series **2.** serial
seriedad *noun f.* seriousness
serio, -ria *adj.* **1.** serious, earnest **2.** important
sermón *noun m.* **1.** sermon **2.** lecture
sermonear *verb.* to lecture
serpentear *verb.* to twist, wind
serpiente *noun f.* snake

serrar *verb.* to saw
servicial *adj.* helpful
servicio *noun m.* **1.** service **2.** serve
—**servicios** restroom, toilet
servir *verb.* **1.** to serve **2.** be of use **3.** work
—**servirse** to help oneself
—**servirse de** to make use of
sesenta *noun m. adj.* sixty
sesión *noun f.* session
set *noun m.* set
seta *noun f.* mushroom
setenta *noun m. adj.* seventy
seto *noun m.* **1.** fence **2.** hedge
severidad *noun f.* severity
severo, -ra *adj.* **1.** severe **2.** strict
sexagésimo, -ma *noun. adj.* sixtieth
sexo *noun m.* sex
sexto, -ta *noun. adj.* sixth
sexual *adj.* sexual
shock *noun m.* shock
si *conj.* **1.** if **2.** whether
—**si bien** although
—**si no** otherwise
sí *interj.* yes
sida *noun m.* AIDS
sidra *noun f.* cider
siempre *adv.* always
—**para siempre** forever
—**siempre que 1.** whenever, every time **2.** provided that
sien *noun f.* temple
sierra *noun f.* **1.** mountain range **2.** saw
siete *noun m. adj.* seven
siglo *noun m.* **1.** century **2.** age
significado *noun m.* **1.** meaning, sense **2.** significance, importance
significar *verb.* to mean
significativo, -va *adj.* significant
signo *noun m.* **1.** sign **2.** mark
siguiente *adj.* following, next
sílaba *noun f.* syllable
silbar *verb.* to whistle
silbato *noun m.* whistle
silbido *noun m.* whistle, whistling
silenciar *verb.* to silence
silencio *noun m.* silence
silencioso, -sa *adj.* quiet, silent
silla *noun f.* chair

—**silla de montar** saddle
—**silla de ruedas** wheelchair
sillón noun m. armchair
silvicultura noun f. forestry
simbólico, -ca adj. symbolic
símbolo noun m. symbol
simetría noun f. symmetry
simétrico, -ca adj. symmetrical, symmetric
similar adj. similar
similitud noun f. similarity
simpático, -ca adj. nice, friendly
simple adj. 1. mere 2. simple
simplificar verb. to simplify
simulación noun f. simulation
simular verb. to feign, pretend
simultáneo, -nea adj. simultaneous
sin prep. without
—**sin embargo** nevertheless, however
sinceridad noun f. sincerity
sincero, -ra adj. sincere
sindicato noun m. union, trade union
sinfonía noun f. symphony
singular noun m. singular
siniestro, -tra adj. 1. sinister 2. left
sino noun m. fate, destiny
sino conj. 1. but 2. except
sintaxis noun f. syntax
síntesis noun f. synthesis
sintético, -ca adj. synthetic
síntoma noun m. symptom
sintonizar verb. to tune in
Siria noun f. Syria
sirio, -ria noun. adj. Syrian
sirviente, -ta noun. 1. servant 2. maid (f.)
sistema noun m. system
sistemático, -ca adj. systematic
sitiar verb. to besiege
sitio noun m. 1. place 2. site, spot 3. room, space 4. siege
situación noun f. situation
situado, -da adj. situated, placed
situar verb. to situate, locate, place
soberano, -na noun. adj. sovereign
soberbia noun f. 1. pride 2. magnificence
soberbio, -bia adj. 1. proud 2. superb, magnificent

sobornar verb. to bribe
soborno noun m. 1. bribe 2. bribery
sobra noun f. excess, surplus
—**de sobra** 1. in excess 2. extra
—**sobras** scraps, leftovers
sobre noun m. 1. envelope 2. packet
sobre prep. 1. on, upon, on top of 2. over 3. about
—**sobre todo** 1. especially 2. above all
sobrepasar verb. to surpass, exceed
sobresaliente adj. 1. projecting, protruding 2. outstanding
sobresalir verb. 1. to project, protrude 2. stand out
sobresaltar verb. to frighten
sobrevivir verb. to survive
sobrino, -na noun. nephew/niece
sobrio, -bria adj. sober
sociable adj. sociable
social adj. social
socialismo noun m. socialism
socialista noun mf. adj. socialist
sociedad noun f. 1. society 2. company
—**sociedad anónima** incorporated company
socio, -cia noun. 1. member 2. partner
socorrer verb. to aid, assist
socorro noun m. aid, help
sodio noun m. sodium
sofá noun m. couch, sofa
sofisticación noun f. sophistication
sofisticado, -da adj. sophisticated
software noun m. software
sol noun m. sun
solamente adv. just, only
solapa noun f. 1. flap 2. lapel
solaparse verb. to overlap
solar noun m. lot, plot
solar adj. solar
soldado noun mf. soldier
—**soldado raso** private
soleado, -da adj. sunny
soledad noun f. loneliness
solemne adj. solemn
soicitante noun mf. applicant
solicitar verb. 1. to apply for 2. request
solicitud noun f. 1. application 2. request
solidaridad noun f. solidarity

sólido *noun m.* solid
sólido, -da *adj.* 1. solid 2. firm 3. sound
solitario *noun m.* solitaire
solitario, -ria *noun.* loner
solitario, -ria *adj.* 1. lone 2. lonely 3. deserted
solo, -la *adj.* 1. alone 2. only, unique, sole, single
sólo *adv.* 1. just, only 2. solely
soltar *verb.* 1. to release 2. loosen
soltero, -ra *noun.* bachelor, single man or woman
soltero, -ra *adj.* single
soltura *noun f.* 1. ease 2. looseness 3. fluency
solución *noun f.* 1. solution 2. answer
solucionar *verb.* to solve
solvente *adj.* 1. solvent 2. reliable
sombra *noun f.* 1. shade 2. shadow
sombrear *verb.* to shade
sombrero *noun m.* hat
sombrío, -bría *adj.* somber, gloomy
someter *verb.* 1. to subjugate 2. subject
　—**someterse** to submit
　—**someterse a** to undergo
sonajero *noun m.* rattle
sonar *verb.* 1. to sound 2. ring
sondeo *noun m.* survey, poll
sonido *noun m.* sound
sonoro, -ra *adj.* 1. loud 2. voiced
sonreír *verb.* to smile
sonriente *adj.* smiling
sonrisa *noun f.* smile
sonrojarse *verb.* to blush, flush
soñar *verb.* to dream
sopa *noun f.* soup
soplar *verb.* to blow
soplón, -plona *noun.* sneak
soportar *verb.* 1. to bear, endure 2. carry 3. support
soporte *noun m.* bracket, support
sorber *verb.* to sip
sorbo *noun m.* sip
sordo, -da *adj.* deaf
sorprendente *adj.* surprising
sorprender *verb.* to surprise
sorpresa *noun f.* surprise
sorteo *noun m.* drawing
sosegado, -da *adj.* calm

sosiego *noun m.* calm
soso, -sa *adj.* 1. flavorless, saltless 2. dull
sospecha *noun f.* suspicion
sospechar *verb.* to suspect
sospechoso, -sa *noun.* suspect
sospechoso, -sa *adj.* suspect, suspicious
sostener *verb.* 1. to support 2. hold 3. defend, uphold 4. maintain, sustain
　—**sostenerse** to stand
sostenido, -da *adj.* 1. sustained 2. sharp
sótano *noun m.* basement
sotavento *noun m.* lee
soviético, -ca *adj.* soviet
su *adj.* 1. his, her, its, their 2. your
suave *adj.* 1. soft 2. smooth 3. delicate 4. gentle, mild
suavizar *verb.* to soften
subasta *noun f.* auction
subastar *verb.* to auction
súbdito, -ta *noun.* subject
subestimar *verb.* to underestimate
subida *noun f.* 1. rise 2. ascent, climb
subir *verb.* 1. to increase, rise 2. raise 3. climb
　—**subir a** to get on
súbitamente *adv.* suddenly
súbito, -ta *adj.* sudden
subjetivo, -va *adj.* subjective
sublevación *noun f.* uprising
submarino *noun m.* submarine
submarino, -na *adj.* submarine
subordinado, -da *noun. adj.* subordinate
subrayar *verb.* 1. to underline 2. emphasize, stress
subsidio *noun m.* subsidy
subsiguiente *adj.* subsequent
subsistir *verb.* 1. to subsist 2. endure, last
subterráneo, -nea *adj.* underground
subvención *noun f.* grant, subsidy
subvencionar *verb.* to subsidize
subyugar *verb.* to subjugate
suceder *verb.* 1. to happen, occur 2. succeed, follow, come after
sucesión *noun f.* 1. succession 2. sequence

sucesivo, -va *adj.* successive
suceso *noun m.* **1.** event, occurrence **2.** incident
sucesor, -sora *noun.* successor
suciedad *noun f.* dirt
sucio, -cia *adj.* dirty, filthy, messy
sucumbir *verb.* to succumb
sucursal *noun f.* branch
sudar *verb.* to sweat
sudor *noun m.* sweat
Suecia *noun f.* Sweden
sueco, -ca *noun. adj.* Swedish
suela *noun f.* sole
sueldo *noun m.* salary, wage
suelo *noun m.* **1.** floor **2.** ground **3.** soil
suelto, -ta *adj.* **1.** loose **2.** odd
sueño *noun m.* **1.** dream **2.** sleep
suero *noun m.* serum
suerte *noun f.* **1.** luck, fortune, chance **2.** fate, lot **3.** kind, sort
suéter *noun m.* sweater
suficiente *adj.* enough, sufficient
sufragio *noun m.* suffrage
sufrido, -da *adj.* patient
sufrimiento *noun m.* suffering
sufrir *verb.* **1.** to suffer **2.** endure, bear
sugerencia *noun f.* suggestion
sugerir *verb.* to suggest
suicida *noun mf.* suicide
suicida *adj.* suicidal
suicidio *noun m.* suicide
suite *noun f.* suite
Suiza *noun f.* Switzerland
suizo, -za *noun. adj.* Swiss
sujetar *verb.* **1.** to hold **2.** attach, fasten, secure **3.** subdue
sujeto *noun m.* **1.** subject **2.** individual
sujeto, -ta *adj.* fastened, secure
  —**sujeto a** subject to
suma *noun f.* **1.** sum, amount **2.** addition
sumar *verb.* **1.** to add **2.** total
suministrar *verb.* to supply, provide
suministro *noun m.* supply, provision
sumisión *noun f.* submission
suntuoso, -sa *adj.* sumptuous
superar *verb.* **1.** to surpass **2.** overcome
superficial *adj.* superficial
superficie *noun f.* **1.** surface **2.** area
superintendente *noun mf.* superintendent

superior *noun m.* superior
superior *adj.* **1.** superior **2.** higher **3.** upper
superioridad *noun f.* superiority
supermercado *noun m.* supermarket
supervisar *verb.* to supervise, oversee
supervisión *noun f.* supervision
supervisor, -sora *noun.* supervisor
supervivencia *noun f.* survival
superviviente *noun mf.* survivor
superviviente *adj.* surviving
suplementario, -ria *adj.* supplementary
suplemento *noun m.* supplement
suplente *noun mf.* **1.** substitute **2.** deputy
súplica *noun f.* plea
suplicar *verb.* to beg, plead
suponer *verb.* **1.** to suppose, presume **2.** assume **3.** involve
suposición *noun f.* supposition, presumption
supremo, -ma *adj.* supreme, high
supresión *noun f.* suppression
suprimir *verb.* to suppress
supuesto *noun m.* supposition
supuesto, -ta *adj.* supposed
  —**por supuesto** of course
sur *noun m.* south
sur *adj.* south, southern
sureño, -ña *adj.* southern
surgir *verb.* to arise, emerge
surtido *noun m.* assortment, variety
susceptible *adj.* **1.** sensitive **2.** susceptible
suscitar *verb.* to provoke, arise
suscripción *noun f.* subscription
suspender *verb.* **1.** to suspend **2.** fail
suspensión *noun f.* suspension
suspenso *noun m.* failure
suspirar *verb.* to sigh
suspiro *noun m.* sigh
sustancia *noun f.* substance
sustancial *adj.* substantial
sustantivo *noun m.* noun
sustentar *verb.* **1.** to sustain **2.** maintain
sustento *noun m.* **1.** sustenance **2.** livelihood
sustitución *noun f.* substitution, replacement

sustituir *verb.* to substitute, replace
sustituto, -ta *noun.* substitute
susto *noun m.* scare
sustraer *verb.* **1.** to take away **2.** rob, steal **3.** subtract
susurrar *verb.* **1.** to whisper **2.** murmur

susurro *noun m.* **1.** whisper **2.** murmur
sutil *adj.* **1.** subtle **2.** fine
suturar *verb.* to suture
suyo, suya *adj.* **1.** his, her, its, theirs **2.** yours
suyo, suya *pron.* **1.** his, her, theirs **2.** yours

T

tabaco *noun m.* tobacco
tabla *noun f.* **1.** table **2.** board, plank
—**tablas 1.** boards, stage **2.** draw
tablero *noun m.* board
tableta *noun f.* **1.** tablet **2.** bar
tabloide *noun m.* tabloid
tablón *noun m.* **1.** plank **2.** board
taburete *noun m.* stool
tacaño, -ña *adj.* stingy
tachar *verb.* to cross out, delete
—**tachar de** to accuse of
tachuela *noun f.* tack
taco *noun m.* **1.** plug, stopper **2.** pad **3.** cue
tacón *noun m.* heel
táctica *noun f.* tactics
táctico, -ca *adj.* tactical
tacto *noun m.* **1.** touch **2.** tact
tailandés, -desa *noun. adj.* Thai
Tailandia *noun f.* Thailand
tajada *noun f.* hack, slash
tajar *verb.* to hack, slash
tajo *noun m.* hack, slash
tal *adj.* **1.** such **2.** said
—**tal vez** perhaps, maybe
tal *adv.* so, thus
—**con tal que** provided that
—**¿qué tal?** how are you?, what's new?
tal *pron.* **1.** such a one **2.** such a thing
tala *noun f.* felling
taladrar *verb.* to drill
taladro *noun m.* drill
talar *verb.* to fell
talento *noun m.* talent, gift
talentoso, -sa *adj.* talented, gifted
talla *noun f.* **1.** carving **2.** cutting **3.** height **4.** stature **5.** size
tallar *verb.* **1.** to carve **2.** cut **3.** measure

(height)
talle *noun m.* **1.** waist **2.** figure, shape
taller *noun m.* **1.** workshop **2.** studio
talón *noun m.* heel
tamaño *noun m.* size
también *adv.* **1.** also, likewise, too **2.** so
tambor *noun m.* drum
tamborilear *verb.* to drum
tampoco *adv.* neither, not either
tan *adv.* **1.** so **2.** as
—**tan sólo** only
tangible *adj.* tangible
tanque *noun m.* tank
tanteo *noun m.* **1.** score **2.** estimate
tanto *noun m.* **1.** point, goal **2.** certain amount **3.** rate
—**tanto por ciento** percentage, rate
tanto, -ta *adj.* **1.** so many, so much, such **2.** as many, as much
tanto *adv.* **1.** so much **2.** so long
—**al tanto** aware
—**entre tanto** meanwhile
—**por lo tanto** therefore
—**un tanto** rather, somewhat
tanto, -ta *pron.* so many, so much
tañer *verb.* to toll
tapa *noun f.* cover, lid
tapadera *noun f.* cover, top
tapar *verb.* **1.** to cover **2.** block **3.** hide, keep secret
tapete *noun m.* rug
tapia *noun f.* wall
tapón *noun m.* **1.** cap **2.** cork **3.** plug
taquilla *verb.* box office
tara *noun f.* fault
tararear *verb.* to hum
tarde *noun f.* **1.** afternoon **2.** evening

tarde *adv.* late
tarea *noun f.* job, task, work
tarifa *noun f.* **1.** fare **2.** rate **3.** duty
tarjeta *noun f.* card
—**tarjeta de crédito** credit card
tarro *noun m.* jar, pot
tarta *noun f.* cake
tasa *noun f.* rate
tasar *verb.* **1.** to set the price **2.** value
taxi *noun m.* taxi
taxímetro *noun m.* taximeter
taza *noun f.* **1.** cup **2.** bowl
tazón *noun m.* mug
te *pron.* **1.** you **2.** for you, from you, to you **3.** yourself
té *noun m.* tea
teatral *adj.* theatrical
teatro *noun m.* theatre
tebeo *noun m.* comic
techar *verb.* to roof
techo *noun m.* **1.** ceiling **2.** roof
tecla *noun f.* key
teclado *noun m.* keyboard
técnica *noun f.* skill, technique
técnico, -ca *noun.* technician, engineer
técnico, -ca *adj.* technical
tecnología *noun f.* technology
tecnológico, -ca *adj.* technological
tedioso, -sa *adj.* tedious
teja *noun f.* tile
tejado *noun m.* roof
tejer *verb.* **1.** to knit **2.** weave
tejido *noun m.* **1.** tissue **2.** fabric **3.** texture
tela *noun f.* cloth, fabric, material, stuff
telar *noun m.* loom
tele *noun f.* TV, television
telecomunicación *noun f.* telecommunication
telefonear *verb.* to call, phone, telephone
telefonista *noun mf.* telephone operator
teléfono *noun m.* phone, telephone
—**teléfono móvil** mobile phone
telegrafiar *verb.* to telegraph, wire
telégrafo *noun m.* telegraph, wire
telegrama *noun m.* cable, wire
telenovela *noun f.* serial
telescopio *noun m.* telescope

televisar *verb.* to televise
televisión *noun f.* television
televisor *noun m.* television
tema *noun m.* theme, topic
temblar *verb.* to shiver, tremble
temblor *noun m.* tremble
temer *verb.* to fear, dread
temerario, -ria *adj.* reckless
temeroso, -sa *adj.* fearful
temible *adj.* fearsome, dreadful
temor *noun m.* fear, dread
temperamento *noun m.* temperament
temperatura *noun f.* temperature
templado, -da *adj.* **1.** warm **2.** mild **3.** moderate
templar *verb.* **1.** to warm up **2.** temper **3.** moderate
templo *noun m.* temple
tempo *noun m.* tempo
temporada *noun f.* season
temporal *adj.* **1.** temporal **2.** temporary
temprano, -na *adj. adv.* early
tendencia *noun f.* **1.** tendency **2.** trend
tender *verb.* **1.** to spread out **2.** hang out **3.** lay
—**tender a** to tend to
—**tender una emboscada** to ambush
—**tenderse** to lie down
tendero, -ra *noun.* storekeeper
tenebroso, -sa *adj.* gloomy
tenedor *noun m.* fork
tener *verb.* **1.** to have **2.** hold **3.** own, possess **4.** feel
—**tener en cuenta** to bear in mind
—**tener que 1.** to have to **2.** must
—**tenerse por** to consider oneself
teniente *noun mf.* lieutenant
tenis *noun m.* tennis
tensar *verb.* **1.** to tense **2.** tighten
tensión *noun f.* **1.** tension **2.** strain, stress
—**tensión arterial** blood pressure
tenso, -sa *adj.* tense
tentación *noun f.* temptation
tentador, -dora *adj.* tempting, inviting
tentar *verb.* **1.** to tempt **2.** touch, feel
tentativa *noun f.* attempt, try
tentempié *noun m.* snack
tenue *adj.* **1.** tenuous **2.** faint, dim **3.** delicate, slender

teñir *verb.* to dye
teología *noun f.* theology
teológico, -ca *adj.* theological
teoría *noun f.* theory
teórico, -ca *noun.* theorist
teórico, -ca *adj.* theoretical
tepe *noun m.* turf
terapeuta *noun mf.* therapist
terapéutico, -ca *adj.* therapeutic
terapia *noun f.* therapy
tercero, -ra *noun. adj.* third
tercio *noun m.* third
terciopelo *noun m.* velvet
terco, -ca *adj.* stubborn
termal *adj.* thermal
térmico, -ca *adj.* thermal
terminal *noun f. adj.* terminal
terminar *verb.* 1. to end 2. conclude 3. complete 4. finish 5. expire
término *noun m.* 1. term 2. end
terminología *noun f.* terminology
ternera *noun f.* veal
ternero, -ra *noun.* calf
terraplén *noun m.* embankment
terrateniente *noun mf.* landowner
terraza *noun f.* terrace
terremoto *noun m.* earthquake
terreno *noun m.* 1. terrain 2. ground, land 3. plot
terrible *adj.* terrible, horrible
territorial *adj.* territorial
territorio *noun m.* territory
terrón *noun m.* lump
terror *noun m.* terror
terrorismo *noun m.* terrorism
terrorista *noun mf. adj.* terrorist
tesis *noun f.* thesis
tesorero, -ra *noun.* treasurer
tesoro *noun m.* treasure
test *noun m.* test
testamento *noun m.* testament, will
testigo *noun mf.* witness
testimonio *noun m.* testimony
tetera *noun f.* kettle
textil *noun m. adj.* textile
texto *noun m.* text
textura *noun f.* texture
tez *noun f.* coloring, skin
ti *pron.* you

tía *noun f.* (see tío)
tiempo *noun m.* 1. time 2. period, epoch, age 3. weather 4. tense 5. tempo
tienda *noun f.* store, shop
  —**tienda de campaña** tent
tierno, -na *adj.* 1. tender 2. soft 3. affectionate
tierra *noun f.* 1. earth 2. land 3. soil 4. homeland
  —**tierra firme** mainland
tieso, -sa *adj.* stiff
tiesto *noun m.* pot
tigre, -gresa *noun.* 1. tiger or tigress 2. jaguar
tijeras *noun f. plural.* scissors
tilde *noun f.* accent mark
timar *verb.* to cheat, con, swindle
timbre *noun m.* 1. bell 2. tone
tímido, -da *adj.* shy
timo *noun m.* con, swindle
timonel *noun m.* coxswain
tímpano *noun m.* eardrum
tina *noun f.* bathtub
tinaja *noun f.* vat
tinta *noun f.* ink
tinte *noun m.* 1. dye 2. overtone
tintinear *verb.* to jingle, tinkle
tintineo *noun m.* jingle, tinkle
tío, tía *noun.* 1. uncle or aunt 2. guy or gal
típico, -ca *adj.* typical
tipo *noun m.* 1. type 2. kind, sort 3. style
  —**tipo de interés** interest rate
tipo, -pa *noun.* guy or gal
tipografía *noun f.* typography, printing
tira *noun f.* band, strip
  —**tira cómica** comic strip
tirada *noun f.* 1. throw 2. edition, issue 3. circulation
tirador *noun m.* handle, knob
tirante *adj.* tense
tirantes *noun m. plural.* suspenders
tirar *verb.* 1. to throw, hurl, toss 2. throw away 3. shoot, fire 4. pull, draw 5. attract 6. print
  —**ir tirando** to get by, manage
  —**tirar a** to be rather
  —**tirar de la cadena** to flush
  —**tirar para** to turn to
tiritar *verb.* to shiver

tiro *noun m.* shot
—**a tiro** within range
tirón *noun m.* pull, tug
titubear *verb.* 1. to stammer 2. hesitate
titular *noun m.* headline
titular *noun mf.* holder, owner
titular *verb.* to entitle
—**titularse** 1. to be entitled, be called 2. obtain a degree
título *noun m.* 1. title 2. degree, qualification 3. diploma, certificate 4. bond
tiza *noun f.* chalk
toalla *noun f.* towel
tobillo *noun m.* ankle
tobogán *noun m.* slide
tocar *verb.* 1. to touch 2. feel 3. play 4. ring, knock 5. concern, affect
—**tocarle a** to be one's turn
tocino *noun m.* bacon
tocón *noun m.* stump
todavía *adv.* 1. still, yet 2. even
todo *noun m.* whole
todo, -da *adj.* 1. every, each 2. all, whole, entire
—**todo el mundo** everybody, everyone
todo *adv.* wholly, entirely
—**a todo esto** in the meanwhile
—**ante todo** in the first place
—**con todo** nevertheless
todo, -da *pron.* all, everything
—**todos, todas** everybody, everyone
toga *noun f.* gown
tolerancia *noun f.* tolerance
tolerante *adj.* tolerant
tolerar *verb.* to tolerate
toma *noun f.* 1. taking 2. intake 3. dose 4. capture, seizure
tomar *verb.* 1. to take 2. drink, have 3. capture, seize
—**tomar por** to go in the direction of
—**tomarse** 1. to take 2. have, drink, eat
tomate *noun m.* tomato
tonelada *noun f.* ton
tónica *noun f.* 1. tonic 2. trend
tónico *noun m.* tonic
tónico, -ca *adj.* tonic
tono *noun m.* 1. tone 2. key, pitch 3. shade
tontear *verb.* to fool around

tontería *noun f.* foolishness, stupidity
tonto, -ta *noun.* fool
tonto, -ta *adj.* foolish, stupid
toparse (con) *verb.* to come across
tope *noun m.* 1. limit, end 2. stop
topo *noun m.* mole
toque *noun m.* touch
—**toque de queda** curfew
torcedura *noun f.* 1. twisting 2. sprain
torcer *verb.* 1. to turn 2. bend, twist 3. sprain, strain
torcido, -da *adj.* twisted
tormenta *noun f.* storm
tormento *noun m.* torment
torneo *noun m.* tournament
tornillo *noun m.* bolt, screw
toro *noun m.* bull
torpe *adj.* 1. awkward, clumsy 2. dull
torre *noun f.* 1. tower 2. rook
torrente *noun m.* torrent
torsión *noun f.* twisting, torsion
torta *noun f.* cake
tortuoso, -sa *adj.* tortuous, winding
tortura *noun f.* torture
torturar *verb.* to torture
tos *noun f.* cough
toser *verb.* to cough
tostada *noun f.* toast
tostado, -da *adj.* brown, tanned
tostar *verb.* 1. to roast 2. toast 3. tan
total *noun m. adj.* total
totalidad *noun f.* whole, totality
tóxico *noun m.* toxic substance
tóxico, -ca *adj.* toxic
trabajador, -dora *noun.* laborer, worker
trabajador, -dora *adj.* hard-working
trabajar *verb.* 1. to work 2. labor
trabajo *noun m.* 1. work, job 2. labor 3. effort
tractor *noun m.* tractor
tradición *noun f.* tradition
tradicional *adj.* traditional
traducción *noun f.* translation
traducir *verb.* to translate
traductor, -tora *noun.* translator
traer *verb.* 1. to bring, fetch 2. cause 3. have 4. wear
—**traer consigo** to entail, involve
traficar *verb.* to trade, deal

tráfico *noun m.* traffic
tragar *verb.* to swallow
tragedia *noun f.* tragedy
trágico, -ca *adj.* tragic
trago *noun m.* **1.** swallow **2.** draft
traición *noun f.* betrayal
traicionar *verb.* to betray
tráiler *noun m.* trailer
traje *noun m.* **1.** costume, outfit **2.** dress, apparel **3.** suit
trama *noun f.* **1.** plot **2.** weave
tramar *verb.* **1.** to plot, devise **2.** weave
tramo *noun m.* **1.** stretch **2.** flight
trampa *noun f.* **1.** trap **2.** trick
tramposo, -sa *noun.* cheat, swindler
tranca *noun m.* bar
tranquilidad *noun f.* tranquility, quietness
tranquilizador, -dora *adj.* **1.** soothing **2.** reassuring
tranquilizante *noun m.* tranquilizer
tranquilizar *verb.* to calm down, soothe
tranquilo, -la *adj.* calm, quiet
transacción *noun f.* transaction, deal
transatlántico *noun m.* liner
transbordador *noun m.* ferry
transcripción *noun f.* transcript
transcurrir *verb.* to elapse, pass
transferir *verb.* **1.** to transfer **2.** convey
transformación *noun f.* conversion, transformation
transformar *verb.* **1.** to convert **2.** transform, change
transición *noun f.* transition
transigir *verb.* to give in
—**transigir con** to put up with
transitable *adj.* passable, traversable
tránsito *noun m.* **1.** transit **2.** traffic
transitorio, -ria *adj.* transitory
transmisión *noun f.* transmission
transmitir *verb.* **1.** to transmit, broadcast **2.** pass on
transparente *adj.* transparent
transportar *verb.* **1.** to carry **2.** transport
transporte *noun m.* carriage, transport, transportation
trapo *noun m.* cloth, rag
tras *prep.* **1.** after **2.** behind
trasero *noun m.* buttocks

trasero, -ra *adj.* back, rear
trasladar *verb.* to move, transfer
—**trasladarse** to relocate, move
traslado *noun m.* move, transfer
traspasar *verb.* **1.** to pierce **2.** cross **3.** go too far **4.** convey
traspié *noun m.* slip
trasplantar *verb.* to transplant
trasplante *noun m.* transplant
trastornar *verb.* to disrupt, upset
trastorno *noun m.* **1.** disorder **2.** disruption, upset
trastos *noun m. plural.* **1.** utensils **2.** junk, stuff
tratado *noun m.* treaty
tratamiento *noun m.* treatment
tratar *verb.* **1.** to treat **2.** handle
—**tratar con** to deal with, have contact with
—**tratar de 1.** to try to, attempt **2.** be about **3.** address as
trato *noun m.* **1.** deal **2.** treatment
travesía *noun f.* crossing, voyage
travieso, -sa *adj.* naughty
trayecto *noun m.* **1.** route **2.** journey
trayectoria *noun f.* trajectory
trazado *noun m.* plan, design
trazar *verb.* **1.** to trace **2.** plan, design
trébol *noun m.* **1.** clover **2.** clubs
trece *noun m. adj.* thirteen
trecho *noun m.* **1.** stretch **2.** distance
tregua *noun f.* truce
treinta *noun m. adj.* thirty
tremendo, -da *adj.* **1.** tremendous **2.** terrible
tren *noun m.* train
trepar *verb.* **1.** to climb **2.** creep
tres *noun m. adj.* three
triángulo *noun m.* triangle
tribal *adj.* tribal
tribu *noun f.* tribe
tribuna *noun f.* **1.** platform **2.** gallery
tribunal *noun m.* court, tribunal
tributo *noun m.* **1.** tribute **2.** tax
tridimensional *adj.* three-dimensional
trigésimo, -ma *noun. adj.* thirtieth
trigo *noun m.* wheat
trimestral *adj.* quarterly
trimestre *noun m.* quarter

trinchar *verb.* to carve
trinchera *noun* f. trench
trío *noun* m. trio
tripa *noun* f. gut
triple *noun* m. *adj.* triple
triplicar *verb.* to treble, triple
tripulación *noun* f. crew
tripular *verb.* to man
triste *adj.* 1. sad, blue, gloomy 2. sorry
tristeza *noun* f. sadness
triturar *verb.* to grind
triunfante *adj.* triumphant
triunfar *verb.* to triumph
triunfo *noun* m. triumph
trivial *adj.* trivial
triza *noun* f. shred
  —**hacer trizas** to tear into shreds
trofeo *noun* m. trophy
trompa *noun* f. 1. horn 2. tube 3. trunk
trompeta *noun* f. trumpet
tronar *verb.* 1. to thunder 2. be furious
tronco *noun* m. 1. torso 2. trunk 3. log
trono *noun* m. throne
tropa *noun* f. troop
tropezar *verb.* to stumble
  —**tropezarse con** to bump into, chance upon
tropezón *noun* m. stumble
tropical *adj.* tropical
trópico *noun* m. tropic

tropiezo *noun* m. setback
troquel *noun* m. die
trozo *noun* m. 1. piece, bit, chunk 2. fragment
trucha *noun* f. trout
truco *noun* m. trick
trueno *noun* m. thunder
trueque *noun* m. barter
trust *noun* m. trust
tu *adj.* your
tú *pron.* you
tubería *noun* f. pipes, tubing
tubo *noun* m. 1. tube 2. pipe 3. canal
  —**tubo de escape** exhaust pipe
tuerca *noun* f. nut
tumba *noun* f. 1. grave 2. tomb
tumbar *verb.* to knock down
  —**tumbarse** to lie down
tumbo *noun* m. tumble
tumor *noun* m. tumor
túnel *noun* m. tunnel
turbulento, -ta *adj.* turbulent
turco, -ca *noun.* Turk
turco, -ca *adj.* Turkish
turismo *noun* m. tourism
turista *noun* m/f. tourist
turístico, -ca *adj.* tourist
turno *noun* m. 1. turn. 2. shift
Turquía *noun* f. Turkey
tutor, -tora *noun.* 1. guardian 2. tutor

U

ubicación *noun* f. 1. location 2. situation
ubicar *verb.* to locate
úlcera *noun* f. 1. sore 2. ulcer
últimamente *adv.* lately
tuyo, tuya *adj.* yours, of yours
tuyo, tuya *pron.* yours
u *conj.* or
último, -ma *adj.* 1. last 2. final 3. latter
  —**por último** finally
ultrajar *verb.* to outrage, insult
ultraje *noun* m. outrage, insult
umbral *noun* m. doorstep, threshold
un *adj.* one

un, una *art.* a, an
  —**una vez** once
  —**unos, unas** 1. some, a few 2. about
unánime *adj.* unanimous
undécimo, -ma *noun. adj.* eleventh
único, -ca *noun.* only one
único, -ca *adj.* 1. only, single, sole 2. unique
unidad *noun* f. 1. unit 2. unity
unido, -da *adj.* joined, united
unificación *noun* f. unification
unificar *verb.* to unify
uniforme *noun* m. *adj.* uniform
unión *noun* f. 1. union 2. joint

unir *verb.* to unite, join, link
—**unirse** to join together
—**unirse a** to join
universal *adj.* 1. universal 2. worldwide
universidad *noun f.* university
universo *noun m.* universe
uno *noun m.* one, number one
uno, -na *adj.* one
uno, una *pron.* one
—**uno y otro** both
—**unos, unas** some, some people
—**unos y otros** all of them
untar *verb.* 1. to smear 2. bribe
uña *noun f.* nail
uranio *noun m.* uranium
urbanización *noun f.* residential area

urbano, -na *adj.* urban
urgencia *noun f.* urgency
urgente *adj.* urgent
usado, -da *adj.* 1. used 2. worn
usar *verb.* 1. to use 2. wear
uso *noun m.* 1. use 2. wear 3. custom, usage
usted *pron.* you
—**ustedes** you
usual *adj.* usual
usuario, -ria *noun.* user
útil *adj.* useful, helpful
utilidad *noun f.* utility, usefulness
utilización *noun f.* use
utilizar *verb.* to use, utilize
uva *noun f.* grape

V

vaca *noun f.* cow
vacación *noun f.* vacation, holiday
vacante *noun f.* vacancy
vaciar *verb.* to drain, empty
vacilación *noun f.* hesitation
vacilar *verb.* to hesitate
vacío *noun m.* 1. emptiness, void 2. gap 3. vacuum
vacío, -cía *adj.* 1. empty 2. vacant
vacuna *noun f.* vaccine
vacuno, -na *adj.* bovine
vadear *verb.* to ford
vado *noun m.* ford
vagabundo, -da *noun.* rover, vagabond
vagar *verb.* to wander
vago, -ga *noun.* idler
vago, -ga *adj.* 1. idle, lazy 2. vague
vagón *noun m.* car
vaivén *noun m.* 1. swing 2. change, instability
vajilla *noun f.* dishes
vale *noun m.* voucher
valentía *noun f.* courage
valer *verb.* 1. to cost 2. be worth 3. be valid
—**valerse de** to make use of
valeroso, -sa *adj.* brave
válido, -da *adj.* valid

valiente *adj.* bold, brave
valioso, -sa *adj.* valuable
valla *noun f.* 1. fence 2. hurdle
valle *noun m.* vale, valley
valor *noun m.* 1. value, worth 2. courage, heart, nerve
—**valores** 1. values 2. bonds, securities
valoración *noun f.* assessment, valuation
valorar *verb.* 1. to assess, evaluate 2. value
válvula *noun f.* valve
vanagloriarse *verb.* to boast
vanguardia *noun f.* vanguard
—**a la vanguardia** in the forefront
vanidad *noun f.* vanity
vanidoso, -sa *adj.* vain
vano, -na *adj.* vain
vapor *noun m.* vapor, steam
vaquero, -ra *noun.* cowboy or cowgirl
vaquero, -ra *adj.* cowboy or cowgirl
—**vaqueros** jeans
vara *noun f.* rod, stick
varar *verb.* to beach
variable *noun f. adj.* variable
variación *noun f.* variation
variado, -da *adj.* diverse, mixed, varied
variante *noun f.* variant
variar *verb.* 1. to vary 2. change

variedad *noun f.* variety, diversity

varilla *noun f.* **1.** rod, bar **2.** rib

vario, -ria *adj.* diverse

  —varios, -rias several, various

varón *noun m.* man, male

vaso *noun m.* glass

vasto, -ta *adj.* vast

vatio *noun m.* watt

vecindad *noun f.* neighborhood, vicinity

vecino, -na *noun.* **1.** neighbor **2.** resident, inhabitant

vecino, -na *adj.* neighboring

veda *noun f.* **1.** prohibition **2.** closed season

vedar *verb.* to ban, prohibit

vegetación *noun f.* vegetation

vegetal *noun m.* vegetable

vegetariano, -na *noun. adj.* vegetarian

vehículo *noun m.* vehicle

veinte *noun m. adj.* twenty

veintena *noun f.* group of twenty, score

vejiga *noun f.* bladder

vela *noun f.* **1.** candle **2.** sail

velar *verb.* to veil

velo *noun m.* veil

velocidad *noun f.* speed, velocity

veloz *adj.* swift, fast

vena *noun f.* **1.** vein **2.** strain

venado *noun m.* deer

vencedor, -dora *noun.* winner, victor

vencedor, -dora *adj.* winning

vencejo *noun m.* swift

vencer *verb.* **1.** to win **2.** defeat **3.** overcome **4.** expire

vendaje *noun m.* bandage, dressing

vendar *verb.* to bandage

vendedor, -dora *noun.* salesperson, salesman or saleswoman

vender *verb.* to sell

veneno *noun m.* poison

venezolano, -na *noun. adj.* Venezuelan

Venezuela *noun f.* Venezuela

venganza *noun f.* revenge, vengeance

vengar *verb.* to avenge

  —vengarse to take revenge

venidero, -ra *adj.* coming, forthcoming, future

venir *verb.* **1.** to come **2.** arrive **3.** fit **4.** follow, come after

  —venirse abajo to fall, collapse

venta *noun f.* sale

ventaja *noun f.* **1.** advantage **2.** lead

ventajoso, -sa *adj.* **1.** advantageous **2.** profitable

ventana *noun f.* window

ventanilla *noun f.* **1.** box office **2.** window

ventilación *noun f.* ventilation

ventilador *noun m.* **1.** ventilator **2.** fan

ventilar *verb.* **1.** to ventilate **2.** air

ventoso, -sa *adj.* windy

ver *verb.* **1.** to see **2.** understand **3.** examine **4.** visit **5.** witness

verano *noun m.* summer

verbal *adj.* verbal

verbo *noun m.* verb

verdad *noun f.* truth

  —¿de verdad? really?

verdadero, -ra *adj.* real, true

verde *noun m. adj.* green

verdura *noun f.* vegetables, greens

veredicto *noun m.* verdict

vergonzoso, -sa *adj.* **1.** shameful **2.** shy

vergüenza *noun f.* **1.** shame, disgrace **2.** embarrassment **3.** shyness

verificar *verb.* **1.** to verify **2.** check

verja *noun f.* gate

versátil *adj.* versatile

versículo *noun m.* verse

versión *noun f.* version

verso *noun m.* verse

versus *prep.* against, versus

vertedero *noun m.* garbage dump

verter *verb.* **1.** to pour **2.** empty out **3.** pour

vertical *adj.* vertical, upright

vertiente *noun f.* **1.** slope **2.** side

vestíbulo *noun m.* hall, lobby

vestido *noun m.* **1.** dress **2.** clothes

vestigio *noun m.* trace

vestimenta *noun f.* clothes

vestir *verb.* to dress

vestuario *noun m.* **1.** wardrobe **2.** locker room

veta *noun f.* **1.** grain **2.** streak

vetar *verb.* to veto

veterano, -na *noun. adj.* veteran

veterinario, -ria *noun.* veterinarian

veterinario, -ria adj. veterinary
veto noun m. veto
vez noun f. 1. time 2. occasion
—**en vez de** instead of
vía noun f. 1. way 2. road, railway, track
3. means
—**por vía** by
vía prep. via
viajante noun mf. commercial traveler,
traveling salesman or saleswoman
viajar verb. to travel
viaje noun m. 1. journey, trip 2. voyage
viajero, -ra noun. 1. traveler 2. passenger
vicio noun m. vice
víctima noun f. 1. victim 2. casualty
victoria noun f. victory
vid noun f. vine
vida noun f. 1. life 2. lifetime
vídeo noun m. video
vidrio noun m. glass
viejo, -ja noun. old man or woman
viejo, -ja adj. 1. old 2. worn
viento noun m. wind
vientre noun m. belly, abdomen
viernes noun m. Friday
viga noun f. beam
vigente adj. valid, in force
vigésimo, -ma noun. adj. twentieth
vigía noun mf. watch
vigilancia noun f. vigilance
vigilante noun mf. watchman, guard
vigilante adj. alert, vigilant
vigilar verb. 1. to watch, guard 2. police
3. look after
vigor noun m. vigor
—**en vigor** valid, in force
vigoroso, -sa adj. vigorous
vil adj. vile
villa noun f. 1. village, town 2. villa
villancico noun m. carol
vinagre noun m. vinegar
vínculo noun m. bond, link, tie
vino noun m. wine
viña noun f. vineyard
viñedo noun m. vineyard
violación noun f. 1. violation 2. rape
violar verb. 1. to violate 2. rape
violencia noun f. violence
violento, -ta adj. 1. violent 2. embarrassing

violeta noun f. violet (flower)
violeta noun m. adj. violet
violín noun m. violin
viraje noun m. turn
virar verb. to turn, tack
virgen noun mf. adj. virgin
vírico, -ca adj. viral
virtual adj. virtual
virtud noun f. virtue
virus noun m. virus
visa noun f. visa
visibilidad noun f. visibility
visible adj. visible
visión noun f. 1. vision 2. view
visita noun f. 1. call, visit 2. visitor
visitante noun mf. visitor
visitante adj. visiting
visitar verb. to visit
vislumbrar verb. 1. to distinguish 2.
glimpse
vislumbre noun m. glimpse
víspera noun f. eve
vista noun f. 1. vision, eyesight 2. view,
sight 3. glance, look 4. hearing
vistazo noun m. glance, look
vistoso, -sa adj. colorful
visual adj. visual
vital adj. vital
vitalidad noun f. vitality
vitamina noun f. vitamin
vitorear verb. cheer
vitrina noun f. 1. cabinet 2. case
viudo, -da noun. widower or widow
vivero noun m. nursery
viveza noun f. 1. liveliness 2. vividness
vivienda noun f. 1. housing 2. dwelling
vivir verb. 1. to live 2. be alive 3. reside
4. go through
vivo, -va adj. 1. alive 2. lively 3. vivid
vocabulario noun m. vocabulary
vocación noun f. calling, vocation
vocal noun f. vowel
vocal noun mf. voting member
vocal adj. vocal
vociferar verb. to shout
volante noun m. wheel
volar verb. 1. to fly 2. hurry 3. disappear
4. burst, explode
volcán noun m. volcano

volcánico, -ca *adj.* volcanic
volcar *verb.* **1.** to overturn **2.** topple **3.** upset
voltaje *noun m.* voltage
voltear *verb.* **1.** to turn over **2.** roll over **3.** tumble
voltereta *noun f.* tumble
voltio *noun m.* volt
volumen *noun m.* **1.** volume **2.** amount **3.** size
voluntad *noun f.* **1.** will **2.** intention
voluntario, -ria *noun.* volunteer
voluntario, -ria *adj.* voluntary
volver *verb.* **1.** to return **2.** go back, come back **3.** revert **4.** cause, drive, make **5.** turn over
—**volver a** to do again
—**volverse 1.** to become **2.** turn around

vomitar *verb.* to vomit
vómito *noun m.* **1.** vomit **2.** vomiting
vos *pron.* you
vosotros, vosotras *pron.* you
votación *noun f.* voting
votante *noun mf.* voter
votar *verb.* to vote
voto *noun m.* **1.** vote **2.** vow
voz *noun f.* **1.** voice **2.** word
vuelo *noun m.* **1.** flight **2.** fullness
vuelta *noun f.* **1.** turn **2.** revolution **3.** return **4.** round **5.** stroll, walk, ride **6.** bend, curve **7.** change **8.** back
vuestro, vuestra *adj.* your, of yours
vuestro, vuestra *pron.* yours
vulgar *adj.* **1.** common **2.** vulgar
vulnerabilidad *noun f.* vulnerability
vulnerable *adj.* vulnerable

W, X, Y, Z

western *noun m.* western
whisky *noun m.* whiskey
xenofobia *noun f.* xenophobia
xenófobo, -ba *noun.* xenophobe
xenófobo, -ba *adj.* xenophobic
y *conj.* and
ya *adv.* **1.** already **2.** now **3.** anymore, no longer **4.** later, soon
—**ya que** since
yacimiento *noun m.* deposit, field
yarda *noun f.* yard
yate *noun m.* yacht
yegua *noun f.* mare
yen *noun m.* yen
yermo *noun m.* wasteland
yeso *noun m.* plaster
yo *pron.* **1.** I **2.** me
zalamero, -ra *noun.* flatterer
zalamero, -ra *adj.* flattering

zambullida *noun f.* dive, plunge
zambullirse *verb.* to dive, plunge
zanahoria *noun f.* carrot
zancada *noun f.* stride
zanja *noun f.* ditch
zapato *noun m.* shoe
zarcillo *noun m.* earring
zarpar *verb.* to set sail
zigzaguear *verb.* to zigzag
zona *noun f.* area, district, zone
zoo *noun m.* zoo
zorra *noun f.* bitch
zorro *noun m.* fox or vixen
zumbar *verb.* **1.** to buzz, hum **2.** thrash
zumbido *noun m.* buzzing, humming
zumo *noun m.* juice
zurdo, -da *noun.* left-handed person
zurdo, -da *adj.* left-handed

ENGLISH-SPANISH DICTIONARY

A

a, an *indef. art.* **1.** un, una **2.** por, al, a la

abacus *noun.* ábaco

abandon *verb.* **1.** abandonar, dejar **2.** suspender

abandoned *adj.* **1.** abandonado **2.** inmoral, desvergonzado

abandonment *noun.* abandono

abbey *noun.* abadía

abbot *noun.* abad

ABC *noun.* **1.** abecedario **2.** abecé

abdominal *adj.* abdominal

ability *noun.* capacidad, habilidad

able *adj.* **1.** capaz **2.** competente

abnormal *adj.* anormal

aboard *adv. prep.* a bordo

abolish *verb.* abolir

abolition *noun.* abolición

abortion *noun.* aborto

about *prep. adv.* **1.** alrededor de, aproximadamente **2.** casi **3.** cerca, por aquí, por ahí

about *prep.* de, sobre, acerca de

above *prep.* **1.** (por) encima de **2.** sobre **3.** superior

above *adv.* **1.** arriba **2.** mayor

abroad *adv.* en el extranjero, fuera

abrupt *adj.* **1.** brusco, repentino **2.** abrupto

abruptly *adv.* bruscamente

absence *noun.* ausencia

absent *verb.* ausentarse

absent *adj.* ausente

absolute *adj.* absoluto

absolutely *adv.* absolutamente

absorb *verb.* absorber

absorption *noun.* absorción

abstract *noun.* resumen

abstract *adj.* abstracto

absurd *adj.* absurdo

abundance *noun.* abundancia

abundant *adj.* abundante

abuse *noun.* **1.** abuso **2.** insulto, injuria

abuse *verb.* **1.** abusar de **2.** insultar, injuriar

academic *noun.* profesor de universidad

academic *adj.* académico

academy *noun.* **1.** academia **2.** colegio

accelerate *verb.* acelerar

acceleration *noun.* aceleración

accent *noun.* **1.** acento, tilde **2.** énfasis

accent *verb.* acentuar

accept *verb.* aceptar

acceptable *adj.* **1.** aceptable **2.** grato

acceptance *noun.* aceptación

accepted *adj.* reconocido

access *noun.* acceso, entrada

accessible *adj.* accesible

accession *noun.* **1.** ascensión, subida **2.** adquisición, adición **3.** accesión, adhesión

accessory *noun.* **1.** complemento, accesorio **2.** cómplice

accident *noun.* **1.** accidente **2.** casualidad

accidental *adj.* accidental, fortuito

accidentally *adv.* **1.** por casualidad, accidentalmente **2.** sin querer

acclaim *noun.* aclamación

acclaim *verb.* **1.** aclamar, vitorear **2.** proclamar

accommodate *verb.* **1.** acomodar **2.** complacer **3.** proveer **4.** hospedar, alojar

accommodation *noun.* **1.** acomodación, acomodamiento **2.** alojamiento, sitio

accompany *verb.* acompañar

accomplish *verb.* realizar, lograr

accomplished *adj.* consumado, experto

accord *noun.* acuerdo

accord with *verb.* **1.** concordar (con) **2.** conceder

accordance *noun.* acuerdo, conformidad
—**in accordance with** de acuerdo con, conforme a
according to *prep.* según, conforme, por
accordingly *adv.* 1. en consecuencia 2. por consiguiente
account *noun.* 1. cuenta 2. factura 3. relato, versión
—**by all accounts** a decir de todos
—**on account of** a causa de
accountancy *noun.* contabilidad
accountant *noun.* contable
accumulate *verb.* acumular, acumularse
accumulation *noun.* acumulación
accuracy *noun.* precisión, exactitud, fidelidad
accurate *adj.* 1. exacto, preciso, fiel 2. certero
accurately *adv.* 1. con exactitud, fielmente 2. certeramente
accusation *noun.* acusación
accuse of *verb.* acusar
accustomed *adj.* acostumbrado, usual
ace *noun.* 1. as 2. ace
ache *noun.* dolor
ache *verb.* 1. doler 2. ansiar, desear
achieve *verb.* conseguir, lograr, realizar
achievement *noun.* logro, hazaña
acid *noun.* ácido
acid *adj.* 1. ácido 2. mordaz, sarcástico
acknowledge *verb.* 1. reconocer, admitir, confesar 2. agradecer 3. acusar recibo de
acoustic *adj.* acústico
acquaintance *noun.* conocido
—**acquaintance with** conocimiento de
acquire *verb.* adquirir
acquisition *noun.* adquisición
across *prep.* 1. a través de 2. al otro lado de
across *adv.* 1. a través, de través, transversalmente 2. al otro lado
act *noun.* 1. acto, acción 2. función
—**act (of law)** *noun.* ley
act *verb.* 1. actuar 2. comportarse 3. representar, fingir
acting *adj.* en funciones
action *noun.* 1. acción, actuación 2. proceso 3. combate, batalla
activate *verb.* activar

active *adj.* 1. activo 2. en vigor 3. en actividad
actively *adv.* activamente
activity *noun.* actividad
actor *noun.* actor
actual *adj.* real
actually *adv.* 1. en realidad, realmente 2. de hecho
acute *adj.* 1. agudo, perspicaz, fino 2. grave
ad *noun.* anuncio
AD *abbr.* d.C., después de Cristo
Adam's apple *noun.* nuez
adapt *verb.* adaptar
adaptation *noun.* adaptación
add *verb.* 1. sumar 2. añadir, agregar
addict *noun.* adicto
addiction *noun.* adicción
addition *noun.* 1. suma 2. adición
additional *adj.* adicional
address *noun.* 1. dirección, señas 2. discurso, alocución
address *verb.* 1. poner la dirección, dirigir 2. dirigirse a, pronunciar
adequate *adj.* suficiente, adecuado
adequately *adv.* suficientemente
adjacent (to) *adj.* adyacente
adjective *noun.* adjetivo
adjust (to) *verb.* 1. amoldarse 2. ajustar
adjustment *noun.* ajuste
administer *verb.* 1. administrar 2. aplicar
administration *noun.* administración
administrative *adj.* administrativo
administrator *noun.* administrador
admirable *adj.* admirable
admiral *noun.* almirante
admiration *noun.* admiración
admire *verb.* admirar
admission *noun.* 1. admisión 2. confesión, reconocimiento
admit *verb.* 1. admitir, dejar entrar 2. reconocer
admittedly *adv.* sin duda, ciertamente
adolescent *noun. adj.* adolescente
adopt *verb.* adoptar
adoption *noun.* adopción
adult *noun. adj.* adulto
advance *noun.* 1. avance, progreso, mejora 2. anticipo, adelanto

—**advances** insinuaciones, requerimientos

advance verb. 1. avanzar, proceder 2. adelantar

advance adj. 1. por adelantado, anticipado 2. avanzadilla

advanced adj. avanzado

advantage noun. ventaja

advent noun. advenimiento, llegada

adventure noun. aventura

adverse adj. adverso, desfavorable, negativo

advert noun. anuncio

advertise verb. anunciar, hacer publicidad

advertisement, ad noun. anuncio

advice noun. consejo

advisable adj. aconsejable, conveniente

advise verb. aconsejar

—**advise of** avisar, informar

adviser, advisor noun. consejero

advisory adj. asesor, consultivo

advocate noun. abogado, defensor

advocate verb. defender, abogar, recomendar

aerial adj. aéreo

affair noun. 1. caso 2. cosa 3. amorío, relación

—**affairs** asuntos

affect verb. afectar

affection noun. afecto, cariño

affirm verb. afirmar

afford verb. permitirse, darse el gusto de

afraid adj. temeroso, con miedo

—**be afraid that** sentir, lamentar, temer

Africa noun. África

African noun. adj. africano

after conj. después de que

after prep. 1. después (de) 2. detrás (de), tras 3. según, al estilo de

after adv. después

aftermath noun. secuelas, consecuencias

afternoon noun. tarde

afterwards adv. después, posteriormente, a continuación

again adv. otra vez, de nuevo

against prep. contra, en contra de

age noun. 1. edad 2. época, período

—**ages** años, siglos, mucho tiempo

age verb. envejecer

aged adj. 1. viejo, anciano 2. de la edad de

agency noun. agencia

agenda noun. orden del día

agent noun. agente

aggregate noun. total

aggression noun. agresión

aggressive adj. agresivo

agitation noun. agitación

ago adv. hace

agony noun. agonía

agree verb. 1. estar de acuerdo con 2. acordar, consentir, aceptar 3. concordar, llevarse bien

—**agree with** sentar bien

agreement noun. 1. acuerdo, pacto, contrato 2. contrato

agricultural adj. agrícola

agriculture noun. agricultura

ahead (of) adv. delante

aid noun. ayuda, auxilio

aid verb. ayudar, auxiliar

AIDS abbr. sida

aim noun. 1. puntería 2. objetivo, meta, intención

aim verb. apuntar

—**aim to/at** tener intención de, proponerse

air noun. aire

air verb. airear, ventilar

air force noun. 1. fuerzas aérea 2. flota aérea

aircraft noun. aeronave, avión

airfield noun. campo de aviación

airlift noun. puente aéreo

airline noun. línea aérea, compañía aérea

airplane noun. avión

airport noun. aeropuerto

airway noun. ruta aérea

alarm noun. 1. alarma, sobresalto 2. toque de alarma

alarm verb. alarmar, asustar

alarming adj. alarmante

album noun. álbum

alcohol noun. alcohol

alcoholic *noun*. alcohólico
alcoholic *adj*. alcohólico
ale *noun*. cerveza
alert *noun*. alerta
alert *verb*. alertar
alert *adj*. despierto, espabilado, alerta
algae *noun plural*. algas
alien *noun*. **1.** extranjero **2.** extraterrestre
alien *adj*. **1.** extraño, extranjero, ajeno **2.**
extraterrestre
alienate *verb*. **1.** enajenar, alienar **2.**
malquistar
alike *adj*. parecido
alike *adv*. igual, del mismo modo
alive *adj*. **1.** vivo **2.** animado, activo
all *adj. pron*. **1.** todo **2.** todos
—**all the better** tanto mejor
all *adv*. completamente, totalmente
—**not at all** en absoluto
allegation *noun*. alegación
allege *verb*. alegar
allegiance *noun*. lealtad
allergy *noun*. alergia
alley *noun*. **1.** callejón, callejuela **2.** pista
(de bolos)
alliance *noun*. alianza
allied *adj*. aliado
—**allied to** emparentado, afín, relacionado
—**allied with** junto con
allocate *verb*. **1.** asignar, designar, destinar **2.** distribuir, repartir
allocation *noun*. **1.** asignación **2.** distribución, reparto
allow *verb*. **1.** permitir, dejar **2.** dar, asignar **3.** admitir
—**allow for** tener en cuenta, calcular
allowance *noun*. **1.** asignación, subsidio, prestación **2.** dinero de bolsillo,
plus **3.** margen **4.** ración **5.** concesión
ally *noun*. aliado
ally *verb*. aliarse (con)
almost *adv*. casi
alone *adj*. solo
alone *adv*. sólo, solamente
along *prep*. por, a lo largo de
along *adv*. **1.** adelante **2.** con (una persona) **3.** aquí, allí

—**along with** junto con, en compañía
de
alongside *prep. adv*. al lado de
aloud *adv*. en voz alta
alpine *adj*. alpino
already *adv*. ya
also *adv*. también
altar *noun*. altar
alter *verb*. cambiar, modificar, alterar
alteration *noun*. cambio, modificación,
alteración
alternate *verb*. alternar
alternate *adj*. **1.** alterno **2.** uno sí y otro
no
alternative *noun*. alternativa
alternative *adj*. alternativo
alternatively *adv*. o bien, alternativamente, si no
although *conj*. aunque
altitude *noun*. altitud
altogether *adv*. **1.** del todo, totalmente
2. en conjunto
aluminum *noun. adj*. aluminio
always *adv*. siempre
a.m., A.M. *abbr*. de la mañana
amateur *noun*. aficionado
amateur *adj*. aficionado, amateur
amaze *verb*. asombrar, pasmar
amazement *noun*. asombro, pasmo,
sorpresa
amazing *adj*. **1.** asombroso **2.** extraordinario
ambassador *noun*. embajador
amber *noun. adj*. ámbar
ambiguity *noun*. ambigüedad
ambiguous *adj*. ambiguo
ambition *noun*. ambición
ambitious *adj*. ambicioso
ambulance *noun*. ambulancia
ambush *noun*. emboscada
ambush *verb*. tender una emboscada,
agarrar por sorpresa
amend *verb*. enmendar, corregir
America *noun*. **1.** Estados Unidos de
América **2.** América
American *noun. adj*. **1.** estadounidense,
norteamericano **2.** americano
amid, amidst *prep*. en medio de, entre
amiss *adj*. **1.** mal **2.** inoportuno

ammunition *noun.* munición

amnesty *noun.* amnistía

among *prep.* entre

amount *noun.* cantidad, suma, importe

amount to *verb.* **1.** sumar, ascender a **2.** equivaler, venir a ser lo mismo

ample *adj.* **1.** bastante, de sobra **2.** amplio, generoso

ampère *noun.* amperio

amuse *verb.* **1.** divertir, entretener **2.** divertirse

amusement *noun.* distracción, diversión, entretenimiento

amusing *adj.* divertido

an, a *indef. art.* **1.** un, una **2.** por, al, a la

analysis *noun.* **1.** análisis **2.** psicoanálisis

analyst *noun.* **1.** analista **2.** psicoanalista

analytical *adj.* analítico

analyze *verb.* analizar

anatomy *noun.* anatomía

ancestor *noun.* antepasado

anchor *noun.* ancla

anchor *verb.* anclar

ancient *adj.* **1.** antiguo **2.** viejo

and *conj.* y, e (before i-, hi, but not hie-)

angel *noun.* ángel

anger *noun.* enojo, ira

anger *verb.* enojar, enfadar

angle *noun.* **1.** ángulo **2.** punto de vista **3.** esquina, rincón

angle *verb.* pescar con caña

angler *noun.* pescador de caña

Anglican *noun. adj.* anglicano

angrily *adv.* enojado, con ira

angry *adj.* **1.** enojado, enfadado **2.** inflamado

anguish *noun.* angustia

animal *noun.* animal

ankle *noun.* tobillo

anniversary *noun.* aniversario

announce *verb.* **1.** anunciar **2.** declarar **3.** presentar

announcement *noun.* **1.** anuncio **2.** declaración

annoy *verb.* fastidiar, molestar

annoyed *adj.* enojado, molesto

annual *noun.* **1.** anuario **2.** planta anual

annual *adj.* anual

annually *adv.* anualmente

anonymous *adj.* anónimo

another *adj. pron.* otro

answer *noun.* **1.** respuesta, contestación **2.** solución

answer *verb.* **1.** responder, contestar **2.** abrir, atender (la puerta) **3.** coger (el teléfono)

—answer for ser responsable de

answering machine *noun.* contestador

ant *noun.* hormiga

Antarctic *adj.* antártico

antenna *noun.* antena

anthropology *noun.* antropología

antibiotic *noun.* antibiótico

anticipate *verb.* **1.** esperar, contar con **2.** prever **3.** anticiparse

anticipation *noun.* **1.** espera **2.** expectación, esperanza **3.** anticipación, previsión

antique *noun.* antigüedad

antique *adj.* **1.** antiguo, de época **2.** anticuado

anxiety *noun.* ansiedad

anxious *adj.* **1.** inquieto, preocupado **2.** angustioso **3.** ansioso, deseoso

anxiously *adv.* **1.** con inquietud **2.** impacientemente **3.** ansiosamente

any *adv.* **1.** para nada **2.** algo

any *pron. adj.* **1.** cualquier, cualquiera **2.** algún **3.** ningún

anybody *pron.* **1.** alguien **2.** nadie (in negative sentences) **3.** cualquiera

anyhow *adv.* **1.** en cualquier caso, de todas formas **2.** de cualquier manera

anyone *pron.* **1.** alguien **2.** nadie (in negative sentences) **3.** cualquiera

anything *pron.* **1.** algo **2.** nada (in negative sentences) **3.** cualquier cosa, lo que

anyway *adv.* de todas formas, de todos modos

anywhere *adv.* **1.** en alguna parte **2.** en ninguna parte (in negative sentences) **3.** en cualquier parte

apart *adv.* **1.** aparte **2.** separado **3.** en pedazos, en piezas

apartment *noun.* apartamento, departamento, piso

apologize *verb.* disculparse, pedir perdón

apology *noun.* disculpa
appall *verb.* horrorizar
appalling *adj.* horrible
apparatus *noun.* aparato, equipo
apparent *adj.* 1. evidente, claro 2. aparente
apparently *adv.* 1. por lo visto, al parecer 2. aparentemehte
appeal *noun.* 1. solicitud, súplica, petición, llamado 2. apelación 3. atractivo, encanto
appeal *verb.* 1. suplicar, rogar 2. apelar, recurrir
—**appeal to** gustar, agradar, atraer
appealing *adj.* 1. atrayente, encantador 2. suplicante
appear *verb.* 1. aparecer, salir 2. comparecer 3. parecer
appearance *noun.* 1. apariencia, imagen, aspecto 2. aparición, comparecencia 3. publicación
appendix *noun.* apéndice
appetite *noun.* apetito
applaud *verb.* aplaudir
applause *noun.* aplauso
apple *noun.* manzana
appliance *noun.* aparato, electrodoméstico
applicable *adj.* aplicable
applicant *noun.* solicitante, candidato, aspirante
application *noun.* 1. solicitud, petición 2. aplicación
apply *verb.* 1. aplicar 2. emplear 3. ser válido, estar en vigor
—**apply for** solicitar
—**apply to** aplicarse
appoint *verb.* 1. nombrar, designar 2. convenir, fijar
appointed *adj.* convenido, fijado
appointment *noun.* 1. cita, hora 2. nombramiento, puesto, empleo
appreciate *verb.* 1. agradecer 2. valorar, apreciar 3. comprender, hacerse cargo de 4. revalorizarse, aumentar en valor
appreciation *noun.* 1. agradecimiento, gratitud, reconocimiento 2. apreciación 3. comprensión 4. revalora-

ción, aumento en valor 5. crítica, informe
apprehension *noun.* 1. aprensión, temor 2. comprensión, percepción
apprentice *noun.* aprendiz
apprentice *verb.* poner de aprendiz
apprenticeship *noun.* aprendizaje
approach *noun.* 1. aproximación, acercamiento 2. acceso 3. propuesta, proposición
approach *verb.* 1. acercarse, aproximarse, dirigirse a 2. abordar
approaching *adj.* 1. venidero 2. que viene en dirección contraria
appropriate *adj.* apropiado, adecuado, conveniente
appropriately *adv.* apropiadamente, adecuadamente
approval *noun.* aprobación
approve *verb.* 1. aprobar, tener un buen concepto de 2. aceptar
approximate *adj.* aproximado
approximately *adv.* aproximadamente
April *noun.* abril
apron *noun.* delantal, mandil
apt *adj.* 1. propenso, inclinado 2. apropiado, oportuno 3. listo, talentoso
aquarium *noun.* acuario
Arab *noun. adj.* árabe
Arabia *noun.* Arabia
Arabian *adj.* árabe, arábigo
Arabic *noun.* árabe
arbitrary *adj.* arbitrario
arbitration *noun.* arbitraje
arc *noun.* arco
arch *noun.* 1. arco 2. empeine
arch *verb.* arquear
archaeological *adj.* arqueológico
archaeology *noun.* arqueología
archbishop *noun.* arzobispo
architect *noun.* arquitecto
architectural *adj.* arquitectónico
architecture *noun.* arquitectura
archives *noun plural.* archivo
Arctic *adj.* 1. ártico 2. glacial, gélido
area *noun.* 1. área, superficie 2. zona
arena *noun.* arena
Argentina *noun.* Argentina
Argentinean *noun. adj.* argentino

argue *verb*. **1.** discutir **2.** sostener
—**argue for/against** argüir, argumentar
argument *noun*. **1.** discusión **2.** argumento
arise *verb*. **1.** surgir, presentarse **2.** levantarse, alzarse
aristocracy *noun*. aristocracia
aristocratic *adj*. aristocrático
arithmetic *noun*. aritmética
arm *noun*. **1.** brazo **2.** arma
—**coat of arms** escudo, blasón
arm *verb*. **1.** armar **2.** armarse
armchair *noun*. sillón, butaca
armed *adj*. armado
armor *noun*. **1.** armadura **2.** blindaje
armored *adj*. blindado
army *noun*. **1.** ejército **2.** multitud, bandada
around *adv*. **1.** alrededor **2.** aproximadamente, más o menos **3.** por ahí
around *prep*. **1.** alrededor de **2.** cerca de **3.** a la vuelta de
arouse *verb*. despertar, provocar
arrange *verb*. **1.** ordenar, disponer **2.** organizar, planear **3.** arreglar, adaptar
arrangement *noun*. **1.** disposición **2.** arreglo
—**arrangements** preparativos
array *noun*. **1.** serie, conjunto, colección **2.** atavío
array *verb*. **1.** alinear, disponer **2.** engalanarse
arrears *noun plural*. atrasos
arrest *noun*. **1.** detención, arresto, captura **2.** paro
arrest *verb*. **1.** detener, arrestar, capturar **2.** parar
arrival *noun*. **1.** llegada **2.** recién nacido, recién llegado
arrive *verb*. llegar
arrogance *noun*. arrogancia
arrogant *adj*. arrogante
arrow *noun*. flecha
arsenal *noun*. arsenal
art *noun*. arte
—**Arts** Letras, Filosofía y Letras
—**fine arts** bellas artes
artery *noun*. arteria
article *noun*. artículo

articulate *verb*. articular
articulate *adj*. que se expresa bien
artificial *adj*. artificial
artillery *noun*. artillería
artist *noun*. artista
artistic *adj*. artístico
as *conj*. **1.** cuando, mientras **2.** como, igual que **3.** aunque, por mucho que (with subjunctive verb) **4.** al igual que
as *prep*. **1.** como **2.** en tanto que
as *adv*. tan, tanto
ascent *noun*. **1.** ascensión **2.** cuesta, pendiente
ascertain *verb*. esclarecer, descubrir
ash *noun*. ceniza
ashamed *adj*. avergonzado
ashore *adv*. a/en tierra firme
ashtray *noun*. cenicero
Asia *noun*. Asia
Asian *noun. adj*. asiático
aside *noun*. aparte
aside *adv*. aparte, a un lado
ask *verb*. **1.** preguntar **2.** pedir, preguntar por **3.** invitar
asleep *adj*. dormido
aspect *noun*. **1.** aspecto **2.** orientación **3.** pinta
aspiration *noun*. aspiración
ass *noun*. **1.** asno, burro **2.** imbécil
assassinate *verb*. asesinar
assassination *noun*. asesinato
assault *noun*. **1.** asalto, ataque **2.** agresión sexual, intento de violación
assault *verb*. **1.** asaltar **2.** agredir sexualmente
assemble *verb*. **1.** reunirse **2.** reunir **3.** montar
assembly *noun*. **1.** asamblea **2.** montaje, ensamblaje
assert *verb*. **1.** aseverar, afirmar, sostener **2.** defender, hacer valer
assertion *noun*. aserción, aserto, afirmación
assess *verb*. **1.** evaluar **2.** calcular
assessment *noun*. evaluación
asset *noun*. ventaja, factor positivo
—**assets** bienes, haberes
assign *verb*. **1.** asignar, atribuir **2.** destinar

assignment noun. cometido, tarea
assist verb. ayudar
assistance noun. ayuda, asistencia
assistant noun. 1. ayudante 2. dependiente
associate noun. socio
associate verb. asociar
 —**associate with** encontrarse, relacionarse
associate adj. 1. adjunto 2. asociado
association noun. asociación
assume verb. 1. suponer 2. asumir 3. adquirir, adoptar
assumed adj. presunto, falso
assumption noun. supuesto
assurance noun. 1. seguridad 2. garantía, promesa, palabra de honor 3. seguro
assure verb. 1. asegurar 2. garantizar
assured adj. seguro
asthma noun. asma
astonishing adj. asombroso, sorprendente
astonishment noun. asombro, sorpresa
astronomer noun. astrónomo
asylum noun. 1. asilo 2. manicomio
at prep. 1. en 2. a, hacia
athlete noun. atleta
athletic adj. atlético
athletics noun singular. atletismo
Atlantic noun. Atlántico
atmosphere noun. 1. atmósfera 2. ambiente
atmospheric adj. atmosférico
atom noun. 1. átomo 2. ápice, pizca, gota
atomic adj. atómico
atrocity noun. atrocidad
attach verb. atar, sujetar, adjuntar
attached (to) adj. apegado
attachment noun. accesorio
 —**attachment for/to** cariño, apego
attack noun. ataque
attack verb. 1. atacar 2. lanzarse (a)
attain verb. conseguir, alcanzar, lograr
attempt noun. 1. tentativa, intento 2. atentado
attempt verb. intentar, tratar de
attend verb. 1. asistir 2. atender, ocu-

parse de
attendance noun. asistencia
attendant noun. encargado
attention noun. 1. atención 2. cuidado 3. posición de firmes
attic noun. ático, desván, buhardilla
attitude noun. 1. actitud (hacia), postura 2. posición
attorney noun. 1. apoderado 2. abogado
attract verb. atraer
attraction noun. atracción
attractive adj. 1. atractivo 2. atrayente, interesante
attribute noun. atributo
attribute verb. 1. atribuir 2. acusar
auction noun. subasta
auction verb. subastar
audience noun. 1. público 2. audiencia
audit noun. auditoría
audit verb. auditar, revisar las cuentas
auditor noun. auditor, revisor de cuentas
august adj. augusto
August noun. agosto
aunt noun. tía
auntie, aunty noun. tita
Australia noun. Australia
Australian noun. adj. australiano
Austria noun. Austria
Austrian noun. adj. austríaco
authentic adj. auténtico
author noun. autor
authoritarian adj. autoritario
authoritative adj. autorizado, acreditado
authority noun. autoridad
authorize verb. autorizar
auto noun. carro, coche, automóvil
autobiography noun. autobiografía
automatic noun. arma automática
automatic adj. automático
automatically adv. automáticamente
automobile noun. automóvil
autonomous adj. autónomo
autonomy noun. autonomía
availability noun. disponibilidad
available adj. disponible
avenue noun. avenida
average noun. media
average verb. hacer un promedio de

average *adj.* **1.** medio, promedio **2.** corriente, común
avert *verb.* **1.** desviar, apartar **2.** prevenir, impedir
aviary *noun.* pajarera
aviation *noun.* **1.** aviación **2.** aeronáutica
avoid *verb.* evitar
avoidance *noun.* evitación
await *verb.* esperar, aguardar
awake *verb.* **1.** despertar **2.** despertarse
awake *adj.* despierto
award *noun.* premio
award *verb.* **1.** conceder, otorgar **2.** adjudicar

aware *adj.* informado, consciente
awareness *noun.* consciencia
away *adv.* **1.** a, lejos **2.** hacia el otro lado, para otra parte **3.** por completo **4.** sin pausa **5.** fuera, en otro sitio
awe *noun.* temor, respeto
awe *verb.* infundir temor/respeto, atemorizar
awful *adj.* **1.** enorme, imponente, terrible, tremendo **2.** horrible, horroroso
awkward *adj.* **1.** patoso, desgarbado, torpe **2.** difícil, delicado, peliagudo
ax, axe *noun.* hacha
axis *noun.* eje

B

BA, B.A. *abbr.* **1.** licenciatura en Letras **2.** licenciado en Letras
baby *noun.* **1.** bebé **2.** cría
back *noun.* **1.** espalda (of a person) **2.** lomo (of an animal) **3.** parte trasera, fondo, dorso, reverso, respaldo **4.** defensa (in sports)
back *verb.* **1.** dar marcha atrás, mover hacia atrás **2.** apoyar **3.** apostar por
back *adj.* de detrás, trasero
back *adv.* **1.** atrás **2.** hacia atrás, para atrás **3.** de vuelta
background *noun.* **1.** fondo **2.** antecedentes **3.** orígenes, formación, educación
backward *adj.* **1.** hacia atrás **2.** atrasado, retrasado
backward *adv.* **1.** hacia atrás **2.** de espaldas **3.** al revés
bacon *noun.* tocino
bacterium *noun plural.* bacteria
bad *adj.* **1.** malo, mal **2.** perverso **3.** podrido, pasado, picado **4.** perjudicial, nocivo, pernicioso **5.** grave, fuerte **6.** incobrable
badge *noun.* insignia, distintivo
badly *adv.* **1.** mal **2.** gravemente, desesperadamente

bag *noun.* **1.** saco, bolsa, bolso, maleta **2.** caza
bag *verb.* **1.** ensacar, meter en una bolsa/en bolsas **2.** cazar
bail *noun.* **1.** fianza **2.** fiador
bait *noun.* cebo, anzuelo
bait *verb.* cebar
bake *verb.* **1.** cocer al horno **2.** endurecer
baker *noun.* panadero, pastelero
bakery *noun.* panadería, pastelería
balance *noun.* **1.** balanza **2.** equilibrio **3.** saldo **4.** contrapeso
balance *verb.* **1.** equilibrar, nivelar **2.** cuadrar **3.** sopesar, comparar **4.** mantener(se) en equilibrio
balcony *noun.* **1.** balcón **2.** galería, anfiteatro
bald *adj.* **1.** calvo **2.** pelado, desnudo **3.** escueto, sencillo
ball *noun.* **1.** bola, esfera, globo **2.** pelota, balón **3.** ovillo **4.** bala **5.** yema **6.** huevo, cojón **7.** baile
ballet *noun.* ballet
balloon *noun.* globo
ballot *noun.* **1.** votación **2.** papeleta para votar
ban *noun.* prohibición

ban *verb.* prohibir

banana *noun.* plátano, banana

band *noun.* 1. banda, tira, faja 2. franja, lista 3. orquesta, conjunto 4. grupo, pandilla

band *verb.* unirse, asociarse

bang *noun.* 1. estallido, detonación, portazo 2. golpe

bang *verb.* 1. estallar, detonar 2. dar un portazo 3. golpear, golpearse, darse

bank *noun.* 1. banco 2. ribera, terraplén, loma 3. hilera

bank *verb.* 1. depositar/ingresar en el banco 2. amontonar, apilar 3. ladearse

banker *noun.* banquero

bankrupt *noun.* quebrado, insolvente
—**to be bankrupt** estar en quiebra
—**to go bankrupt** quebrar, declararse en quiebra

bankrupt *adj.* en bancarrota, en quiebra

bankruptcy *noun.* quiebra, insolvencia

banner *noun.* bandera, estandarte

bar *prep.* excepto, con excepción de

bar *noun.* 1. barra, tableta, pastilla 2. barrote, reja 3. tranca 4. palanca 5. bar, cantina 6. mostrador 7. compás 8. impedimento, obstáculo, prohibición 9. abogacía 10. tribunal

bar *verb.* 1. atrancar 2. obstruir, impedir 3. excluir, prohibir

bare *verb.* descubrir, desnudar, revelar

bare *adj.* 1. desnudo, descubierto, descalzo 2. vacío 3. mero, escaso, escueto 4. pelado, árido 5. raído

barely *adv.* apenas

bargain *noun.* 1. ganga 2. trato, negocio

bargain *verb.* 1. regatear 2. negociar

barge *noun.* barcaza, gabarra

barge *verb.* 1. moverse torpemente 2. chocar contra, dar contra
—**barge in** irrumpir con rudeza

bark *noun.* 1. corteza 2. ladrido

bark *verb.* 1. ladrar 2. berrear, vociferar 3. raspar

barley *noun.* cebada

barn *noun.* 1. granero 2. cuadra, establo

baron *noun.* 1. barón 2. magnate

barracks *noun.* cuartel

barrel *noun.* 1. barril, tonel 2. cañón

barricade *noun.* barricada

barricade *verb.* obstruir, cerrar con barricadas

barrier *noun.* 1. barrera 2. obstáculo

barrow *noun.* 1. carretilla, carretón 2. túmulo

base *noun.* 1. base, sède 2. pie

base *adj.* bajo, vil

base (on) *verb.* basar, fundar

baseball *noun.* béisbol

basement *noun.* sótano

bash *noun.* porrazo

bash (in) *verb.* golpear, aporrear

basic *adj.* 1. básico, fundamental 2. elemental

basically *adv.* básicamente, en el fondo

basin *noun.* 1. palangana, jofaina 2. cuenco, bol 3. cuenca 4. dársena

basis *noun.* base, cimientos, piedra angular

basket *noun.* cesta, capazo

basketball *noun.* baloncesto

bass *noun.* 1. bajo 2. róbalo, lubina

bastard *noun. adj.* bastardo

bat *noun.* 1. bate, pala, raqueta 2. murciélago

bat *verb.* apalear, golpear

batch *noun.* hornada, lote

bath *noun.* 1. bañera, tina 2. baño

bathe *verb.* bañar, bañarse, lavar

bathroom *noun.* servicio, baño

battalion *noun.* batallón

batter *noun.* mezcla para rebozar

batter *verb.* moler a palos, apalear

battered *adj.* maltratado

battery *noun.* 1. pila, batería 2. criadero 3. retahíla

battle *noun.* batalla

battle *verb.* luchar, batirse, combatir

battlefield *noun.* campo de batalla

bay *noun.* 1. bahía 2. crujía

bay *verb.* aullar

bay *adj.* bayo

bay (tree) *noun.* laurel

BC *abbr.* a.C., antes de Cristo

be *verb.* 1. estar + gerundio 2. ir a + infinitivo 3. ser 4. deber + infinitivo, tener como propósito
—**be about** estar a punto de

BE, B.E. *abbr.* licenciatura en Ingeniería

beach *noun.* playa

beach *verb.* varar

beam *noun.* **1.** viga **2.** rayo **3.** manga

beam *verb.* **1.** sonreír de oreja a oreja **2.** emitir

bean *noun.* **1.** frijol, judía, habichuela **2.** grano

bear *noun.* oso

bear *verb.* **1.** aguantar, soportar **2.** dar a luz, parir **3.** cargar, llevar **4.** llevar **5.** desviarse

beard *noun.* **1.** barba **2.** arista

bearing *noun.* **1.** comportamiento, modales **2.** cojinete

beast *noun.* **1.** bestia **2.** bruto, animal **3.** descortés, rudo

beat *noun.* **1.** compás, ritmo **2.** ronda

beat *verb.* **1.** batir, golpear, percutir **2.** derrotar **3.** latir, pulsar **4.** marcar, llevar (el compás)

beaten *adj.* **1.** derrotado **2.** batido

beating *noun.* golpeo, latido, batida

beautiful *adj.* bello, hermoso, guapo, lindo

beautifully *adv.* **1.** bellamente **2.** maravillosamente, perfectamente

beauty *noun.* **1.** belleza **2.** monada, guapada

because *conj.* porque

beck *noun.* **to be at someone's beck and call** estar a disposición de

become *verb.* **1.** volverse, ponerse, convertirse **2.** hacerse, llegar a ser **3.** sentar bien, quedar bien
—**become of** ser de

becoming *adj.* favorecedor

bed *noun.* **1.** cama **2.** lecho **3.** macizo, cuadro **4.** capa, estrato

B.Ed. *abbr.* licenciatura en Magisterio

bedroom *noun.* dormitorio

bedside *noun.* cabecera

bee *noun.* **1.** abeja **2.** trabajo colectivo

beef *noun.* carne de vaca

beer *noun.* cerveza

before *conj.* antes (de que)

before *prep.* **1.** antes (de) **2.** delante (de), antes (de/que) **3.** antes que

before *adv.* antes

beforehand *adv.* de antemano, previamente

beg *verb.* **1.** pedir **2.** suplicar

begin *verb.* empezar, comenzar

beginner *noun.* principiante

behalf *noun.* favor, beneficio
—**on behalf of (someone)** en nombre de, en beneficio de

behave *verb.* comportarse

behavior *noun.* comportamiento

behind *prep.* **1.** detrás de **2.** tras **3.** con

behind *noun.* trasero

behind *adv.* **1.** detrás, atrás **2.** atrasado, retrasado

being *noun.* **1.** existencia **2.** ser

Belgian *noun. adj.* belga

Belgium *noun.* Bélgica

belief(s) *noun.* **1.** confianza, fe **2.** creencia

believe *verb.* creer (que), pensar (que)

bell *noun.* **1.** campana **2.** timbre, campanilla

belly *noun.* **1.** barriga, vientre **2.** estómago

belong (to) *verb.* **1.** pertenecer, ser propiedad (de) **2.** ser miembro, formar parte de
—**belong with** ir con

beloved *noun.* amado, amor

beloved *adj.* adorado

below *prep.* debajo (de), por debajo

below *adv.* de abajo

belt *noun.* **1.** cinturón **2.** correa **3.** faja

belt *verb.* **1.** ponerse el cinturón **2.** dar una paliza

bench *noun.* **1.** banco **2.** banco de trabajo, banco de carpintero

bend *noun.* curva

bend *verb.* **1.** doblar(se), curvar **2.** doblegar, compeler, obligar

beneath *adv.* de abajo

beneath *prep.* bajo, debajo (de)

beneficial *adj.* beneficioso

beneficiary *noun.* beneficiario

benefit *noun.* beneficio

benefit from, benefit by *verb.* **1.** aprovecharse, beneficiarse **2.** hacer bien (a)

benign *adj.* benigno, bondadoso

bent *noun.* inclinación

berry *noun.* baya
beside *prep.* junto a, al lado de
besides *prep.* aparte de, además de
besides *adv.* además
besiege *verb.* sitiar, asediar
  —**besiege with** asediar
best *verb.* vencer
best *adj. pron. adv.* mejor
bet *noun.* apuesta
bet (on) *verb.* apostar
betray *verb.* **1.** traicionar **2.** revelar, delatar
betrayal *noun.* traición
better *verb.* mejorar
better *adj.* **1.** mejor **2.** mejorado, recuperado **3.** más vale
better *adv.* mejor
between *prep.* entre
beware (of) *verb.* tener cuidado
beyond *prep.* **1.** más allá de **2.** fuera de **3.** más de, algo más de
bias *noun.* **1.** parcialidad, prejuicio **2.** desviación
bias *verb.* influenciar, predisponer
Bible *noun.* Biblia
biblical, Biblical *adj.* bíblico
bicycle, cycle *verb.* ir/montar en bicicleta
bicycle *noun.* bicicleta
bid *noun.* **1.** oferta **2.** intento/tentativa (de conseguir)
bid *verb.* **1.** pujar, hacer una oferta **2.** pedir, rogar **3.** dar
  —**bid for** hacer una oferta de adquisición, hacer una licitación
bidding *noun.* puja, oferta, orden
big *adj.* **1.** grande **2.** importante
bike *noun.* bicicleta
bilateral *adj.* bilateral
bile *noun.* **1.** bilis, hiel **2.** mal genio
bill *noun.* **1.** pico **2.** factura, cuenta **3.** billete **4.** cartel
bill *verb.* facturar
billion *noun. adj.* millardo, mil millones
bin *noun.* cubo
binary *adj.* binario
bind *verb.* **1.** atar, amarrar **2.** encuadernar
binding *noun.* encuadernación

binoculars *noun plural.* prismáticos
biography *noun.* biografía
biological *adj.* biológico
biology *noun.* biología
bird *noun.* ave, pájaro
birth *noun.* **1.** nacimiento **2.** comienzo, inicio
birthday *noun.* cumpleaños
bishop *noun.* **1.** obispo **2.** alfil
bit *noun.* freno, bocado
bit *noun.* **1.** pedazo, trozo **2.** pequeño **3.** un poco, un poquito, un segundo **4.** bit, unidad de información
bitch *noun.* **1.** perra, loba, zorra **2.** zorra, lagarta
bite *noun.* **1.** mordisco, picadura **2.** picada
bite *verb.* morder, picar
biting *adj.* **1.** penetrante, cortante **2.** mordaz, incisivo
bitter *adj.* **1.** amargo **2.** hostil, encarnizado **3.** helado
bitterly *adv.* amargamente
bitterness *noun.* amargura
bizarre *adj.* extraño, raro
black *noun.* negro
black *verb.* ennegrecer, volver negro
black *adj.* **1.** negro **2.** oscuro **3.** solo
bladder *noun.* vejiga
blade *noun.* **1.** hoja, filo **2.** brizna **3.** pala
blame *noun.* culpa, responsabilidad
blame *verb.* **1.** culpar, responsabilizar, echar la culpa **2.** reprochar (algo a alguien)
bland *adj.* **1.** de sabor imperceptible, insípido **2.** inexpresivo, insulso, desabrido
blank *noun.* **1.** espacio en blanco **2.** cartucho sin bala
blank *adj.* **1.** en blanco **2.** vacío, inexpresivo **3.** liso
blanket *noun.* **1.** manta **2.** manto
blanket *verb.* cubrir de, envolver en
blanket *adj.* general
blast *noun.* **1.** ráfaga **2.** toque **3.** explosión, detonación
blast *verb.* volar
  —**blast out** emitir a todo volumen, prorrumpir

blaze *noun.* **1.** llamarada, incendio, resplandor **2.** arranque, explosión **3.** fulgor

blaze *verb.* fulgurar, resplandecer
—**blaze a trail** abrir (el) camino, dar los primeros pasos

blazing *adj.* **1.** fulgurante, resplandeciente **2.** violento, encolerizado

bleak *adj.* **1.** inhóspito, desolado **2.** desesperanzador, nada prometedor

bleed *verb.* sangrar

bleeding *adj.* sangrante, sangriento

blend *noun.* mezcla

blend *verb.* mezclar, combinar

bless *verb.* bendecir

blessed *adj.* bendito

blessing *noun.* **1.** bendición **2.** merced, gracia

blind *noun.* **1.** persiana **2.** pretexto, evasiva, subterfugio

blind *verb.* cegar, volver ciego

blind *adj.* **1.** ciego **2.** sin visibilidad **3.** para invidentes/ciegos
—**blind to** ciego, que no se da cuenta de algo

blink *noun.* parpadeo, pestañeo

blink *verb.* parpadear, pestañear

bloc *noun.* bloque

block *noun.* **1.** bloque **2.** zoquete, tarugo **3.** barrera, control policial **4.** manzana

block *verb.* bloquear, obstruir

blockade *noun.* bloqueo

blockade *verb.* bloquear

blocked *adj.* taponado, congestionado

blonde *noun.* rubia

blood *noun.* sangre
—**blood pressure** presión sanguínea, tensión arterial

bloody *adj.* **1.** ensangrentado **2.** que sangra **3.** sangriento **4.** maldito

bloom *noun.* **1.** flor **2.** floración, en flor **3.** estar en la flor de (la vida), lozanía, frescura

bloom *verb.* florecer

blossom *noun.* flor

blossom *verb.* **1.** florecer **2.** transformarse en, convertirse en

blouse *noun.* blusa

blow *noun.* **1.** golpe **2.** golpe (duro)

blow *verb.* **1.** soplar **2.** llevarse **3.** salir volando/despedido, moverse con el aire, viento, etc. **4.** tocar, hacer sonar

blue *noun.* **1.** azul **2.** cielo **3.** mar

blue *adj.* **1.** azul **2.** triste, deprimido, melancólico

blunt *verb.* desafilar, despuntar

blunt *adj.* **1.** desafilado, despuntado **2.** abrupto, brusco, directo

blur *noun.* imagen borrosa/imprecisa

blur *verb.* empañar, hacer borroso

board *noun.* **1.** tabla, plancha **2.** tablón, tablero **3.** pensión, comida **4.** consejo, junta

board *verb.* **1.** subir a **2.** alojarse en, estar hospedado en

boast *noun.* objeto de orgullo, alarde

boast *verb.* vanagloriarse, jactarse de, fanfarronear

boat *noun.* **1.** barco, barca, embarcación, navío, buque **2.** salsera

boat *verb.* navegar

bob *verb.* fluctuar

bodily *adj.* corporal, físico

bodily *adv.* en peso

body *noun.* **1.** cuerpo **2.** cadáver **3.** parte principal **4.** conjunto, colección

bodyguard *noun.* guardaespaldas

bog *noun.* pantano, ciénaga

boil *noun.* furúnculo

boil *verb.* hervir, bullir, cocer

boiler *noun.* caldera

bold *adj.* **1.** valiente, audaz, atrevido **2.** nítido, vivo **3.** en negrita

bolster *noun.* travesaño

bolster (up) *verb.* apoyar, reforzar

bolt *noun.* **1.** pestillo **2.** tornillo **3.** rayo **4.** rollo

bolt *verb.* **1.** echar el cerrojo **2.** engullir, tragar **3.** escaparse, huir

bomb *noun.* bomba
—**A-bomb** bomba atómica

bomb *verb.* **1.** bombardear **2.** fracasar

bomber *noun.* **1.** bombardero **2.** persona que pone bombas

bond *noun.* **1.** lazo **2.** vínculo

bone *noun.* hueso

bone *verb.* deshuesar

bonus noun. 1. plus, prima 2. regalo, bendición

book noun. 1. cuaderno 2. libro 3. talonario

book verb. reservar

booking noun. registro, reserva

booklet noun. folleto

bookstore noun. librería

boom noun. 1. boom, auge 2. estruendo

boom verb. 1. estar en auge 2. retumbar

boomerang noun. bumerang

boost noun. impulso

boost verb. aumentar

boot noun. 1. bota 2. maletero

boot verb. dar una patada

booth noun. 1. puesto 2. cabina

border noun. 1. borde 2. frontera 3. arriate

border on verb. lindar con

bore noun. 1. pelmazo, pesado 2. taladro

bore verb. 1. perforar 2. aburrir

boredom noun. aburrimiento

boring adj. aburrido

borough noun. municipio

borrow verb. tomar prestado

borrower noun. persona que toma algo prestado

borrowing noun. préstamo

boss noun. jefe

boss (about/around) verb. mandar

bossy adj. mandón

botanist noun. botánico, botanista

both adj. pron. ambos

bother noun. 1. molestia 2. incomodidad

bother verb. 1. molestar 2. molestarse

bottle noun. botella

bottle verb. embotellar

bottleneck noun. 1. atasco, embotellamiento 2. obstáculo

bottom noun. 1. fondo 2. trasero, culo

bough noun. rama

bounce noun. 1. bote 2. vitalidad

bounce verb. 1. hacer botar, botar, rebotar 2. ser rechazado por el banco

bound noun. 1. salto 2. límite

bound verb. dar saltos, brincar

boundary noun. 1. frontera 2. punto

bounty noun. 1. generosidad 2. recompensa

bout noun. 1. ataque (of illness), tanda 2. asalto, lucha, combate

bow noun. 1. arco 2. lazo 3. proa 4. inclinación, reverencia

bow verb. inclinar(se), hacer una reverencia

—bow to ceder ante, transigir con

bowed (down) adj. inclinado, arqueado

bowel noun. 1. intestino 2. (**bowels**) entrañas

bowl noun. 1. bol, cuenco 2. cazoleta

—bowls bolos

bowl verb. 1. jugar a los bolos 2. lanzar la pelota 3. dejar fuera de juego

bowler noun. lanzador, jugador de bochas

bowling noun. bolos, boliche

box noun. 1. caja, cajón, estuche 2. palco 3. cachete

—box office noun. taquilla

box verb. 1. boxear 2. poner/meter en una caja

boxer noun. boxeador

boxing noun. boxeo

boy noun. niño, muchacho, chico

boycott noun. boicot

boycott verb. boicotear

boyfriend noun. novio, amigo

brace noun. refuerzo, abrazadera

brace verb. fortalecer, prepararse

bracket noun. soporte, repisa

bracket verb. agrupar, poner juntos

brain noun. 1. cerebro 2. seso

brake noun. freno

brake verb. frenar

branch noun. 1. rama, ramo, sección 2. sucursal

branch verb. ramificarse

brand noun. marca

brand verb. 1. marcar 2. grabar, registrar 3. estigmatizar

brand-new adj. completamente nuevo, recién comprado

brandy noun. coñac

brass noun. 1. latón 2. metales (music)

brave noun. guerrero indio

brave verb. desafiar, arrostrar

brave adj. valiente, valeroso

Brazil noun. Brasil

Brazilian noun. adj. brasileño

breach noun. 1. infracción, violación 2. brecha

breach verb. abrir brecha en

bread noun. pan

breadth noun. 1. anchura, ancho 2. amplitud

break noun. 1. rotura, ruptura, abertura 2. interrupción, pausa 3. cambio 4. oportunidad

break verb. 1. romper, quebrar 2. quebrantar, infringir 3. batir 4. interrumpir 5. comunicar, hacer público 6. mudar, cambiar 7. amortiguar 8. estallar, desatarse

—**break away/off** partir, romper

—**break down** 1. frustrarse, malograrse 2. averiarse

—**break into** abrir, forzar

—**break out** 1. aparecer, salir 2. estallar 3. escaparse

—**break up** 1. romperse 2. separarse 3. disolverse

—**break through** penetrar, abrirse paso

breakdown noun. 1. colapso, crisis nerviosa 2. avería

breakfast noun. desayuno

breakfast verb. desayunar, tomar el desayuno

breakthrough noun. avance, descubrimiento

breast noun. 1. pecho, seno 2. pechuga

breast verb. 1. enfrentarse a, arrostrar 2. subir a la cumbre, coronar la cumbre

breath noun. aliento, respiración

breathe verb. 1. respirar 2. soplar, revelar

breathless adj. sin aliento, sofocado

bred adj. 1. educado, criado 2. de raza

breed noun. raza

breed verb. criar, reproducirse

breeding noun. educación, modales

breeze noun. brisa

brew verb. 1. elaborar bebidas fermentadas 2. preparar 3. avecinarse, prepararse

brewery noun. cervecería

bribe noun. soborno

bribe verb. sobornar

brick noun. ladrillo

bride noun. novia

bridge noun. 1. puente 2. puente de mando 3. caballete

bridge verb. 1. construir/tender un puente 2. llenar, salvar

brief noun. informe, expediente

brief verb. dar instrucciones

brief adj. breve

briefing noun. instrucciones, sesión informativa

briefly adv. brevemente, en pocas palabras

brigade noun. 1. brigada 2. cuerpo

bright adj. 1. luminoso, resplandeciente, brillante 2. vivo 3. radiante, alegre 4. inteligente

brightly adv. 1. brillantemente 2. alegremente 3. inteligentemente

brilliant adj. 1. brillante, luminoso 2. genial, sobresaliente

brilliantly adv. 1. brillantemente 2. genialmente

bring verb. 1. traer, llevar, conducir 2. ocasionar, producir, dar, causar

—**bring about** ocasionar, provocar

—**bring out** sacar, publicar

—**bring up** 1. mencionar, sacar a relucir 2. criar

brink noun. borde

brisk adj. activo, movido, rápido

Britain, Great Britain noun. Gran Bretaña

British noun. adj. británico

Briton noun. británico

broad adj. 1. ancho, amplio, extenso 2. general

broadcast noun. retransmisión, emisión

broadcast verb. 1. retransmitir, radiar 2. difundir, divulgar

broadcaster noun. locutor, presentador

broadcasting noun. retransmisión, emisión

broadly adv. en general

brochure noun. folleto

broke adj. arruinado, sin blanca

broken adj. 1. roto, quebrado, fracturado 2. estropeado, averiado 3. entrecortado, interrumpido 4. deshecho, quebrantado, destrozado

broker noun. agente, corredor de bolsa

bronze noun. adj. 1. bronce 2. color bronce 3. objeto de bronce

brook noun. arroyo

brook verb. aguantar, tolerar, permitir

brother noun. 1. hermano 2. compañero

brow noun. 1. ceja 2. frente 3. cresta

brown noun. marrón, color café, castaño

brown verb. broncearse, ponerse moreno

brown adj. 1. marrón, color café, castaño 2. moreno, bronceado

bruise noun. moretón, cardenal, magulladura

bruise verb. amorotonar, magullar

brush noun. 1. cepillo 2. hopo 3. roce

brush verb. 1. cepillar, barrer 2. rozar

brutal adj. brutal

bubble noun. burbuja

bubble verb. burbujear

buck noun. macho

buck verb. corcovear

bucket noun. cubo

bud noun. brote, capullo

bud verb. brotar

budget noun. presupuesto

budget verb. hacer un presupuesto
—**budget for** asignar

buffer noun. amortiguador

buffet noun. 1. bar, cantina 2. bufé 3. bofetada

buffet verb. 1. golpear 2. zarandear

buffet adj. bufé

bug noun. 1. chinche 2. bicho 3. microbio 4. micrófono oculto 5. entusiasta

bug verb. 1. pinchar, intervenir 2. molestar

buggy noun. cochecito de bebé

build noun. constitución, complexión

build verb. construir, edificar

builder noun. constructor

building noun. 1. construcción 2. edificio

built-in adj. incorporado

bulb noun. 1. bulbo 2. bombilla, bombillo 3. cubeta

bulk noun. 1. la mayor parte, la mayoría 2. masa, bulto

bulk adj. a granel, en grandes cantidades

bull noun. 1. toro 2. macho 3. diana

bullet noun. bala

bulletin noun. boletín

bully noun. matón

bully verb. intimidar

bum noun. vago

bum adj. inútil, que no vale

bump noun. 1. golpe 2. chichón, bollo, bache

bump verb. dar(se) un golpe, chocar

bumper noun. parachoques

bunch noun. manojo, ramo, racimo

bunch verb. apretujarse

bundle noun. fardo

bundle verb. 1. empaquetar, liar 2. echar, despachar

bungalow noun. bungalow

bunker noun. búnker

burden noun. carga, peso

burden verb. cargar (con)

bureau noun. 1. cómoda 2. agencia, departamento

bureaucracy noun. burocracia

bureaucratic adj. burocrático

burglary noun. robo

burial noun. entierro

Burma noun. Birmania

Burmese noun. adj. birmano

burn noun. quemadura

burn verb. 1. quemar, incendiar 2. arder

burst noun. 1. reventón 2. estallido

burst verb. 1. reventar, estallar 2. desbordarse, salirse de madre
—**burst in/into/through** entrar precipitadamente

bury verb. 1. enterrar, sepultar 2. esconder

bus noun. autobús, camión (México)

bus verb. transportar en autobús

bush noun. arbusto

business noun. 1. negocio, empresa 2. asunto

businessman noun. hombre de negocios, empresario
bust noun. 1. busto 2. pecho
bust verb. (slang) 1. agarrar, trincar 2. destrozar
bust adj. estropeado
busy adj. 1. ocupado 2. concurrido
busy (with) verb. ocuparse
but conj. pero
but prep. excepto, menos, salvo
butcher noun. carnicero
butcher verb. 1. matar 2. masacrar
butter noun. mantequilla

butter verb. untar con mantequilla
butterfly noun. mariposa
button noun. botón
button verb. abrocharse
buy verb. comprar
buzz noun. zumbido
buzz verb. zumbar
by.prep. 1. al lado de, junto a 2. por, en 3. por delante 4. para 5. de 6. según
by adv. 1. al lado, cerca 2. por ahí 3. aparte
bypass noun. variante, circunvalación
bypass verb. evitar

C

C abbr. centígrado
cab noun. 1. taxi 2. cabina
cabbage noun. repollo
cabin noun. 1. cabaña 2. camarote 3. cabina
cabinet noun. 1. armario, vitrina 2. gabinete
cable noun. 1. cable 2. cablegrama, telegrama
—**cable television** televisión por cable
cable verb. cablegrafiar
cage noun. jaula
cage verb. enjaular
cake noun. 1. torta, pastel, tarta 2. pastilla
cake verb. formar costra
calcium noun. calcio
calculate verb. calcular
calculation noun. cálculo
calculator noun. calculadora
calendar noun. calendario, agenda
calf noun. 1. pantorrilla, canilla 2. ternero 3. piel de becerro
call noun. 1. llamada, grito 2. canto 3. visita 4. demanda 5. necesidad, motivo
call verb. 1. llamar, gritar 2. convocar 3. hacer una visita 4. marcar, declarar
—**call for** requerir, necesitar
—**call off** cancelar, suspender
caller noun. visita, visitante

calling noun. vocación, profesión
calm noun. calma, tranquilidad
calm verb. calmar, tranquilizar
calm adj. en calma, tranquilo, apacible
calmly adv. con calma, tranquilamente
calorie noun. caloría
camera noun. cámara fotográfica, cámara
camp noun. 1. campamento 2. bando, facción
camp verb. acampar
campaign noun. campaña
campaign verb. hacer campaña
campaigner noun. defensor, militante
campus noun. recinto universitario, campus
can noun. lata, bote
can verb. 1. poder 2. saber 3. enlatar
Canada noun. Canadá
Canadian noun. adj. canadiense
canal noun. 1. canal 2. tubo
cancel verb. 1. cancelar 2. matasellar 3. anular
cancellation, cancelation noun. cancelación, anulación
cancer noun. cáncer
candidate noun. candidato, aspirante
candle noun. vela
candy noun. caramelo, golosina, dulce
cane noun. 1. caña 2. bastón

cane verb. castigar con la palmeta
cannon noun. cañón
cannon verb. chocar
canon noun. 1. canon 2. canónigo 3. obra básica, clásico, canon
canopy noun. dosel
canteen noun. 1. cantina, comedor 2. cantimplora
canvas noun. adj. 1. lona 2. lienzo
cap noun. 1. gorra, gorro, cofia 2. capuchón, tapón, tapa
capability noun. capacidad
capable (of) adj. 1. capaz 2. competente
capacity noun. 1. capacidad 2. calidad
cape noun. 1. capa 2. cabo
capital noun. 1. capital 2. mayúscula 3. principal 4. capitel
capital adj. 1. capital 2. principal 3. mayúsculo
capitalism noun. capitalismo
capitalist noun. capitalista
capitalistic adj. capitalista
captain noun. capitán
captain verb. capitanear
caption noun. leyenda
captive noun. adj. cautivo
capture noun. captura, apresamiento
capture verb. 1. capturar 2. cautivar
car noun. 1. carro, automóvil, coche 2. vagón, coche-restaurante
caravan noun. caravana
carbohydrate noun. carbohidrato
carbon noun. carbono
carbon dioxide noun. dióxido de carbono
card noun. 1. carta 2. cartulina 3. tarjeta
—**cards** cartas
cardboard noun. adj. cartón
cardinal noun. cardenal
cardinal adj. cardinal
care noun. 1. cuidado, atención 2. preocupación 3. tratamiento
care verb. 1. preocuparse 2. querer, gustar
career noun. carrera
career verb. ir a toda velocidad
careful adj. 1. cuidadoso 2. minucioso
carefully adv. cuidadosamente

careless adj. descuidado, despreocupado
cargo noun. carga, cargamento
carnival noun. carnaval
carol noun. villancico
carp noun. carpa
carpet noun. alfombra
carpet verb. cubrir con una alfombra
carriage noun. 1. coche, carruaje 2. carro 3. porte
carrot noun. zanahoria
carry verb. 1. llevar, transportar 2. transmitir, ser portador 3. soportar 4. comportar, conllevar 5. aprobar 6. comportarse
cart noun. carro, carrito, cochecito
cart verb. llevar, acarrear
cartoon noun. 1. tira cómica, viñeta, caricatura 2. dibujos animados
carve verb. 1. tallar, grabar, esculpir 2. cortar, trinchar
carving noun. escultura, talla
case noun. 1. caso 2. proceso 3. razón 4. maleta, estuche, funda, vitrina
cash noun. 1. efectivo, metálico 2. dinero
cash verb. 1. cobrar, 2. pagar, hacer efectivo
casino noun. casino
casket noun. 1. ataúd 2. estuche, cofre
cassette noun. casete
cast noun. 1. molde 2. escayola, yeso 3. reparto 4. desecho, excremento
cast verb. 1. lanzar, arrojar, tirar 2. moldear, fundir 3. dar el papel 4. mudar (skin) 5. dar (el voto)
caste noun. casta
castle noun. 1. castillo 2. torre (chess)
casual adj. 1. despreocupado, rápido 2. informal 3. ocasional, fortuito 4. eventual
casually adv. casualmente
casualty noun. baja, víctima
cat noun. 1. gato 2. felino
catalog noun. catálogo
catalog verb. catalogar
catastrophe noun. catástrofe
catch noun. 1. presa, captura, redada 2. pestillo 3. trampa

catch *verb.* **1.** agarrar, coger, asir, tomar **2.** pillar, sorprender, pescar **3.** contagiarse de, contraer **4.** engancharse **5.** dar con, darse con **6.** oír, entender, captar **7.** prender (fuego)
catching *adj.* contagioso
category *noun.* categoría
cater *verb.* **1.** proveer comida, abastecer **2.** atender las necesidades
catering *noun.* servicio de comidas
cathedral *noun.* catedral
catholic *adj.* amplio, variado
Catholic *noun. adj.* católico
cattle *noun plural.* ganado (vacuno)
cause *noun.* **1.** causa **2.** razón, motivo
cause *verb.* causar
caution *noun.* **1.** cautela, precaución, prudencia **2.** advertencia
caution *verb.* advertir
cautious *adj.* cauteloso, prudente, cauto
cautiously *adv.* prudentemente
cavalry *noun.* caballería
cave *noun.* cueva, caverna
CD *noun.* CD, disco compacto
cease *verb.* cesar
ceasefire *noun.* alto al fuego
ceiling *noun.* techo
celebrate *verb.* celebrar
celebrated *adj.* célebre, famoso
celebration *noun.* fiesta, festejo, celebración
celebrity *noun.* celebridad
cell *noun.* **1.** celda **2.** célula
cellar *noun.* sótano, bodega
cellular *adj.* celular
Celsius *adj.* Celsius
Celtic *adj.* celta
cement *noun.* **1.** cemento **2.** adhesivo **3.** empaste
cement *verb.* cementar
cemetery *noun.* cementerio
censorship *noun.* censura
census *noun.* censo
cent *noun.* céntimo
centennial *noun. adj.* centenario
center *noun.* centro
center *verb.* centrar
  —**center on** concentrarse en

centigrade *adj.* centígrado
centimeter *noun.* centímetro
central *adj.* **1.** central **2.** principal
centrally *adv.* céntrico
century *noun.* siglo
ceramic *adj.* de cerámica
ceramics *noun.* cerámica
cereal *noun.* cereal
cerebral *adj.* cerebral
ceremony *noun.* ceremonia
certain *adj.* **1.** cierto **2.** seguro
certainly *interj.* por supuesto
certainly *adv.* **1.** seguro **2.** desde luego, por supuesto
certainty *noun.* certeza, seguridad
certificate *noun.* certificado
chain *noun.* cadena
chain *verb.* encadenar, atar
chair *noun.* **1.** silla **2.** presidencia **3.** cátedra
chair *verb.* presidir
chairman, chairperson, chairwoman *noun.* presidente
chalk *noun.* **1.** creta, roca caliza **2.** tiza
challenge *noun.* **1.** desafío, reto **2.** recusación
challenge *verb.* **1.** desafiar, retar **2.** recusar **3.** poner en duda, cuestionar
challenger *noun.* desafiador, contrincante, aspirante
challenging *adj.* desafiante, estimulante, que supone un reto
chamber *noun.* **1.** cuarto **2.** cámara
champagne *noun.* champán, champaña
champion *noun.* **1.** campeón **2.** defensor
champion *verb.* defender
championship *noun.* **1.** campeonato **2.** defensa
chance *noun.* **1.** azar, casualidad **2.** oportunidad, ocasión **3.** posibilidad **4.** riesgo
  —**by chance** por casualidad
chance *verb.* **1.** arriesgar **2.** suceder algo por casualidad
  —**chance on/upon** encontrarse por casualidad, dar con
chance *adj.* fortuito, casual
chancellor *noun.* **1.** canciller **2.** rector

change *noun.* **1.** cambio **2.** transformación, modificación

change *verb.* **1.** cambiar, cambiarse **2.** transformar, modificar

channel *noun.* **1.** canal, cauce, vía **2.** estrecho

channel *verb.* canalizar, dirigir, encauzar

chant *noun.* **1.** canto litúrgico, cántico **2.** eslogan, consigna

chant *verb.* **1.** cantar **2.** corear, gritar

chaos *noun.* caos

chap *noun.* tío, tipo

chapel *noun.* capilla

chapter *noun.* capítulo

character *noun.* **1.** carácter, naturaleza, personalidad **2.** personaje **3.** tipo, figura

characteristic *noun.* característica

characteristic *adj.* característico

characterize *verb.* **1.** caracterizar **2.** describir

charcoal *noun.* carbón vegetal

charge *noun.* **1.** precio, honorarios **2.** acusación **3.** carga **4.** cargo, cuidado

charge *verb.* **1.** cobrar **2.** poner en la cuenta **3.** cargar contra, atacar **4.** irrumpir **5.** cargar **6.** encargar
—**charge with** acusar

charitable *adj.* **1.** caritativo, comprensivo **2.** benéfico

charity *noun.* **1.** caridad **2.** institución benéfica

charm *noun.* **1.** encanto, simpatía **2.** hechizo **3.** amuleto

charm *verb.* encantar

charming *adj.* encantador

chart *noun.* **1.** carta, mapa **2.** gráfico

chart *verb.* **1.** trazar **2.** representar en un gráfico

charter *noun.* fuero, estatutos

charter *verb.* fletar, alquilar

charter *adj.* chárter

chase *noun.* **1.** persecución **2.** caza

chase *verb.* **1.** perseguir **2.** cazar
—**chase away/off** ahuyentar

chat *noun.* charla, conversación

chat *verb.* charlar, conversar

cheap *adj.* **1.** barato **2.** ordinario

cheat *noun.* **1.** tramposo **2.** trampa, estafa

cheat *verb.* engañar, estafar, timar

check *noun.* **1.** control, revisión, inspección **2.** impedimento, freno **3.** jaque **4.** cuadro **5.** ticket, comprobante, papeleta, resguardo **6.** cuenta, nota **7.** cheque

check *verb.* **1.** controlar, revisar **2.** comprobar, verificar **3.** detener, frenar **4.** marcar, señalar **5.** chequear, facturar

checked *adj.* a cuadros

cheek *noun.* **1.** mejilla **2.** descaro, frescura

cheer *noun.* **1.** ovación, aclamación **2.** alegría, regocijo

cheer *verb.* vitorear, aclamar

cheerful *adj.* alegre, animado, risueño

cheerfully *adv.* alegremente

cheese *noun.* queso

chef *noun.* cocinero, jefe de cocina

chemical *noun.* producto químico

chemical *adj.* químico

chemist *noun.* químico

chemistry *noun.* química

chicken *noun.* **1.** pollo **2.** cobarde

child *noun.* **1.** niño/a **2.** hijo/a

Chile *noun.* Chile

Chilean *noun. adj.* chileno

chili *noun.* chile

chill *noun.* **1.** frío **2.** resfriado

chill *verb.* enfriar

chill *adj.* frío

chimney *noun.* chimenea

chin *noun.* barbilla, mentón

china *noun.* porcelana

China *noun.* China

Chinese *noun. adj.* chino

chip *noun.* **1.** astilla, lasca **2.** desportilladura **3.** ficha **4.** chip

chip *verb.* desportillar, desconchar

chocolate *noun.* chocolate

chocolate *adj.* de chocolate

choice *noun.* elección

choir *noun.* coro

choke *noun.* estrangulador

choke *verb.* **1.** ahogar, asfixiar **2.** ahogarse, asfixiarse **3.** obstruir, atascar

choose *verb.* **1.** escoger, elegir, seleccionar **2.** optar

chop *noun.* **1.** golpe cortante **2.** chuleta

chop (up) *verb.* cortar, picar
chops *noun plural.* mandíbulas
chord *noun.* acorde
chorus *noun.* 1. coro 2. estribillo
chorus *verb.* corear
Christ *noun.* Cristo
Christian *noun. adj.* cristiano
Christianity *noun.* cristianismo
Christmas *noun.* Navidad
chronic *adj.* crónico
chronicle *noun.* crónica
chronicle *verb.* hacer la crónica de
chuck *verb.* tirar, botar
chunk *noun.* trozo
church *noun.* iglesia
churchyard *noun.* cementerio
CIA *abbr.* CIA
cider *noun.* sidra
cigarette *noun.* cigarro
cinema *noun.* cine
circle *noun.* círculo
circle *verb.* 1. rodear, cercar 2. trazar un círculo
circuit *noun.* 1. recorrido 2. circuito 3. vuelta
circular *noun. adj.* circular
circulate *verb.* 1. circular 2. hacer circular
circulation *noun.* circulación
circumstance *noun.* circunstancia
circus *noun.* circo
citizen *noun.* ciudadano, vecino, habitante
citizenship *noun.* ciudadanía
city *noun.* ciudad
civic *adj.* 1. municipal, cívico 2. cortés, educado 3. civil
civil servant *noun.* funcionario
civilian *noun.* civil
civilization *noun.* civilización
claim *noun.* 1. reivindicación, demanda, reclamación 2. derecho 3. afirmación
claim *verb.* 1. reivindicar, reclamar 2. afirmar 3. requerir, exigir
clamp *noun.* 1. grapa, clip 2. abrazadera
clamp *verb.* sujetar
clan *noun.* clan
clarification *noun.* aclaración
clarify *verb.* aclarar

clarity *noun.* claridad, lucidez
clash *noun.* 1. choque, conflicto 2. ruido, estruendo, fragor 3. coincidencia
clash *verb.* 1. oponerse, chocar, enfrentarse 2. sonar, entrechocar 3. coincidir 4. desentonar
class *noun.* 1. clase 2. categoría
class *verb.* clasificar
classic *noun. adj.* clásico
classical *adj.* clásico
classification *noun.* clasificación
classified *adj.* secreto, confidencial
classify *verb.* clasificar
clause *noun.* 1. oración 2. cláusula
clay *noun.* arcilla, barro
clean *verb.* limpiar, lavar
clean *adj.* 1. limpio 2. nuevo, en blanco 3. puro 4. neto, bien definido, preciso
clean *adv.* por completo
cleaner *noun.* 1. encargado de la limpieza 2. producto de limpieza
cleanse *verb.* limpiar
clear *verb.* 1. quitar, despejar, aclarar, desalojar 2. despejarse 3. salvar
—**clear (of)** absolver
clear *adj.* 1. claro 2. despejado, sereno 3. transparente, nítido 4. tranquilo 5. explícito 6. amplio, absoluto
—**clear (of)** libre (de)
clearance *noun.* 1. despeje 2. margen 3. autorización
clearing *noun.* claro
clearly *adv.* 1. claramente, con claridad 2. obviamente
clergy *noun.* clero
clerical *adj.* 1. clerical, eclesiástico 2. de oficina, administrativo
clerk *noun.* 1. oficinista, empleado 2. funcionario, secretario 3. dependiente, vendedor
clever *adj.* 1. inteligente 2. hábil 3. ingenioso
click *noun.* clic
click *verb.* hacer clic
client *noun.* cliente
cliff *noun.* acantilado
climate *noun.* 1. clima 2. ambiente
climax *noun.* clímax

climb *noun.* escalada, ascenso, subida
climb *verb.* escalar, ascender, subir
climber *noun.* **1.** alpinista, andinista, escalador **2.** enredadera **3.** arribista, trepador
clinch *verb.* cerrar, firmar
cling (to) *verb.* pegarse, agarrarse, aferrarse
clinic *noun.* clínica
clinical *adj.* clínico
clip *noun.* **1.** clip, pasador, grapa, horquilla **2.** tijeretada **3.** cachete, golpe **4.** secuencia
clip *verb.* **1.** sujetar **2.** cortar, podar **3.** dar un cachete
cloak *noun.* capa, manto
cloak *verb.* ocultar
clock *noun.* reloj
clock *verb.* cronometrar
  —clock in/out/on/off fichar, entrar a trabajar
close *noun.* fin, final
close *verb.* **1.** cerrar **2.** terminar, concluir
close *adj.* **1.** cercano, próximo **2.** íntimo **3.** parecido, igualado **4.** detallado **5.** ajustado, reñido **6.** bochornoso **7.** tacaño **8.** reservado
close *adv.* cerca (de)
closely *adv.* **1.** detenidamente **2.** de cerca **3.** con atención
closet *noun.* armario
closure *noun.* **1.** cierre **2.** clausura
cloth *noun.* tela, paño
clothes *noun plural.* **1.** ropa, vestidos **2.** ropa de cama
clothespin *noun.* pinza
clothing *noun.* ropa, vestimenta
cloud *noun.* nube
cloud *verb.* **1.** nublar, enturbiar, empañar **2.** nublarse
club *noun.* **1.** porra **2.** palo **3.** club
  —clubs *noun plural.* tréboles, palos
club *verb.* aporrear
clue *noun.* pista, indicio
cluster *noun.* grupo, racimo
cluster *verb.* agruparse
clutch *noun.* **1.** dominio **2.** embrague, cloche
clutch (at) *verb.* **1.** agarrar, asir **2.** apretar

  —clutch (at) *verb.* tratar de agarrar, aferrarse a
cm *abbr.* centímetro
Co *abbr.* compañía
coach *noun.* **1.** entrenador **2.** profesor particular **3.** vagón, coche
coach *verb.* preparar, entrenar, enseñar
coal *noun.* carbón
coalition *noun.* coalición
coarse *adj.* **1.** áspero, grueso **2.** grosero, ordinario
coast *noun.* costa, litoral
coast *verb.* ir en punto muerto
coastal *adj.* costero
coat *noun.* **1.** abrigo **2.** chaqueta, saco **3.** pelo, pelaje **4.** capa
coat *verb.* cubrir, revestir, bañar
cocaine *noun.* cocaína
cock *noun.* **1.** gallo, macho **2.** grifo, espita **3.** polla, pinga
cock *verb.* **1.** erguir, enderezar **2.** amartillar **3.** ladear
cockpit *noun.* cabina
cocktail *noun.* **1.** cóctel **2.** macedonia
cocoa *noun.* **1.** cacao **2.** chocolate
code *noun.* código
code *verb.* codificar
coffee *noun.* café
coherent *adj.* coherente
coin *noun.* moneda
coin *verb.* **1.** acuñar **2.** inventar
coincide *verb.* coincidir
coincidence *noun.* coincidencia
coke *noun.* coque
cold *noun.* **1.** frío **2.** resfriado, resfrío, catarro
cold *adj.* frío
cold war *noun.* guerra fría
coldly *adv.* fríamente
collaboration *noun.* colaboración
collapse *noun.* **1.** caída, derrumbamiento, hundimiento **2.** colapso **3.** fracaso
collapse *verb.* **1.** caer, derrumbarse, hundirse **2.** sufrir un colapso **3.** fracasar **4.** plegarse
collar *noun.* **1.** cuello **2.** collar **3.** collarín
collar *verb.* **1.** abordar, acorralar **2.** agarrar, apropiarse
colleague *noun.* colega

collect *verb.* **1.** reunir, juntar **2.** coleccionar **3.** cobrar, recaudar **4.** recoger

collected *adj.* **1.** completo **2.** seguro de sí

collection *noun.* **1.** recogida, recaudación, colecta **2.** colección

collective *noun. adj.* colectivo

collector *noun.* **1.** recaudador **2.** coleccionista

college *noun.* facultad

collision *noun.* choque, colisión

Colombia *noun.* Colombia

Colombian *noun. adj.* colombiano

colon *noun.* **1.** dos puntos **2.** colon

colonel *noun.* coronel

colonial *adj.* colonial

colony *noun.* colonia

color *noun.* color
—**colors** bandera, enseña

color *verb.* **1.** pintar, colorear **2.** ponerse colorado, ruborizarse

color *adj.* en color

colored *noun.* persona de color, negro

colored *adj.* **1.** de colores **2.** de color, negro

colorful *adj.* lleno de color, vistoso

coloring *noun.* **1.** colorante **2.** tez

column *noun.* **1.** columna **2.** fila

columnist *noun.* columnista

comb *noun.* peine

comb *verb.* **1.** peinar **2.** peinarse

combat *noun.* combate

combat *verb.* combatir

combination *noun.* combinación

combine *noun.* asociación

combine *verb.* combinar, compaginar

come *interj.* ¡vamos!

come *verb.* **1.** venir **2.** llegar **3.** acercarse
—**come across** toparse con
—**come back 1.** volver **2.** contestar, replicar
—**come in** entrar
—**come out** aparecer, salir
—**come through** pasar por
—**come to terms** llegar a un acuerdo

comeback *noun.* vuelta, retorno

comedian *noun.* cómico

comedy *noun.* comedia

comet *noun.* cometa

comfort *noun.* **1.** comodidad, confort **2.** consuelo

comfort *verb.* consolar, confortar

comfortable *adj.* **1.** cómodo **2.** tranquilo, relajado **3.** amplio, suficiente, holgado

comfortably *adv.* **1.** cómodamente **2.** sin problemas, holgadamente

comforting *adj.* reconfortante

comic *noun. adj.* cómico

command *noun.* **1.** orden **2.** control, mando

command *verb.* **1.** ordenar, mandar **2.** estar al mando de **3.** imponer, infundir, inspirar

commander *noun.* **1.** comandante **2.** capitán de fragata

commanding *adj.* **1.** dominante **2.** autoritario

commemorate *verb.* conmemorar

commence *verb.* comenzar

comment *noun.* comentario

comment on *verb.* comentar

commentary *noun.* comentario, crítica

commentator *noun.* comentarista

commerce *noun.* comercio

commercial *noun.* anuncio

commercial *adj.* **1.** comercial **2.** rentable

commission *noun.* **1.** comisión **2.** encargo **3.** nombramiento

commission *verb.* **1.** encargar **2.** nombrar

commissioner *noun.* comisario

commit *verb.* **1.** cometer **2.** enviar, destinar, internar **3.** comprometer, comprometerse

commitment *noun.* compromiso, obligación

committed *adj.* comprometido, entregado

committee *noun.* comité, comisión

commodity *noun.* producto, artículo, mercadería, mercancía

common *noun.* tierras comunales

common *adj.* **1.** común, corriente **2.** público **3.** ordinario, vulgar
—**common sense** *noun.* sentido común

commonplace *adj.* común, corriente

commonwealth *noun.* commonwealth

communal *adj.* comunal, común
communicate *verb.* **1.** comunicar **2.** comunicarse
communication *noun.* **1.** comunicación **2.** comunicado, mensaje
—**communications** *noun plural.* comunicaciones
communicative *adj.* comunicativo
communion *noun.* comunión
communism *noun.* comunismo
communist *noun. adj.* comunista
community *noun.* comunidad
commute *verb.* **1.** desplazarse diariamente al lugar de trabajo **2.** conmutar
compact *noun.* **1.** pacto, acuerdo, convenio **2.** polvera
compact *adj.* compacto, sólido
—**compact disc** disco compacto, compact disc
companion *noun.* **1.** compañero **2.** guía, manual
company *noun.* **1.** compañía **2.** visita **3.** compañía
comparable *adj.* comparable
comparative *adj.* **1.** relativo **2.** comparativo
comparatively *adv.* relativamente
compare *verb.* **1.** comparar **2.** compararse
comparison *noun.* comparación
compartment *noun.* compartimiento
compass *noun.* **1.** brújula **2.** compás **3.** alcance
compassion *noun.* compasión
compatibility *noun.* compatibilidad
compatible *adj.* compatible
compel *verb.* obligar, forzar
compensate *verb.* **1.** indemnizar, compensar **2.** recompensar
compensation *noun.* indemnización
compete *verb.* competir
competence *noun.* competencia
competent *adj.* competente
competition *noun.* **1.** competición **2.** competencia
competitive *adj.* competitivo
competitor *noun.* competidor
compile *verb.* compilar
complain *verb.* quejarse
complaint *noun.* **1.** queja, reclamación,

denuncia **2.** enfermedad, achaque, dolencia
complement *noun.* complemento
complement *verb.* complementar
complementary *adj.* complementario
complete *verb.* **1.** completar **2.** terminar, acabar, cumplir **3.** rellenar
complete *adj.* **1.** completo, entero **2.** acabado
completely *adv.* completamente, totalmente
completion *noun.* finalización
complex *noun. adj.* complejo
complexity *noun.* complejidad
compliance *noun.* conformidad
complicate *verb.* complicar
complicated *adj.* complicado
complication *noun.* complicación
compliment *noun.* cumplido, halago
compliment *verb.* elogiar
comply *verb.* obedecer
component *noun.* pieza, componente
compose *verb.* **1.** componer **2.** calmarse, serenarse
composed *adj.* sereno, tranquilo
composer *noun.* compositor
composition *noun.* **1.** composición **2.** redacción
compost *noun.* abono orgánico
compound *noun.* **1.** compuesto **2.** recinto
compound *adj.* compuesto, múltiple
comprehension *noun.* comprensión
comprehensive *adj.* completo, exhaustivo, integral
compression *noun.* compresión
comprise *verb.* comprender, incluir, constar de
compromise *noun.* acuerdo mutuo, término medio
compulsory *adj.* obligatorio
compute *verb.* computar, calcular
computer *noun.* ordenador
computerize *verb.* computarizar, informatizar
con *noun.* estafa, timo
con *verb.* estafar, timar
conceal *verb.* ocultar, disimular
concede *verb.* **1.** reconocer, admitir **2.** ceder, darse por vencido

conceive *verb*. **1.** concebir **2.** entender

concentrate *verb*. **1.** concentrar **2.** concentrarse

concentrated *adj*. concentrado

concentration *noun*. concentración

concept *noun*. concepto

conception *noun*. **1.** concepción **2.** noción

concern *noun*. **1.** asunto **2.** preocupación, inquietud **3.** interés **4.** negocio

concern *verb*. concernir, afectar

—**concern about/for** preocuparse

—**concern in/with** interesarse en

concerning *prep*. con respecto a, en lo que se refiere a

concert *noun*. concierto

concession *noun*. concesión

conclude *verb*. **1.** concluir, terminar **2.** concertar, pactar, cerrar

conclusion *noun*. conclusión

concrete *noun*. hormigón

concrete *verb*. revestir de hormigón

concrete *adj*. **1.** concreto **2.** de hormigón

condemn *verb*. **1.** condenar **2.** declarar en ruina (a building)

condemnation *noun*. condena

condition *noun*. **1.** condición **2.** estado

condition *verb*. **1.** condicionar **2.** acondicionar

conditional *adj*. condicional

conduct *noun*. comportamiento, conducta

conduct *verb*. **1.** conducir, guiar **2.** dirigir, llevar **3.** comportarse

conductor *noun*. **1.** conductor **2.** director de orquesta **3.** revisor

confederation *noun*. confederación

confer (with) *verb*. consultar (con), deliberar

—**confer on** conceder, conferir

conference *noun*. conferencia

confess *verb*. confesar

confession *noun*. confesión

confidence *noun*. **1.** confianza **2.** seguridad

confident *adj*. seguro, seguro de sí mismo

confidential *adj*. **1.** confidencial **2.** de confianza

confidentiality *noun*. confidencialidad, reserva

confine *verb*. **1.** confinar, recluir **2.** limitar

confined (to) *adj*. **1.** recluido **2.** reducido, limitado

confirm *verb*. confirmar

confirmation *noun*. confirmación

confirmed *adj*. **1.** empedernido, inveterado **2.** confirmado

conflict *noun*. conflicto

conflict *verb*. estar en conflicto, entrar en desacuerdo

conform *verb*. ajustarse, someterse

—**conform to** adaptarse a

conformity *noun*. conformidad

confront *verb*. hacer frente, plantar cara

confrontation *noun*. enfrentamiento

confuse *verb*. **1.** confundir, desconcertar **2.** complicar, enredar

confused *adj*. confuso, desconcertado

confusion *noun*. confusión

congratulate (on) *verb*. felicitar

congregation *noun*. **1.** congregación, feligresía **2.** reunión

congress *noun*. congreso

congressional *adj*. del Congreso

congressman *noun*. congresista

conjunction *noun*. conjunción

connect *verb*. **1.** conectar, unir, enlazar **2.** asociar

connection *noun*. **1.** conexión, enlace **2.** relación **3.** contacto

—**connections** parientes

conquer *verb*. conquistar, vencer

conquest *noun*. conquista

conscience *noun*. conciencia

conscious *adj*. consciente

consciously *adv*. conscientemente

consciousness *noun*. conciencia

consecutive *adj*. consecutivo

consensus *noun*. consenso

consent *noun*. consentimiento

consent *verb*. consentir

consequence *noun*. **1.** consecuencia **2.** importancia, trascendencia

consequently *adv*. por consiguiente

conservation *noun*. conservación

conservatism *noun*. conservadurismo

conservative *adj.* conservador
consider *verb.* **1.** considerar **2.** tener en cuenta
considerable *adj.* considerable
considerably *adv.* considerablemente
consideration *noun.* **1.** consideración **2.** factor
considering *prep.* teniendo en cuenta, en vista de
consist (of) *verb.* componerse de, constar de
consistency *noun.* **1.** coherencia **2.** consistencia
consistent (with) *adj.* **1.** consecuente **2.** coherente
consistently *adv.* **1.** consecuentemente **2.** sistemáticamente
consolation *noun.* **1.** consolación **2.** consuelo
console *verb.* consolar
consolidate *verb.* consolidar
consolidation *noun.* consolidación
consortium *noun.* consorcio
conspicuous *adj.* llamativo, manifiesto
conspiracy *noun.* conspiración
constant *adj.* **1.** constante, continuo **2.** leal, fiel
constantly *adv.* constantemente
constituency *noun.* distrito electoral
constituent *noun.* **1.** componente **2.** elector
constituent *adj.* constitutivo, integrante
constitute *verb.* constituir
constitution *noun.* constitución
constitutional *adj.* constitucional
construct *verb.* construir
construction *noun.* construcción
constructive *adj.* constructivo
consult *verb.* **1.** consultar **2.** pasar visita
consultant *noun.* asesor, consultor
consultation *noun.* consulta
consume *verb.* consumir
consumer *noun.* consumidor
consumption *noun.* consumo, gasto
contact *noun.* contacto
contact *verb.* contactar
contain *verb.* **1.** contener **2.** contenerse
container *noun.* **1.** recipiente, envase **2.** contenedor

contaminate *verb.* contaminar
contamination *noun.* contaminación
contemplate *verb.* **1.** considerar **2.** contemplar
contemporary *noun.* contemporáneo
contemporary *adj.* contemporáneo
contempt *noun.* desprecio, desdén
contend (with) *verb.* competir
—**contend that** sostener, afirmar
contender *noun.* contendiente
content *noun.* **1.** contenido **2.** satisfacción
—**contents** índice
content *verb.* contentar, satisfacer
content *adj.* satisfecho, contento
contention *noun.* **1.** opinión, argumento **2.** discusión, disensión
contentious *adj.* contencioso, polémico
contest *noun.* competencia, competición, concurso, combate
context *noun.* contexto
continent *noun.* continente
continent *adj.* continente
continental *adj.* continental
contingency *noun.* contingencia
contingent *noun.* contingente
continual *adj.* continuo, constante
continually *adv.* continuamente, constantemente
continuation *noun.* continuación
continue *verb.* continuar, seguir
continuity *noun.* continuidad
continuous *adj.* continuo
continuously *adv.* continuamente
contract *noun.* contrato
contract *verb.* **1.** contraer **2.** contraerse **3.** contratar **4.** comprometerse por contrato
contraction *noun.* contracción
contractor *noun.* contratista
contradiction *noun.* contradicción
contradictory *adj.* contradictorio
contrary *noun.* contrario
contrary *adj.* **1.** contrario **2.** terco, obstinado
contrast *noun.* contraste
contrast *verb.* **1.** contrastar **2.** comparar
contribute *verb.* **1.** contribuir, aportar **2.** escribir, colaborar

contribution *noun.* **1.** contribución, aporte **2.** colaboración, artículo **3.** intervención, aportación

contributor *noun.* **1.** contribuyente **2.** contribuidor **3.** colaborador

control *noun.* **1.** control, dominio **2.** restricción
—**controls** mandos

control *verb.* controlar, dominar, dirigir, regular

controller *noun.* controlador, interventor

controversial *adj.* controvertido, polémico

controversy *noun.* controversia

convene *verb.* **1.** convocar **2.** reunirse

convenience *noun.* comodidad, conveniencia, ventaja

convenient *adj.* **1.** conveniente, cómodo, idóneo **2.** bien situado, accesible

conveniently *adv.* convenientemente, oportunamente

convent *noun.* convento

convention *noun.* **1.** convención **2.** congreso

conventional *adj.* convencional, tradicional

convergence *noun.* convergencia

conversation *noun.* conversación

conversely *adv.* a la inversa

conversion *noun.* **1.** conversión **2.** reforma, remodelación

convert *noun.* converso

convert *verb.* **1.** convertir **2.** convertirse **3.** reformar

convertible *noun.* descapotable

convertible *adj.* convertible

convey *verb.* **1.** transportar, llevar, conducir **2.** comunicar, expresar **3.** traspasar

convict *noun.* presidiario

convict *verb.* declarar culpable, condenar

conviction *noun.* **1.** condena **2.** antecedentes penales **3.** convicción

convince *verb.* convencer

convincing *adj.* convincente

convoy *noun.* convoy

cook *noun.* cocinero

cook *verb.* cocinar, guisar, preparar (la comida), cocer

cookery *noun.* cocina

cookie *noun.* galleta

cool *noun.* frescor

cool *verb.* **1.** refrescar, enfriar **2.** calmarse

cool *adj.* **1.** fresco **2.** tranquilo, sereno **3.** frío, seco **4.** enrollado, macanudo **5.** guay, ¡qué pasada!

coop *noun.* gallinero

co-operation *noun.* cooperación, colaboración

co-operative *adj.* colaborador, servicial, cooperativo

coordinate *verb.* coordinar

coordination *noun.* coordinación

cop *noun.* policía

cope *verb.* arreglárselas, poder con, solucionar

copper *noun.* cobre

copper *adj.* de cobre, cobrizo

copy *noun.* **1.** copia **2.** ejemplar, número **3.** manuscrito

copy *verb.* copiar, imitar

copyright *noun.* derechos de autor

coral *noun.* coral

coral *adj.* de coral

cord *noun.* **1.** cuerda, cordón, cable **2.** pana
—**spinal cord** médula espinal

core *noun.* **1.** corazón (fruit) **2.** centro, núcleo **3.** esencia, meollo

core *verb.* deshuesar

cork *noun.* **1.** corcho **2.** tapón

cork *verb.* tapar con corcho, taponar

corn *noun.* **1.** maíz **2.** callo

corner *noun.* **1.** esquina, ángulo **2.** rincón **3.** córner, saque de esquina

corner *verb.* **1.** arrinconar, acorralar **2.** tomar las curvas

coronary *noun.* infarto de miocardio, trombosis coronaria

coronary *adj.* coronario

coronation *noun.* coronación

coroner *noun.* juez de instrucción

corporal *noun.* cabo

corporal *adj.* corporal

corporate *adj.* conjunto, colectivo

corporation *noun.* **1.** corporación **2.** sociedad limitada

corps *noun.* cuerpo
corpse *noun.* cadáver
correct *verb.* corregir
correct *adj.* correcto
—**to be correct** tener razón
correction *noun.* corrección
correctly *adv.* correctamente
correspond *verb.* mantener correspondencia, escribir
—**correspond to** equivaler a
—**correspond with** corresponder con
correspondence *noun.* correspondencia, conexión
correspondent *noun.* 1. correspondiente 2. corresponsal
corresponding *adj.* correspondiente
corridor *noun.* pasillo, corredor
corrupt *verb.* corromper
corrupt *adj.* 1. corrupto, corrompido 2. degenerado, depravado
corruption *noun.* 1. corrupción 2. degeneración
cosmetic *noun. adj.* cosmético
cost *noun.* precio, coste
—**costs** costas
cost *verb.* 1. costar, valer 2. calcular el coste de
costly *adj.* costoso, suntuoso
costume *noun.* 1. traje 2. disfraz
cot *noun.* cama plegable
cottage *noun.* casa de campo
cotton *noun.* algodón
couch *noun.* sofá, camilla, diván
couch *verb.* expresar
cough *noun.* tos
cough *verb.* toser
could *verb.* 1. pasado del verbo **can** 2. (se usa para expresar posibilidad)
council *noun.* 1. consejo, junta, concilio 2. ayuntamiento
councilor *noun.* concejal, miembro de junta
counsel *noun.* 1. consejo 2. abogado
counsel *verb.* aconsejar
counselor *noun.* consejero, asesor
count *noun.* 1. recuento, cuenta, escrutinio 2. cargo, acusación 3. conde
count *verb.* 1. contar 2. considerar
counter *noun.* 1. ficha 2. mostrador, ventanilla 3. contador

counter *verb.* responder a, contestar a
counter to *adv.* al contrario de, al revés de
counterpart *noun.* homólogo, equivalente
countess *noun.* condesa
countless *adj.* incontable, innumerable
country *noun.* 1. país, pueblo 2. patria 3. terreno, tierra
—**the country** el campo
countryside *noun.* campo, zona rural
county *noun.* 1. comarca 2. condado
coup *noun.* 1. logro, éxito 2. golpe de estado
couple *noun.* 1. par 2. pareja, matrimonio
couple *verb.* acoplar, enganchar, unir
coupon *noun.* 1. cupón 2. boleto
courage *noun.* coraje, valor
courier *noun.* 1. guía de turismo 2. mensajero
course *noun.* 1. curso 2. plato 3. campo, pista 4. camino, modo de proceder 5. rumbo, órbita, ruta
—**of course** por supuesto, cómo no
court *noun.* 1. juzgado, corte, tribunal 2. pista, cancha 3. palacio 4. patio
court *verb.* 1. cortejar 2. buscar 3. exponerse a
courtesy *noun.* cortesía
courtyard *noun.* patio
cousin *noun.* primo
covenant *noun.* pacto, convenio, alianza
cover *noun.* 1. tapa, tapadera, funda 2. cubrecama, colcha 3. portada 4. refugio, cobijo, cobertura, amparo
cover *verb.* 1. cubrir, tapar, forrar 2. recorrer 3. abarcar, tratar 4. suplir
coverage *noun.* 1. cobertura 2. reportaje
covering *noun.* capa, envoltura
cow *noun.* 1. vaca 2. hembra (de algunos animales)
cow *verb.* intimidar
cowboy *noun.* vaquero, cowboy
coxswain, cox *noun.* timonel
cozy *adj.* acogedor, íntimo
crack *noun.* 1. grieta, hendidura, raja 2.

rendija **3.** chasquido, crujido **4.** golpe **5.** chiste, chanza **6.** crack, cocaína dura

crack *verb.* **1.** rajarse, resquebrajarse **2.** abrir, romper, cascar **3.** crujir, chasquear **4.** contar chistes **5.** forzar **6.** resolver, descifrar **7.** rendirse, sucumbir, caer

crack *adj.* de primera

crackdown *noun.* medidas enérgicas, campaña

cracked *adj.* **1.** rajado, agrietado **2.** tarado, chiflado

craft *noun.* **1.** arte, oficio **2.** artesanía **3.** barco, embarcación **4.** astucia, destreza

craftsman *noun.* artesano

crafty *adj.* astuto

crane *noun.* grúa

crane *verb.* estirar (el cuello)

crash *noun.* **1.** estruendo, estrépito **2.** colisión, choque, accidente **3.** quiebra

crash *verb.* **1.** caer con estrépito **2.** chocar contra, colisionar **3.** estrellar(se) **4.** derrumbarse, sufrir una crisis **5.** abrirse camino/paso

crash *adj.* acelerado, intensivo

crawl *noun.* **1.** paso lento **2.** crol

crawl *verb.* **1.** avanzar lentamente **2.** gatear, arrastrarse **3.** estar plagado

crazy *adj.* **1.** loco **2.** entusiasmado

cream *noun.* **1.** nata **2.** crema

  —the cream of society la flor y nata de la sociedad

cream *verb.* batir

create *verb.* **1.** crear **2.** nombrar

creation *noun.* creación

creative *adj.* creativo

creativity *noun.* creatividad

creator *noun.* creador

creature *noun.* criatura

credibility *noun.* credibilidad

credible *adj.* creíble

credit *noun.* **1.** crédito **2.** solvencia **3.** saldo **4.** mérito **5.** reputación, honor

  —credit card tarjeta de crédito

  —credits títulos de crédito

credit *verb.* **1.** abonar, ingresar **2.** creer

  —credit with atribuir

creditor *noun.* acreedor

creed *noun.* credo

creep *noun.* adulador, lameculos

creep *verb.* **1.** deslizarse, arrastrarse **2.** avanzar sigilosamente **3.** trepar

crescent *noun.* media luna

crescent *adj.* en forma de media luna, creciente

crest *noun.* **1.** cresta **2.** pico, cumbre **3.** penacho **4.** blasón

crew *noun.* **1.** tripulación, dotación **2.** pandilla, equipo

crew *verb.* tripular

cricket *noun.* **1.** cricket **2.** grillo

crime *noun.* **1.** crimen, delito **2.** delincuencia

criminal *noun.* criminal, delincuente

criminal *adj.* criminal, delictivo

cripple *noun.* inválido, lisiado, mutilado

cripple *verb.* **1.** lisiar, mutilar **2.** inutilizar, paralizar

crisis *noun.* crisis, momento crítico

crisp *adj.* **1.** crujiente **2.** fresco **3.** seco, tajante

criterion *noun.* criterio

critic *noun.* crítico

critical *adj.* **1.** crítico **2.** grave, serio

critically *adv.* **1.** críticamente, de manera crítica **2.** gravemente, de gravedad

criticism *noun.* crítica

criticize *verb.* **1.** criticar **2.** censurar

crook *noun.* **1.** cayado, báculo **2.** criminal, maleante **3.** pliegue del codo

crook *verb.* doblar, encorvar

crop *noun.* **1.** cultivo, cosecha **2.** fusta, látigo **3.** corte a lo garçon **4.** buche

crop *verb.* **1.** pacer **2.** cortar

cross *noun.* **1.** cruz **2.** cruce, híbrido

cross *verb.* **1.** cruzar, atravesar **2.** cruzarse **3.** santiguarse **4.** contrariar

cross *adj.* enojado, enfadado

cross-country *adj.* a campo traviesa

crossing *noun.* **1.** cruce **2.** travesía

crossroads *noun singular.* encrucijada, cruce

cross-section *noun.* **1.** corte transversal **2.** sección representativa, muestra

crouch *verb.* **1.** agacharse, ponerse en cuclillas **2.** agazaparse

crowd *noun.* **1.** multitud, muchedumbre **2.** público, espectadores **3.** gente

crowd *verb*. **1.** agolparse, congregarse, reunirse **2.** atestar, llenar

crowded *adj*. **1.** abarrotado, atestado, concurrido **2.** lleno de actividad

crown *noun*. **1.** corona **2.** coronilla **3.** cima, cumbre

crown *verb*. **1.** coronar **2.** rematar **3.** poner una corona **4.** golpear en la cabeza, dar un coscorrón

—crown prince príncipe heredero

crucial *adj*. crucial

crude *adj*. **1.** crudo **2.** rudimentario, primitivo

cruel *adj*. cruel

cruelty *noun*. crueldad

cruise *noun*. crucero

cruise *verb*. **1.** hacer un crucero **2.** navegar, volar

crumble *verb*. desmigajar, desmenuzar

crunch *noun*. crujido

crunch *verb*. mascar, ronzar, hacer crujir

crusade *noun*. **1.** cruzada **2.** campaña, cruzada

crusade *verb*. hacer una campaña en pro/contra de algo

crush *noun*. aglomeración, multitud

crush *verb*. **1.** aplastar **2.** estrujar, exprimir, prensar **3.** doblegar, aniquilar, eliminar **4.** comprimir

crust *noun*. **1.** corteza, cuscurro, costra **2.** pasta

cry *noun*. **1.** grito **2.** lloro **3.** aullido

cry *verb*. **1.** llorar **2.** (*often with out*) gritar

crystal *noun*. cristal

Cuba *noun*. Cuba

Cuban *noun. adj*. cubano

cube *noun*. cubo, dado, terrón

cube *verb*. **1.** elevar al cubo **2.** cortar en dados

cue *noun*. **1.** pie (theater) **2.** taco

cuisine *noun*. cocina

cult *noun*. culto

cultivate *verb*. cultivar

cultivated *adj*. **1.** cultivado **2.** culto, refinado

cultivation *noun*. cultivo

cultural *adj*. cultural

culture *noun*. **1.** cultura **2.** cultivo

cumulative *adj*. acumulativo

cup *noun*. **1.** taza **2.** copa

cup *verb*. **1.** ahuecar las manos, hacer bocina con las manos **2.** envolver con las manos

curator *noun*. **1.** conservador **2.** director de museo

curb *noun*. **1.** freno **2.** bordillo

curb *verb*. refrenar, dominar

cure *noun*. cura, remedio

cure *verb*. **1.** curar, remediar **2.** salar

curfew *noun*. toque de queda

curiosity *noun*. curiosidad

curious *adj*. curioso

curiously *adv*. curiosamente

curl *noun*. **1.** rizo **2.** bucle

curl *verb*. **1.** rizar **2.** rizarse

curly *adj*. rizado

currency *noun*. moneda

current *noun*. **1.** corriente **2.** aceptación

current *adj*. actual

currently *adv*. actualmente

curriculum *noun*. currículum, plan de estudios

curry *noun*. curry

curry *verb*. **1.** almohazar **2.** guisar con curry

curse *noun*. **1.** maldición **2.** desgracia

curse *verb*. **1.** maldecir **2.** blasfemar, decir palabrotas

curtain *noun*. cortina

curve *noun*. curva

curve *verb*. torcerse, hacer curva

curved *adj*. curvo, encorvado

cushion *noun*. **1.** cojín **2.** amortiguador

cushion *verb*. suavizar, amortiguar

custody *noun*. **1.** custodia **2.** detención

custom *noun*. **1.** costumbre **2.** clientela

—customs (derechos de) aduana

customary *adj*. habitual, de costumbre

customer *noun*. cliente

cut *noun*. **1.** corte **2.** trozo **3.** tajada **4.** rebaja, reducción

cut *verb*. **1.** cortar **2.** recortar, acortar **3.** suprimir **4.** tallar, abrir **5.** ignorar, hacer como si no viera

—cut down reducir

cute *adj*. **1.** lindo, precioso **2.** listo, vivo

cutting *noun*. **1.** esqueje **2.** recorte

cutting *adj*. cortante

cutting board *noun*. tabla de cortar

cycle *noun*. **1.** bicicleta **2.** ciclo
cycle *verb*. ir en bicicleta
cylinder *noun*. cilindro
cynical *adj*. cínico

Cypriot *noun*. chipriota
Cypriot *adj*. chipriota
Cyprus *noun*. Chipre
Czech *noun*. *adj*. checo

D

dad, daddy *noun*. papá
daily *noun*. diario, periódico
daily *adj*. diario
daily *adv*. diariamente, a diario
dairy *noun*. **1.** lechería **2.** vaquería
daisy *noun*. margarita
dam *noun*. **1.** dique **2.** presa, embalse
dam (up) *verb*. embalsar
damage *noun*. daño
  —damages daños y perjuicios
damage *verb*. dañar, averiar, perjudicar
damaged *adj*. deteriorado, averiado
dame *noun*. **1.** dama **2.** mujer, tía (informal)
damn *noun*. nada de nada
damn *verb*. **1.** maldecir **2.** condenar
damn *interj*. ¡vaya!, ¡carajo!, ¡mecachis!
damned *adj*. **1.** puñetero, fregado **2.** maldito, condenado
damp *noun*. humedad
damp *adj*. húmedo
dance *noun*. baile, danza
dance *verb*. bailar, danzar
dancer *noun*. bailarín, bailaor
dancing *noun*. danza
dandelion *noun*. diente de león
danger *noun*. peligro
dangerous *adj*. peligroso, arriesgado
Danish *noun*. *adj*. danés
dare *noun*. desafío, reto
dare *verb*. **1.** atreverse, osar **2.** desafiar
daring *noun*. osadía, audacia
daring *adj*. arriesgado, audaz
dark *noun*. oscuridad
dark *adj*. **1.** oscuro **2.** misterioso, siniestro
darkness *noun*. oscuridad
darling *noun*. **1.** cariño **2.** encanto
darling *adj*. **1.** querido **2.** encantador

dart *noun*. **1.** dardo, flecha **2.** movimiento rápido
dart *verb*. lanzarse, precipitarse
dash *noun*. **1.** carrera **2.** poco, gota, chorrito, pizca **3.** raya, guión **4.** viveza
dash *verb*. **1.** correr, ir de prisa **2.** estrellar **3.** frustrar, defraudar
data *noun plural*. datos
database *noun*. base de datos
date *noun*. **1.** fecha **2.** compromiso, cita **3.** pareja, acompañante **4.** dátil
date *verb*. **1.** fechar, datar, poner fecha **2.** pasar de moda **3.** salir con
  —date from/back datar de, remontarse a
dated *adj*. pasado de moda, anticuado
daughter *noun*. hija
daunting *adj*. desalentador, abrumador
dawn *noun*. **1.** alba, amanecer **2.** albores
dawn *verb*. amanecer
day *noun*. **1.** día **2.** jornada
  —in those days en aquellos tiempos
daylight *noun*. **1.** luz (del día) **2.** amanecer
daytime *noun*. día
dazzling *adj*. deslumbrante
dead *adj*. **1.** muerto **2.** marchito, seco **3.** desconectado, cortado, apagado **4.** total, completo
dead *adv*. completamente
deadline *noun*. fecha límite
deadly *adj*. **1.** mortal, mortífero **2.** absoluto **3.** aburridísimo
deadly *adv*. completamente
deaf *adj*. sordo
deal *noun*. **1.** trato, acuerdo, pacto **2.** ganga **3.** reparto
deal *verb*. **1.** comerciar **2.** repartir

dealer *noun.* **1.** comerciante, tratante **2.** repartidor

dealings *noun plural.* relaciones, transacciones, negocios

dean *noun.* **1.** deán **2.** decano

dear *noun.* encanto, amor, cariño
—**dear, dear!/oh dear!** ¡Dios mío!, ¡ay, Dios!, ¡vaya!

dear *adj.* **1.** querido **2.** encantador

death *noun.* muerte

debate *noun.* debate

debate *verb.* **1.** debatir **2.** considerar, dar vueltas

debris *noun.* **1.** escombros **2.** restos

debt *noun.* deuda

debtor *noun.* deudor

debut, début *noun.* presentación, debut

Dec. *abbr.* diciembre

decade *noun.* década

decadence *noun.* decadencia

decay *noun.* **1.** descomposición, caries, deterioro **2.** decadencia

decay *verb.* **1.** pudrirse, cariarse, deteriorarse **2.** decaer

deceased *adj.* difunto

December *noun.* diciembre

decent *adj.* **1.** decente **2.** amable **3.** adecuado

deception *noun.* engaño, falsedad

decide *verb.* **1.** decidir **2.** decidirse

decision *noun.* decisión

decisive *adj.* **1.** decisivo **2.** decidido

deck *noun.* **1.** cubierta **2.** piso **3.** baraja

declaration *noun.* declaración

declare *verb.* **1.** declarar, anunciar **2.** pronunciarse

decline *noun.* **1.** descenso, disminución **2.** decadencia, declive

decline *verb.* **1.** declinar, rehusar, rechazar **2.** disminuir **3.** decaer

decorate *verb.* **1.** decorar **2.** pintar, empapelar **3.** condecorar

decoration *noun.* decoración

decorative *adj.* decorativo

decrease *noun.* disminución, bajada, reducción

decrease *verb.* disminuir, reducir

decree *noun.* **1.** decreto **2.** sentencia

decree *verb.* decretar

dedicate *verb.* **1.** dedicar, consagrar **2.** inaugurar oficialmente

dedicated *adj.* dedicado, entregado

dedication *noun.* **1.** dedicación, consagración **2.** dedicatoria

deduct *verb.* restar, descontar, deducir

deduction *noun.* deducción, descuento, desgravación

deed *noun.* **1.** acción, hecho, hazaña **2.** escritura

deem *verb.* juzgar, considerar

deep *adj.* **1.** profundo **2.** hondo **3.** absorbido **4.** profundo, intenso **5.** grave

deep *adv.* profundamente

deepen *verb.* **1.** profundizar **2.** aumentar, agudizarse, intensificarse

deeply *adv.* profundamente

deer *noun.* ciervo, venado

defeat *noun.* derrota, fracaso, rechazo

defeat *verb.* vencer, derrotar, frustrar

defect *noun.* defecto

defect *verb.* desertar

defective *adj.* defectuoso

defend *verb.* defender

defendant *noun.* demandado, acusado

defender *noun.* defensor

defense *noun.* defensa

defensive *adj.* defensivo

defiance *noun.* desafío

defiant *adj.* insolente, desafiante

deficiency *noun.* deficiencia

deficit *noun.* déficit

define *verb.* definir, delimitar

definite *adj.* definitivo

definitely *adv.* definitivamente

definition *noun.* definición

defy *verb.* **1.** desafiar **2.** desobedecer, contravenir

degree *noun.* **1.** grado **2.** título

delay *noun.* retraso

delay *verb.* **1.** demorar, retrasar, aplazar **2.** tardar, demorarse

delegate *noun.* delegado

delegate *verb.* delegar

delegation *noun.* delegación

delete *verb.* suprimir, tachar

deliberate *verb.* deliberar, reflexionar

deliberate *adj.* **1.** deliberado, intencionado **2.** pausado, lento

deliberately *adv.* **1.** deliberadamente, a propósito **2.** pausadamente, lentamente

delicate *adj.* **1.** delicado, suave **2.** frágil **3.** difícil

delicious *adj.* delicioso, rico

delight *noun.* **1.** placer, gusto, deleite **2.** encanto

delight *verb.* **1.** deleitar, encantar **2.** deleitarse, disfrutar

delightful *adj.* encantador, delicioso

deliver *verb.* **1.** entregar, dar, repartir **2.** pronunciar **3.** asestar **4.** traer al mundo, asistir en el parto

delivery *noun.* **1.** entrega, reparto **2.** presentación oral, declamación **3.** parto, alumbramiento

delta *noun.* delta

demand *noun.* **1.** petición, solicitud **2.** exigencia **3.** demanda

demand *verb.* **1.** exigir, requerir **2.** reclamar

demanding *adj.* exigente, difícil

democracy *noun.* democracia

democrat *noun.* demócrata

democratic *adj.* democrático

demolish *verb.* demoler

demolition *noun.* demolición

demonstrate *verb.* **1.** demostrar **2.** hacer una demostración **3.** manifestarse

demonstration *noun.* **1.** manifestación **2.** demostración

demonstrator *noun.* manifestante

den *noun.* **1.** guarida **2.** cuarto, estudio

denial *noun.* **1.** negación, desmentido **2.** denegación, rechazo

Denmark *noun.* Dinamarca

denounce *verb.* denunciar

dense *adj.* **1.** denso, nutrido **2.** corto, torpe, estúpido

density *noun.* densidad

dental *adj.* dental

dentist *noun.* dentista, odontólogo

deny *verb.* **1.** negar, rechazar, desmentir **2.** denegar

depart *verb.* partir, salir, irse
—**depart from** apartarse de, desviarse de

department *noun.* departamento, sección
—**department store** grandes almacenes

departmental *adj.* departamental

departure *noun.* **1.** partida, marcha, salida **2.** desviación, novedad

depend (on) *verb.* **1.** contar con, fiarse de **2.** depender de

dependent *adj.* dependiente

depict *verb.* **1.** pintar, representar **2.** describir

deplete *verb.* reducir, mermar, agotar

deport *verb.* deportar

deposit *noun.* **1.** depósito **2.** señal, fianza **3.** poso, sedimento **4.** yacimiento

deposit *verb.* depositar, ingresar

depot *noun.* **1.** almacén, depósito **2.** cochera, parque **3.** terminal, estación

depress *verb.* **1.** deprimir, abatir, desalentar **2.** reducir

depressed *adj.* **1.** deprimido **2.** abatido

depressing *adj.* deprimente

depression *noun.* **1.** depresión **2.** recesión, crisis **3.** depresión atmosférica

deprivation *noun.* privación

deprive (of) *verb.* privar de

deprived *adj.* necesitado, marginado

depth *noun.* **1.** profundidad, fondo **2.** intensidad

deputy *noun.* **1.** suplente, lugarteniente **2.** diputado, representante

derelict *adj.* abandonado, en ruinas

derive (from) *verb.* **1.** proceder, venir de **2.** sacar, obtener, encontrar

descend *verb.* **1.** descender, bajar **2.** rebajarse
—**descend on** atacar, caer sobre

descent *noun.* **1.** descenso, bajada **2.** pendiente, cuesta **3.** ascendencia

describe *verb.* **1.** describir **2.** calificar, definir

description *noun.* **1.** descripción **2.** clase, tipo

desert *noun.* desierto

desert *verb.* **1.** abandonar **2.** desertar

deserted *adj.* desierto, abandonado

deserve *verb.* merecer

design *noun.* **1.** diseño, dibujo **2.** plan, proyecto, intención, propósito

design verb. diseñar, concebir, proyectar, planear

designate verb. designar, nombrar

designer noun. diseñador

desirable adj. deseable, apetecible, conveniente

desire noun. deseo

desire verb. desear

desk noun. 1. escritorio, pupitre 2. mostrador

despair noun. desesperación

despair verb. desesperarse, perder la esperanza

desperate adj. 1. desesperado 2. atroz, pésimo

desperately adv. 1. desesperadamente 2. terriblemente

desperation noun. desesperación

despite prep. a pesar de

dessert noun. postre

destination noun. destino

destined adj. 1. destinado 2. con destino a

destiny noun. destino, sino

destroy verb. 1. destruir 2. matar, sacrificar, exterminar

destruction noun. destrucción

destructive adj. destructivo, destructor

detached adj. 1. independiente, separado, suelto 2. objetivo, imparcial

detachment noun. 1. objetividad, imparcialidad 2. indiferencia 3. destacamento

detail noun. detalle, pormenor

detailed adj. detallado, minucioso, pormenorizado

detain verb. 1. demorar, retener 2. detener, arrestar

detect verb. detectar, descubrir

detective noun. detective

detention noun. detención

deter verb. 1. disuadir 2. impedir

deteriorate verb. empeorar, deteriorarse

deterioration noun. deterioro

determination noun. determinación

determine verb. 1. determinar, decidir 2. fijar, definir

determined adj. determinado, resuelto, decidido

deterrent noun. elemento disuasivo, elemento disuasorio

deterrent adj. disuasivo, disuasorio

devaluation noun. devaluación

devalue verb. devaluar

devastating adj. devastador, demoledor, tremendo

develop verb. 1. desarrollar, desarrollarse 2. elaborar, perfeccionar 3. contraer, adquirir 4. aparecer, mostrarse 5. revelar 6. surgir

development noun. 1. desarrollo, evolución 2. novedad, cambio, acontecimiento 3. explotación

deviation noun. desviación

device noun. 1. mecanismo, aparato, artefacto 2. estratagema, recurso

devil noun. 1. demonio, diablo 2. pobre diablo, pobrecito

devise verb. 1. concebir, inventar 2. elaborar, encontrar

devote (to) verb. 1. dedicar 2. dedicarse

devoted adj. leal, fiel

devotion noun. 1. devoción, lealtad 2. dedicación

diabetes noun. diabetes

diabetic noun. adj. diabético

diagnose verb. diagnosticar

diagnosis noun. diagnóstico

diagram noun. diagrama, gráfica

dial noun. 1. esfera, carátula 2. dial

dial verb. marcar, discar

dialect noun. dialecto

dialog, dialogue noun. diálogo

diameter noun. diámetro

diamond noun. 1. diamante 2. rombo

diaper noun. pañal

diarrhea noun. diarrea

diary noun. diario

dice noun plural. dado

dictate verb. 1. dictar 2. mandar

dictator noun. dictador

dictatorship noun. dictadura

dictionary noun. diccionario

die noun. troquel

die verb. 1. morir 2. apagarse, desaparecer 3. pararse 4. morirse de ganas de hacer algo

diet *noun.* dieta, régimen
diet *verb.* estar a régimen
differ *verb.* discrepar, no estar de acuerdo
—**differ from** ser distinto
difference *noun.* diferencia
different *adj.* diferente
differentiate *verb.* diferenciar, distinguir
differentiation *noun.* diferenciación
difficult *adj.* **1.** difícil, complicado **2.** problemático
difficulty *noun.* dificultad, problemas
dig *noun.* **1.** excavación **2.** empujón, codazo, golpe
dig *verb.* **1.** cavar, excavar, escarbar **2.** empujar, dar un codazo
digest *noun.* resumen
digest *verb.* digerir, asimilar
digestion *noun.* digestión
digital *adj.* digital
dignity *noun.* dignidad
dilemma *noun.* dilema
dilute *verb.* diluir
dilute *adj.* diluido
dim *verb.* **1.** apagar, atenuar **2.** borrar
dim *adj.* **1.** débil, tenue **2.** borroso, vago
dimension *noun.* dimensión
diminish *verb.* disminuir
diminished *adj.* reducido
dine *verb.* cenar
dining-room *noun.* comedor
dinner *noun.* **1.** comida, cena **2.** banquete
dinosaur *noun.* dinosaurio
diocese *noun.* diócesis
dip *noun.* **1.** depresión, hondonada **2.** salsa **3.** chapuzón, zambullida
dip *verb.* **1.** mojar, sumergir **2.** descender, bajar **3.** meter
diploma *noun.* diploma
diplomacy *noun.* diplomacia
diplomat *noun.* diplomático
diplomatic *adj.* diplomático
dire *adj.* **1.** pésimo, espantoso, atroz **2.** nefasto, funesto **3.** extremo
direct *verb.* **1.** dirigir **2.** indicar el camino **3.** mandar
direct *adj.* **1.** directo **2.** claro, franco, sincero

direction *noun.* **1.** dirección **2.** orientación
—**directions** instrucciones
directive *noun.* orden, directiva
directly *adv.* **1.** directamente **2.** con franqueza **3.** inmediatamente **4.** justo
director *noun.* **1.** director **2.** directivo
directory *noun.* guía telefónica, listín
dirt *noun.* suciedad
dirty *verb.* **1.** ensuciar **2.** ensuciarse
dirty *adj.* **1.** sucio **2.** obsceno, porno, cochino, indecente **3.** malo
disability *noun.* invalidez, discapacidad, minusvalía
disabled *adj.* minusválido, discapacitado
disadvantage *noun.* desventaja, inconveniente
disagree *verb.* **1.** no estar de acuerdo, estar en desacuerdo **2.** discutir, reñir **3.** diferir, no cuadrar **4.** sentar mal
disagreement *noun.* **1.** desacuerdo, disconformidad **2.** discusión, riña, altercado **3.** discrepancia
disappear *verb.* desaparecer
disappearance *noun.* desaparición
disappoint *verb.* decepcionar, defraudar
disappointed *adj.* decepcionado, defraudado
disappointing *adj.* decepcionante
disappointment *noun.* decepción, desilusión
disapproval *noun.* desaprobación
disaster *noun.* desastre
disastrous *adj.* desastroso
disbelief *noun.* incredulidad
disc, disk *noun.* disco
—**disc jockey, DJ** *noun.* discjockey, pinchadiscos
discard *verb.* desechar, deshacerse de
discharge *noun.* **1.** descarga, disparo **2.** alta, liberación **3.** despido **4.** emisión, vertido, supuración **5.** ejercicio, cumplimiento
discharge *verb.* **1.** descargar, disparar **2.** dar de alta, poner en libertad **3.** despedir **4.** verter, emitir **5.** desempeñar, cumplir

disciplinary *adj.* disciplinario

discipline *noun.* disciplina.

discipline *verb.* **1.** disciplinar **2.** castigar, sancionar

disclose *verb.* revelar

disclosure *noun.* revelación

disco *noun.* discoteca

discomfort *noun.* incomodidad, malestar, molestia

discontent *noun.* descontento, malestar

discotheque *noun.* discoteca

discount *noun.* descuento, rebaja

discount *verb.* **1.** descontar, rebajar **2.** descartar

discourage *verb.* **1.** desanimar, desalentar **2.** oponerse

—**discourage from** disuadir

discover *verb.* **1.** descubrir, hallar, encontrar **2.** darse cuenta

discovery *noun.* descubrimiento, hallazgo

discredit *noun.* descrédito, deshonor, desprestigio

discredit *verb.* **1.** desacreditar, deshonrar **2.** rebatir, refutar

discreet *adj.* discreto

discretion *noun.* **1.** discreción **2.** criterio, juicio

discrimination *noun.* discriminación

discuss *verb.* **1.** hablar de, discutir **2.** tratar, analizar

discussion *noun.* discusión

disease *noun.* enfermedad, mal

disembark *verb.* desembarcar

disgrace *noun.* **1.** desgracia **2.** deshonra **3.** vergüenza

disgrace *verb.* **1.** caer en desgracia **2.** deshonrar

disguise *noun.* disfraz

—**in disguise** disfrazado

disguise *verb.* **1.** disfrazar **2.** disimular, ocultar

disgust *noun.* **1.** asco, repugnancia **2.** indignación

disgust *verb.* dar asco, repugnar

disgusting *adj.* asqueroso, repugnante

dish *noun.* **1.** plato **2.** fuente

disintegrate *verb.* desintegrar

disk, disc *noun.* disco

dislike *noun.* aversión, antipatía

dislike *verb.* tener antipatía, caer mal, no gustar

dismantle *verb.* desmontar, desarmar, desmantelar

dismay *noun.* consternación

dismay *verb.* consternar

dismiss *verb.* **1.** despedir, destituir **2.** despachar **3.** descartar, rechazar **4.** desestimar

dismissal *noun.* **1.** despido, destitución **2.** rechazo

disorder *noun.* **1.** desorden **2.** disturbio, motín **3.** trastorno, dolencia

dispatch *noun.* **1.** despacho, informe, reportaje **2.** envío, expedición **3.** prontitud, presteza

dispatch *verb.* **1.** enviar, remitir **2.** despachar

disperse *verb.* **1.** dispersar, diseminar **2.** dispersarse

displace *verb.* **1.** desplazar **2.** destituir, quitar el puesto

display *noun.* **1.** exhibición, demostración **2.** exposición **3.** muestrario, surtido **4.** visualizador

display *verb.* **1.** exhibir **2.** exponer **3.** mostrar, manifestar

disposal *noun.* **1.** disposición **2.** venta, traspaso **3.** eliminación

dispose *verb.* predisponer, inclinar

—**dispose of** *verb.* **1.** vender, traspasar **2.** deshacerse de, tirar, botar

disposition *noun.* **1.** carácter, temperamento **2.** predisposición

dispute *noun.* **1.** disputa, discusión **2.** polémica **3.** contencioso

dispute *verb.* **1.** disputar **2.** poner en duda

disrupt *verb.* interrumpir, trastocar, alterar

disruption *noun.* interrupción, alteración

dissatisfaction *noun.* insatisfacción, descontento

dissent *noun.* disentimiento, disconformidad, disidencia

dissent *verb.* disentir, estar disconforme, disidir

dissident noun. adj. disidente
dissolution noun. disolución
dissolve verb. 1. disolver 2. disolverse
distance noun. distancia
—**from a distance** desde lejos
—**in the distance** a lo lejos
distant adj. 1. distante, lejano, remoto 2. frío 3. ausente
distinct adj. 1. diferente, distinto 2. claro, definido, nítido, evidente
distinction noun. 1. distinción 2. sobresaliente
distinctive adj. distintivo, característico
distinctly adv. claramente, definitivamente
distinguish verb. 1. distinguir 2. caracterizar 3. destacarse
distinguished adj. distinguido, eminente
distort verb. 1. deformar 2. distorsionar 3. tergiversar
distortion noun. 1. deformación 2. distorsión
distract verb. distraer
distracted adj. 1. distraído 2. demente, trastornado
distress noun. 1. aflicción, dolor 2. preocupación, angustia 3. desdicha, apuro
distress verb. afligir, doler
distribute verb. repartir, distribuir
distribution noun. distribución
district noun. distrito
disturb verb. 1. molestar 2. alterar, interrumpir 3. preocupar 4. agitar, desordenar
disturbance noun. 1. disturbio, alboroto, bronca 2. interrupción
ditch noun. zanja, foso, cuneta
ditch verb. deshacerse de, dejar plantado
dive noun. zambullida, salto de cabeza
dive verb. 1. zambullirse, tirarse de cabeza 2. precipitarse hacia, abalanzarse 3. caer en picado
diverse adj. diverso, variado
diversify verb. diversificar
diversion noun. 1. distracción 2. diversión
diversity noun. diversidad
divert verb. entretener

divide verb. 1. dividir 2. separar, cortar
—**divide between/among** repartir
dividend noun. dividendo
divine verb. adivinar
divine adj. divino, precioso
division noun. 1. división 2. separación 3. desacuerdo, diferencia
divorce noun. divorcio
divorce verb. 1. divorciarse 2. separar
dizzy adj. 1. mareado 2. vertiginoso
DJ abbr. pinchadiscos
do noun. fiesta, evento
do verb. 1. hacer 2. servir, ir bien, ser suficiente 3. dedicarse, estudiar 4. ir, estar 5. arreglar
—**do away with** abolir, suprimir
—**do without** prescindir
dock noun. 1. muelle 2. banquillo de los acusados
dock verb. 1. atracar 2. descontar dinero
doctor noun. 1. médico 2. doctor
doctor verb. 1. adulterar, manipular 2. tratar, curar
doctrine noun. doctrina
document noun. documento
documentary noun. documental
documentary adj. documental
dodge verb. esquivar, evadir
doe noun. gama, liebre, coneja
dog noun. perro
dog verb. seguir (de cerca)
dole (out) verb. repartir
doll noun. muñeca
dollar noun. dólar
dolly noun. muñeca
dolphin noun. delfín
domain noun. dominio, propiedad
dome noun. cúpula
domestic adj. 1. doméstico 2. familiar 3. nacional
dominance noun. dominio, control, preponderancia
dominant adj. dominante
dominate verb. dominar
domination noun. dominación, dominio
donate verb. donar, hacer una donación
donation noun. donación
done adj. 1. hecho 2. cocido, asado (food) 3. rendido

donkey *noun.* **1.** burro **2.** tonto, imbécil, idiota

donor *noun.* donante

door *noun.* puerta

doorstep *noun.* peldaño, umbral

doorway *noun.* entrada, puerta, portal

dose *noun.* **1.** dosis **2.** ataque

dose *verb.* medicinar

dot *noun.* punto

double *noun.* doble

double *verb.* **1.** duplicar, doblar **2.** hacer las veces de, usarse de

double *adj.* doble

double *adv.* **1.** dos veces, el doble **2.** en dos, por la mitad

doubt *noun.* duda

doubt *verb.* dudar

doubtful *adj.* **1.** dudoso **2.** incierto **3.** poco probable **4.** sospechoso

doubtless *adv.* sin duda, seguramente

down *noun.* plumón

down *verb.* **1.** tragarse, devorar **2.** derribar, vencer

down *prep.* **1.** abajo, hacia abajo **2.** en la dirección de **3.** por

down *adv.* **1.** abajo, hacia abajo **2.** por tierra, en tierra **3.** a través de los tiempos

downstairs *adj. adv.* abajo

downtown *adj.* céntrico

downtown *adv.* en el centro

downward *adj.* descendente

dozen *noun.* docena

Dr *abbr.* Dr, doctor

draft *noun.* **1.** borrador, esbozo **2.** destacamento **3.** letra de cambio, giro **4.** leva, conscripción **5.** corriente de aire **6.** trago **7.** calado

draft *verb.* **1.** esbozar, redactar **2.** reclutar

drag *noun.* **1.** estorbo, freno **2.** calada **3.** lata, plomo, rollo **4.** vestido de travesti

drag *verb.* **1.** arrastrar, llevar a rastras **2.** dragar **3.** hacerse largo/pesado

dragon *noun.* dragón

drain *noun.* **1.** desagüe, sumidero **2.** desgaste, sangría

drain *verb.* **1.** vaciar, drenar, desaguar **2.** escurrir, escurrirse **3.** apurar, vaciar **4.** agotar, consumir

drainage *noun.* drenaje

drama *noun.* **1.** drama **2.** obra de teatro, obra dramática **3.** arte dramático

dramatic *adj.* **1.** dramático **2.** teatral **3.** impresionante, espectacular

dramatically *adv.* dramáticamente

drastic *adj.* drástico, radical

draw *noun.* **1.** atracción **2.** sorteo, lotería **3.** acción de sacar/desenvainar **4.** empate, tablas

draw *verb.* **1.** dibujar, trazar **2.** extraer, sacar, cobrar **3.** acercarse **4.** empatar, entablar **5.** causar, provocar, motivar **6.** correr, descorrer, tirar **7.** atraer

—draw near acercarse

drawer *noun.* cajón

drawing *noun.* dibujo

drawn *adj.* **1.** desenvainado, sacado **2.** ojeroso, demacrado **3.** empatado

dread *noun.* terror, pavor

dread *verb.* temer, tener miedo

dreadful *adj.* terrible, espantoso

dream *noun.* **1.** sueño **2.** maravilla **3.** ensueño

dream *verb.* **1.** soñar **2.** imaginar, imaginarse

dress *noun.* **1.** ropa **2.** vestido

dress *verb.* **1.** vestir, vestirse **2.** preparar, aliñar, aderezar **3.** vendar

dressed *adj.* vestido

dressing *noun.* **1.** aliño **2.** apósito, vendaje **3.** abono

dried *adj.* seco

drift *noun.* **1.** montón **2.** sentido, tendencia **3.** significado

drift *verb.* **1.** amontonarse **2.** vagar, ir sin rumbo, ir a la deriva, dejarse llevar

drill *noun.* **1.** taladro, barrena, perforador **2.** instrucción, ejercicios

drill *verb.* **1.** taladrar, perforar **2.** entrenarse

drink *noun.* **1.** bebida **2.** trago, copa

drink *verb.* beber, tomar

drip *noun.* **1.** gota **2.** goteo **3.** gota a gota

drip *verb.* gotear

dripping *noun.* pringue, grasa de carne asada

drive *noun.* **1.** paseo en coche, viaje **2.** camino de entrada **3.** ímpetu, empuje, dinamismo **4.** campaña **5.** drive, golpe directo **6.** unidad de disco

drive verb. **1.** conducir, manejar, pilotar **2.** llevar (en coche) **3.** hincar, clavar **4.** hacer funcionar, mover, impulsar **5.** conducirse, manejarse

driver noun. conductor

drop noun. **1.** gota **2.** lágrima **3.** caída, descenso, disminución **4.** desnivel, pendiente

drop verb. **1.** dejar, abandonar **2.** dejar caer, soltar, lanzar, echar **3.** bajar **4.** suprimir **5.** escribir

drought noun. sequía

drown verb. **1.** ahogar **2.** ahogarse

drug noun. **1.** medicamento **2.** droga, estupefaciente

drug verb. drogar

drum noun. **1.** tambor **2.** bidón **3.** tímpano

drum verb. **1.** tocar el tambor **2.** tamborilear **3.** repiquetear

drummer noun. batería

drunk noun. adj. borracho

drunken adj. **1.** borracho **2.** causado por embriaguez

dry verb. **1.** secar **2.** secarse

dry adj. **1.** seco, árido **2.** aburrido **3.** sardónico, mordaz

dual adj. doble

dub verb. **1.** doblar **2.** apodar

dubious adj. **1.** dudoso, sospechoso **2.** indeciso

duchess noun. duquesa

duck noun. pato

duck verb. **1.** hundir, zambullir **2.** agachar **3.** eludir, esquivar

due noun. merecido

—dues cuota, derechos

due adj. **1.** debido, merecido, justo **2.** pagadero, pendiente **3.** esperado

due adv. hacia

duke noun. duque

dull adj. **1.** lento, torpe **2.** apagado, sin brillo **3.** monótono, aburrido

duly adv. **1.** debidamente **2.** puntualmente

dumb adj. **1.** mudo **2.** callado **3.** tonto, estúpido

dump noun. **1.** basural, vertedero, basurero **2.** depósito

dump verb. **1.** dejar, soltar **2.** verter, descargar

durable adj. duradero

duration noun. duración

during prep. durante

dusk noun. crepúsculo

dust noun. polvo

dust verb. quitar el polvo

dusty adj. polvoriento

Dutch noun. holandés

Dutch adj. holandés, neerlandés

duty noun. **1.** deber, obligación **2.** función, responsabilidad **3.** derecho, impuesto

dwarf noun. enano

dwarf verb. empequeñecer, eclipsar

dwelling noun. morada, vivienda

dye noun. tinte

dye verb. teñir

dynamic adj. dinámico

dynamics noun singular. dinámica

dynasty noun. dinastía

E

each adj. cada

each adv. pron. cada uno

—each other el uno al otro, mutuamente

eager adj. ávido, ansioso, entusiasta, ilusionado

eagerly adv. con avidez, ansiosamente, con entusiasmo, con ilusión

eagle noun. águila

ear noun. **1.** oído **2.** oreja **3.** espiga

early adj. **1.** temprano **2.** prematuro **3.** antiguo, primitivo **4.** pronto

early adv. **1.** temprano **2.** pronto **3.** en los inicios, al principio

—early riser madrugador

earn verb. **1.** ganar, obtener **2.** merecer

earnest adj. serio

earnings *noun plural.* ingresos

earth *noun.* **1.** tierra **2.** suelo **3.** madriguera

—**the Earth** la Tierra

earthquake *noun.* terremoto

ease *noun.* **1.** facilidad **2.** alivio, bienestar **3.** soltura

ease *verb.* **1.** facilitar **2.** aliviar, aligerar, aflojar **3.** mover con cuidado

—**ease off** disminuir, amainar

easily *adv.* **1.** fácilmente **2.** con diferencia, con mucho

east *noun.* este

east *adj.* **1.** este, oriental **2.** del este

east *adv.* hacia el este, en dirección este

Easter *noun.* Pascua, Semana Santa

eastern *adj.* del este, oriental

easy *interj.* ¡despacio!

easy *adj.* **1.** fácil **2.** tranquilo, relajado **3.** natural

eat *verb.* comer

eccentric *noun. adj.* excéntrico

ecclesiastical *adj.* eclesiástico

echo *noun.* eco

echo *verb.* **1.** hacer eco, resonar **2.** repetir

ecological *adj.* ecológico

ecology *noun.* ecología

economic *adj.* **1.** económico **2.** rentable

economical *adj.* económico, ahorrador

economically *adv.* económicamente

economics *noun singular.* economía

economist *noun.* economista

economy *noun.* economía

ecstasy *noun.* éxtasis

edge *noun.* **1.** borde **2.** filo, canto, arista **3.** orilla **4.** ventaja

edge *verb.* **1.** ribetear, bordear **2.** moverse con cautela, moverse poco a poco

edit *verb.* **1.** editar **2.** dirigir **3.** corregir

edition *noun.* edición

editor *noun.* **1.** editor, redactor **2.** director

editorial *noun. adj.* editorial

educate *verb.* educar, formar

education *noun.* educación

educational *adj.* **1.** educativo, docente **2.** pedagógico

eel *noun.* anguila

effect *noun.* **1.** efecto, consecuencia, resultado **2.** sentido

—**effects** **1.** bienes **2.** efectos

effect *verb.* efectuar, lograr

effective *adj.* **1.** efectivo **2.** eficaz **3.** logrado, llamativo, impresionante **4.** en vigor, vigente **5.** real

effectively *adv.* **1.** eficazmente **2.** realmente

efficacy *noun.* eficacia

efficiency *noun.* eficiencia, eficacia

efficient *adj.* **1.** eficiente, competente **2.** eficaz, de buen rendimiento

efficiently *adv.* eficientemente, eficazmente

effort *noun.* **1.** esfuerzo **2.** intento

e.g. *abbr.* por ejemplo

egg *noun.* **1.** huevo **2.** óvulo

egg on *verb.* animar, incitar

ego *noun.* ego, amor propio, orgullo

Egypt *noun.* Egipto

Egyptian *noun. adj.* egipcio

eight *noun. adj.* ocho

eighteen *noun. adj.* dieciocho

eighteenth *noun.* decimoctavo

eighth *noun.* octavo

eighties *noun plural.* **1.** entre ochenta y noventa **2.** los años ochenta

eightieth *noun.* octogésimo

eighty *noun. adj.* ochenta

either *adj.* **1.** cualquiera de los dos, ambos (positive) **2.** ninguno de los dos (negative) **3.** cada

either *adv.* tampoco

either *pron.* **1.** cualquiera de los dos (positive) **2.** ninguno de los dos (negative)

either...or *conj.* **1.** o...o (positive) **2.** ni ...ni (negative)

elaborate *verb.* **1.** desarrollar, elaborar **2.** explicar detalladamente

elaborate *adj.* **1.** elaborado **2.** complicado, rebuscado **3.** detallado

elastic *noun.* elástico

elastic *adj.* **1.** elástico **2.** flexible

elbow *noun.* codo

elbow *verb.* dar un codazo

elder *noun.* **1.** mayor **2.** anciano **3.** saúco

elder adj. mayor
elderly adj. mayor, anciano
eldest adj. mayor
elect verb. 1. elegir 2. decidir
elect adj. electo
election noun. elección
—**general election** elecciones generales
electoral adj. electoral
electorate noun. electorado
electric adj. 1. eléctrico 2. electrizante
electrical adj. eléctrico
electricity noun. electricidad
electron noun. electrón
electronic adj. electrónico
electronics noun singular. electrónica
elegance noun. elegancia
elegant adj. elegante
element noun. 1. elemento 2. factor 3. parte, ingrediente 4. resistencia
—**elements** rudimentos
—**the elements** los elementos, las fuerzas de la naturaleza
elementary adj. elemental, básico
elephant noun. elefante
elevate verb. 1. elevar 2. ascender
elevator noun. 1. ascensor, elevador 2. montacargas 3. elevador de granos
eleven noun. adj. once
eleventh noun. 1. undécimo 2. onceavo
eligible adj. 1. idóneo, apto 2. elegible
eliminate verb. eliminar
elimination noun. eliminación
elite noun. elite
elitist noun. adj. elitista
eloquence noun. elocuencia
else adj. adv. 1. más 2. otra cosa, otro
elsewhere adv. 1. en otro sitio, en otra parte 2. a otro sitio, a otra parte
elude verb. eludir, evitar
elusive adj. esquivo
emancipation noun. emancipación
embargo noun. embargo
embark verb. embarcar
embarrassed adj. turbado
embarrassing adj. embarazoso
embarrassment noun. vergüenza, pena
embassy noun. embajada
embody verb. 1. encarnar, personificar 2. plasmar

embrace noun. abrazo
embrace verb. 1. abrazar 2. abarcar
embryo noun. embrión
emerge verb. 1. emerger, salir, surgir 2. resultar
emergence noun. aparición
emergency noun. emergencia
emigrate verb. emigrar
eminent adj. eminente
emission noun. emisión
emotion noun. 1. emoción 2. sentimiento
emotional adj. 1. emocional, afectivo 2. emotivo 3. sentimental
emotionally adv. 1. emocionalmente 2. emotivamente
emperor noun. emperador
emphasis noun. 1. acento 2. énfasis
emphasize verb. enfatizar, hacer hincapié
empire noun. imperio
employ verb. 1. emplear 2. ocupar
employed adj. empleado
employee noun. empleado
employer noun. empresario, patrón
employment noun. empleo
empty noun. envase vacío, casco vacío
empty verb. 1. vaciar 2. vaciarse
empty adj. 1. vacío 2. desierto 3. desocupado 4. vano, hueco
enable verb. 1. permitir, autorizar 2. posibilitar
enact verb. 1. representar 2. promulgar
enclose verb. 1. adjuntar 2. cercar, vallar
enclosure noun. 1. anexo, carta adjunta 2. cercado 3. recinto reservado
encounter noun. encuentro
encounter verb. 1. encontrar, encontrarse con 2. tropezar con
encourage verb. animar, alentar
encouragement noun. ánimo
encouraging adj. 1. alentador 2. halagüeño
end noun. 1. final, extremo, cabo, punta 2. conclusión, fin 3. muerte 4. objetivo, finalidad, propósito 5. resto
end verb. 1. terminar, acabar con 2. terminarse
endanger verb. poner en peligro

159

endeavor noun. tentativa, intento, esfuerzo

endeavor verb. esforzarse

ending noun. final, desenlace

endless adj. 1. interminable, inagotable 2. continuo, sin fin

endorse verb. 1. endosar 2. aprobar, respaldar

endorsement noun. aprobación, respaldo

endowment noun. 1. dotación 2. fundación, creación 3. donación 4. dote

endure verb. 1. soportar, resistir, aguantar 2. durar

enemy noun. enemigo

energetic adj. 1. activo 2. enérgico 3. vigoroso

energy noun. 1. energía 2. vigor

enforce verb. 1. imponer 2. hacer cumplir 3. aplicar, ejecutar

enforcement noun. aplicación, ejecución

engage verb. 1. contratar 2. ocupar, captar 3. entablar 4. meterse en, tomar parte en 5. engranar

engaged adj. 1. prometido 2. ocupado

engagement noun. 1. compromiso, noviazgo 2. cita 3. batalla 4. contrato

engaging adj. atractivo

engine noun. 1. motor 2. máquina, locomotora

engineer noun. 1. ingeniero 2. maquinista

engineer verb. maquinar, organizar

engineering noun. ingeniería

England noun. Inglaterra

English noun. adj. inglés

Englishman, Englishwoman noun. inglés, inglesa

enhance verb. realzar, acrecentar, aumentar

enjoy verb. 1. disfrutar, gozar de 2. poseer, tener

enjoyable adj. 1. agradable 2. divertido

enjoyment noun. placer

enlarge verb. 1. aumentar 2. ampliar

enlightened adj. bien informado, culto

enlightenment noun. aclaración
—**the Enlightenment** la Ilustración

enormous adj. enorme

enough adj. pron. bastante, suficiente

enough adv. bastante, suficientemente

ensure verb. asegurar

entail verb. suponer, implicar, acarrear, traer consigo

enter verb. 1. entrar, entrar en 2. presentarse 3. inscribirse, participar 4. registrar, anotar, escribir 5. comenzar

enterprise noun. 1. empresa 2. iniciativa

entertain verb. 1. recibir 2. divertir, entretener 3. considerar, abrigar, albergar

entertaining adj. divertido, entretenido

entertainment noun. 1. espectáculo 2. entretenimiento 3. diversión

enthusiasm noun. entusiasmo

enthusiast noun. entusiasta

enthusiastic adj. entusiasta

entire adj. 1. entero 2. completo

entirely adv. 1. enteramente, exclusivamente 2. completamente

entitle verb. 1. dar derecho, tener derecho 2. titular

entitlement noun. derecho

entrance noun. 1. entrada 2. admisión 3. ingreso

entrance verb. encantar

entrepreneur noun. empresario

entry noun. 1. entrada, ingreso 2. participante 3. registro, anotación, partida

envelope noun. sobre

environment noun. entorno, medio ambiente

environmental adj. ambiental

environmentalist noun. ecologista

envisage verb. 1. prever 2. imaginar

envoy noun. enviado, mensajero

envy noun. envidia

envy verb. envidiar

epic noun. epopeya, poema épico

epidemic noun. epidemia

epilog noun. epílogo

episcopal adj. episcopal

episode noun. episodio

epoch noun. época

equal verb. 1. igualar 2. equivaler

equal noun. adj. igual

equality *noun.* igualdad

equally *adv.* **1.** igualmente **2.** equitativamente, por igual

equation *noun.* ecuación

equilibrium *noun.* equilibrio

equip *verb.* equipar

equipment *noun.* **1.** equipo **2.** material, herramienta, pertrechos

equitable *adj.* equitativo, justo

equity *noun.* equidad

equivalent *noun. adj.* equivalente

era *noun.* era

eradicate *verb.* erradicar

erase *verb.* borrar

erect *verb.* **1.** erigir **2.** levantar, edificar **3.** montar

erect *adj.* erecto, erguido, parado

erode *verb.* **1.** erosionar, corroer, desgastar **2.** mermar, reducir

erosion *noun.* erosión

erotic *adj.* erótico

error *noun.* error

erupt *verb.* entrar en erupción, estallar

eruption *noun.* erupción

escalate *verb.* **1.** subir vertiginosamente **2.** intensificarse

escape *noun.* fuga, evasión

escape *verb.* **1.** escapar, escaparse **2.** fugarse, huir **3.** librarse de, evitar **4.** salirse

escort *noun.* **1.** escolta **2.** acompañamiento **3.** acompañante, prostituto

escort *verb.* **1.** escoltar **2.** acompañar

especially *adv.* especialmente

essay *noun.* **1.** ensayo **2.** trabajo

essence *noun.* **1.** esencia **2.** extracto

essential *noun.* necesidad, elemento necesario

essential *adj.* **1.** esencial, imprescindible **2.** fundamental

essentially *adv.* **1.** básicamente, en esencia **2.** en lo fundamental, en lo esencial

establish *verb.* **1.** establecer **2.** fundar **3.** afirmar **4.** comprobar, demostrar, verificar **5.** averiguar, determinar

established *adj.* **1.** establecido **2.** oficial **3.** consolidado, arraigado **4.** probado

establishment *noun.* **1.** establecimiento

2. institución **3.** residencia

—the Establishment la clase dirigente

estate *noun.* **1.** finca, hacienda **2.** urbanización **3.** patrimonio, propiedad **4.** herencia **5.** estado

esteem *noun.* aprecio, estima

esteem *verb.* apreciar, estimar

estimate *noun.* cálculo, estimación, presupuesto

estimate *verb.* estimar, calcular

estuary *noun.* estuario

eternal *adj.* **1.** eterno **2.** constante

ethical *adj.* ético

ethics *noun.* ética

ethnic *adj.* étnico

euro *noun.* euro

Europe *noun.* Europa

European *noun. adj.* europeo

evacuate *verb.* evacuar

evaluate *verb.* **1.** valorar, evaluar **2.** calcular, hallar el valor numérico

evaluation *noun.* **1.** valoración **2.** cálculo

eve *noun.* **1.** víspera **2.** tarde

even *verb.* **1.** igualar **2.** allanar, nivelar

even *adj.* **1.** uniforme, constante, regular **2.** liso, llano **3.** igual **4.** par **5.** constante, tranquilo

even *adv.* **1.** hasta, incluso **2.** ni siquiera **3.** todavía, aún

evening *noun.* **1.** tarde **2.** atardecer **3.** noche

evenly *adv.* **1.** uniformemente **2.** por igual, equitativamente **3.** con calma

event *noun.* **1.** acontecimiento, suceso **2.** prueba, evento

eventual *adj.* final

eventually *adv.* **1.** finalmente **2.** con el tiempo

ever *adv.* **1.** siempre **2.** jamás, nunca **3.** alguna vez

every *adj.* **1.** cada **2.** todo

everybody, everyone *pron.* todos, todo el mundo

everyday *adj.* **1.** cotidiano, diario **2.** habitual

everything *pron.* todo

everywhere *adv.* en todas partes, por todas partes

evidence *noun.* **1.** prueba **2.** indicio, señal **3.** testimonio

evident *adj.* evidente

evidently *adv.* **1.** por lo visto **2.** claramente, evidentemente

evil *noun.* **1.** mal, maldad **2.** desgracia, plaga

evil *adj.* **1.** malo, malvado **2.** diabólico, funesto

evocative *adj.* evocador

evoke *verb.* **1.** provocar, suscitar **2.** evocar

evolution *noun.* evolución, desarrollo

evolutionary *adj.* evolutivo

evolve *verb.* **1.** evolucionar **2.** desarrollar

exact *verb.* **1.** exigir **2.** obtener, conseguir **3.** arrancar

exact *adj.* **1.** exacto **2.** preciso, meticuloso

exactly *adv.* exactamente

exaggerate *verb.* exagerar

examination *noun.* **1.** inspección **2.** examen **3.** interrogatorio **4.** reconocimiento

examine *verb.* **1.** inspeccionar **2.** examinar **3.** interrogar

example *noun.* ejemplo

—for example por ejemplo

excavation *noun.* excavación

exceed *verb.* exceder, sobrepasar, rebasar

excellence *noun.* excelencia

excellent *adj.* excelente

except *prep.* excepto, salvo

except *verb.* excluir, exceptuar

exception *noun.* excepción

exceptional *adj.* excepcional

exceptionally *adv.* excepcionalmente

excerpt *noun.* extracto

excess *noun.* **1.** exceso **2.** excedente

excess *adj.* exceso

excessive *adj.* excesivo

exchange *noun.* **1.** intercambio, canje **2.** cambio **3.** bolsa **4.** central telefónica, conmutador

exchange *verb.* **1.** cambiar **2.** intercambiar, canjear

excise *noun.* impuestos indirectos

excise *verb.* extirpar, cortar

excite *verb.* **1.** emocionar, entusiasmar **2.** despertar, suscitar, provocar

excited *adj.* **1.** emocionado, entusiasmado **2.** excitado, nervioso

excitement *noun.* excitación, emoción

exciting *adj.* emocionante, apasionante

exclaim *verb.* exclamar

exclude *verb.* **1.** excluir, expulsar **2.** exceptuar

excluding *prep.* excepto, con excepción de

exclusion *noun.* exclusión, expulsión

exclusive *adj.* **1.** exclusivo **2.** selecto

exclusively *adv.* exclusivamente

excuse *noun.* excusa

excuse *verb.* **1.** perdonar, excusar **2.** justificar **3.** dispensar

execute *verb.* **1.** ejecutar, realizar, llevar a cabo **2.** fusilar

execution *noun.* **1.** ejecución **2.** fusilamiento

executive *noun.* **1.** poder ejecutivo **2.** ejecutivo

executive *adj.* ejecutivo, directivo

exempt *verb.* eximir, dispensar

exempt *adj.* exento

exemption *noun.* exención

exercise *noun.* ejercicio

exercise *verb.* **1.** hacer ejercicio **2.** ejercitar, ejercer

exert *verb.* **1.** ejercer, emplear **2.** esforzarse

exhaust *noun.* tubo de escape

exhaust *verb.* agotar

exhausted *adj.* agotado

exhaustion *noun.* agotamiento

exhibit *noun.* **1.** objeto expuesto **2.** exposición **3.** prueba instrumental

exhibit *verb.* **1.** exponer **2.** manifestar, mostrar

exhibition *noun.* **1.** exposición **2.** demostración

exile *noun.* **1.** exiliado, desterrado **2.** exilio, destierro

exile *verb.* exiliar, desterrar

exist *verb.* **1.** existir **2.** vivir, subsistir

existence *noun.* existencia

exit *noun.* salida

exit *verb.* **1.** salir, salir de **2.** hacer mutis

exotic *adj.* exótico

expand *verb.* **1.** ampliar, aumentar **2.** extender **3.** desplegar

expansion *noun.* **1.** ampliación **2.** desarrollo **3.** dilatación

expect *verb.* **1.** esperar **2.** suponer, creer **3.** imaginarse **4.** exigir

expectancy *noun.* expectativa

expectation *noun.* **1.** expectativa **2.** esperanza

expedition *noun.* expedición

expel *verb.* **1.** expulsar, expeler **2.** despedir

expenditure *noun.* gasto

expense *noun.* gasto, costo

expensive *adj.* caro

experience *noun.* experiencia

experience *verb.* experimentar

experienced *adj.* experimentado

experiment *noun.* experimento

experiment (on/with) *verb.* experimentar con

experimental *adj.* experimental

expert *noun.* experto, especialista

expert *adj.* experto

expire *verb.* **1.** terminar **2.** caducar, vencer **3.** expirar, morir

explain *verb.* **1.** explicar **2.** justificar, defender

explanation *noun.* explicación, aclaración

explanatory *adj.* explicativo

explicit *adj.* explícito

explicitly *adv.* explícitamente

explode *verb.* **1.** explotar, estallar **2.** hacer explotar, hacer estallar **3.** refutar, echar por tierra

exploit *noun.* hazaña

exploit *verb.* **1.** explotar **2.** aprovechar

exploitation *noun.* explotación

exploration *noun.* exploración

explore *verb.* **1.** explorar **2.** examinar

explosion *noun.* **1.** explosión **2.** ataque, arrebato **3.** aumento rápido

explosive *noun. adj.* explosivo

export *noun.* **1.** exportación **2.** artículo de exportación

export *verb.* exportar

expose *verb.* **1.** exponer **2.** descubrir **3.** revelar

exposure *noun.* **1.** exposición **2.** riesgo **3.** fotografía

express *noun.* **1.** expreso **2.** urgente, rápido

express *verb.* **1.** expresar **2.** enviar por correo urgente

express *adj.* **1.** expreso, explícito **2.** rápido, urgente, exprés

express *adv.* urgente

expression *noun.* expresión

expressive *adj.* expresivo

expressly *adv.* expresamente

expulsion *noun.* expulsión

exquisite *adj.* **1.** exquisito **2.** excelente

extend *verb.* **1.** extender, extenderse **2.** ampliar, prolongar **3.** tender, alargar **4.** ofrecer, dar

extension *noun.* **1.** extensión, ampliación, prolongación **2.** prorroga

extensive *adj.* **1.** extenso, vasto, amplio **2.** comprensivo

extent *noun.* **1.** extensión **2.** amplitud, alcance **3.** punto, grado

—**to a certain extent** hasta cierto punto

—**to a large extent** en gran parte

—**to what extent?** ¿hasta qué punto?

exterior *noun. adj.* exterior

external *adj.* externo

extinction *noun.* extinción

extra *noun.* **1.** extra **2.** suplemento **3.** edición especial

extra *adj.* **1.** extra **2.** adicional **3.** de más **4.** de sobra

extra *adv.* **1.** más **2.** extraordinariamente

extract *noun.* **1.** extracto **2.** fragmento

extract *verb.* extraer, sacar

extraction *noun.* **1.** extracción **2.** origen

extradite *verb.* extraditar

extraordinarily *adv.* extraordinariamente

extraordinary *adj.* extraordinario

extreme *noun. adj.* extremo

extremely *adv.* extremadamente

extremist *noun. adj.* extremista

eye *noun.* **1.** ojo **2.** vista, buen ojo **3.** opinión, juicio

eye *verb.* mirar, observar

eyebrow *noun.* ceja

F

F *abbr.* Fahrenheit
fabric *noun.* **1.** tela, tejido **2.** estructura
fabulous *adj.* fabuloso
face *noun.* **1.** cara, rostro **2.** semblante, expresión **3.** superficie **4.** aspecto, faceta **5.** descaro
face *verb.* **1.** estar enfrente de, dar a **2.** mirar, mirar hacia **3.** afrontar, hacer cara
facial *adj.* facial
facility *noun.* **1.** facilidad **2.** habilidad
—**facilities** instalaciones, servicios
facing *prep.* de cara a, frente a
fact *noun.* **1.** hecho **2.** dato **3.** realidad
faction *noun.* facción
factor *noun.* factor
factory *noun.* fábrica
factual *adj.* objetivo, basado en hechos
faculty *noun.* **1.** facultad **2.** habilidad **3.** claustro, profesorado
fade *verb.* **1.** marchitarse **2.** apagarse, descolorarse
Fahrenheit *adj.* Fahrenheit
fail *verb.* **1.** fracasar **2.** fallar **3.** faltar **4.** suspender, reprobar **5.** decepcionar
failing *prep.* a falta de
failing *noun.* defecto, falta
failure *noun.* **1.** fracaso, suspenso **2.** fracasado **3.** omisión, descuido **4.** avería, corte **5.** quiebra
faint *noun.* desmayo, desvanecimiento
faint *verb.* desmayarse, perder el sentido
faint *adj.* **1.** débil, tenue, borroso **2.** desfallecido, lánguido
faintly *adv.* **1.** débilmente **2.** ligeramente
fair *noun.* **1.** feria **2.** mercado
fair *adj.* **1.** justo, imparcial, recto, limpio **2.** considerable **3.** bueno, despejado, sereno **4.** regular, pasable **5.** rubio (hair), blanco (skin) **6.** hermoso, lindo, bello
fairly *adv.* **1.** justamente, equitativamente **2.** bastante
fairness *noun.* justicia, imparcialidad
fairy *noun.* hada

faith *noun.* **1.** fe **2.** religión, doctrina **3.** confianza **4.** palabra
faithful *adj.* fiel, leal
faithfully *adv.* fielmente
fake *noun.* **1.** falsificación **2.** impostor, farsante
fake *verb.* falsificar
fake *adj.* **1.** falso **2.** fingido
fall *noun.* **1.** caída, disminución, bajada **2.** rendición **3.** otoño
—**falls** catarata
fall *verb.* **1.** caer **2.** caerse **3.** disminuir, bajar, descender **4.** incumbir, corresponder, tocar **5.** rendirse, ser tomado **6.** morir
false *adj.* **1.** falso **2.** postizo **3.** desleal, infiel
fame *noun.* fama
familiar *adj.* **1.** conocido, familiar **2.** íntimo
—**familiar with** familiarizado con
familiarity *noun.* familiaridad
family *noun.* familia
famine *noun.* hambre, hambruna
famous *adj.* famoso
fan *noun.* **1.** abanico **2.** ventilador
fan *noun.* aficionado, admirador
fan *verb.* **1.** abanicar **2.** abanicarse **3.** atizar, avivar
fancy *noun.* **1.** capricho, antojo **2.** fantasía **3.** imaginación
fancy *verb.* **1.** gustar, apetecer **2.** imaginarse, figurarse
fancy *adj.* **1.** elegante **2.** elaborado
fantastic *adj.* fantástico
fantasy *noun.* **1.** fantasía **2.** imaginación
far *adj.* **1.** lejano, distante **2.** extremo
far *adv.* **1.** lejos **2.** muy, mucho
fare *noun.* **1.** tarifa, precio del billete **2.** pasajero
farewell *noun.* despedida
farewell *interj.* adiós
farm *noun.* granja, chacra, hacienda
farm *verb.* **1.** cultivar, labrar **2.** ser granjero
farmer *noun.* granjero, agricultor, chacarero

farmhouse *noun.* granja, alquería, casa de labranza
farming *noun.* **1.** agricultura **2.** ganadería, cría
fascinate *verb.* fascinar
fascinating *adj.* fascinante
fascination *noun.* fascinación
Fascism *noun.* fascismo
fascist *noun. adj.* fascista
fashion *noun.* **1.** modo, manera **2.** moda
fashionable *adj.* de moda, a la moda
fast *noun.* ayuno
fast *verb.* ayunar
fast *adj.* **1.** rápido **2.** firme, seguro **3.** adelantado
fast *adv.* **1.** rápidamente **2.** firmemente, seguramente **3.** profundamente
fat *noun.* **1.** grasa **2.** manteca, grasa
fat *adj.* **1.** gordo, relleno **2.** sustancioso, grande
fatal *adj.* **1.** mortal **2.** fatal
fate *noun.* **1.** destino **2.** suerte
father *noun.* **1.** padre **2.** sacerdote
father *verb.* engendrar
fatigue *noun.* fatiga, cansancio
fatty *adj.* graso
faucet *noun.* grifo, llave
fault *noun.* **1.** culpa **2.** defecto, tara **3.** falla
fault *verb.* criticar, encontrar defectos
faulty *adj.* defectuoso
favor *noun.* **1.** favor **2.** aprobación **3.** preferencia, favoritismo
favor *verb.* **1.** apoyar, preferir **2.** preferir
favorable *adj.* **1.** favorable **2.** propicio
favorite *noun. adj.* favorito, preferido
fax *noun.* **1.** fax **2.** telefax
fax *verb.* mandar por fax, faxear
FBI *abbr.* FBI
fear *noun.* temor, miedo
fear *verb.* temer, tener miedo
fearful *adj.* **1.** temeroso **2.** terrible, espantoso **3.** horrible
feasibility *noun.* factibilidad
feasible *adj.* factible
feast *noun.* **1.** banquete, festín **2.** fiesta
feast *verb.* banquetear, festejar
feat *noun.* hazaña, proeza
feather *noun.* pluma

feather *verb.* emplumar
feature *noun.* **1.** característica **2.** rasgo **3.** crónica, artículo de fondo **4.** largometraje
feature *verb.* presentar
Feb. *abbr.* febrero
February *noun.* febrero
fed up *adj.* harto
federal *adj.* federal
federation *noun.* federación
fee *noun.* **1.** honorarios **2.** matrícula
feed *noun.* comida, alimento
feed *verb.* dar de comer, alimentar
—feed on alimentarse, nutrirse
feel *verb.* **1.** sentir **2.** tocar, palpar **3.** sentirse, encontrarse **4.** creer
feeling *noun.* **1.** sensación **2.** sentimiento **3.** impresión **4.** opinión **5.** sensibilidad, percepción
fell *verb.* talar, derribar
fellow *noun.* **1.** tipo **2.** compañero, camarada **3.** socio, miembro
fellow *adj.* compañero
fellowship *noun.* **1.** asociación **2.** compañerismo **3.** beca
felt *noun. adj.* fieltro
female *noun.* hembra
female *adj.* femenino
feminine *adj.* femenino
feminism *noun.* feminismo
feminist *noun. adj.* feminista
fen *noun.* pantano
fence *noun.* valla, cerca
fence *verb.* **1.** cercar **2.** practicar la esgrima **3.** defenderse con evasivas
ferry *noun.* transbordador, ferry
ferry *verb.* transportar
fertile *adj.* fértil
fertility *noun.* fertilidad
fertilizer *noun.* fertilizante, abono
festival *noun.* **1.** fiesta **2.** festival
fetch *verb.* **1.** traer, ir por, ir a buscar **2.** venderse por
feudal *adj.* feudal
fever *noun.* fiebre
few *adj. pron.* **1.** pocos **2.** algunos
fiber *noun.* **1.** fibra **2.** nervio, carácter
fiction *noun.* **1.** ficción **2.** literatura de ficción, narrativa

fictional *adj.* ficticio

field *noun.* **1.** campo **2.** cancha **3.** yacimiento **4.** terreno **5.** campo de batalla

fierce *adj.* **1.** feroz, salvaje **2.** intenso, fuerte

fiercely *adv.* **1.** ferozmente, violentamente **2.** intensamente

fiery *adj.* **1.** ardiente, llameante **2.** violento, colérico

fifteen *noun. adj.* quince

fifteenth *noun.* decimoquinto

fifth *noun.* quinto

fifties *noun plural.* **1.** entre cincuenta y sesenta **2.** los años cincuenta

fiftieth *noun.* quincuagésimo

fifty *noun. adj.* cincuenta

fig *noun.* higo

fight *noun.* **1.** pelea **2.** lucha **3.** combatividad, ánimo de lucha **4.** resistencia

fight *verb.* **1.** pelear, pelearse **2.** luchar, combatir **3.** discutir

fighter *noun.* **1.** combatiente, luchador **2.** avión de caza

figure *noun.* **1.** figura **2.** talle **3.** cifra, número **4.** diagrama

figure *verb.* **1.** aparecer **2.** figurar, calcular

file *noun.* **1.** carpeta **2.** archivo **3.** fila, hilera **4.** lima

file *verb.* **1.** archivar, clasificar **2.** presentar **3.** desfilar **4.** limar

fill *verb.* **1.** llenar, ocupar **2.** llenarse **3.** satisfacer, cubrir, cumplir **4.** rellenar, tapar, empastar

filling *noun.* **1.** empaste **2.** relleno

film *noun.* **1.** carrete **2.** película **3.** capa

film *verb.* **1.** filmar **2.** cubrirse, nublarse

filter *noun.* filtro

filter *verb.* **1.** filtrar **2.** filtrarse

filthy *adj.* **1.** sucio, asqueroso **2.** obsceno

fin *noun.* aleta

final *noun.* final

final *adj.* **1.** final, último **2.** definitivo

finally *adv.* **1.** finalmente **2.** al final

finals *noun plural.* finales

finance *noun.* **1.** finanzas **2.** fondos

finance *verb.* financiar

financial *adj.* financiero

financially *adv.* económicamente

find *noun.* hallazgo

find *verb.* **1.** encontrar, hallar **2.** descubrir, inventar **3.** fallar, dar sentencia —**find out** descubrir, averiguar

fine *noun.* multa

fine *interj.* muy bien, bien hecho

fine *verb.* multar

fine *adj.* **1.** excelente **2.** bueno, magnífico **3.** bien **4.** fino, delgado **5.** delicado **6.** sutil

fine *adv.* muy bien, a la perfección

finely *adv.* **1.** delicadamente **2.** elegantemente **3.** muy fino **4.** con precisión

finger *noun.* dedo

finger *verb.* manosear

finish *noun.* **1.** final **2.** acabado

finish *verb.* **1.** acabar **2.** terminar

finished *adj.* **1.** acabado, completo **2.** pulido, perfecto **3.** rendido, hecho polvo

finite *adj.* **1.** finito, limitado **2.** conjugado

Finland *noun.* Finlandia

Finn *noun.* finlandés

Finnish *noun. adj.* finlandés, finés

fire *noun.* **1.** fuego **2.** lumbre, chimenea **3.** incendio **4.** ardor, pasión

fire *verb.* **1.** incendiar, prender fuego **2.** enardecer, excitar **3.** disparar **4.** despedir, echar —**fire at/on** disparar

fireplace *noun.* chimenea

firm *noun.* empresa, firma

firm *adj.* **1.** firme, sólido **2.** severo **3.** tenaz

firmly *adv.* firmemente

first *noun. adj. adv.* primero

first-class *adj.* **1.** de primera clase **2.** de primera calidad, excelente

firstly *adv.* en primer lugar, primero

fish *noun.* **1.** pez **2.** pescado

fish *verb.* **1.** pescar **2.** buscar

fisherman *noun.* pescador

fist *noun.* puño

fit *noun.* **1.** ataque **2.** acceso, arrebato **3.** corte (de un traje)

fit *verb.* **1.** quedar bien, encajar, entrar

en 2. adecuarse a 3. instalar, poner,
colocar 4. equipar 5. concordar, corres-
ponderse

fit *adj.* 1. sano, en forma 2. adecuado,
conveniente

fitness *noun.* 1. buena forma 2. aptitud,
capacidad

fitting *noun.* 1. mobiliario, accesorios 2.
prueba

fitting *adj.* adecuado, propio, digno

five *noun. adj.* cinco

fiver *noun.* billete de cinco dólares

fix *noun.* apuro, aprieto

fix *verb.* 1. fijar 2. asegurar 3. clavar,
atar, amarrar, sujetar 4. arreglar 5. convenir

fixed *adj.* 1. fijo 2. amañado

fixture *noun.* instalación fija

flag *noun.* bandera

flag *verb.* decaer, flaquear

flame *noun.* llama

flame *verb.* 1. arder 2. encenderse,
llamear, brillar

flank *noun.* 1. costado 2. flanco

flank *verb.* flanquear

flap *noun.* 1. solapa, faldón 2. aleteo

flap *verb.* ondear, agitar, aletear, batir

flare *verb.* 1. llamear 2. acampanarse,
ensancharse

flash *noun.* 1. destello 2. arrebato 3.
instante 4. flash 5. noticia de última
hora

flash *verb.* 1. brillar, centellear, relam-
paguear 2. mostrar 3. lanzar, dirigir
—**flash by/past** pasar como un rayo

flashing *adj.* relampagueante, intermi-
tente

flash-light *noun.* 1. linterna 2. antorcha

flat *noun.* 1. llanura 2. palma 3. hoja (of
a sword) 4. bemol

flat *adj.* 1. llano, plano, liso 2.
monótono, aburrido, soso 3. rotundo,
terminante 4. desinflado 5. sin gas 6.
desafinado 7. fijo

flat *adv.* 1. horizontalmente 2. rotundamente, terminantemente

flavor *noun.* 1. sabor 2. aire

flavor *verb.* sazonar, condimentar

flee *verb.* huir

fleet *noun.* 1. flota 2. armada

flesh *noun.* 1. carne 2. pulpa

flexibility *noun.* flexibilidad

flexible *adj.* flexible

flick *noun.* movimiento rápido

flick *verb.* hacer un movimiento rápido

flight *noun.* 1. vuelo 2. huida, fuga 3.
tramo 4. bandada

fling *verb.* 1. arrojar, lanzar 2. arrojarse

flint *noun. adj.* 1. sílex 2. pedernal

flip *noun.* tirada, echada, coletazo

flip *verb.* 1. tirar al aire 2. hojear

float *noun.* boya, flotador

float *verb.* 1. flotar, poner a flote, hacer
flotar 2. emitir, poner en circulación

flock *noun.* 1. rebaño, bandada 2. tropel, multitud

flock (to/into) *verb.* congregarse,
reunirse

flood *noun.* 1. inundación 2. torrente,
avalancha

flood *verb.* inundar

floor *noun.* 1. suelo 2. piso, planta

floor *verb.* 1. solar, entarimar 2. derribar,
tumbar

flop *noun.* fracaso, fiasco

flop *verb.* 1. tumbarse, dejarse caer 2.
caer 3. fracasar

floppy *adj.* 1. blando, que se cae 2. flexible

flora *noun.* flora

flounder *verb.* revolcarse, andar dificul-
tosamente

flour *noun.* harina

flourish *noun.* 1. floritura 2. ademán,
movimiento ostentoso 3. floreo

flourish *verb.* 1. florecer 2. prosperar 3.
agitar, blandir

flow *noun.* corriente, flujo, circulación

flow *verb.* 1. fluir 2. subir 3. circular

flower *noun.* flor

flower *verb.* florecer

flu *noun.* gripe

fluid *noun.* 1. fluido 2. líquido

fluid *adj.* 1. fluido, líquido 2. flexible

flush *noun.* 1. rubor 2. arrebato 3. cisterna

flush *verb.* 1. ruborizar, sonrojar 2. tirar
de la cadena 3. hacer salir, desalojar

flushed *adj.* sonrojado

flux *noun.* inestabilidad, cambio constante

fly *noun.* **1.** mosca **2.** mosca artificial

fly *verb.* **1.** volar **2.** pilotar, ir en avión **3.** huir, salir de, abandonar **4.** pasar volando

foam *noun.* espuma

foam *verb.* hacer espuma

focal *adj.* focal

focus *noun.* **1.** foco **2.** centro
  —**in/out of focus** enfocado/desenfocado

focus *verb.* **1.** enfocar **2.** centrar, concentrar

fog *noun.* niebla

fog *verb.* empañarse

foil *noun.* **1.** papel de aluminio **2.** florete

foil *verb.* frustrar, desbaratar los planes

fold *noun.* **1.** pliegue **2.** redil

fold *verb.* **1.** doblar, plegar **2.** cruzar

folded *adj.* doblado, plegado, cruzado

folding *adj.* plegable

foliage *noun.* follaje

folk *adj.* popular, folclórico, tradicional

folks *noun plural.* gente

follow *verb.* **1.** seguir **2.** entender **3.** deducirse

follower *noun.* seguidor

following *prep.* después de

following *noun.* seguidores

following *adj.* siguiente

following *pron.* lo siguiente

follow-up *noun.* **1.** seguimiento **2.** continuación

folly *noun.* locura

fond *adj.* **1.** cariñoso, afectuoso **2.** ilusorio, vano

food *noun.* comida, alimento

fool *noun.* tonto, imbécil

fool *verb.* engañar
  —**fool about/around** hacer el tonto, bromear

foolish *adj.* **1.** tonto, imprudente **2.** ridículo

foot *noun.* **1.** pie **2.** pata

football *noun.* **1.** fútbol americano **2.** balón de fútbol

footstep *noun.* paso, pisada

for *prep.* **1.** para **2.** hacia, en dirección a **3.** durante **4.** por **5.** a favor de **6.** a causa de **7.** a pesar de **8.** de

for *conj.* ya que, puesto que

for example por ejemplo

forbid *verb.* prohibir

forbidden *adj.* prohibido

force *noun.* **1.** fuerza **2.** cuerpo, personal
  —**in force** vigente, en vigor
  —**forces** fuerzas armadas

force *verb.* **1.** forzar **2.** obligar **3.** imponer

forced *adj.* forzado, forzoso

ford *noun.* vado

ford *verb.* vadear

forecast *noun.* pronóstico, previsión

forecast *verb.* pronosticar

forefront *noun.* vanguardia

forehead *noun.* frente

foreign *adj.* **1.** extranjero **2.** ajeno **3.** exterior **4.** de asuntos exteriores

foreigner *noun.* **1.** extranjero **2.** extraño

foreman, forewoman *noun.* **1.** capataz, maestro de obras **2.** presidente del jurado

foremost *adj.* principal, más destacado

forensic *adj.* forense

foresee *verb.* prever

forest *noun.* **1.** bosque **2.** reserva

forestry *noun.* silvicultura

forestry *adj.* forestal

forge *noun.* forja

forge *verb.* **1.** forjar **2.** falsificar
  —**forge ahead** abrirse camino, avanzar

forget *verb.* **1.** olvidar **2.** olvidarse **3.** perder los estribos

forgive *verb.* perdonar

fork *noun.* **1.** tenedor **2.** bifurcación **3.** horca, horquilla

fork *verb.* **1.** bifurcarse, ramificarse **2.** torcer, girar **3.** cargar con la horca

form *noun.* **1.** forma **2.** clase, tipo **3.** formulario **4.** formalidad **5.** banco

form *verb.* **1.** formar, constituir **2.** formarse **3.** construir, hacer, elaborar, formular

formal *adj.* **1.** formal **2.** oficial **3.** de eti-

queta, de ceremonia, solemne **4.** regular **5.** correcto
formally *adv.* formalmente
format *noun.* formato
format *verb.* formatear
formation *noun.* formación
former *adj.* antiguo, anterior
—**the former** el primero
formerly *adv.* antiguamente, anteriormente
formidable *adj.* **1.** temible, imponente
2. formidable
formula *noun.* fórmula
fort *noun.* fortaleza, fuerte
forth *adv.* adelante
forthcoming *adj.* **1.** próximo, venidero
2. abierto, comunicativo
forties *noun plural.* **1.** entre cuarenta y
cincuenta **2.** los años cuarenta
fortieth *noun.* cuadragésimo
fortnight *noun.* quincena
fortress *noun.* fortaleza, fuerte
fortunate *adj.* afortunado
fortunately *adv.* afortunadamente
fortune *noun.* fortuna, suerte
forty *noun. adj.* cuarenta
forum *noun.* foro
forward, forwards *adv.* **1.** adelante,
hacia adelante **2.** en adelante
forward *noun.* delantero
forward *verb.* remitir, expedir, enviar
forward *adj.* **1.** hacia delante **2.**
delantero **3.** precoz, adelantado **4.**
atrevido, insolente
fossil *noun.* fósil
foster *verb.* **1.** acoger, criar **2.** fomentar,
promover, favorecer
foul *noun.* falta
foul *verb.* **1.** cometer una falta **2.** ensuciar, contaminar
foul *adj.* **1.** asqueroso, fétido **2.** vil, terrible **3.** ordinario, grosero **4.** antir-
reglamentario, sucio
found *verb.* fundar
—**found on/upon** basar
foundation *noun.* **1.** fundación **2.** fundamento, base **3.** cimientos
founder *noun.* fundador
founding *noun.* fundación

fountain *noun.* fuente
four *noun. adj.* cuatro
fourteen *noun. adj.* catorce
fourteenth *noun.* **1.** catorceavo **2.** decimocuarto
fourth *noun.* cuarto
fox *noun.* zorro
fox *verb.* confundir, despistar, dejar perplejo
fraction *noun.* **1.** fracción **2.** poquito,
parte
fracture *noun.* fractura
fracture *verb.* fracturar
fragile *adj.* frágil
fragment *noun.* fragmento, pedazo,
trozo
fragment *verb.* fragmentarse, hacerse
añicos
fragrance *noun.* fragancia, perfume
frail *adj.* débil, delicado
frame *noun.* **1.** armazón, estructura,
montura **2.** marco **3.** cuerpo, constitución
frame *verb.* **1.** enmarcar **2.** encuadrar **3.**
incriminar, culpar
framework *noun.* estructura, marco
franc *noun.* franco
France *noun.* Francia
franchise *noun.* **1.** sufragio **2.** licencia,
concesión, franquicia
frank *verb.* franquear
frank *adj.* franco
frankly *adv.* francamente
frantic *adj.* **1.** desesperado **2.** frenético
fraud *noun.* **1.** fraude, estafa **2.** impostor
freak *noun.* **1.** fenómeno, monstruo,
anomalía **2.** fanático
free *verb.* **1.** liberar, poner en libertad **2.**
deshacerse de, librarse de **3.** desatar,
soltar
free *adj.* **1.** libre **2.** abierto **3.** vacante,
desocupado **4.** gratuito, gratis
—**free with** generoso
freedom *noun.* libertad
freely *adv.* **1.** libremente **2.** voluntariamente **3.** generosamente
freeway *noun.* autopista
freeze *noun.* helada

freeze *verb.* **1.** congelar **2.** helar **3.** helarse, congelarse **4.** quedarse inmóvil

freezing *adj.* helado, glacial

freight *noun.* **1.** carga, mercancías **2.** flete

French *noun. adj.* francés

French fries *noun plural.* papas fritas, patatas fritas

Frenchman, Frenchwoman *noun.* francés

frequency *noun.* frecuencia

frequent *verb.* frecuentar

frequent *adj.* frecuente

frequently *adv.* frecuentemente

fresh *adj.* **1.** fresco **2.** recién hecho **3.** lozano, saludable **4.** nuevo, reciente **5.** dulce

freshly *adv.* recién

friction *noun.* fricción

Friday *noun.* viernes

fridge *noun.* frigorífico, refrigeradora, nevera

friend *noun.* **1.** amigo **2.** conocido

friendly *adj.* simpático, amigable

friendship *noun.* amistad

frighten *verb.* asustar

frightened *adj.* asustado

frightening *adj.* espantoso, aterrador

fringe *noun.* **1.** fleco, franja **2.** linde, periferia, borde

fringe *verb.* bordear, circundar

frog *noun.* rana

from *prep.* **1.** de **2.** desde **3.** por

front *noun.* **1.** parte delantera **2.** fachada **3.** portada **4.** frente

frontier *noun.* frontera

frost *noun.* **1.** helada **2.** escarcha

frost (over/up) *verb.* **1.** helarse **2.** escarchar

frown *noun.* ceño

frown *verb.* fruncir el ceño

fruit *noun.* **1.** fruta **2.** fruto

fruit *verb.* dar fruto

frustrate *verb.* frustrar

frustrated *adj.* frustrado

frustration *noun.* frustración

fry *verb.* **1.** freír **2.** freírse

ft. *abbr.* pie

fuel *noun.* combustible, carburante

fuel *verb.* abastecer de combustible

fulfill *verb.* **1.** cumplir, desempeñar **2.** satisfacer **3.** realizar, alcanzar

fulfillment *noun.* **1.** cumplimiento **2.** satisfacción **3.** realización

full *adj.* **1.** lleno **2.** completo, entero, íntegro **3.** detallado, extenso **4.** holgado, amplio **5.** de mucho vuelo **6.** ocupado

full *adv.* **1.** completamente, al máximo **2.** totalmente **3.** de cuerpo entero **4.** justo, de lleno

full-time *adj. adv.* a tiempo completo

fully *adv.* **1.** completamente, enteramente, plenamente **2.** por lo menos, como mínimo

fun *noun.* diversión

function *noun.* **1.** función **2.** recepción, acto

function *verb.* funcionar, marchar

functional *adj.* funcional

fund *noun.* **1.** fondo **2.** reserva

fundamental *noun.* fundamento, piedra angular, aspecto básico

fundamental *adj.* fundamental

fundamentally *adv.* fundamentalmente, básicamente, en esencia

funeral *noun.* funeral

funny *adj.* **1.** divertido, gracioso **2.** extraño, raro, curioso

fur *noun.* **1.** pelo, pelaje **2.** piel

furious *adj.* **1.** furioso **2.** violento

furnish *verb.* **1.** amueblar **2.** proporcionar, proveer, suministrar

furnished *adj.* amueblado

furniture *noun.* mobiliario, muebles

further *verb.* fomentar, promover, favorecer

further *adj.* **1.** más **2.** adicional **3.** ulterior, más distante

further *adv.* **1.** lejos, a lo lejos **2.** mucho **3.** más **4.** más lejos **5.** más allá

furthermore *adv.* además

fury *noun.* furia, furor

fusion *noun.* **1.** fusión **2.** fundición

fuss *noun.* **1.** jaleo, alboroto, ruido **2.** conmoción, bulla

fuss *verb.* preocuparse por cosas sin importancia

future *noun. adj.* futuro

G

g. *abbr.* gramo

gain *noun.* 1. aumento 2. beneficio, ganancia

gain *verb.* 1. ganar, adquirir 2. obtener, conseguir 3. aumentar 4. adelantarse, ir adelantado

galaxy *noun.* 1. galaxia 2. constelación

gall *noun.* 1. bilis, hiel 2. atrevimiento, caradura

gall *verb.* fastidiar, molestar

gallery *noun.* 1. galería 2. tribuna, gallinero

gallery *adj.* de galería, de gallinero

gallon *noun.* galón

gamble *noun.* riesgo, apuesta

gamble *verb.* apostar, jugar dinero

gambling *noun.* juego

game *noun.* 1. juego 2. partido, partida 3. caza mayor, caza menor

game *adj.* valiente, animoso, bien dispuesto

gang *noun.* 1. grupo, cuadrilla, equipo 2. banda

gap *noun.* 1. hueco, espacio, vacío 2. brecha

garage *noun.* 1. garaje, cochera 2. taller, gasolinera, estación de servicio

garbage *noun.* basura

garbage-can *noun.* cubo de la basura

garden *noun.* jardín, huerto
—**gardens** parque, jardines

garden *verb.* trabajar en el jardín/huerto

gardener *noun.* jardinero

gardening *noun.* jardinería

garlic *noun.* ajo

garment *noun.* prenda de vestir

garrison *noun.* guarnición

garrison *verb.* guarnecer

garrison *adj.* fortificado

gas *noun.* 1. gas 2. anestesia 3. gasolina

gas *verb.* asfixiar con gas, gasear

gasoline *noun.* gasolina

gasp *noun.* boqueada, jadeo, grito ahogado

gasp *verb.* 1. jadear, respirar con dificultad 2. gritar

gastric *adj.* gástrico

gate *noun.* 1. puerta, entrada 2. verja

gateway *noun.* 1. puerta de acceso 2. portal

gather *noun.* pliegue, fruncido

gather *verb.* 1. coger, recoger, recopilar 2. reunir, juntar 3. reunirse, juntarse, congregarse 4. enterarse, tener entendido 5. acumularse, amontonarse 6. recolectar 7. fruncir

gathering *noun.* 1. reunión, asamblea 2. concurrencia, muchedumbre

gauge *noun.* 1. calibrador, indicador 2. calibre 3. ancho de vía

gauge *verb.* 1. medir, calibrar 2. juzgar, estimar

gay *noun.* gay, homosexual

gay *adj.* 1. gay, homosexual 2. vivo, vistoso, alegre

gaze *noun.* mirada fija

gaze *verb.* mirar fijamente, clavar la vista

gear *noun.* 1. engranaje 2. marcha 3. mecanismo 4. equipo, bártulos, trastos, herramientas

gender *noun.* género

gene *noun.* gen

general *noun.* general

general *adj.* 1. general 2. común

generally *adv.* generalmente, en general, por lo general

generate *verb.* generar, producir, causar, suscitar

generation *noun.* generación

generator *noun.* generador

generic *adj.* genérico

generosity *noun.* generosidad

generous *adj.* 1. generoso 2. abundante

genetic *adj.* genético

genetics *noun singular.* genética

genius *noun.* genio

gentle *adj.* 1. amable, dulce, tierno 2. suave, ligero, moderado

gentleman *noun.* caballero

gently *adv.* 1. amablemente, dulcemente, tiernamente 2. suavemente, ligeramente, moderadamente

genuine *adj.* **1.** genuino, auténtico, verdadero **2.** sincero

genuinely *adv.* **1.** realmente, verdaderamente **2.** sinceramente

geography *noun.* geografía

geological *adj.* geológico

geology *noun.* geología

German *noun. adj.* alemán

Germany *noun.* Alemania

gesture *noun.* gesto

gesture *verb.* hacer un gestos

get *verb.* **1.** conseguir **2.** obtener **3.** tomar **4.** recibir, ganar, cobrar **5.** traer, ir a buscar, procurar **6.** llevar **7.** encontrar **8.** coger, recoger, agarrar, atrapar **9.** adquirir, comprar **10.** entender, comprender **11.** poner, ponerse **12.** hacer **13.** hacerse, volverse, convertirse **14.** convencer, persuadir **15.** llegar **16.** lograr, llegar a **17.** tener **18.** acertar, dar en

—**get along** llevarse bien

—**get down** bajar, descender

—**get off** apearse de, bajar de

—**get out** salir

—**get over 1.** superar **2.** atravesar

—**get up** levantarse

ghetto *noun.* gueto

ghost *noun.* fantasma

giant *noun.* **1.** gigante **2.** as, coloso

giant *adj.* gigante, gigantesco, descomunal

gift *noun.* **1.** regalo, presente, obsequio **2.** don, talento

gift *verb.* regalar, obsequiar

gifted *adj.* talentoso

giggle *noun.* risa tonta, risa nerviosa

giggle *verb.* reírse tontamente, dar la risa tonta

gill *noun.* branquia, agalla

gilt *noun.* dorado

gin *noun.* ginebra

ginger *noun.* jengibre

ginger *adj.* **1.** de jengibre **2.** rojo, pelirrojo, bermejo

girl *noun.* niña, chica, muchacha

—**Girl Scout** exploradora

give *noun.* elasticidad, resistencia

give *verb.* **1.** dar **2.** regalar, entregar,

otorgar, conceder **3.** proporcionar, proveer, servir, suministrar **4.** provocar, causar **5.** ceder, dar de sí **6.** lanzar, proferir

—**give in** darse por vencido

—**give out** acabarse, agotarse

—**give up 1.** renunciar, dejar de **2.** rendirse, entregarse

given *adj.* **1.** dado **2.** determinado

—**given to** dado a, propenso a

glad *adj.* feliz, alegre, contento

glamour, glamor *noun.* glamour, encanto, atractivo

glamorous *adj.* glamuroso, atractivo

glance *noun.* mirada, vistazo, ojeada

glance *verb.* echar un vistazo, dar una mirada

glancing *adj.* oblicuo

gland *noun.* glándula

glare *noun.* **1.** mirada feroz **2.** deslumbramiento

glare *verb.* **1.** mirar ferozmente, fulminar con la mirada **2.** deslumbrar

glass *noun.* **1.** vidrio, cristal **2.** vaso, copa **3.** espejo **4.** barómetro

glasses *noun plural.* gafas, anteojos

gleam *noun.* **1.** brillo, destello **2.** rayo, resquicio

gleam *verb.* relucir, brillar, destellar

glimpse *noun.* vislumbre, destello

glimpse *verb.* vislumbrar, entrever

glitter *noun.* brillo, resplandor

glitter *verb.* brillar, relucir

glittering *adj.* brillante, reluciente

global *adj.* global, mundial, universal

globe *noun.* **1.** globo, esfera **2.** globo terráqueo

gloom *noun.* **1.** penumbra, oscuridad **2.** pesimismo, tristeza, melancolía

gloomy *adj.* **1.** sombrío, lóbrego **2.** triste, pesimista

glorious *adj.* **1.** glorioso **2.** magnífico, espléndido

glory *noun.* gloria, esplendor

glory *verb.* enorgullecerse, jactarse

glossy *adj.* lustroso, brillante, reluciente

glove *noun.* guante

glow *noun.* brillo, resplandor, incandescencia

glow *verb.* brillar, resplandecer, estar al rojo vivo

glowing *adj.* brillante, resplandeciente, incandescente

glucose *noun.* glucosa

glue *noun.* cola, pegamento

glue *verb.* colar, pegar

go *noun.* 1. intento 2. turno 3. energía, empuje

go *verb.* 1. ir 2. irse, marcharse, salir, partir 3. acudir 4. conducir a, ir a 5. enviarse, tramitar, pasar 6. venderse, darse 7. desarrollarse, marchar 8. desaparecer, gastarse, pasar, esfumarse, transcurrir 9. averiarse, fallar, desgastarse, romperse, ceder 10. funcionar 11. volverse, ponerse 12. valer, estar permitido, ser aceptable 13. hacer 14. pasar 15. extenderse, llegar 16. hacer juego, pegar, armonizar 17. caber

—**go by** pasar por, pasar junto a

—**go off** 1. marcharse, irse 2. estallar

—**go on** seguir, proseguir

—**go out** salir

—**go through** 1. pasar por 2. padecer, sufrir

—**go with** 1. acompañar 2. armonizar, hacer juego

go-ahead *noun.* luz verde, visto bueno

goal *noun.* 1. gol 2. objetivo, finalidad, meta

goalkeeper *noun.* portero, arquero

goat *noun.* cabra

God *noun.* Dios

goddess *noun.* diosa

going *noun.* 1. salida, partida, ida 2. estado

going *adj.* 1. próspero, que funciona bien 2. actual, del momento

gold *noun.* oro

golden *adj.* dorado, de oro

golf *noun.* golf

golf *verb.* jugar al golf

golfer *noun.* golfista, jugador de golf

good *interj.* bueno, bien

good *noun.* 1. bien, provecho, beneficio 2. bondad, lado bueno

—**goods** artículos, bienes, mercancías

good *adj.* 1. buen, bueno 2. correcto 3. competente 4. amable, bondadoso 5. útil, beneficioso 6. agradable 7. apropiado, adecuado, oportuno 8. apto, cualificado 9. sano, saludable 10. positivo 11. profundo 12. virtuoso

goodbye *interj. noun.* adiós

good-looking *adj.* guapo, bien parecido

goodness *interj.* ¡Dios mío!

goodness *noun.* bondad

goodwill, good will *noun.* 1. clientela, renombre comercial 2. buena voluntad

goose *noun.* ganso

gore *noun.* sangre derramada, sangre coagulada

gore *verb.* cornear, dar una cornada

gorgeous *adj.* 1. hermoso, precioso, guapísimo 2. magnífico, espléndido

gosh *interj.* ¡cielos!

gospel *noun.* evangelio

gossip *noun.* 1. chisme, chismorreo, cotilleo 2. charla, conversación 3. chismoso, cotilla

gossip *verb.* 1. chismorrear, cotillear 2. charlar, conversar

govern *verb.* 1. gobernar 2. dominar 3. regir 4. guiar

government *noun.* 1. gobierno 2. dirección

governmental *adj.* gubernamental, gubernativo

governor *noun.* gobernador

gown *noun.* 1. vestido largo 2. toga

grab *noun.* asimiento, acto de agarrar

grab *verb.* 1. asir, agarrar, coger 2. apropiarse de, arrebatar, echar mano a

grace *noun.* 1. gracia, elegancia 2. delicadeza, cortesía, gentileza 3. bendición 4. plazo, demora 5. Ilustrísima, Excelencia

grade *noun.* 1. nivel, clase, categoría, calidad, grado 2. curso, año 3. nota 4. pendiente

grade *verb.* 1. clasificar 2. calificar

gradient *noun.* pendiente

gradual *adj.* gradual

gradually *adv.* gradualmente

graduate *noun.* licenciado, graduado, egresado

graduate *verb.* **1.** licenciarse, graduarse **2.** graduar

grain *noun.* **1.** grano **2.** cereal **3.** veta, fibra **4.** pizca, ápice

grammar *noun.* gramática

grammatical *adj.* gramatical

grand *noun.* mil dólares

grand *adj.* **1.** grandioso, magnífico, espléndido, imponente **2.** ambicioso **3.** distinguido, respetable

grandchild *noun.* nieto, nieta

granddad *noun.* abuelo

granddaughter *noun.* nieta

grandfather *noun.* abuelo

grandmother *noun.* abuela

grandparent *noun.* abuelo, abuela

grandson *noun.* nieto

granite *noun.* granito

granny, grannie *noun.* abuelita

grant *noun.* otorgamiento, concesión

grant *verb.* **1.** conceder, otorgar **2.** reconocer, admitir

grape *noun.* uva

graph *noun.* gráfica, gráfico

graphic *adj.* gráfico

grasp *noun.* **1.** apretón **2.** control, dominio **3.** alcance **4.** comprensión, conocimientos

grasp *verb.* **1.** asir, agarrar, sujetar, empuñar **2.** comprender, entender

grass *noun.* **1.** hierba, césped **2.** marihuana, mota

grate *noun.* parrilla

grate *verb.* **1.** rallar **2.** crispar, irritar, poner nervioso

grateful *adj.* agradecido

gratitude *noun.* gratitud

grave *noun.* tumba

grave *adj.* grave, serio

gravel *noun.* grava

gravity *noun.* **1.** gravedad **2.** seriedad

gray, grey *noun.* gris

gray, grey *verb.* encanecer

gray, grey *adj.* **1.** gris **2.** canoso

graze *noun.* rasguño, roce

graze *verb.* **1.** pastar, pacer **2.** raspar **3.** rozar

great *adj.* **1.** gran, grande **2.** importante **3.** enorme, vasto **4.** mucho **5.** maravi-

lloso, espléndido, fantástico **6.** excelente, buenísimo

Great Britain *noun.* Gran Bretaña

greatly *adv.* muy, mucho

Greece *noun.* Grecia

greed *noun.* **1.** avaricia, codicia **2.** gula

greedy *adj.* **1.** avaricioso, codicioso **2.** glotón

Greek *noun. adj.* griego

green *noun.* **1.** verde, verdor **2.** césped, prado **3.** green (golf)
—**greens** verduras

green *adj.* **1.** verde **2.** inexperto, bisoño **3.** inocente **4.** ecologista

greenhouse *noun.* invernadero

greet *verb.* saludar

greeting *noun.* saludo

grid *noun.* **1.** cuadrícula **2.** reja

grief *noun.* dolor, pesar, aflicción

grill *noun.* **1.** parrilla, grill **2.** parrillada

grill *verb.* **1.** asar a la parrillar, hacer al grill **2.** interrogar

grim *adj.* **1.** desalentador **2.** horrible, macabro, espantoso **3.** ceñudo, austero, severo **4.** inflexible, inexorable

grimly *adv.* **1.** severamente **2.** horriblemente, espantosamente **3.** inflexiblemente

grin *noun.* sonrisa de oreja a oreja

grin *verb.* sonreír de oreja a oreja

grind *noun.* trabajo pesado

grind *verb.* **1.** moler, triturar, picar **2.** rechinar **3.** afilar

grip *noun.* **1.** apretón **2.** asidero, asa, empuñadura **3.** saco de mano, bolsa **4.** conocimiento, comprensión

grip *verb.* empuñar, agarrar, aferrar, asir

groan *noun.* **1.** gemido **2.** gruñido

groan *verb.* **1.** gemir **2.** gruñir

groove *noun.* surco, ranura, estría

gross *noun.* totalidad

gross *adj.* **1.** flagrante, grande, craso **2.** grosero, ordinario **3.** muy gordo, obeso **4.** bruto

ground *noun.* **1.** suelo, tierra **2.** terreno, campo
—**grounds** **1.** jardines **2.** razones, motivos **3.** poso, sedimento

ground *verb.* **1.** basarse, fundarse **2.**

encallar **3.** obligar a quedarse en tierra
group *noun.* grupo, conjunto
group *verb.* **1.** agrupar **2.** agruparse
grow *verb.* **1.** crecer **2.** aumentar **3.** desarrollarse **4.** dejarse **5.** hacerse, ponerse, volverse **6.** cultivar
grower *noun.* cultivador
grown *adj.* adulto
growth *noun.* **1.** crecimiento, desarrollo **2.** aumento **3.** tumor
guarantee *noun.* garantía
guarantee *verb.* garantizar
guard *noun.* **1.** guardia, centinela **2.** carcelero **3.** vigilancia, protección
guard *verb.* **1.** guardar **2.** vigilar, proteger, defender
guarded *adj.* cauteloso, prudente
guardian *noun.* **1.** tutor **2.** guardián, protector
guess *noun.* suposición, conjetura, estimación
guess *verb.* **1.** adivinar, acertar **2.** suponer, creer

guest *noun.* invitado, huésped
guidance *noun.* orientación, consejo
guide *noun.* **1.** guía **2.** modelo, pauta
guide *verb.* guiar, dirigir
guideline *noun.* directriz, pauta
guilt *noun.* culpa, culpabilidad
guilty *adj.* culpable
guitar *noun.* guitarra
guitarist *noun.* guitarrista
gulf *noun.* golfo
gum *noun.* **1.** goma **2.** pegamento **3.** chicle, goma de mascar **4.** encía
gum *verb.* pegar
gun *noun.* **1.** arma de fuego **2.** fusil **3.** escopeta **4.** pistola
gunman *noun.* pistolero
gut *noun.* **1.** intestino, tripa **2.** cuerda de tripa
—**guts** agallas, coraje
gut *verb.* **1.** destripar **2.** destruir el interior
guy *noun.* tipo, tío, individuo
gym *noun.* **1.** gimnasio **2.** gimnasia
gypsy *noun. adj.* gitano

H

habit *noun.* **1.** costumbre **2.** hábito
habitat *noun.* hábitat
hack *noun.* **1.** corte, tajo, machetazo, hachazo **2.** taxi
hack *verb.* cortar, tajar
hail *interj.* salve
hail *noun.* **1.** granizo **2.** lluvia **3.** grito
hail *verb.* **1.** granizar **2.** llamar **3.** aclamar
hair *noun.* pelo, cabello, vello
half *noun.* mitad
half *adj.* **1.** medio **2.** mitad
half *adv.* **1.** medio **2.** a medias **3.** casi
half-time *noun.* descanso, intervalo
hall *noun.* **1.** vestíbulo, entrada **2.** sala **3.** ayuntamiento **4.** pasillo, corredor **5.** residencia, colegio mayor
hallo *interj. noun.* hola
halt *noun.* **1.** alto, interrupción **2.** parada **3.** apeadero
halt *verb.* **1.** parar, detener **2.** pararse, detenerse

halve *verb.* **1.** partir en dos **2.** reducir a la mitad
ham *noun.* jamón
hammer *noun.* **1.** martillo **2.** macillo
hammer *verb.* **1.** martillar, martillear, clavar, batir **2.** hacer entender algo a alguien a fuerza de repetirlo
hamper *noun.* cesta, canasta
hamper *verb.* estorbar, impedir, obstaculizar
hand *noun.* **1.** mano **2.** manecilla, aguja **3.** trabajador, operario **4.** habilidad **5.** influencia **6.** ayuda **7.** partida **8.** palmo **9.** caligrafía, escritura
hand *verb.* **1.** dar, entregar **2.** devolver, pasar
handbag *noun.* bolso
handbook *noun.* manual
handful *noun.* puñado
handicap *noun.* **1.** obstáculo, impedimento **2.** desventaja **3.** handicap **4.** discapacidad, minusvalía

handicap *verb.* obstaculizar, impedir, perjudicar

handicapped *adj.* 1. discapacitado 2. deficiente mental

handkerchief *noun.* pañuelo

handle *noun.* 1. mango, asa, manilla, pomo 2. asa 3. manilla 4. pomo

handle *verb.* 1. manejar 2. tocar, manipular 3. tratar 4. comerciar con

handsome *adj.* 1. guapo, hermoso, bien parecido 2. generoso, considerable

handwriting *noun.* caligrafía

handy *adj.* 1. a mano, cerca 2. práctico, útil 3. hábil, diestro

hang *verb.* 1. colgar 2. tender 3. ahorcar 4. caer 5. inclinar, bajar

hanging *noun.* ahorcamiento

happen *verb.* 1. ocurrir, pasar, acontecer, suceder 2. dar la casualidad, resultar que

happening *noun.* acontecimiento, suceso

happily *adv.* felizmente, por suerte

happiness *noun.* felicidad, alegría, dicha

happy *adj.* 1. feliz, alegre, dichoso 2. contento

harassment *noun.* acoso

harbor *noun.* puerto

hard *adj.* 1. duro 2. firme 3. difícil 4. agotador 5. severo 6. riguroso 7. irrefutable 8. fuerte

hard *adv.* 1. duro, duramente 2. con ahínco 3. fuerte, fuertemente 4. fijamente 5. severamente 6. completamente, totalmente

harden *verb.* 1. endurecer 2. endurecerse

hardly *adv.* 1. apenas 2. casi 3. difícilmente

hardship *noun.* 1. infortunio 2. privación 3. sufrimiento

hardware *noun.* 1. ferretería 2. hardware, soporte físico

hardy *adj.* fuerte, resistente, robusto

harm *noun.* daño, mal, perjuicio

harm *verb.* hacer daño, perjudicar

harmful *adj.* nocivo, perjudicial, dañino

harmless *adj.* inofensivo, inocuo

harmony *noun.* armonía

harness *noun.* arneses, guarniciones, arreos

harness *verb.* 1. enjaezar, poner los arreos 2. aprovechar, utilizar

harry *verb.* acosar, hostigar, atormentar

harsh *adj.* 1. severo, duro, cruel 2. fuerte, chillón 3. áspero

harvest *noun.* cosecha

harvest *verb.* cosechar

hastily *adv.* apresuradamente, precipitadamente

hasty *adj.* 1. apresurado, precipitado 2. irritable, con genio

hat *noun.* sombrero

hatch *noun.* 1. ventanilla 2. escotilla

hatch *verb.* 1. empollar, incubar 2. romper el cascarón 3. tramar, urdir, madurar

hate *noun.* odio, aversión

hate *verb.* odiar, detestar, aborrecer

hatred *noun.* odio, aversión

haul *noun.* 1. tirón, estirón 2. redada, botín

haul *verb.* tirar, arrastrar

haunt *noun.* 1. guarida, lugar frecuentado 2. lugar predilecto

haunt *verb.* 1. aparecer, rondar 2. perseguir, obsesionar 3. frecuentar

haunted *adj.* encantado, embrujado

have *verb.* 1. tener 2. haber (auxiliary) 3. tomar 4. poseer 5. pasar 6. tolerar, sufrir 7. recibir 8. hacer 9. lograr, conseguir 10. dar 11. hacer que alguien haga algo, mandar hacer algo 12. tomar el pelo, engañar

—have to deber, tener que

haven *noun.* puerto, refugio

hawk *noun.* halcón

hawk *verb.* vender de puerta en puerta

hay *noun.* heno

hazard *noun.* riesgo, peligro

hazard *verb.* arriesgar, aventurar

hazardous *adj.* arriesgado, peligroso

hazel *noun.* avellano

hazel *adj.* color de avellana

he *noun.* 1. macho 2. varón

he *pron.* 1. él 2. el que, aquel que

head *noun.* 1. cabeza 2. mente 3. director, jefe **4.** fuente, nacimiento, origen **5.** cabecera, principio **6.** parte superior **7.** cara **8.** cabo, punta **9.** espuma

head *verb.* **1.** encabezar **2.** estar al frente de, dirigir, capitanear **3.** titular **4.** cabecear, rematar con la cabeza
—**head for** dirigirse, encaminarse

headache *noun.* **1.** dolor de cabeza **2.** quebradero de cabeza

heading *noun.* encabezamiento, título

headline *noun.* titular, cabecera

head-on *adv. adj.* de frente, frontal

headquarters *noun.* **1.** cuartel general **2.** sede, oficina central

heal *verb.* curar, sanar

health *noun.* salud

healthy *adj.* **1.** sano **2.** saludable **3.** próspero, sustancioso

heap *noun.* montón, pila

heap *verb.* **1.** amontonar, apilar **2.** colmar, llenar

hear *verb.* **1.** oír **2.** escuchar **3.** ver **4.** enterarse, tener noticias

hearing *noun.* **1.** oído **2.** oportunidad de hablar **3.** audiencia, vista
—**within hearing** al alcance del oído

heart *noun.* **1.** corazón **2.** entrañas **3.** centro, meollo **4.** valor
—**hearts** corazones, copas (cards)
—**lose heart** descorazonarse

heart attack *noun.* infarto, ataque al corazón

heat *noun.* **1.** calor **2.** pasión, ardor, vehemencia **3.** furia, ira **4.** eliminatoria

heat (up) *verb.* **1.** calentar **2.** calentarse

heated *adj.* **1.** caliente **2.** climatizado **3.** acalorado

heater *noun.* **1.** calentador **2.** estufa

heather *noun.* brezo

heating *noun.* calefacción

heaven *noun.* **1.** cielo **2.** paraíso, gloria

heavily *adv.* **1.** muy, mucho **2.** fuertemente **3.** profundamente **4.** pesadamente

heavy *adj.* **1.** pesado **2.** fuerte, abundante **3.** empedernido **4.** profundo **5.** considerable, cuantioso **6.** grueso, tosco **7.** cargado, encapotado **8.** denso **9.** difícil

heavyweight *noun. adj.* peso pesado

hectare *noun.* hectárea

hedge *noun.* seto

hedge *verb.* **1.** contestar con evasivas **2.** cercar (con un seto)

heel *noun.* **1.** talón **2.** tacón

heel *verb.* poner un tacón

height *noun.* **1.** altura, estatura **2.** cúspide, apogeo, punto culminante **3.** cumbre, cima **4.** colmo

heighten *verb.* **1.** elevar, realzar **2.** aumentar, intensificar

heir *noun.* heredero

helicopter *noun.* helicóptero

hell *noun.* infierno

hello *interj. noun.* **1.** hola **2.** ¡vaya!, ¡ándale!

helmet *noun.* casco

help *noun.* **1.** ayuda **2.** criado, asistente, empleado, ayudante **3.** remedio

help *verb.* **1.** ayudar **2.** socorrer, auxiliar **3.** contribuir **4.** aliviar **5.** servir
—**cannot help** no poder evitar

helpful *adj.* **1.** servicial **2.** útil

helping *noun.* ración, porción

helpless *adj.* indefenso, desvalido

hemisphere *noun.* hemisferio

hen *noun.* **1.** gallina **2.** hembra (de ave)

hence *adv.* **1.** por lo tanto, por consiguiente **2.** de aquí a

her *adj.* su, sus (de ella)

her *pron.* **1.** la (direct object) **2.** le, se (indirect object) **3.** ella (after prep)

herald *noun.* **1.** heraldo **2.** precursor

herald *verb.* anunciar, proclamar

herb *noun.* hierba

herd *noun.* **1.** rebaño, manada, piara **2.** multitud, tropel

herd *verb.* **1.** llevar en rebaño **2.** reunirse

here *interj.* **1.** ¡oye!, ¡eh! **2.** ¡presente!
—**here, there and everywhere** por todas partes, en todas partes

here *adv.* **1.** aquí, acá **2.** entonces, llegado a ese punto **3.** aquí presente

hereditary *adj.* hereditario

heritage *noun.* herencia, patrimonio

hero *noun.* **1.** héroe **2.** protagonista, personaje principal

heroic adj. heroico

heroin noun. heroína

hers pron. **1.** (el) suyo, (la) suya, (los) suyos, (las) suyas (de ella) **2.** de ella

herself pron. **1.** se **2.** sí misma **3.** ella misma **4.** ella sola

hesitate verb. vacilar, titubear, dudar

hesitation noun. indecisión, vacilación, duda

hey interj. ¡eh!, ¡oye!

hi interj. ¡hola!

hidden adj. escondido, oculto

hide noun. **1.** cuero **2.** piel, pellejo

hide verb. **1.** esconder, ocultar **2.** esconderse, ocultarse

hiding noun. **1.** escondrijo **2.** paliza

hierarchical adj. jerárquico

hierarchy noun. jerarquía

high adj. **1.** alto **2.** elevado **3.** grande **4.** superior **5.** excelente **6.** bueno **7.** noble **8.** fuerte **9.** agudo **10.** pasado **11.** importante

high adv. **1.** alto **2.** arriba, hacia arriba

high school noun. instituto, escuela de secundaria

higher education noun. enseñanza superior

highlight noun. punto culminante, guinda

highlight verb. destacar, dar relieve

highly adv. **1.** muy **2.** mucho **3.** sumamente **4.** extremadamente

high-tech, hi-tech, high technology noun. alta tecnología

highway noun. **1.** carretera **2.** autopista

hike noun. caminata, excursión a pie

hike verb. dar una caminata, ir de excursión

hill noun. **1.** colina, loma **2.** cuesta

hillside noun. ladera

him pron. **1.** lo, le (direct object) **2.** le, se (indirect object) **3.** él (after prep)

himself pron. **1.** se **2.** sí mismo **3.** él mismo **4.** él solo

Hindu noun. adj. hindú

hint noun. **1.** insinuación, indirecta **2.** indicación, sugerencia **3.** indicio

hint verb. **1.** insinuar, dar a entender **2.** soltar indirectas

hip noun. cadera

hip adj. a la última

hire noun. alquiler

hire verb. **1.** alquilar **2.** contratar

his adj. pron. **1.** su, sus (de él) **2.** (el) suyo, (la) suya, (los) suyos, (las) suyas (de él) **3.** de él

historian noun. historiador

historic, historical adj. histórico

historically adv. históricamente

history noun. historia

hit noun. **1.** golpe, tiro **2.** acierto **3.** éxito

hit verb. **1.** golpear, lanzar **2.** pegar, chocar **3.** dar con, dar contra **4.** afectar, dañar **5.** dar en, alcanzar

hitherto adv. hasta la fecha, hasta ahora

HIV abbr. VIH, virus del sida

hobby noun. pasatiempo

hockey noun. hockey

hold noun. **1.** agarre, asimiento **2.** dominio, influencia **3.** llave **4.** bodega

hold verb. **1.** tener en las manos, agarrar, sujetar, coger, asir **2.** sostener **3.** mantener, mantenerse **4.** creer, opinar **5.** tener **6.** retener **7.** guardar **8.** defender **9.** resistir **10.** ser válido, regir **11.** contener **12.** tener capacidad, tener cabida **13.** aguantar **14.** soportar **15.** ocupar, desempeñar, ejercer **16.** tener lugar, celebrarse **17.** deparar **18.** atenerse

—**hold on 1.** seguir, persistir **2.** aguantar, resistir

—**hold together 1.** unir, juntar **2.** mantenerse juntos

hole noun. **1.** agujero **2.** cavidad, hueco **3.** hoyo **4.** bache

hole verb. **1.** agujerear **2.** meter en el hoyo

holiday noun. **1.** fiesta, día festivo **2.** vacaciones

Holland noun. Holanda

hollow noun. **1.** hueco **2.** hondonada

hollow adj. **1.** hueco, hundido **2.** falso, vacío

holly noun. acebo

holy adj. **1.** sagrado **2.** santo

home noun. **1.** casa **2.** domicilio **3.** cuna, patria **4.** asilo, orfanato **5.** hogar

home *adj.* **1.** casero, del hogar **2.** local, nacional **3.** en casa, de casa

home *adv.* **1.** a casa, en casa **2.** de vuelta

homeland *noun.* patria, tierra natal

homeless *noun.* sin techo

homeless *adj.* sin hogar, sin vivienda

homework *noun.* deberes

homogeneous *adj.* homogéneo

homosexual *noun. adj.* homosexual

homosexuality *noun.* homosexualidad

honest *adj.* honesto

honestly *interj.* ¡hay que ver!, ¡vamos!

honestly *adv.* **1.** honestamente **2.** francamente, sinceramente

honesty *noun.* honestidad

honey *noun.* **1.** miel **2.** querido, cariño

honeymoon *noun.* luna de miel

honor *noun.* **1.** honor **2.** condecoración

honor *verb.* **1.** honrar **2.** condecorar **3.** cumplir

   —Your/His/Her Honor Su Señoría

honorable *adj.* **1.** honrado **2.** honorable

honorary *adj.* **1.** honorario, honorífico **2.** no remunerado

hood *noun.* **1.** capucha, caperuza **2.** capó **3.** muceta

hook *noun.* **1.** anzuelo **2.** gancho **3.** alcayata **4.** croché

hook *verb.* **1.** pescar **2.** enganchar

hooked *adj.* ganchudo

   —hooked on enganchado, adicto

hop *noun.* **1.** lúpulo **2.** salto, brinco

hop *verb.* dar saltos, brincar

hope *noun.* **1.** esperanza **2.** sueño, ilusión **3.** posibilidad

hope *verb.* esperar

hopeful *adj.* **1.** optimista, esperanzado **2.** prometedor

hopefully *adv.* **1.** con esperanza **2.** con suerte

hopeless *adj.* **1.** inútil **2.** desesperado, imposible

   —hopeless at negado, desastre

horizon *noun.* horizonte

horizontal *adj.* horizontal

hormone *noun.* hormona

horn *noun.* **1.** cacho, cuerno, asta **2.** trompa **3.** bocina, claxon

horrible *adj.* horrible, horroroso

horrify *verb.* **1.** horrorizar **2.** escandalizar

horror *noun.* horror

horse *noun.* **1.** caballo **2.** potro

hospital *noun.* hospital

hospitality *noun.* hospitalidad

host, hostess *noun.* **1.** anfitrión, anfitriona **2.** huésped **3.** multitud

hostage *noun.* rehén

hostel *noun.* **1.** albergue **2.** residencia

hostile *adj.* **1.** hostil, contrario **2.** adverso, desfavorable

hostility *noun.* hostilidad

hot *adj.* **1.** caliente **2.** caluroso, cálido **3.** picante **4.** acalorado, impetuoso, violento **5.** reciente, de última hora

hotel *noun.* hotel

hound *noun.* perro de caza

hound *verb.* perseguir, acosar

hour *noun.* hora

house *noun.* **1.** casa **2.** hogar **3.** sala **4.** cámara

house *verb.* **1.** alojar **2.** guardar, poner

household *noun.* casa, familia

housekeeper *noun.* gobernanta, ama de llaves

housewife *noun.* ama de casa

housework *noun.* quehaceres domésticos, faenas de la casa

housing *noun.* alojamiento, vivienda

hover *verb.* **1.** planear, flotar en el aire **2.** revolotear, rondar

   —hover between dudar, vacilar

how *adv. conj.* **1.** cómo **2.** qué **3.** cuánto, cómo de, a qué

however *conj.* de todas formas, de cualquier modo

however *adv.* **1.** sin embargo, no obstante **2.** cómo **3.** por más que

howl *noun.* rugido, aullido, gemido, alarido

howl *verb.* rugir, aullar, gemir, dar alaridos

hug *noun.* abrazo

hug *verb.* **1.** abrazar **2.** arrimarse, pegarse

huge *adj.* enorme

hull *noun.* casco

hum *noun.* murmullo, zumbido

hum *verb*. **1.** tararear, canturrear **2.** zumbar **3.** bullir

human, human being *noun*. ser humano

human *adj*. humano

humanity *noun*. humanidad

humble *verb*. humillar

humble *adj*. humilde, modesto

humiliation *noun*. humillación

humor *noun*. **1.** humor **2.** comicidad, gracia

humor *verb*. complacer, consentir

hundred *noun*. ciento, centenar, centena

hundred *adj*. cien, ciento

Hungarian *noun. adj*. húngaro

Hungary *noun*. Hungría

hunger *noun*. **1.** hambre, apetito **2.** deseo

hunger (for) *verb*. ansiar, anhelar

hungry *adj*. hambriento

hunt *noun*. **1.** caza **2.** busca, búsqueda, persecución

hunt *verb*. **1.** cazar **2.** buscar, perseguir

hunter *noun*. cazador

hunting *noun*. caza, cacería

hurdle *noun*. **1.** valla **2.** obstáculo

hurl *verb*. arrojar, tirar, lanzar

hurricane *noun*. huracán

hurried *adj*. **1.** apresurado, precipitado **2.** apremiado

hurry *noun*. **1.** prisa **2.** apuro

hurry *verb*. **1.** meter prisa, apurar **2.** darse prisa, apurarse **3.** hacer deprisa **4.** llevar deprisa, marchar deprisa

hurt *verb*. **1.** herir, hacer daño, lastimar **2.** doler **3.** perjudicar **4.** ofender

hurt *adj*. **1.** herido, lastimado **2.** dolido

husband *noun*. marido, esposo

husband *verb*. administrar bien, dosificar

hut *noun*. cabaña, choza

hydrogen *noun*. hidrógeno

hygiene *noun*. higiene

hypothesis *noun*. hipótesis

hypothetical *adj*. hipotético

I

I *pron*. yo

ice *noun*. **1.** hielo **2.** helado

ice *verb*. glasear

Icelandic *noun. adj*. islandés

icing *noun*. alcorza, glaseado

icy *adj*. **1.** helado, glacial **2.** frío, seco, desabrido

ID *noun*. **1.** identidad **2.** cédula de identidad, carné de identidad

idea *noun*. **1.** idea **2.** concepto, juicio **3.** impresión

ideal *noun. adj*. ideal

ideally *adv*. idealmente, perfectamente

identical *adj*. idéntico

identification *noun*. identificación

identify *verb*. identificar

identity *noun*. identidad

idiot *noun*. idiota

idle *verb*. **1.** holgazanear, estar ocioso, haraganear **2.** funcionar en vacío

idle *adj*. **1.** parado, inactivo, desocupado **2.** flojo, perezoso, holgazán **3.** inútil, vano **4.** infundado

i.e. *abbr*. es decir, esto es

if *conj*. **1.** si **2.** en caso de que **3.** cuando **4.** a pesar de, aunque

ignorance *noun*. ignorancia

ignorant *adj*. ignorante

ignore *verb*. desatender, no hacer caso, hacer caso omiso

ill *noun*. **1.** mal **2.** padecimiento, dolencia

ill *adj*. **1.** adverso, dañino **2.** malo **3.** enfermo, delicado

ill *adv*. mal, a duras penas

illegal *adj*. ilegal

illegally *adv*. ilegalmente

illness *noun*. enfermedad, mal, dolencia

illuminate *verb*. iluminar

illuminated *adj*. ilustrado

illusion *noun*. ilusión

illustrate *verb*. **1.** ilustrar **2.** demostrar **3.** aclarar, explicar

illustration noun. 1. ejemplo 2. ilustración 3. aclaración

image noun. 1. imagen 2. efigie 3. retrato 4. reflejo

imaginary adj. imaginario

imagination noun. imaginación

imaginative adj. imaginativo

imagine verb. 1. imaginar 2. imaginarse 3. suponer, creer

imitation noun. 1. imitación 2. copia, reproducción

imitation adj. de imitación

immaculate adj. inmaculado, impecable

immediate adj. 1. inmediato 2. directo 3. urgente

immediately adv. 1. inmediatamente 2. directamente

immense adj. inmenso

immensely adv. inmensamente

immigrant noun. adj. inmigrante

immigration noun. inmigración

imminent adj. inminente

immune (to/from) adj. inmune

immunity noun. inmunidad

impact noun. impacto

impatient adj. impaciente

impatiently adv. impacientemente

imperative noun. adj. imperativo

imperial adj. imperial

impetus noun. ímpetu

implement noun. instrumento, herramienta

implication noun. 1. consecuencia, implicación 2. complicidad

implicit adj. implícito

implicitly adv. implícitamente

imply verb. insinuar, dar a entender

import noun. importación

import verb. importar

importance noun. importancia

important adj. importante

importantly adv. importantemente, con importancia

impose verb. imponer

—**impose on** abusar de

imposing adj. imponente, impresionante

imposition noun. imposición

impossible adj. imposible

impress verb. 1. impresionar 2. grabar 3. imprimir 4. subrayar, recalcar

impression noun. 1. impresión 2. huella, marca 3. edición, tirada

impressive adj. impresionante

imprison verb. encarcelar

imprisonment noun. encarcelamiento, prisión

improve verb. 1. mejorar, perfeccionar 2. aumentar

improvement noun. 1. mejora 2. aumento

impulse noun. impulso

in prep. 1. en 2. dentro 3. por 4. con 5. de

in adv. adj. 1. dentro, adentro 2. en 3. de moda

inability noun. incapacidad

inadequate adj. insuficiente, inadecuado, inepto

inappropriate adj. inadecuado, impropio, inoportuno

incapable (of) adj. incapaz

incentive noun. incentivo

inch noun. 1. pulgada 2. pizca, poco

inch verb. avanzar poco a poco

incident noun. incidente, suceso

incidentally adv. por cierto, a propósito

inclination noun. 1. inclinación 2. propensión 3. afición, deseo

include verb. incluir

including prep. inclusive, incluido

inclusion noun. inclusión

income noun. renta, ingreso

—**income tax** impuesto sobre la renta

incoming adj. que llega, entrante

incompatible adj. incompatible

incomplete adj. incompleto

inconsistent (with) adj. 1. inconsecuente, contradictorio 2. irregular, desigual

incorporate verb. incorporar

incorporated, Inc. adj. sociedad anónima

incorrect adj. incorrecto

increase noun. aumento

increase verb. aumentar

increasingly adv. cada vez más

incredible adj. increíble

incredibly adv. increíblemente
incur verb. 1. incurrir en, provocar 2. contraer, sufrir
indeed interj. ¿de verdad?, ¡no me digas!
indeed adv. 1. de hecho 2. realmente
indefinitely adv. indefinidamente
independence noun. independencia
independent adj. independiente
independently adv. independiente-mente
index noun. índice
India noun. India
Indian noun. adj. 1. indio, indígena 2. hindú
indicate verb. indicar
indication noun. indicación
indicative noun. adj. indicativo
indicator noun. indicador
indifference noun. indiferencia
indifferent (to) adj. 1. indiferente 2. mediocre
indirect adj. indirecto
individual noun. 1. individuo 2. persona
individual adj. 1. individual 2. personal, propio
individually adv. individualmente
Indonesia noun. Indonesia
Indonesian noun. adj. indonesio
indoor adj. 1. de interior 2. cubierto
indoors adv. 1. dentro 2. bajo techo
indulge verb. 1. consentir 2. satisfacer 3. darse el gusto
industrial adj. industrial
industrialized adj. industrializado
industry noun. 1. industria 2. diligencia
ineffective adj. ineficaz
inefficient adj. ineficaz
inequality noun. desigualdad
inevitable adj. inevitable
inevitably adv. inevitablemente
inexperienced adj. inexperto
infant noun. menor, párvulo
infantry noun. infantería
infect verb. infectar
infection noun. infección
infectious adj. infeccioso
inference noun. inferencia, deducción
inferior (to) adj. inferior, peor

infinite adj. infinito
infinitely adv. infinitamente
infinitive noun. infinitivo
infirmary noun. hospital, enfermería
inflation noun. 1. inflación 2. hinchazón
inflict (on) verb. infligir, imponer
influence noun. influencia
influence verb. influir, influenciar
influential adj. influyente
inform verb. informar
    —inform against/on denunciar, delatar
informal adj. 1. informal 2. familiar, coloquial
information noun. información
informative adj. informativo
ingredient noun. ingrediente
inhabit verb. habitar, ocupar, vivir en
inhabitant noun. habitante
inherent adj. inherente
inherit verb. heredar
inheritance noun. herencia
inhibit verb. impedir, inhibir
inhibited adj. inhibido
inhibition noun. inhibición
initial noun. adj. inicial
initial verb. firmar con las iniciales
initially adv. al principio
initiate noun. iniciado
initiate verb. 1. iniciar, poner en marcha, empezar 2. admitir
initiative noun. iniciativa
inject verb. inyectar
injection noun. inyección
injure verb. herir, lastimar, dañar, perjudicar
injured adj. herido, lesionado, dolido
injury noun. herida, lesión
injustice noun. injusticia
ink noun. tinta
inland adj. interior
inland adv. tierra adentro
inmate noun. 1. interno, paciente 2. recluso
inn noun. 1. albergue 2. posada, venta
inner adj. 1. interior 2. íntimo, profundo
    —inner tube cámara, llanta
innocence noun. inocencia
innocent adj. 1. inocente 2. ingenuo
innovation noun. innovación

input *noun*. 1. input 2. entrada 3. insumo, inversión

inquest *noun*. investigación, pesquisa

inquire, enquire *verb*. preguntar
—**inquire into** investigar, indagar

inquiry, enquiry *noun*. 1. interrogación, pregunta 2. investigación, pesquisa

insect *noun*. insecto

insecure *adj*. 1. inseguro 2. inestable, precario

insert *verb*. insertar

inset *noun*. recuadro

inside *prep*. dentro de, en el interior de
—**inside of** en menos de

inside *noun*. 1. interior, parte interior 2. entrañas, tripas

inside *adj*. interior

inside *adv*. dentro, adentro

insight *noun*. 1. perspicacia 2. comprensión

insignificant *adj*. insignificante

insist (on/that) *verb*. 1. insistir 2. exigir

insistence *noun*. insistencia

inspect *verb*. 1. inspeccionar, examinar, revisar 2. pasar revista

inspection *noun*. inspección

inspector *noun*. inspector

inspiration *noun*. inspiración

inspire *verb*. 1. inspirar 2. animar, alentar

instability *noun*. inestabilidad

install *verb*. instalar

installation *noun*. instalación

instance *noun*. ejemplo, caso

instant *noun*. instante, momento

instant *adj*. instantáneo, inmediato

instantly *adv*. instantáneamente, inmediatamente

instead *adv*. en cambio
—**instead of** en vez de, en lugar de

instinct *noun*. instinto

instinctive *adj*. instintivo

instinctively *adv*. instintivamente

institute *noun*. instituto

institute *verb*. fundar, establecer

institution *noun*. institución

institutional *adj*. institucional

instruct *verb*. 1. instruir, enseñar 2. ordenar, mandar

instruction *noun*. 1. instrucción, enseñanza 2. orden
—**instructions** instrucciones

instructor *noun*. 1. instructor, monitor 2. profesor auxiliar

instrument *noun*. instrumento

instrumental *adj*. instrumental
—**to be instrumental in** contribuir decisivamente a

insufficient *adj*. insuficiente

insulation *noun*. aislamiento

insulin *noun*. insulina

insult *noun*. insulto

insult *verb*. insultar

insurance *noun*. seguro

insure *verb*. asegurar

intact *adj*. intacto

intake *noun*. 1. admisión 2. entrada, toma 3. consumo

integrate *verb*. 1. integrar 2. integrarse

integration *noun*. integración

integrity *noun*. integridad

intellectual *adj*. intelectual

intelligence *noun*. 1. inteligencia 2. información 3. servicio de inteligencia

intelligent *adj*. inteligente

intend *verb*. 1. proponerse, tener la intención 2. pretender, querer decir 3. ir dirigido, destinar

intense *adj*. intenso

intensely *adv*. intensamente

intensity *noun*. intensidad

intensive *adj*. intensivo

intent *noun*. intención, propósito

intent *adj*. decidido, resuelto
—**intent on** absorto

intention *noun*. intención

inter *verb*. enterrar

interact *verb*. 1. influirse mutuamente 2. relacionarse

interaction *noun*. interacción, interrelación

interactive *adj*. interactivo

intercourse *noun*. 1. relaciones, trato 2. relación sexual

interest *noun*. 1. interés 2. provecho 3. participación 4. grupo de intereses

interest (in) *verb*. interesar

interested *adj*. interesado

interesting adj. interesante
interestingly adv. 1. curiosamente 2. de manera interesante
interfere (in/with) verb. 1. interferir, entrometerse 2. afectar
interference noun. interferencia, intromisión
interior noun. interior
interior adj. interior
intermediate adj. intermedio
internal adj. 1. interno 2. interior
internally adv. internamente
international noun. adj. internacional
internationally adv. internacionalmente
interpret verb. 1. interpretar 2. explicar
interpretation noun. interpretación
interpreter noun. intérprete
interrupt verb. 1. interrumpir 2. obstruir
interruption noun. interrupción
interval noun. 1. intervalo 2. descanso
intervene verb. 1. intervenir 2. interponerse 3. transcurrir
intervention noun. intervención
interview noun. entrevista
interview verb. entrevistar
interviewer noun. entrevistador
intestinal adj. intestinal
intimacy noun. 1. intimidad 2. familiaridad
intimate noun. amigo íntimo
intimate verb. insinuar
intimate adj. 1. íntimo 2. privado, personal 3. profundo
intimidate verb. intimidar
into prep. 1. en, dentro de 2. contra 3. entre
intolerable adj. intolerable
intricate adj. intrincado, complejo
intriguing adj. intrigante
introduce (to/into) verb. 1. presentar 2. introducir 3. iniciar en
introduction noun. 1. presentación 2. introducción 3. prólogo, prefacio
introductory adj. introductorio, preliminar
invade verb. invadir
invalid noun. inválido, disminuido
invalid verb. 1. licenciar por invalidez 2. quedarse inválido
invalid adj. 1. inválido 2. nulo
—**to became invalid** caducar
invaluable adj. inestimable

invariably adv. invariablemente
invasion noun. invasión
invent verb. 1. inventar 2. inventarse
invention noun. 1. invención, invento 2. mentira
inventory noun. inventario
invest verb. investir
—**invest in** invertir
investigate verb. 1. investigar 2. examinar, estudiar
investigation noun. investigación
investigator noun. investigador
investment noun. inversión
investor noun. inversor
invisible adj. invisible
invitation noun. invitación
invite verb. 1. invitar 2. pedir, solicitar 3. provocar
inviting adj. tentador, atractivo
invoke verb. invocar
involve verb. 1. implicar, suponer, traer consigo 2. involucrar
involved adj. complicado
involvement noun. 1. implicación, participación 2. enredo, complicación
inward, inwards adv. hacia dentro
inward adj. 1. interior 2. hacia dentro
Iran noun. Irán
Iranian noun. adj. iraní
Iraq noun. Irak, Iraq
Iraqi noun. adj. iraquí
Ireland noun. Irlanda
iris noun. 1. iris 2. lirio
Irish noun. adj. irlandés
iron noun. adj. 1. hierro, fierro 2. plancha
iron verb. planchar
ironically adv. irónicamente
irony noun. ironía
irregular adj. irregular
irrelevant adj. irrelevante
irresistible adj. irresistible
irrespective (of) adj. sin tomar en cuenta
irritate verb. irritar, molestar
irritation noun. irritación
Islam noun. Islam
Islamic adj. Islámico
island noun. isla
isle noun. isla
isolated adj. aislado

isolation noun. aislamiento
Israel noun. Israel
Israeli noun. adj. israelí
issue noun. 1. tema, asunto 2. emisión 3. ejemplar, número
issue verb. 1. emitir 2. hacer público 3. expedir 4. distribuir 5. salir
it pron. 1. él, ella, ello 2. lo, la (direct object) 3. le (indirect object) 4. (often not translated)

Italian noun. adj. italiano
Italy noun. Italia
item noun. artículo
its adj. su, sus
itself pron. 1. se 2. sí mismo, sí misma 3. él mismo, ella misma 4. él solo, ella sola
ivory noun. marfil
ivory adj. de marfil, de color marfil
ivy noun. hiedra

J

jack noun. 1. gato, gata 2. jota, sota
jacket noun. 1. chaqueta, saco 2. sobrecubierta, funda
jaguar noun. jaguar, tigre
jail noun. cárcel, prisión
jail verb. encarcelar
jam noun. 1. atasco, embotellamiento 2. apuro, aprieto 3. mermelada, confitura
jam verb. 1. abarrotar, apiñar 2. atascar, atascarse 3. causar interferencia
Jamaica noun. Jamaica
Jamaican noun. adj. jamaicano
Jan. abbr. enero
January noun. enero
Japan noun. Japón
Japanese noun. adj. japonés
jar noun. 1. tarro, bote, jarra 2. sacudida, choque
jar (on) verb. 1. chirriar, discordar 2. sacudir, afectar
jargon noun. jerga
jaw noun. maxilar
—**jaws** 1. mandíbula 2. fauces
jazz noun. jazz
jealous (of) adj. 1. celoso 2. envidioso
jealousy noun. 1. celos 2. envidia
jeans noun plural. vaqueros, tejanos, bluejeans
jelly noun. mermelada
jerk noun. sacudida
jerk verb. sacudir
jersey noun. jersey, suéter
jet noun. adj. azabache

jet noun. 1. chorro 2. boquilla 3. avión a reacción, reactor
Jew noun. judío
jewel noun. joya, alhaja, piedra preciosa
jewelry noun. joyas
Jewish adj. judío
jingle noun. 1. tintineo 2. tonadilla publicitaria
jingle verb. tintinear
job noun. 1. trabajo, empleo 2. tarea
jockey noun. jockey
join noun. juntura, unión
join verb. 1. juntar, unir 2. hacerse socio, afiliarse, ingresar 3. juntarse, confluir 4. acompañar
joint noun. 1. junta, juntura, unión, bisagra 2. articulación, nudillo, coyuntura
joint adj. 1. mutuo 2. compartido
jointly adv. conjuntamente
joke noun. 1. chiste 2. broma
joke verb. 1. contar chistes 2. bromear
jolly adj. alegre, divertido, gracioso
journal noun. 1. periódico 2. revista 3. diario
journalism noun. periodismo
journalist noun. periodista, reportero
journey noun. 1. viaje 2. tramo, trayecto 3. expedición
journey verb. viajar
joy noun. 1. alegría, júbilo 2. deleite
Jr. abbr. hijo, junior
jubilee noun. jubileo, aniversario
judge noun. 1. juez 2. jurado 3. conocedor, entendido
judge verb. 1. juzgar 2. calcular

judicial adj. judicial
jug noun. jarro, jarra
juice noun. 1. zumo 2. jugo
July noun. julio
jump noun. 1. salto 2. brinco 3. obstáculo 4. aumento, subida
jump verb. 1. saltar 2. sobresaltarse 3. subir, aumentar
jumper noun. pichi
junction noun. empalme, cruce, crucero
June noun. junio
jungle noun. jungla, selva
junior noun. menor
junior adj. 1. menor 2. subordinado, auxiliar 3. juvenil 4. hijo

junk noun. 1. trastos, baratijas 2. junco
jurisdiction noun. jurisdicción
jury noun. jurado
just adj. 1. justo 2. merecido 3. correcto 4. apropiado
just adv. 1. justamente, justo 2. exactamente 3. precisamente 4. sencillamente 5. ahora mismo 6. recién 7. a penas 8. sólo, nomás 9. absolutamente 10. por poco
justice noun. 1. justicia 2. juez
justification noun. justificación
justify verb. justificar
juvenile noun. adj. 1. juvenil 2. infantil

K

keen adj. 1. entusiasta, aplicado 2. vivo, grande 3. cortante, afilado, agudo, fino
keep noun. sustento
keep verb. 1. guardar 2. mantener, conservar 3. mantenerse 4. quedarse con 5. continuar, seguir 6. cuidar 7. criar 8. tener 9. llevar al día 10. retener, entretener 11. cumplir, observar 12. celebrar 13. dirigir
  —**keep from** abstenerse, guardarse de
  —**keep on** continuar, seguir
keeper noun. guarda, guardián
keeping noun. cuidado
Kenya noun. Kenia
Kenyan noun. adj. keniata
kettle noun. hervidor, caldero
key noun. 1. llave 2. tecla 3. clave 4. leyenda
key adj. clave
keyboard noun. 1. teclado 2. instrumento de teclado
kg abbr. kilogramo
kick noun. 1. puntapié, patada, coz 2. culetazo 3. diversión, emoción
kick verb. 1. dar un puntapié, dar una patada, cocear 2. recular
kid noun. 1. niño, crío, chaval, chamaco

2. cabrito, chivo
kid verb. engañar, tomar el pelo
kidnap verb. secuestrar, raptar
kidney noun. riñón
kill verb. matar, asesinar
killer noun. asesino
kilo noun. kilo
kilogram noun. kilogramo
kilometer noun. kilómetro
kin noun plural. familiares, parientes
kin adj. de la familia
kind noun. tipo, género, clase
kind adj. amable, atento
kindly adj. bondadoso, amable
kindly adv. 1. amablemente 2. favorablemente
kindness noun. bondad, amabilidad
king noun. rey
kingdom noun. reino
kiss noun. beso
kiss verb. besar
kit noun. 1. equipo, kit 2. herramientas, avíos
kitchen noun. cocina
kite noun. cometa
km abbr. kilómetro
knee noun. 1. rodilla 2. rodillera
kneel verb. arrodillarse

knife noun. 1. cuchillo 2. puñal, navaja
knife verb. acuchillar, apuñalar
knight noun. 1. caballero 2. caballo (chess)
knit verb. 1. tejer, hacer punto, tricotar 2. soldarse
knitting noun. 1. labor de punto 2. prenda de punto
knock noun. 1. golpe 2. choque 3. llamada
knock verb. 1. golpear 2. chocar 3. llamar 4. tirar, hacer caer
knot noun. nudo

knot verb. anudar, atar
know verb. 1. saber 2. conocer 3. comprender 4. reconocer
know-how noun. conocimientos, experiencia
knowing adj. de complicidad
knowledge noun. 1. conocimiento 2. conocimientos 3. saber
Korea noun. Corea
Korean noun. adj. coreano
Kuwait noun. Kuwait
Kuwaiti noun. adj. kuwaití
lab abbr. laboratorio

L

label noun. 1. etiqueta 2. marca
label verb. etiquetar
labor noun. 1. trabajo 2. obreros, mano de obra 3. parto, dolores de parto
labor verb. 1. trabajar duro 2. esforzarse, afanarse 3. avanzar penosamente, funcionar con dificultad
laboratory noun. laboratorio
lace noun. 1. cordón 2. cinta 3. encaje
lace verb. atar, amarrar
lack noun. falta, carencia, escasez
lack verb. 1. carecer de 2. hacer falta
lad noun. muchacho, chico, chaval, pibe
ladder noun. escalera (de mano)
lady noun. 1. señora 2. dama 3. lady
lag noun. retraso
lag verb. retrasarse, quedarse atrás
lake noun. lago
lamb noun. cordero
lamp noun. lámpara
land noun. 1. tierra 2. terreno 3. tierras, fincas 4. país 5. territorio, región
land verb. 1. aterrizar 2. desembarcar 3. caer 4. ir a parar
landing noun. 1. aterrizaje 2. desembarco 3. desembarcadero 4. descansillo, rellano
landlord noun. 1. dueño, propietario 2. patrón

landmark noun. 1. punto de referencia 2. hito
landowner noun. terrateniente, hacendado
landscape noun. paisaje
landscape verb. ajardinar, diseñar
lane noun. 1. callejuela, callejón 2. calle 3. carril, vía 4. ruta
language noun. 1. lenguaje 2. lengua, idioma
lap noun. 1. regazo, rodillas 2. vuelta 3. etapa
lap verb. 1. lamer 2. chapalear
large adj. 1. grande 2. corpulento 3. extenso 4. numeroso
largely adv. en gran parte, en gran medida
laser noun. láser
lash noun. 1. pestaña 2. latigazo, azote 3. látigo
lash verb. 1. azotar 2. atar, amarrar 3. agitar, mover
last verb. durar
last adj. 1. último 2. pasado
last adv. 1. en último lugar 2. por último 3. la última vez
lasting adj. 1. duradero 2. permanente
late adj. 1. tarde, atrasado, tardío 2. difunto 3. anterior
—**late riser** dormilón

late adv. tarde
lately adv. 1. últimamente 2. recientemente
latent adj. latente
lateral adj. lateral
Latin noun. 1. latín 2. latino
Latin adj. latino
Latin American noun. adj. latinoamericano
latter adj. último
laugh noun. risa, carcajada
laugh verb. 1. reír 2. reírse
laughter noun. 1. risa 2. risas
launch noun. 1. lancha 2. lanzamiento 3. botadura 4. estreno 5. fundación 6. emisión
launch verb. 1. lanzar 2. botar, echar al mar 3. estrenar 4. fundar 5. emitir
laundry noun. 1. lavandería 2. ropa sucia, colada
lavatory noun. lavabo, baño, aseos
lavender noun. espliego, lavanda
lavish verb. prodigar
lavish adj. 1. pródigo, generoso 2. suntuoso 3. abundante
law noun. ley
lawful adj. 1. legal, lícito 2. legítimo
lawn noun. césped, pasto
lawsuit noun. pleito, proceso
lawyer noun. abogado
lay noun. romance, trova
lay verb. 1. poner 2. colocar 3. tender 4. depositar 5. preparar, hacer 6. calmar, aquietar 7. apostar
  —lay down 1. establecer, sentar 2. entregar 3. trazar, dibujar
  —lay out 1. presentar, exponer 2. planear, diseñar
lay adj. 1. laico, lego, seglar 2. profano
layer noun. 1. capa, estrato 2. ponedora
layer verb. poner en capas
layout noun. plan, disposición, trazado
lazy adj. perezoso, vago
lb. abbr. libra
lead noun. 1. delantera 2. ejemplo 3. liderazgo 4. ventaja 5. pista 6. papel principal 7. protagonista 8. plomo 9. mina 10. correa
lead verb. 1. llevar 2. conducir 3. liderar, dirigir 4. encabezar 5. aventajar 6. ser mano

  —lead to ocasionar, causar
lead adj. de plomo
leader noun. 1. líder 2. cabecilla, jefe 3. reportaje principal
leadership noun. 1. liderazgo 2. dirección, jefatura
leaf noun. 1. hoja 2. página
leaflet noun. folleto, octavilla
league noun. 1. legua 2. liga
leak noun. 1. fuga, escape 2. rotura, gotera, grieta 3. filtración
leak verb. 1. perder, gotear, salir 2. filtrar, divulgar
lean verb. 1. inclinarse 2. apoyarse
lean adj. 1. delgado, flaco 2. magro 3. malo, escaso, pobre
leaning noun. inclinación, tendencia
leap noun. 1. salto, brinco 2. subida
leap verb. 1. saltar, brincar 2. incrementarse, aumentar
learn verb. 1. aprender 2. enterarse, saber
learned adj. 1. docto, erudito 2. liberal
learner noun. principiante, estudiante
learning noun. 1. conocimientos 2. aprendizaje
lease noun. contrato de arrendamiento
lease verb. arrendar
least adj. pron. lo menos, lo mínimo
least adv. menos
leather noun. piel, cuero
leather adj. de piel, de cuero
leave noun. permiso
leave verb. 1. dejar 2. salir 3. marcharse 4. legar
  —to be left quedar
  —leave behind dejar atrás, olvidar
  —leave out omitir, excluir
Lebanese noun. adj. libanés
Lebanon noun. Líbano
lecture noun. 1. conferencia, clase 2. reprimenda, sermón
lecture verb. 1. dar clase 2. sermonear
lecturer noun. conferenciante, profesor
lee noun. sotavento
leek noun. puerro
left noun. izquierda
left adj. 1. izquierdo 2. de izquierda
left adv. a la izquierda

left-hand adj. a la izquierda
left-wing adj. de izquierda
leg noun. 1. pierna 2. pernera 3. pata, muslo 4. etapa
legacy noun. herencia
legal adj. 1. legal 2. jurídico
legally adv. legalmente, por ley
legend noun. leyenda
legendary adj. legendario
legion noun. legión
legislation noun. legislación
legislative adj. legislativo
legislature noun. cuerpo legislativo
legitimacy noun. legitimidad
legitimate adj. legítimo, justificado
leisure noun. ocio
lemon noun. adj. limón
lemonade noun. limonada, gaseosa
lend verb. prestar
length noun. 1. longitud, largo 2. extensión 3. duración 4. pedazo, trozo
lengthy adj. largo
lens noun. 1. lente, objetivo 2. cristalino
Lent noun. Cuaresma
less adj. adv. prep. pron. menos
lesser adj. adv. menor
lesson noun. 1. lección 2. clase 3. lectura
let verb. 1. dejar, permitir 2. alquilar 3. (as an expression of imperative is rendered in Spanish by the subjunctive or the imperative)
—**let down** fallar
lethal adj. letal, mortal
letter noun. 1. letra 2. carta
leukemia noun. leucemia
level noun. 1. nivel 2. piso 3. llano, llanura
level verb. 1. nivelar, aplanar 2. igualar 3. arrasar
—**level at** apuntar
level adj. 1. llano, plano 2. a nivel, nivelado 3. uniforme
lever noun. palanca
lever verb. sopalancar
leverage noun. 1. acción de palanca 2. influencia, poder
levy noun. impuesto
levy verb. 1. recaudar, imponer 2. reclutar
lexicon noun. léxico

liability noun. 1. responsabilidad 2. carga
liable adj. 1. propenso 2. responsable 3. expuesto, sujeto
liaison noun. 1. enlace, coordinación 2. relación
libel noun. libelo, difamación
libel verb. difamar
liberal adj. 1. liberal 2. abundante, generoso
liberate verb. liberar, poner en libertad
liberation noun. liberación
liberty noun. 1. libertad 2. atrevimiento
—**liberties** privilegios, derechos
librarian noun. bibliotecario
library noun. biblioteca
Libya noun. Libia
Libyan noun. adj. libio
license noun. licencia, permiso
license verb. autorizar, dar permiso
licensed adj. con licencia
lick noun. 1. lamedura, lengüetada 2. mano
lick verb. lamer
lid noun. 1. tapa 2. párpado
lie noun. mentira
lie verb. 1. echarse, tumbarse 2. ubicarse, estar situado 3. quedarse 4. mentir
lieutenant noun. 1. teniente 2. alférez de navío
life noun. 1. vida 2. vitalidad
—**life imprisonment** cadena perpetua
lifeboat noun. bote salvavidas, lancha de salvamento
lifetime noun. vida
lift noun. 1. acción de levantar 2. ascensor, montacargas 3. estímulo
lift verb. 1. levantar 2. alzar 3. levantarse, alzarse 4. coger 5. descolgar 6. elevarse 7. disiparse
light noun. 1. luz 2. lámpara 3. fuego 4. perspectiva, punto de vista
light verb. 1. encender 2. iluminar 3. encenderse, iluminarse
light adj. 1. claro 2. luminoso 3. ligero 4. leve
lighter noun. encendedor, mechero
lighting noun. iluminación, alumbrado
lightly adv. 1. ligeramente 2. suavemente
lightning noun. rayo, relámpago

lightweight adj. ligero
like conj. como
like prep. como
like noun. semejante, igual
like verb. 1. gustar 2. querer
like adj. parecido, igual
likelihood noun. probabilidad
likely adj. 1. probable 2. apropiado
likewise adv. igualmente, asimismo, también
liking noun. gusto, simpatía, aprecio
lily noun. lirio, azucena
limb noun. 1. miembro, extremidad 2. rama
lime noun. 1. cal 2. lima 3. tilo
limestone noun. piedra caliza
limit noun. límite
limit verb. limitar, restringir
limitation noun. limitación, restricción
limited adj. 1. limitado, restringido 2. escaso
limp noun. cojera
limp verb. cojear
limp adj. 1. débil 2. flojo, fláccido 3. mustio
line noun. 1. línea 2. renglón 3. arruga, surco 4. fila, hilera 5. cola 6. linaje 7. vía 8. profesión, ramo 9. especialidad 10. gama 11. cuerda, cordel, sedal
line verb. 1. alinear, poner en fila 2. forrar, revestir 3. surcar
linear adj. lineal
lined adj. 1. forrado, revestido 2. arrugado 3. rayado, pautado
linen noun. 1. lino, hilo 2. ropa blanca
liner noun. transatlántico
lines noun plural. texto, papel
linger verb. 1. rezagarse 2. persistir, perdurar, quedarse
linguistic adj. lingüístico
linguistics noun singular. lingüística
lining noun. 1. revestimiento 2. forro
link noun. 1. enlace 2. conexión, relación 3. vínculo, lazo 4. eslabón
link verb. unir, conectar
lion noun. león
lip noun. 1. labio 2. borde
lipstick noun. lápiz de labios
liquid noun. adj. líquido

liquor noun. licor, bebida alcohólica
list noun. lista, catálogo
list verb. 1. hacer una lista 2. enumerar
listen verb. escuchar
liter noun. litro
literacy noun. capacidad de leer y escribir
literal adj. literal
literally adv. literalmente
literary adj. literario, de literatura
literature noun. literatura
Lithuania noun. Lituania
Lithuanian noun. adj. lituano
litigation noun. litigio
litter noun. 1. basura, papeles 2. cama, lecho 3. camada
litter verb. poner en desorden
little adj. 1. pequeño, chico 2. poco, escaso 3. insignificante
little adv. 1. poco 2. ni la menor idea
little pron. poco
live verb. 1. vivir 2. sobrevivir
live adj. 1. vivo 2. en directo 3. cargado 4. conectado
live adv. en directo
lively adj. alegre, vivo, vivaz
liver noun. hígado
livestock noun. ganado
living noun. 1. medio de vida, sustento 2. vida
living adj. vivo
load noun. 1. carga 2. peso, cantidad 3. montón, montones
load verb. cargar
loaded adj. cargado
loan noun. 1. préstamo 2. empréstito
loan verb. prestar
lobby noun. 1. vestíbulo, pasillo 2. grupo de presión
lobby verb. presionar, cabildear
local adj. local, del barrio, municipal, regional
locality noun. localidad
locally adv. en la localidad, en la zona
locate verb. 1. situar, ubicar 2. localizar
location noun. 1. lugar 2. situación, ubicación
lock noun. 1. cerradura, chapa 2. esclusa 3. llave 4. mecha, mechón

lock verb. **1.** cerrar con llave **2.** inmovilizar, bloquear

locks noun. cabellos

locomotive noun. locomotora

lodge noun. **1.** garita **2.** logia

lodge verb. **1.** alojar, hospedar **2.** alojarse, hospedarse **3.** presentar, interponer

loft noun. desván

log noun. tronco, leño

logic noun. lógica

logical adj. lógico

logically adv. lógicamente

lone adj. solitario

loneliness noun. soledad

lonely adj. **1.** solo **2.** aislado, solitario

long adj. **1.** largo **2.** de largo **3.** prolongado

long adv. mucho, mucho tiempo

long (for) verb. anhelar, desear

longing noun. anhelo, añoranza

long-range adj. **1.** de largo alcance **2.** a largo plazo

look noun. **1.** ojeada **2.** mirada **3.** aspecto, apariencia **4.** moda, estilo

look verb. **1.** mirar **2.** parecer **3.** dar (a)
—**look after** cuidar
—**look for 1.** buscar **2.** esperar
—**look forward to** desear, esperar con ilusión

loom noun. telar

loom (up) verb. surgir, asomar

loop noun. **1.** lazo **2.** recodo, curva

loop verb. atar con un lazo

loose adj. **1.** suelto **2.** flojo **3.** descosido **4.** flexible, libre, aproximado **5.** a granel

loosely adv. **1.** aproximadamente **2.** ligeramente **3.** vagamente

loosen verb. **1.** desatar **2.** aflojar

loot noun. botín

loot verb. saquear

lord noun. **1.** señor **2.** lord
—**Our Lord** Nuestro Señor, Dios

lose verb. **1.** perder **2.** atrasarse

loser noun. perdedor

loss noun. pérdida

lost adj. **1.** perdido **2.** desaparecido

lot noun. **1.** suerte, destino **2.** lote **3.** parte, porción **4.** solar
—**a lot** mucho
—**lots** mucho

lottery noun. lotería

lotus noun. loto

loud adj. **1.** alto, fuerte **2.** chillón

loudly adv. fuertemente, ruidosamente

lounge noun. sala, salón

lounge verb. **1.** apoltronarse **2.** holgazanear

love noun. **1.** amor **2.** afición **3.** cero (tennis)

love verb. **1.** amar, querer **2.** gustar, encantar

lovely adj. **1.** lindo, bello, hermoso **2.** encantador, amoroso

lover noun. **1.** aficionado **2.** amante, enamorado

loving adj. cariñoso, tierno

low verb. mugir

low adj. **1.** bajo **2.** grave **3.** deprimido, triste **4.** inferior **5.** humilde

low adv. bajo

lower verb. **1.** bajar **2.** rebajar **3.** encapotarse

loyal adj. leal, fiel

loyalty noun. lealtad, fidelidad

luck noun. suerte

luckily adv. afortunadamente

lucky adj. **1.** afortunado **2.** de la suerte

lucrative adj. lucrativo

luggage noun. equipaje

lump noun. **1.** terrón **2.** trozo, pedazo **3.** bulto, chichón

lump (together) verb. amontonar, agrupar

lunch noun. almuerzo, comida

lunch verb. almorzar, comer

lunchtime noun. hora del almuerzo, hora de comer

lung noun. pulmón

lure noun. aliciente, reclamo

lure verb. atraer, tentar

lust noun. codicia, lujuria

luxurious adj. lujoso

luxury noun. **1.** lujo **2.** artículo de lujo

lyric noun. poema lírico
—**lyrics** letra

lyric adj. lírico

M

MA *abbr.* máster en letras

machine *noun.* 1. máquina, aparato 2. organización

machine *verb.* 1. elaborar a máquina 2. coser a máquina

machinery *noun.* 1. maquinaria 2. mecanismo

mad *adj.* 1. loco 2. furioso

madam *noun.* señora

madness *noun.* locura

Madonna *noun.* la Virgen

magazine *noun.* 1. revista 2. recámara

maggot *noun.* gusano, cresa

magic *noun.* magia

magic *adj.* mágico

magical *adj.* 1. mágico 2. fascinante

magistrate *noun.* magistrado

magnetic *adj.* magnético

magnificent *adj.* magnífico

magnitude *noun.* magnitud

mahogany *noun.* caoba

maid *noun.* criada, sirvienta

maiden *noun.* doncella

mail *noun.* 1. correo 2. correspondencia

mail *verb.* mandar por correo

main *noun.* conducto principal, tubería principal, cañería principal

main *adj.* principal

mainland *noun.* continente, tierra firme

mainly *adv.* 1. principalmente 2. en su mayoría

mainstream *noun.* corriente principal

maintain *verb.* 1. mantener 2. guardar, conservar 3. sostener

maintenance *noun.* mantenimiento, cuidado

majesty *noun.* majestad

major *noun.* 1. comandante, mayor 2. especialidad

major *adj.* 1. mayor 2. principal 3. muy importante 4. serio, grave

major (in) *verb.* especializarse (en)

majority *noun.* mayoría

make *noun.* marca

make *verb.* 1. hacer 2. crear, producir, construir, fabricar, confeccionar 3. rodar, grabar 4. preparar 5. cometer 6. obligar 7. ganar 8. calcular

—**make for** encaminarse a, dirigirse a

—**make out** 1. distinguir, divisar 2. comprender 3. arreglárselas, ir

—**make up** 1. inventar 2. pintarse, maquillarse 3. reconciliarse

—**make up for** compensar

—**make up one's mind** decidirse

maker *noun.* fabricante, creador

make-up *noun.* 1. maquillaje 2. carácter 3. composición

making *noun.* fabricación, preparación

Malaysia *noun.* Malasia

Malaysian *noun. adj.* malasio

male *noun. adj.* macho, varón

Malta *noun.* Malta

Maltese *noun. adj.* maltés

mamma, mama *noun.* mamá

mammal *noun.* mamífero

man *noun.* 1. hombre 2. persona 3. el hombre, la humanidad 4. pieza, ficha

man *verb.* 1. tripular, dirigir 2. guarnecer, armar

manage *verb.* 1. dirigir, llevar, administrar 2. manejar, poder 3. arreglárselas (para), conseguir

management *noun.* 1. dirección, administración, gestión 2. gerencia, cuerpo directivo

manager *noun.* 1. director, gerente, administrador 2. representante, mánager

maneuver *noun.* maniobra

maneuver *verb.* 1. maniobrar 2. manipular

manifest *verb.* manifestar, hacer patente

manifest *adj.* manifiesto, patente

manifestation *noun.* 1. manifestación 2. demostración

manifesto *noun.* manifiesto

manipulate *verb.* 1. manipular 2. manejar

manipulation *noun.* 1. manipulación 2. manejo

mankind *noun.* género humano, humanidad

manner *noun.* **1.** manera, modo **2.** porte, aire **3.** clase

—**manners** modales, educación

manpower *noun.* mano de obra

mansion *noun.* mansión

manslaughter *noun.* homicidio sin premeditación

manual *noun. adj.* manual

manufacture *noun.* **1.** manufactura **2.** fabricación

manufacture *verb.* fabricar, manufacturar

manufacturer *noun.* fabricante

manuscript *noun.* manuscrito

many *adj. pron.* muchos, muchas

—**how many?** ¿cuántos?, ¿cuántas?

—**too many** demasiados, demasiadas

map *noun.* **1.** mapa **2.** plano **3.** carta

map *verb.* hacer un mapa

mar *verb.* estropear, aguar

Mar. *abbr.* marzo

marathon *noun.* maratón

marble *noun.* **1.** mármol **2.** canica

march *noun.* marcha

march *verb.* **1.** marchar **2.** manifestarse

March *noun.* marzo

mare *noun.* yegua

margin *noun.* margen

marginal *adj.* **1.** marginal **2.** mínimo

marine *noun.* infante de marina

marine *adj.* marino, marítimo

marital *adj.* conyugal

maritime *adj.* marítimo

mark *noun.* **1.** marca **2.** calificación **3.** mancha **4.** señal **5.** blanco **6.** marco

mark *verb.* **1.** marcar **2.** señalar, indicar **3.** calificar, poner nota **4.** poner precio

marked *adj.* marcado, notable

markedly *adv.* notablemente, visiblemente

marker *noun.* **1.** marcador **2.** marca **3.** rotulador

market *noun.* mercado

market *verb.* vender, comercializar

marketing *noun.* marketing, mercadotecnia

marriage *noun.* **1.** boda **2.** matrimonio **3.** unión

married *adj.* casado

marry *verb.* **1.** casar **2.** casarse

marsh *noun.* ciénaga, pantano

marshal *noun.* **1.** maestro de ceremonias, organizador **2.** oficial de justicia **3.** jefe de policía/bomberos **4.** mariscal

marshal *verb.* **1.** poner en orden, arreglar **2.** dirigir

martial *adj.* marcial

marvelous *adj.* **1.** maravilloso **2.** excelente

masculine *adj.* masculino

mask *noun.* máscara, careta, mascarilla

mask *verb.* enmascarar

mason *noun.* **1.** albañil **2.** masón

mass *noun.* **1.** masa **2.** montón **3.** misa **4.** muchedumbre

mass *verb.* congregarse, concentrarse

mass *adj.* multitudinario, de masas

massacre *noun.* masacre

massacre *verb.* masacrar

massage *noun.* masaje

massage *verb.* dar masajes, masajear

massive *adj.* **1.** enorme **2.** macizo, sólido **3.** cuantioso

master *noun.* **1.** señor, dueño, amo **2.** máster **3.** maestro, profesor **4.** capitán, patrón

master *verb.* dominar

master *adj.* maestro, experto

masterpiece *noun.* obra maestra

mat *noun.* estera, felpudo

match *noun.* **1.** cerilla, fósforo **2.** partido, encuentro, juego **3.** igual **4.** casamiento, matrimonio

match *verb.* **1.** hacer juego, combinar **2.** emparejar **3.** igualar **4.** enfrentar

mate *noun.* **1.** pareja **2.** compañero **3.** colega **4.** ayudante **5.** segundo de a bordo **6.** mate

mate *verb.* **1.** aparear **2.** dar jaque mate

material *noun.* **1.** material, materia **2.** tela, tejido

material *adj.* **1.** material **2.** esencial, primordial

maternal *adj.* **1.** maternal **2.** materno

maternity *noun.* maternidad

mathematical *adj.* matemático

mathematics, math *noun singular.* matemáticas

matter noun. 1. materia, sustancia 2. asunto, cuestión 3. pus
matter verb. importar
mature verb. 1. madurar 2. vencer
mature adj. 1. maduro 2. añejo, curado
maturity noun. madurez
maxim noun. máxima
maximum noun. adj. máximo
may verb. 1. poder 2. ser posible 3. ojalá que (expressing wish, hope)
May noun. mayo
maybe adv. quizás, tal vez
mayor noun. alcalde
me pron. 1. me 2. mí, conmigo (after prep) 3. yo
meadow, meadows noun. prado
meal noun. 1. comida 2. harina
mean noun. término medio, medio, promedio
mean verb. 1. significar, querer decir 2. pretender, tener la intención 3. destinar
mean adj. 1. malo, ruin 2. mediano 3. medio 4. mezquino, tacaño 5. humilde, pobre
meaning noun. 1. significado, sentido 2. propósito
meaningful adj. 1. significativo 2. valioso
meaningless adj. sin sentido
means noun plural. 1. recursos, medios de vida 2. medio, manera
meantime noun. adv. entretanto, mientras tanto
meanwhile adv. entretanto, mientras tanto
measure noun. 1. medida 2. grado, cantidad 3. compás, ritmo
measure verb. medir
measurement noun. 1. medida 2. medición
meat noun. carne
mechanic noun. mecánico
mechanical adj. mecánico
mechanics noun plural. mecanismo
mechanics noun singular. mecánica
mechanism noun. mecanismo
medal noun. medalla
mediate verb. mediar, arbitrar

medical noun. reconocimiento médico
medical adj. médico
medicine noun. medicina
medieval, mediaeval adj. medieval
meditation noun. meditación
medium noun. 1. medio 2. médium
medium adj. medio, mediano
meet noun. encuentro
meet verb. 1. encontrar 2. encontrarse con 3. quedar con 4. ir/venir a buscar 5. conocer 6. juntarse 7. satisfacer 8. enfrentarse con 9. reunirse 10. confluir
meeting noun. 1. encuentro 2. reunión 3. cita 4. confluencia
melody noun. melodía
melt verb. 1. derretir, fundir 2. derretirse, fundirse
member noun. miembro, socio, afiliado
membership noun. 1. calidad de miembro/socio 2. afiliación 3. cuota
membrane noun. membrana
memo noun. memorándum
memoirs noun plural. memorias, autobiografía
memorable adj. memorable
memorandum noun. memorándum
memorial noun. monumento conmemorativo
memory noun. 1. memoria 2. recuerdo
menace noun. amenaza, peligro
menace verb. amenazar
mental adj. 1. mental 2. psiquiátrico
mentally adv. mentalmente
mention noun. mención, alusión
mention verb. mencionar, hablar de
menu noun. 1. menú 2. carta
merchandise noun. mercancía
merchant noun. comerciante
mercury noun. mercurio
mercy noun. 1. misericordia, clemencia 2. suerte
mere adj. mero, simple
merely adv. meramente, solamente
merge verb. 1. fusionar, unir 2. fusionarse, fundirse
merger noun. fusión
merit noun. mérito
merit verb. merecer
merry adj. alegre

mess *noun.* desastre, enredo, lío
mess (with) *verb.* interferir
message *noun.* 1. mensaje 2. recado
messenger *noun.* mensajero
messy *adj.* 1. sucio 2. desordenado
metal *noun.* metal
metal *adj.* metálico, de metal
metaphor *noun.* metáfora
meter *noun.* 1. metro 2. contador, medidor
meter *verb.* medir
method *noun.* 1. método, forma 2. procedimiento 3. técnica
metropolitan *adj.* metropolitano
Mexican *noun. adj.* mexicano
Mexico *noun.* México
mg. *abbr.* miligramo
microcomputer *noun.* microordenador, microcomputador
microphone, mike *noun.* micrófono
microscope *noun.* microscopio
microwave (oven) *noun.* microondas
mid *adj.* a mediados de
midday *noun.* mediodía
middle *noun.* 1. medio, centro 2. cintura
middle *adj.* medio, central
Middle East *noun.* Oriente Medio
middle-aged *adj.* de mediana edad
midnight *noun.* medianoche
might *noun.* fuerza, poder
might *verb.* poder, ser posible
mighty *adj.* poderoso, potente, enorme
migrant *noun.* emigrante
migrate *verb.* emigrar
migration *noun.* migración
mild *adj.* 1. apacible, afable 2. ligero, leve 3. suave, moderado
mildly *adv.* 1. ligeramente 2. suavemente
mile *noun.* milla
militant *adj.* militante
military *adj.* militar
milk *noun.* leche
milk *verb.* ordeñar
mill *noun.* 1. molinillo 2. molino 3. fábrica
mill *verb.* moler
  —**mill about/around** arremolinarse, apiñarse

miller *noun.* molinero
milliliter *noun.* mililitro
millimeter *noun.* milímetro
million *noun. adj.* millón
millionaire *noun.* millonario
millionth *noun.* millonésimo
mind *interj.* ¡cuidado!
mind *noun.* mente, cabeza, cerebro
mind *verb.* 1. cuidar 2. importar, molestar 3. tener cuidado 4. hacer caso de
mine *noun.* mina
mine *verb.* 1. extraer 2. minar 3. sembrar minas
mine *pron.* (el) mío, (la) mía, (los) míos, (las) mías
miner *noun.* minero
mineral *noun.* mineral
mini *noun.* minifalda
mini *adj.* mini-
miniature *noun. adj.* miniatura
minimal *adj.* mínimo
minimize *verb.* minimizar
minimum *noun. adj.* mínimo
mining *noun.* minería, explotación de minas
miniskirt *noun.* minifalda
minister *noun.* 1. ministro 2. pastor, clérigo
minister *verb.* atender, servir
ministerial *adj.* ministerial
ministry *noun.* 1. ministerio 2. sacerdocio, clerecía
minor *noun.* menor
minor *verb.* estudiar como asignatura secundaria
minor *adj.* 1. menor, de poca importancia 2. secundario
minority *noun.* minoría
mint *noun.* 1. casa de la moneda 2. menta 3. caramelo de menta
mint *verb.* acuñar
minus *noun. prep.* menos
minus *adj.* negativo
minute *noun.* 1. minuto 2. momento, instante
minute *adj.* 1. diminuto, minúsculo 2. minucioso, detallado
minutes *noun plural.* acta

miracle *noun.* milagro
mirror *noun.* espejo
mirror *verb.* reflejar
miscarriage *noun.* **1.** aborto **2.** error
miserable *adj.* **1.** abatido, triste, infeliz **2.** miserable
misery *noun.* **1.** miseria **2.** tristeza, pena **3.** dolor
misleading *adj.* engañoso
miss *noun.* fallo, tiro errado
miss *verb.* **1.** fallar, errar **2.** perder **3.** lamentar, sentir **4.** echar de menos, extrañar **5.** no asistir, faltar **6.** no entender
Miss *noun.* señorita
missile *noun.* misil
missing *adj.* **1.** perdido, extraviado, desaparecido **2.** que falta
mission *noun.* misión
missionary *noun.* misionero
mist *noun.* neblina
mistake *noun.* error, equivocación
mistake (for) *verb.* **1.** confundir **2.** equivocarse, entender mal
mistaken *adj.* equivocado
Mister, Mr. *noun.* señor
mistress *noun.* **1.** señora, ama **2.** amante
misunderstanding *noun.* malentendido
mix *noun.* mezcla, preparado
mix *verb.* **1.** mezclar **2.** mezclarse **3.** combinar **4.** juntarse, alternar
mixed *adj.* **1.** variado **2.** diverso **3.** mixto
mixture *noun.* **1.** mezcla **2.** preparado
ml. *abbr.* mililitro
mm. *abbr.* milímetro
moan *noun.* **1.** gemido **2.** queja
moan *verb.* **1.** gemir **2.** quejarse
mob *noun.* banda, chusma
mob *verb.* **1.** acosar **2.** atacar
mobile *adj.* **1.** móvil **2.** ambulante
mobility *noun.* movilidad
mobilize *verb.* movilizar
mock *verb.* burlarse
mock *adj.* fingido, falso
mode *noun.* **1.** modo **2.** medio **3.** moda
model *noun.* modelo
model *verb.* **1.** modelar **2.** hacer de modelo, posar

moderate *noun.* moderado
moderate *verb.* moderar
moderate *adj.* **1.** moderado **2.** regular
modern *adj.* moderno
modernize *verb.* modernizar
modest *adj.* **1.** modesto **2.** recatado **3.** pequeño
modification *noun.* modificación
modify *verb.* modificar
module *noun.* módulo
moist *adj.* húmedo
moisture *noun.* humedad
mold *noun.* **1.** molde **2.** moho
mold *verb.* moldear
mole *noun.* **1.** lunar **2.** topo
molecular *adj.* molecular
molecule *noun.* molécula
mom, momma, mommy *noun.* mamá
moment *noun.* momento, instante
momentarily *adv.* momentáneamente
momentum *noun.* impulso, ímpetu
monarch *noun.* monarca
monarchy *noun.* monarquía
monastery *noun.* monasterio
Monday *noun.* lunes
monetary *adj.* monetario
money *noun.* dinero, plata
monitor *noun.* **1.** responsable, encargado **2.** monitor
monitor *verb.* controlar, observar
monk *noun.* monje
monkey *noun.* **1.** mono **2.** diablillo, pillo
monkey *verb.* juguetear
monopoly *noun.* monopolio
monster *noun.* monstruo
month *noun.* mes
monthly *adj.* mensual
monthly *adv.* mensualmente
monument *noun.* monumento
mood *noun.* humor
moody *adj.* malhumorado
moon *noun.* luna
moonlight *noun.* luz de la luna
moonlight *verb.* estar pluriempleado
moor *noun.* páramo
moor *verb.* amarrar
moral *noun.* moraleja
moral *adj.* moral
morale *noun.* moral

morality *noun.* moral, moralidad
morally *adv.* moralmente
more *adj. adv. pron.* más
moreover *adv.* además
morning *noun.* mañana
Morse *noun.* morse
mortal *noun. adj.* mortal
mortality *noun.* mortalidad
mortar *noun.* 1. argamasa 2. mortero
mortgage *noun.* hipoteca
mortgage *verb.* hipotecar
mosaic *noun.* mosaico
Moslem, Muslim *noun. adj.* musulmán
mosque *noun.* mezquita
moss *noun.* musgo
most *adj.* 1. más 2. la mayoría de, la mayor parte de
most *adv.* 1. más 2. muy 3. sumamente
most *pron.* la mayor parte
—**at (the) most** como máximo
mostly *adv.* principalmente, en su mayor parte
mother *noun.* madre
mother *verb.* 1. cuidar como una madre 2. consentir
motion *noun.* 1. movimiento 2. gesto 3. moción
motion *verb.* hacer señas
motivate *verb.* motivar
motivation *noun.* motivación
motive *noun.* motivo
motor *noun.* motor
motor *verb.* ir en coche
motorist *noun.* automovilista, conductor
mound *noun.* montículo
mount *noun.* 1. monte 2. montura 3. soporte, base
mount *verb.* 1. montar 2. subir, aumentar, crecer 3. fijar, engastar 4. preparar
mountain *noun.* montaña
mouse *noun.* ratón
mouth *noun.* 1. boca 2. desembocadura 3. entrada
mouth *verb.* decir con los labios
move *noun.* 1. movimiento 2. jugada, turno 3. mudanza, traslado
move *verb.* 1. mover 2. trasladar 3. inducir 4. conmover
—**move back** retroceder

movement *noun.* 1. movimiento 2. expresión corporal 3. tendencia
movie *noun.* película
—**the movies** el cine
moving *adj.* conmovedor
Mrs. *noun.* señora
Ms. *noun.* señora
M.S. *abbr.* doctorado en ciencias
much *adj. adv. pron.* mucho
mud *noun.* barro, lodo
muddy *verb.* ensuciar de barro, llenar de barro
muddy *adj.* fangoso, lleno de barro
mug *noun.* 1. tazón 2. jeta
mug *verb.* asaltar, atracar
multiple *noun.* múltiplo
multiple *adj.* múltiple
multiply *verb.* 1. multiplicar 2. multiplicarse
multitude *noun.* multitud, muchedumbre
municipal *adj.* municipal
murder *noun.* asesinato, homicidio
murder *verb.* asesinar, matar
murderer *noun.* asesino
murmur *noun.* murmullo, susurro
murmur *verb.* murmurar, susurrar
muscle *noun.* músculo
muscular *adj.* 1. muscular 2. musculoso
muse *verb.* reflexionar, meditar
museum *noun.* museo
mushroom *noun.* seta, champiñón
mushroom *verb.* crecer de la noche a la mañana
music *noun.* música
musical *noun.* musical
musical *adj.* 1. musical 2. dotado para la música
musician *noun.* músico
Muslim, Moslem *noun. adj.* musulmán
must *noun.* algo imprescindible
must *verb.* 1. deber, tener que (obligation) 2. deber de (probability)
mustache *noun.* bigote
mustard *noun.* mostaza
mute *adj.* mudo
mutter *noun.* murmullo
mutter *verb.* hablar entre dientes, murmurar

mutual *adj.* mutuo, recíproco
mutually *adv.* mutuamente, recíprocamente
my *interj.* ¡Dios mío!
my *adj.* mi, mis

myself *pron.* 1. me 2. mi (after prep) 3. yo mismo/a 4. yo solo/a
mysterious *adj.* misterioso
mystery *noun.* misterio
myth *noun.* mito

N

nail *noun.* 1. uña 2. clavo
nail *verb.* clavar
naked *adj.* 1. desnudo 2. patente, manifiesto
name *noun.* 1. nombre 2. fama, reputación
name *verb.* 1. llamar 2. mencionar 3. nombrar
namely *adv.* a saber
nanny *noun.* niñera
narrative *noun.* narrativa, narración
narrow *verb.* estrechar
narrow *adj.* 1. estrecho 2. escaso 3. reducido
narrowly *adv.* por poco
nasty *adj.* 1. asqueroso, desagradable, repugnante 2. malo 3. feo, grave 4. peligroso, difícil
nation *noun.* 1. nación 2. pueblo
national *adj.* nacional
nationalism *noun.* nacionalismo
nationalist *noun.* nacionalista
nationality *noun.* nacionalidad
nationally *adv.* nacionalmente
native *noun.* 1. nativo 2. indígena
native *adj.* 1. natal 2. indígena 3. autóctono 4. natural, innato
natural *noun.* natural
natural *adj.* 1. natural 2. innato 3. normal 4. biológico
naturally *adv.* 1. naturalmente 2. por naturaleza 3. con naturalidad
nature *noun.* 1. naturaleza 2. carácter 3. tipo
naught, nought *noun.* 1. nada 2. cero
naughty *adj.* travieso
naval *adj.* naval
naïve, naive *adj.* 1. naif 2. ingenuo

navigation *noun.* navegación
navy *noun.* marina
navy *adj.* azul marino
near *prep.* 1. cerca de 2. casi
near *verb.* acercarse a
near *adj.* 1. cercano 2. próximo
near *adv.* cerca
nearby *adv.* cerca
nearly *adv.* casi
neat *adj.* 1. pulcro, ordenado 2. bien hecho
neatly *adv.* con esmero, hábilmente
necessarily *adv.* necesariamente
necessary *adj.* necesario
necessity *noun.* necesidad
neck *noun.* cuello
neck *verb.* besuquearse
need *noun.* 1. necesidad 2. motivo, razón
need *verb.* 1. necesitar 2. hacer falta
needle *noun.* aguja
needless *adj.* innecesario
negative *noun.* 1. negativa 2. negativo
negative *adj.* negativo
neglect *noun.* descuido, dejadez
neglect *verb.* 1. descuidar, desatender, no cumplir con 2. omitir
negligence *noun.* descuido, negligencia
negotiate *verb.* 1. negociar 2. salvar
negotiation *noun.* negociación
negotiator *noun.* negociador
neighbor *noun.* vecino
neighborhood *noun.* 1. barrio, vecindario 2. alrededores, cercanías
neighboring *adj.* vecino
neither *adj. pron.* ninguno de los dos
nephew *noun.* sobrino
nerve *noun.* 1. nervio 2. valor 3. descaro

nerve *verb.* hacer de tripas corazón
nervous *adj.* nervioso
nervously *adv.* nerviosamente, con inquietud
nest *noun.* nido
nest *verb.* anidar
net *noun.* red, malla
net *verb.* coger (con red)
net *adj.* neto
Netherlands *noun.* Países Bajos
network *noun.* red
neutral *noun.* 1. neutral 2. punto muerto
neutral *adj.* 1. neutral 2. neutro
neutrality *noun.* neutralidad
never *adv.* nunca, jamás
nevertheless *adv.* sin embargo, no obstante
new *adj.* nuevo
new *adv.* recién
newcomer *noun.* recién llegado
newly *adv.* recién
news *noun singular.* noticias
newscaster *noun.* locutor, presentador
newsletter *noun.* boletín informativo
newspaper *noun.* periódico, diario
next *adj.* próximo, siguiente
next *adv.* luego, a continuación, después
next *pron.* el siguiente
next door *adv.* al lado
nice *adj.* 1. amable, simpático, agradable 2. bonito, lindo 3. preciso
nicely *adv.* 1. bien 2. agradablemente
nick *noun.* muesca, hendidura
nick *verb.* cortar
nickname *noun.* apodo
nickname *verb.* apodar
Nigeria *noun.* Nigeria
Nigerian *noun. adj.* nigeriano
night *noun.* noche
nightmare *noun.* pesadilla
nil *noun.* cero
nine *noun. adj.* nueve
nineteen *noun. adj.* diecinueve
nineteenth *noun.* decimonono
nineties *noun plural.* 1. entre noventa y cien 2. los años noventa, los noventa
ninetieth *noun.* nonagésimo

ninety *noun. adj.* noventa
ninth *noun.* nono, noveno
nitrogen *noun.* nitrógeno
no *interj.* ¡no!
no *noun.* no
no *adj.* 1. ningún 2. ninguno/a
no *adv.* no
nobility *noun.* nobleza
noble *noun. adj.* noble
nobody *noun.* don nadie
nobody *pron.* nadie
nod *noun.* señal de asentimiento
nod *verb.* 1. saludar con la cabeza, asentir 2. dar cabezadas
node *noun.* nudo
noise *noun.* ruido, sonido
noisy *adj.* ruidoso
nominal *adj.* 1. nominal 2. simbólico
nominate *verb.* nombrar
nomination *noun.* 1. nombramiento 2. nominación, propuesta
nominee *noun.* candidato
none *adv.* de ningún modo
none *pron.* 1. ninguno 2. nada
nonetheless *adv.* no obstante, sin embargo
nonsense *noun.* tontería, disparate, bobada
noon *noun.* mediodía
no-one *pron.* nadie
nor *conj.* ni, tampoco
normal *adj.* normal
normally *adv.* normalmente
north *noun.* norte
north *adj.* 1. norte 2. del norte
north *adv.* al norte, hacia el norte
northern *adj.* del norte
Norway *noun.* Noruega
Norwegian *noun. adj.* noruego
nose *noun.* 1. nariz 2. hocico 3. olfato 4. morro, parte delantera
nose *verb.* 1. avanzar con cuidado 2. fisgonear, husmear
nostalgia *noun.* nostalgia
not *adv.* no
notable *adj.* notable, distinguido
notably *adv.* 1. especialmente 2. notablemente
notation *noun.* notación

note *noun.* 1. nota 2. billete
—**notes** *noun plural.* apuntes
note (down) *verb.* 1. apuntar, anotar 2. observar
notebook *noun.* cuaderno, libreta
noted *adj.* famoso, célebre
nothing *noun. pron.* 1. nada 2. cero
nothing *adv.* de ningún modo, de ninguna manera
notice *noun.* 1. anuncio 2. letrero, cartel 3. atención 4. aviso
notice *verb.* notar, fijarse en, darse cuenta de
noticeable *adj.* 1. evidente 2. notable, digno de atención
notify *verb.* notificar, avisar
notion *noun.* 1. noción 2. idea, concepto
notorious *adj.* notorio
notoriously *adv.* notoriamente
notwithstanding *prep.* a pesar de, no obstante
noun *noun.* nombre, sustantivo
Nov, *abbr.* noviembre
novel *noun.* novela
novel *adj.* novedoso, original
novelist *noun.* novelista
novelty *noun.* novedad
November *noun.* noviembre
novice *noun.* 1. novato, principiante 2. novicio
now *conj.* ahora que, ya que

—**now, now!** vale, basta
now *adv.* 1. ahora 2. ya, ahora mismo 3. entonces
nowadays *adv.* hoy en día, en la actualidad
nowhere *adv.* en ninguna parte
nuclear *adj.* nuclear
nucleus *noun.* núcleo
nuisance *noun.* molestia, fastidio
number *noun.* 1. número 2. cantidad, multitud 3. ejemplar
number *verb.* 1. numerar 2. contar
numerical *adj.* numérico
numerous *adj.* numeroso
nun *noun.* monja, religiosa
nurse *noun.* 1. enfermero 2. niñera, nodriza
nurse *verb.* 1. cuidar 2. amamantar 3. acunar, mecer 4. abrigar, alimentar
nursery *noun.* 1. cuarto de los niños 2. vivero
nursing *noun.* 1. enfermería 2. asistencia, cuidado 3. lactancia
nurture *noun.* crianza, educación
nurture *verb.* criar, educar
nut *noun.* 1. fruto seco 2. tuerca
nutrient *noun.* nutriente
nutrition *noun.* nutrición, alimentación
nutty *adj.* 1. con nueces 2. chalado
nylon *noun.* nilón, nailon
nylon *adj.* de nilón, de nailon

O

o *interj.* ¡oh!
oak *noun.* roble
oak *adj.* de roble
oath *noun.* 1. juramento 2. palabrota
obedience *noun.* obediencia
obey *verb.* obedecer
obituary *noun.* necrología, obituario
object *noun.* 1. objeto 2. objetivo, fin 3. complemento
object (to) *verb.* objetar
objection *noun.* objeción
objective *noun.* objetivo, fin

objective *adj.* objetivo
obligation *noun.* obligación
oblige *verb.* 1. obligar 2. hacer un favor, ayudar
obscene *adj.* obsceno
obscure *verb.* obscurecer, ocultar
obscure *adj.* 1. oscuro, poco claro 2. desconocido 3. borroso
observation *noun.* 1. observación 2. comentario
observe *verb.* 1. observar 2. ver 3. cumplir, guardar 4. señalar

observer *noun.* observador
obsess *verb.* obsesionar
obsession *noun.* obsesión
obstacle *noun.* obstáculo
obstruction *noun.* obstrucción
obtain *verb.* obtener, conseguir
obvious *adj.* evidente, obvio
obviously *adv.* evidentemente
occasion *noun.* 1. ocasión 2. acontecimiento
occasional *adj.* ocasional, poco frecuente
occasionally *adv.* de vez en cuando, a veces
occupation *noun.* ocupación, profesión
occupational *adj.* profesional
occupy *verb.* 1. ocupar 2. habitar, vivir en
occur *verb.* 1. ocurrir, suceder, tener lugar 2. darse, encontrarse 3. ocurrirse
occurrence *noun.* suceso
ocean *noun.* océano
Oct. *abbr.* octubre
October *noun.* octubre
odd *adj.* 1. extraño, raro 2. impar 3. suelto, desparejado 4. ocasional
oddly *adv.* de manera extraña
odds *noun plural.* 1. probabilidades 2. ventaja
odor *noun.* olor
of *prep.* 1. de 2. por
of course por supuesto, claro, naturalmente
off *prep.* 1. de 2. sin 3. fuera de
off *adv.* 1. fuera 2. apagado, cerrado 3. libre 4. completamente 5. malo, mediocre 6. pasado, caducado 7. anulado
offend *verb.* 1. ofender 2. desagradar
offender *noun.* delincuente, infractor
offense, offence *noun.* 1. ofensa 2. delito, infracción
offensive *noun.* ofensiva
offensive *adj.* 1. ofensivo, insultante 2. repugnante, desagradable
offer *noun.* oferta, ofrecimiento
offer *verb.* 1. ofrecer 2. ofrecerse
offering *noun.* 1. regalo 2. ofrenda
office *noun.* 1. despacho, oficina 2. cargo

officer *noun.* 1. oficial 2. funcionario
official *noun.* 1. oficial 2. funcionario
official *adj.* oficial
officially *adv.* oficialmente
offshore *adj.* de la costa
often *adv.* a menudo, con frecuencia
oh *interj.* ¡ah!, ¡oh!
oil *noun.* 1. aceite 2. óleo 3. petróleo
oil *verb.* engrasar, lubricar
O.K., okay *noun.* aprobación, visto bueno
O.K., okay *adj. adv.* bien
O.K., okay *interj.* ¡vale!, ¡okey!
old *adj.* 1. viejo, mayor 2. de edad 3. antiguo
old-fashioned *adj.* anticuado, pasado de moda
olive *noun.* 1. aceituna, oliva 2. olivo 3. verde oliva
Olympic Games, the Olympics *noun plural.* Juegos Olímpicos
omission *noun.* omisión
omit *verb.* 1. omitir 2. olvidarse de 3. suprimir
on *prep.* 1. encima de, en 2. sobre 3. acerca de 4. de 5. a, al 6. por, mediante 7. tras
on *adj.* 1. en curso, funcionando, en marcha 2. en pie
on *adv.* 1. puesto 2. adelante, hacia adelante 3. en marcha, en funcionamiento 4. en exhibición, en cartelera 5. a bordo
on the spot en el acto
once *conj.* una vez que, en cuanto
once *adv.* 1. una vez 2. antes, en otro tiempo
—**at once** inmediatamente
—**all at once** 1. de repente 2. simultáneamente, a la vez
one *noun.* 1. uno 2. un año
—**one another** el uno al otro
one *adj.* 1. un 2. cierto 3. único
one *pron.* 1. el, la 2. uno, una
one-off *noun. adj.* único, aislado
oneself *pron.* 1. se 2. sí mismo/a 3. uno mismo/a
ongoing *adj.* en curso
onion *noun.* cebolla

on-line, online adj. conectado, en línea
only conj. pero, sólo que
only adj. único
only adv. sólo, solamente
onset noun. inicio, comienzo
open verb. 1. abrir 2. abrirse 3. empezar
open adj. 1. abierto 2. destapado, desabrochado, descubierto 3. franco
opening noun. 1. abertura, brecha 2. comienzo 3. apertura, inauguración 4. oportunidad
openly adv. abiertamente
opera noun. ópera
operate verb. 1. funcionar 2. operar, intervenir
operation noun. 1. operación 2. funcionamiento
operational adj. operativo
operative adj. en vigor
operator noun. 1. operario 2. telefonista
opinion noun. opinión
opponent noun. adversario, oponente
opportunity noun. oportunidad, ocasión
oppose verb. 1. oponerse, estar en contra 2. luchar contra
opposite prep. adv. en frente de, frente a
opposite noun. lo contrario
opposite adj. 1. opuesto, contrario 2. de enfrente
opposition noun. oposición
oppression noun. opresión
opt verb. optar, escoger
—**opt out (of)** abandonar, dejar de participar
optical adj. óptico
optimism noun. optimismo
optimistic adj. optimista
option noun. opción
optional adj. opcional
or conj. o
oracle noun. oráculo
oral noun. examen oral
oral adj. oral
orange noun. 1. naranja 2. naranjo
orange adj. 1. naranja 2. de naranja
orbit noun. órbita

orbit verb. orbitar, estar en órbita
orchard noun. huerto
orchestra noun. orquesta
ordeal noun. experiencia dura
order noun. 1. orden 2. pedido
order verb. 1. ordenar, mandar 2. pedir, encargar
orderly noun. 1. celador 2. ordenanza
orderly adj. formal, ordenado
ordinary adj. 1. ordinario, común, normal 2. mediocre, vulgar
ore noun. mineral, mena
organ noun. órgano
organic adj. orgánico
organism noun. organismo
organization noun. organización
organize verb. organizar
organized adj. organizado
organizer noun. organizador
oriental noun. adj. oriental
orientation noun. orientación
origin noun. origen
original noun. adj. original
originally adv. originalmente
originate verb. 1. originar, crear, suscitar 2. originarse
orthodox adj. ortodoxo
other adj. pron. otro
otherwise conj. si no, de lo contrario
otherwise adv. 1. aparte de eso, por lo demás 2. de otra manera
ought (to) verb. deber
ounce, oz. noun. onza
our adj. nuestro/a, nuestros/as
ours pron. el (nuestro), la (nuestra), (los) nuestros, (las) nuestras
ourselves pron. 1. nos 2. nosotros mismos, nosotras mismas 3. nosotros solos, nosotras solas
oust verb. desbancar, expulsar
out adv. 1. fuera, afuera 2. apagado 3. en voz alta 4. eliminado 5. en huelga 6. pasado de moda 7. expirado, vencido 8. equivocado 9. publicado 10. conocido 11. completamente
—**out of** 1. fuera de 2. de cada 3. sin 4. por 5. de
outbreak noun. estallido
outcome noun. resultado

outdoor *adj.* al aire libre

outer *adj.* exterior, externo

outfit *noun.* traje

outgoing *adj.* **1.** extrovertido, sociable **2.** saliente

outing *noun.* excursión, paseo

outlaw *noun.* prófugo, fugitivo

outlaw *verb.* proscribir

outlet *noun.* salida

outline *noun.* **1.** contorno, silueta **2.** resumen, esbozo

outline *verb.* perfilar, resumir

outlook *noun.* **1.** vista **2.** actitud, punto de vista **3.** perspectivas

output *noun.* producción

outrage *noun.* atrocidad, escándalo, ultraje

outrage *verb.* ultrajar

outrageous *adj.* escandaloso, ofensivo

outright *adj.* absoluto

outright *adv.* **1.** francamente **2.** de inmediato, en el acto

outset *noun.* principio, comienzo

outside *prep.* fuera

outside *noun.* exterior

outside *adj.* **1.** exterior **2.** externo **3.** ínfimo, remoto

outside *adv.* **1.** fuera, afuera **2.** por fuera

outsider *noun.* **1.** forastero, desconocido **2.** competidor con pocas posibilidades de ganar

outskirts *noun plural.* afueras, alrededores

outstanding *adj.* **1.** excepcional, extraordinario, excelente **2.** pendiente, atrasado

outward *adj.* **1.** exterior, externo **2.** de ida

oval *noun.* óvalo

oval *adj.* oval, ovalado

oven *noun.* horno

over *prep.* **1.** sobre **2.** encima de, arriba de **3.** al otro lado, enfrente **4.** más de

5. por **6.** durante **7.** superior a

over *adv.* **1.** por encima, por arriba **2.** al otro lado, enfrente **3.** de un lado al otro **4.** otra vez **5.** hacia abajo **6.** más **7.** de sobra, en exceso **8.** acabado, terminado **9.** arruinado, perdido

overall *noun.* mono, overol

overall *adj.* total

overall *adv.* en total

overcome *verb.* superar, vencer

overcome *adj.* turbado, confundido

overhead *adv.* por lo alto, en alto

overlap *noun.* superposición

overlap *verb.* superponerse, solaparse

overlook *verb.* **1.** tener vistas a, dar a **2.** hacer la vista gorda, pasar por alto

overnight *adj.* **1.** nocturno **2.** repentino

overnight *adv.* **1.** de noche **2.** repentinamente

overseas *adj.* **1.** extranjero **2.** exterior

overseas *adv.* en el extranjero

oversee *verb.* supervisar

overt *adj.* abierto, manifiesto, público

overtake *verb.* adelantar

overthrow *verb.* derrocar, derribar

overtime *noun.* horas extras

overturn *verb.* volcar

overwhelm *verb.* **1.** vencer, aplastar **2.** agobiar, abrumar

overwhelming *adj.* **1.** aplastante **2.** abrumador **3.** irresistible

owe *verb.* deber

owing *adj.* debido

owl *noun.* búho, lechuza

own *verb.* **1.** poseer, tener, ser dueño de **2.** confesar, admitir

own *adj. pron.* propio

owner *noun.* propietario, dueño

ownership *noun.* propiedad

oxygen *noun.* oxígeno

oz *abbr.* onza

ozone *noun.* ozono

P

p. *abbr.* página
pace *noun.* paso
pace *verb.* ir de un lado a otro
pack *noun.* **1.** paquete **2.** cajetilla **3.** fardo, bulto **4.** manada, jauría **5.** hatajo, cuadrilla, pelotón
pack *verb.* **1.** empaquetar, embalar **2.** hacer la maleta **3.** envasar **4.** amontonarse, hacinarse, apiñarse
package *noun.* **1.** paquete **2.** oferta
package *verb.* **1.** empaquetar, embalar **2.** envasar
packet *noun.* **1.** paquete **2.** cajetilla
packing *noun.* **1.** preparación de las maletas **2.** embalaje
pact *noun.* pacto
pad *noun.* **1.** almohadilla **2.** taco, bloc **3.** plataforma
pad *verb.* **1.** almohadillar, acolchar **2.** caminar sin hacer ruido
pagan *noun. adj.* pagano
page *noun.* **1.** página **2.** mensajero **3.** paje
page *verb.* llamar por megafonía/altavoz
pain *noun.* dolor
pain *verb.* doler, afligir, apenar
painful *adj.* doloroso
painfully *adv.* dolorosamente
paint *noun.* pintura
paint *verb.* pintar
painter *noun.* pintor
painting *noun.* **1.** pintura **2.** cuadro
pair *noun.* **1.** par **2.** pareja
pair *verb.* emparejar
Pakistan *noun.* Pakistán
Pakistani *noun. adj.* paquistaní
pal *noun.* amigo, colega
palace *noun.* palacio
pale *verb.* palidecer
pale *adj.* pálido, claro
Palestine *noun.* Palestina
Palestinian *noun. adj.* palestino
palm (tree) *noun.* palma, palmera
pan *noun.* cazuela, cazo, sartén, olla
panama (hat) *noun.* panamá

panel *noun.* **1.** panel, entrepaño **2.** tablero **3.** jurado
panic *noun.* pánico
panic *verb.* **1.** entrarle a alguien el pánico **2.** provocar pánico
pants *noun plural.* **1.** calzoncillos **2.** bragas, calzones **3.** pantalones
papal *adj.* papal
paper *noun.* **1.** papel **2.** periódico **3.** revista **4.** examen
—papers *noun plural.* documentación, papeles
paperback *noun.* libro en rústica
paperback *adj.* en rústica
paperwork *noun.* trabajo de oficina
par *noun.* par
parachute *noun.* paracaídas
parachute *verb.* **1.** lanzar en paracaídas **2.** lanzarse en paracaídas
parade *noun.* **1.** desfile **2.** revista
parade *verb.* **1.** desfilar **2.** formar, pasar revista **3.** lucir, hacer alarde de
paradise *noun.* paraíso
paradox *noun.* paradoja
paragraph *noun.* párrafo
parallel *noun.* **1.** paralela **2.** paralelismo, semejanza, analogía **3.** paralelo
parallel *verb.* equiparar, igualar, comparar
parallel *adj.* **1.** paralelo **2.** análogo
parallel *adv.* paralelamente
parcel *noun.* paquete
pardon *interj.* ¡perdón!, ¿cómo?
pardon *noun.* **1.** perdón **2.** indulto
pardon *verb.* **1.** perdonar, disculpar **2.** indultar
parent *noun.* padre, madre
parental *adj.* de los padres, paterno
parish *noun.* parroquia
park *noun.* **1.** parque **2.** jardín
park *verb.* aparcar, estacionar
parking lot *noun.* parking, aparcamiento
parliament *noun.* parlamento
parliamentary *adj.* parlamentario
parlor *noun.* salón

parsley *noun.* perejil
parson *noun.* 1. párroco, cura 2. clérigo
part *noun.* 1. parte 2. papel 3. función
part *verb.* 1. partir 2. dividir 3. separar, separarse 4. abrir, correr 5. apartarse
partial *adj.* parcial
participant, participator *noun.* participante
participate *verb.* participar
participation *noun.* participación
particle *noun.* partícula
particular *adj.* 1. particular, especial 2. exigente
particularly *adv.* especialmente
particulars *noun plural.* detalles, pormenores
parting *noun.* 1. partida, separación, despedida 2. raya (del pelo)
partly *adv.* en parte
partner *noun.* 1. socio 2. pareja
partner *verb.* acompañar
partnership *noun.* 1. sociedad 2. asociación 3. relación de pareja
part-time *adj. adv.* a tiempo parcial, media jornada
party *noun.* 1. fiesta, reunión 2. grupo 3. partido
pass *noun.* 1. pase 2. permiso 3. desfiladero, paso, puerto
pass *verb.* 1. pasar 2. traspasar, ceder 3. superar 4. adelantar 5. transcurrir 6. aprobar 7. juzgar, dictar sentencia 8. desaparecer 9. morir 10. aprobar 11. sufrir, tolerar
passage *noun.* 1. pasaje 2. pasillo, pasadizo 3. paso 4. viaje, travesía
passenger *noun.* pasajero
passing *adj.* transitorio, pasajero, temporal
passion *noun.* pasión
passionate *adj.* apasionado
passive *adj.* pasivo
passport *noun.* pasaporte
past *prep.* 1. por delante de 2. más allá de
past *noun.* 1. pasado 2. historia
past *adj.* 1. anterior 2. antiguo 3. último 4. pasado
pasta *noun.* pasta

pastoral *adj.* 1. pastoril 2. pastoral
pastry *noun.* 1. masa 2. pastel
pasture *noun.* pasto
pat, off pat *adj.* preparado
pat *noun.* 1. palmadita, caricia 2. porción pequeña
pat *verb.* acariciar, dar palmaditas, tocar
pat *adv.* de memoria, al dedillo
patch *noun.* 1. remiendo, parche 2. parcela, terreno
patch *verb.* remendar
patent *noun.* patente
patent *verb.* patentar
path *noun.* 1. camino, sendero 2. trayectoria, recorrido
pathetic *adj.* 1. lastimoso, patético 2. inútil
patience *noun.* paciencia
patient *noun.* paciente
patient *adj.* paciente, sufrido
patiently *adv.* pacientemente
patriot *noun.* patriota
patriotic *adj.* patriótico
patrol *noun.* patrulla
patrol *verb.* patrullar
patron *noun.* 1. mecenas 2. cliente habitual, parroquiano
patronage *noun.* mecenazgo, patrocinio, apoyo
pattern *noun.* 1. patrón, molde 2. modelo
pause *noun.* pausa, silencio
pause *verb.* hacer una pausa, parar
pave *verb.* pavimentar, empedrar, adoquinar
pavement *noun.* pavimento, acera
pavilion *noun.* pabellón
pay *noun.* salario, sueldo, paga
pay *verb.* 1. pagar, retribuir, remunerar 2. saldar, liquidar 3. compensar, sacar provecho 4. prestar, rendir, ofrecer
payable *adj.* pagadero
payment *noun.* pago, recompensa
PC *abbr.* 1. ordenador, computadora 2. políticamente correcto
pea *noun.* guisante
peace *noun.* paz
peaceful *adj.* tranquilo, sosegado, relajado

peach *noun.* melocotón
peak *noun.* **1.** pico, cumbre **2.** cumbre, cúspide, apogeo **3.** visera
peak *verb.* alcanzar el punto más alto
pear *noun.* pera
pearl *noun.* perla
peasant *noun.* campesino, labrador
peasantry *noun.* campesinado
peculiar *adj.* **1.** curioso, extraño **2.** peculiar, propio, característico
pedestrian *noun.* peatón
pedestrian *adj.* pedestre
peel *noun.* piel, corteza
peel *verb.* **1.** pelar **2.** pelarse, desconcharse
peer *noun.* par, noble
peer *verb.* escudriñar
peg *noun.* **1.** clavija, estaca **2.** percha, colgador
peg *verb.* sujetar
pen *noun.* **1.** pluma **2.** corral
penalty *noun.* pena, castigo, multa
pencil *noun.* lápiz
pencil *verb.* escribir con lápiz
penetrate *verb.* penetrar
penetration *noun.* penetración
penguin *noun.* pingüino
peninsula *noun.* península
penis *noun.* pene
penny *noun.* centavo
pension *noun.* pensión
pensioner *noun.* pensionista
pentagon *noun.* pentágono
people *noun plural.* **1.** gente **2.** personas **3.** pueblo
pepper *noun.* **1.** pimienta **2.** pimentero **3.** pimiento
pepper *verb.* sazonar con pimienta
 —**pepper with** acribillar
per *prep.* por
per cent *adv.* por ciento
perceive *verb.* percibir, comprender
percentage *noun.* porcentaje
perception *noun.* **1.** percepción **2.** perspicacia, agudeza
perch *noun.* **1.** perca **2.** percha
perch *verb.* **1.** posarse, sentarse **2.** encaramar
perennial *adj.* perenne, eterno, perpetuo

perfect *verb.* perfeccionar
perfect *adj.* **1.** perfecto **2.** completo
perfection *noun.* perfección
perfectly *adv.* **1.** perfectamente **2.** completamente, totalmente
perform *verb.* **1.** realizar, efectuar, ejecutar **2.** actuar **3.** representar, interpretar **4.** rendir
performance *noun.* **1.** realización, ejecución **2.** resultado, desempeño **3.** representación, actuación **4.** rendimiento
performer *noun.* artista, intérprete, músico, actor
perfume *noun.* perfume
perfume *verb.* **1.** perfumar **2.** perfumarse
perhaps *adv.* quizás, tal vez
period *noun.* **1.** período **2.** era, fase, etapa **3.** punto
period *adj.* de época
periodic *adj.* periódico
peripheral *adj.* periférico
permanent *adj.* permanente
permanently *adv.* permanentemente
permission *noun.* permiso, autorización
permit *noun.* permiso, pase, licencia
permit *verb.* permitir
perpetual *adj.* perpetuo, eterno, continuo
persist *verb.* **1.** persistir, continuar **2.** insistir, empeñarse
persistence *noun.* persistencia, insistencia
persistent *adj.* persistente, insistente
person *noun.* persona
personal *adj.* **1.** personal **2.** en persona
 —**personal computer, PC** ordenador personal, computadora personal
personality *noun.* personalidad
personally *adv.* personalmente, en persona
personnel *noun.* personal
perspective *noun.* perspectiva
persuade *verb.* **1.** persuadir, convencer **2.** disuadir
persuasion *noun.* persuasión
persuasive *adj.* persuasivo
Peru *noun.* Perú

Peruvian *noun. adj.* peruano

pest *noun.* **1.** plaga, animal/insecto nocivo **2.** pelma, fregón **3.** lata, rollo

pesticide *noun.* pesticida

pet *noun.* animal doméstico, mascota

pet *verb.* **1.** acariciar **2.** acariciarse, sobarse

pet *adj.* favorito, predilecto

petition *noun.* petición, instancia

petition *verb.* **1.** presentar una petición **2.** dirigir una instancia

petroleum *noun.* petróleo

petty *adj.* **1.** insignificante, nimio, de poca monta **2.** mezquino

pharmaceutical *adj.* farmacéutico

phase *noun.* fase

phenomenon *noun.* fenómeno

Philippines *noun.* Filipinas

philosopher *noun.* filósofo

philosophical, philosophic *adj.* filosófico

philosophy *noun.* filosofía

phoenix *noun.* fénix

phone *noun.* teléfono

phone *verb.* telefonear, llamar por teléfono

phone call *noun.* llamada de teléfono

photo *noun.* foto, fotografía

photograph *verb.* fotografiar

photographer *noun.* fotógrafo

photographic *adj.* fotográfico

photography *noun.* fotografía

phrase *noun.* frase

phrase *verb.* expresar

physical *adj.* **1.** físico **2.** material

physically *adv.* físicamente

physician *noun.* médico

physicist *noun.* físico

physics *noun singular.* física

piano *noun.* piano

pick, pickax *noun.* pico, piqueta

pick *noun.* **1.** elección, selección **2.** lo mejor

pick *verb.* **1.** elegir, escoger **2.** coger, recoger **3.** levantar **4.** forzar

picnic *noun.* picnic, jira, merienda campestre

picnic *verb.* ir de picnic, hacer un picnic

picture *noun.* **1.** pintura, cuadro, retrato **2.** fotografía **3.** película **4.** imagen **5.** descripción

picture *verb.* **1.** representar, describir **2.** imaginar, figurarse

picturesque *adj.* pintoresco

pie *noun.* tarta, empanada, pastel

piece *noun.* **1.** trozo, pedazo **2.** pieza **3.** moneda

pier *noun.* muelle, embarcadero

pierce *verb.* **1.** atravesar, traspasar **2.** perforar, agujerear

pig *noun.* cerdo, puerco

pigeon *noun.* paloma

pike *noun.* lucio

pile *noun.* **1.** montón, pila **2.** poste, pilar **3.** pelo

pile *verb.* amontonar, apilar

pilgrim *noun.* peregrino

pilgrimage *noun.* peregrinación

pill *noun.* píldora, pastilla

pillar *noun.* pilar, columna

pillow *noun.* almohada

pillow *verb.* apoyar

pilot *noun.* **1.** piloto **2.** práctico

pilot *verb.* pilotar, pilotear

pilot *adj.* piloto, experimental

pin *noun.* **1.** alfiler **2.** insignia, pin

pin *verb.* **1.** prender, sujetar **2.** inmovilizar

pinch *noun.* **1.** pellizco **2.** pizca

pinch *verb.* **1.** pellizcar **2.** apretar

pine *noun.* pino

pine (away) *verb.* languidecer, consumirse

pine (for) *verb.* suspirar por, anhelar

pink *noun. adj.* rosa, rosado

pint *noun.* pinta

pioneer *noun.* pionero, precursor

pioneer *verb.* se el primero en, marcar un nuevo rumbo

pipe *noun.* **1.** tubería, tubo, cañería **2.** pipa, cachimbo **3.** flauta **4.** gaita

pipe *verb.* **1.** canalizar, llevar por tubería/gaseoducto/oleoducto **2.** tocar

pipeline *noun.* **1.** tubería, cañería **2.** oleoducto **3.** gaseoducto

piper *noun.* **1.** flautista **2.** gaitero

pipes *noun plural.* **1.** gaita **2.** flauta

pirate *noun.* pirata

pirate *verb.* piratear
pistol *noun.* pistola
pit *noun.* **1.** hoyo, foso, fosa **2.** mina, pozo **3.** boxes **4.** hueso, pepita, pepa
pit *verb.* deshuesar, quitar las pepitas
pitch *noun.* brea
pitch *noun.* **1.** tono **2.** grado, punto, extremo **3.** puesto **4.** lanzamiento, tiro **5.** alquitrán, brea
pitch *verb.* **1.** armar, montar **2.** tirar, lanzar, arrojar **3.** caer **4.** cabecear **5.** graduar el tono
pity *noun.* **1.** piedad, compasión **2.** pena, lástima
pity *verb.* **1.** compadecer **2.** compadecerse de, tener lástima
pizza *noun.* pizza
place *noun.* **1.** sitio, lugar **2.** asiento **3.** posición **4.** lugar **5.** pasaje, página **6.** función, deber, obligación **7.** puesto, trabajo **8.** casa **9.** plaza
place *verb.* **1.** colocar, poner **2.** situar, ubicar **3.** echar, achacar, dar **4.** invertir **5.** recordar, identificar, reconocer
plague *noun.* **1.** peste **2.** plaga
plague *verb.* importunar
plain *noun.* **1.** llanura **2.** punto del derecho
plain *adj.* **1.** sencillo, liso, sin ornamentos **2.** claro, evidente **3.** franco **4.** común, ordinario, poco atractivo
plainly *adv.* **1.** sencillamente **2.** claramente **3.** francamente
plaintiff *noun.* demandante, querellante
plan *noun.* **1.** plan, proyecto **2.** plano
plan *verb.* **1.** planear **2.** planificar, proyectar **3.** diseñar
plane *noun.* **1.** avión **2.** plano **3.** nivel **4.** cepillo **5.** plátano
plane *verb.* cepillar, alisar
planet *noun.* planeta
planner *noun.* planificador
planning *noun.* planificación
plant *noun.* **1.** planta **2.** instalaciones, maquinaria **3.** fábrica
plant *verb.* **1.** plantar, sembrar **2.** plantarse **3.** colocar, poner, infiltrar
plantation *noun.* plantación
plasma *noun.* plasma

plaster *noun.* **1.** revoque, enlucido **2.** yeso **3.** esparadrapo, curita
plaster *verb.* **1.** enyesar, enlucir **2.** embadurnar, untar
plastic *noun.* plástico
plastic *adj.* plástico, moldeable
plate *noun.* **1.** plato **2.** quemador, fuego **3.** vajilla **4.** placa **5.** lámina, grabado **6.** dentadura (postiza)
plateau *noun.* meseta, altiplano
platform *noun.* **1.** plataforma **2.** andén
plausible *adj.* **1.** plausible **2.** convincente
play *noun.* **1.** juego **2.** diversión **3.** obra, pieza dramática **4.** función, representación
play *verb.* **1.** jugar (a), mover **2.** representar, actuar **3.** ser representado **4.** tocar, interpretar **5.** dirigir
player *noun.* jugador
playground *noun.* patio de recreo
playwright *noun.* dramaturgo
plea *noun.* **1.** súplica, petición **2.** alegato, defensa
plead *verb.* **1.** declarar, alegar **2.** defender, hablar por alguien
　—plead with suplicar
pleasant *adj.* agradable, amable, simpático
please *verb.* **1.** complacer, agradar **2.** querer, dar la gana
please *adv.* por favor
pleased *adj.* contento, satisfecho
pleasing *adj.* agradable
pleasure *noun.* placer
pledge *noun.* **1.** promesa **2.** empeño, prenda
pledge *verb.* **1.** prometer **2.** empeñar
plenty *adj.* suficiente
plenty *pron.* **1.** bastante, suficiente **2.** mucho
plight *noun.* apuro, situación grave
plot *noun.* **1.** complot **2.** trama, argumento **3.** terreno, solar
plot *verb.* **1.** maquinar, urdir **2.** trazar
plow *noun.* arado
plow *verb.* **1.** arar **2.** abrirse camino
plug *noun.* **1.** enchufe **2.** tapón
plug *verb.* tapar
　—plug in enchufar

plump adj. regordete, rechoncho
—plump for optar por, decidirse por
plunge noun. zambullida, chapuzón
plunge verb. 1. lanzarse, zambullirse 2. caer, hundirse
plus, plus sign noun. (signo) más
plus prep. más
plus adj. positivo
pm, p.m., P.M. abbr. de la tarde/noche
pocket noun. 1. bolsillo 2. tronera 3. bolsa
pocket verb. 1. meterse/guardar en el bolsillo 2. embolsar, quedarse con
poem noun. poema
poet noun. poeta
poetic adj. poético
poetry noun. poesía
point noun. 1. punto 2. punta 3. cabo 4. momento preciso 5. cuestión 6. finalidad, motivo 7. cualidad
point verb. 1. apuntar 2. señalar, indicar 3. rejuntar
pointed adj. puntiagudo
pointless adj. sin sentido, inútil
poised adj. 1. equilibrado, ecuánime 2. listo, preparado
poison noun. veneno
poison verb. envenenar
Poland noun. Polonia
polar adj. polar
pole noun. 1. polo 2. palo, poste
police noun plural. policía
police verb. vigilar, mantener el orden
police station noun. comisaría
policeman, policewoman noun. policía, agente de policía
policy noun. 1. política 2. póliza
polish noun. 1. brillo, lustre 2. cera, betún 3. abrillantador
polish verb. 1. lustrar, abrillantar, limpiar 2. perfeccionar, mejorar
Polish noun. adj. polaco
polished adj. pulido
polite adj. educado
politely adv. educadamente
political adj. político
politically adv. políticamente
politically correct adj. políticamente correcto

politician noun. político
politics noun. política
poll noun. 1. votación, elecciones 2. índice de participación 3. encuesta, sondeo
poll verb. obtener, recibir
pollute verb. contaminar
pollution noun. contaminación
polo noun. polo
polytechnic noun. politécnico
pond noun. estanque
ponder verb. ponderar, considerar
pony noun. poni, póney
pool noun. 1. charca, alberca, piscina 2. charco 3. reserva 4. fondo común
pool verb. juntar, poner en común
poor adj. 1. pobre 2. malo 3. escaso
poorly adj. pachucho, indispuesto
poorly adv. mal
pop noun. pequeño estallido
pop verb. 1. reventar, estallar 2. saltar, salir disparado
pop adj. pop
Pope noun. Papa
popular adj. 1. popular 2. generalizado, extendido 3. de moda
popularity noun. popularidad
population noun. población
porch noun. 1. pórtico 2. terraza, porche
pork noun. cerdo
port noun. 1. puerto 2. ciudad portuaria 3. babor 4. vino de Oporto
portable adj. portátil
porter noun. 1. mozo de equipajes, maletero 2. cargador
portfolio noun. 1. carpeta 2. cartera
portion noun. 1. parte, porción 2. ración
portrait noun. retrato
portray verb. 1. retratar, pintar, describir 2. representar
Portugal noun. Portugal
Portuguese noun. adj. portugués
pose noun. 1. postura, pose 2. afectación
pose verb. 1. posar 2. plantear, presentar
—pose as hacerse pasar por
position noun. 1. posición 2. postura 3. situación 4. puesto

position *verb.* colocar, situar
positive *noun.* positivo
positive *adj.* **1.** positivo **2.** constructivo **3.** seguro
positively *adv.* **1.** categóricamente **2.** positivamente **3.** con seguridad
possess *verb.* poseer, tener
possession *noun.* **1.** posesión **2.** tenencia
possibility *noun.* posibilidad
possible *adj.* posible
possibly *adv.* **1.** posiblemente **2.** quizás
post *noun.* **1.** correo **2.** poste **3.** empleo, cargo **4.** puesto
—**post office** oficina de correos
post *verb.* **1.** poner **2.** hacer público, anunciar **3.** destinar **4.** mandar por correo
postal *adj.* postal
postcard *noun.* postal
poster *noun.* póster, cartel
postpone *verb.* posponer, aplazar
posture *noun.* **1.** postura **2.** posición
pot *noun.* **1.** pote, cacerola, puchero **2.** tarro **3.** maceta, tiesto
pot *verb.* plantar en una maceta, plantar en un tiesto
potato *noun.* papa, patata
potent *adj.* potente
potential *noun. adj.* potencial
potentially *adv.* potencialmente
potter *noun.* alfarero; ceramista
pottery *noun.* **1.** cerámica, loza **2.** alfarería
pound *noun.* **1.** libra **2.** corral **3.** libra esterlina
pound *verb.* **1.** aporrear, golpear **2.** machacar, triturar
pour *verb.* **1.** verter, derramar, echar **2.** chorrear, manar **3.** servir **4.** llover a cántaros
poverty *noun.* pobreza
powder *noun.* **1.** polvo **2.** polvos **3.** pólvora
powder *verb.* empolvar
power *noun.* **1.** poder **2.** potencia, fuerza, poderío **3.** energía **4.** capacidad, facultad **5.** autoridad
power station *noun.* central eléctrica

powered *adj.* accionado, movido por
powerful *adj.* **1.** potente, poderoso **2.** convincente
PR *abbr.* relaciones públicas
practicable *adj.* practicable, factible
practical *adj.* práctico
practically *adv.* **1.** prácticamente, casi **2.** en la práctica
practice *noun.* **1.** práctica **2.** costumbre **3.** entrenamiento, ejercicio **4.** profesión **5.** clientela
practice *verb.* **1.** entrenarse, ejercitarse **2.** practicar, ejercer
practiced *adj.* experto
praise *noun.* elogio, alabanza
praise *verb.* **1.** elogiar **2.** alabar
pray *verb.* **1.** rezar, orar **2.** rogar
prayer *noun.* oración, rezo
preach *verb.* **1.** predicar **2.** sermonear, dar un sermón **3.** aconsejar
precaution *noun.* precaución
precede *verb.* preceder, anteceder
precedent *noun.* precedente
preceding *adj.* precedente, anterior
precious *adj.* precioso
precise *adj.* preciso, exacto
precisely *adv.* **1.** precisamente **2.** exactamente
precision *noun.* precisión
predator *noun.* depredador, predador
predecessor *noun.* **1.** predecesor **2.** antepasado, antecesor
predict *verb.* predecir, pronosticar
predictable *adj.* predecible, previsible
prediction *noun.* predicción, pronóstico
predominantly *adv.* predominantemente
prefer *verb.* preferir
preferable *adj.* preferible
preferably *adv.* preferiblemente
preference *noun.* preferencia
pregnancy *noun.* embarazo
pregnant *adj.* embarazada, encinta
prejudice *noun.* prejuicio
prejudice *verb.* **1.** predisponer, prevenir **2.** perjudicar
preliminary *adj.* preliminar
premature *adj.* prematuro
premier *noun.* primer ministro

premier adj. primero, principal

premises noun plural. local, establecimiento, propiedad

preoccupation noun. preocupación

preparation noun. 1. preparación 2. preparativo

prepare verb. 1. preparar 2. prepararse

prepared adj. preparado

prescribe verb. 1. recetar 2. prescribir

prescription noun. 1. receta 2. prescripción

presence noun. presencia

present noun. 1. presente 2. regalo

present verb. 1. entregar, hacer entrega de 2. presentar 3. ofrecer

present adj. 1. presente 2. actual

presentation noun. presentación

presently adv. 1. en breve, dentro de poco 2. en este momento, actualmente

preservation noun. conservación

preserve noun. 1. dominio, terreno 2. coto, reserva 3. confitura

preserve verb. 1. proteger, guardar 2. conservar

preside verb. presidir

presidency noun. presidencia

president noun. presidente

presidential adj. presidencial

press noun. 1. apretón 2. imprenta 3. prensa

press verb. 1. apretar, pulsar 2. exprimir, estrujar 3. prensar 4. presionar 5. apremiar, instar 6. insistir 7. planchar

press conference noun. conferencia de prensa

pressing adj. urgente, apremiante

pressure noun. presión

prestige noun. prestigio

presumably adv. se supone que, es de suponer

presume verb. 1. presumir, suponer 2. atreverse

presumption noun. presunción, suposición

pretend verb. 1. fingir, simular 2. pretender

pretty adj. 1. bonito, lindo 2. buen

pretty adv. bastante

prevail (against/over) verb. 1. prevalecer, imponerse 2. predominar

prevailing adj. 1. predominante, imperante 2. común

prevalence noun. 1. predominio 2. frecuencia

prevalent adj. prevaleciente, común

prevent verb. 1. impedir 2. evitar

prevention noun. prevención

preview noun. preestreno

previous adj. anterior, previo

previously adv. anteriormente, previamente

prey noun. presa

price noun. precio

price verb. 1. poner/marcar el precio 2. valorar

pride noun. 1. orgullo, arrogancia 2. manada

priest noun. 1. cura 2. sacerdote

priestess noun. sacerdotisa

primarily adv. principalmente, en primer lugar

primary adj. 1. principal 2. primario

prime noun. flor de la vida, plenitud

prime verb. 1. preparar 2. cebar

prime adj. 1. principal 2. primer, primero 3. óptimo, perfecto

primitive adj. primitivo, rudimentario

prince noun. príncipe

princess noun. princesa

principal noun. 1. director, rector 2. capital

principal adj. principal

principally adv. principalmente

principle noun. principio

print noun. 1. huella, marca 2. copia 3. grabado 4. estampado 5. letra

print verb. 1. imprimir 2. publicar, editar 3. sacar una copia 4. estampar 5. escribir con letra de imprenta

printer noun. 1. impresor 2. impresora

printing noun. impresión, tipografía

prior noun. prior

prior adj. 1. previo, anterior 2. prioritario

priority noun. prioridad

prison noun. prisión, cárcel

prisoner noun. preso, recluso, prisionero

privacy noun. intimidad, privacidad
private noun. soldado raso
private adj. 1. privado 2. particular
privately adv. privadamente, en privado
privilege noun. privilegio
privileged adj. privilegiado
prize noun. premio
prize verb. apreciar, valorar
probability noun. probabilidad
probable adj. probable
probably adv. probablemente
probation noun. libertad provisional
probe noun. 1. sonda 2. investigación
probe verb. 1. investigar 2. explorar 3. sondar
problem noun. problema
procedural adj. procesal
procedure noun. procedimiento
proceed verb. 1. proseguir, continuar 2. proceder, actuar 3. empezar
proceedings noun plural. 1. actas 2. proceso
proceeds noun plural. ganancias
process noun. 1. proceso 2. procedimiento
process verb. 1. procesar, tratar 2. revelar
procession noun. desfile
proclaim verb. proclamar
produce noun. productos agrícolas
produce verb. 1. producir 2. sacar, presentar 3. tener, dar a luz 4. provocar 5. fabricar 6. escribir, componer 7. poner en escena
producer noun. productor
product noun. producto
production noun. 1. producción 2. montaje, puesta en escena
productive adj. productivo
productivity noun. productividad
profession noun. 1. profesión 2. cuerpo 3. declaración, afirmación
professional noun. profesional
professional adj. 1. profesional 2. muy bueno
professionally adv. profesionalmente, con profesionalidad
professor, Prof. noun. profesor universitario

profile noun. perfil
profit noun. 1. beneficio, ganancia 2. provecho
profit (by/from) verb. 1. ganar, sacar ganancia 2. aprovechar
profitable adj. 1. lucrativo, rentable 2. provechoso, ventajoso
profound adj. profundo
profoundly adv. profundamente
program noun. programa
program verb. programar
progress noun. progreso
progress verb. 1. avanzar 2. progresar, mejorar
progressive adj. progresivo
progressive (tense) noun. continuo
progressively adv. progresivamente
prohibit verb. prohibir
prohibition noun. prohibición
project noun. 1. proyecto 2. estudio, trabajo
project verb. 1. proyectar, planear 2. sobresalir 3. lanzar
projection noun. proyección
prolonged adj. prolongado
prominence noun. prominencia, importancia
prominent adj. 1. prominente 2. saliente 3. destacado, notable
promise noun. 1. promesa 2. futuro
promise verb. prometer
promising adj. prometedor
promote verb. 1. promover, fomentar 2. ascender 3. promocionar
promoter noun. promotor
promotion noun. 1. promoción 2. ascenso
prompt verb. 1. mover, incitar, provocar 2. apuntar
prompt adj. 1. pronto, inmediato 2. puntual
promptly adv. 1. con prontitud, inmediatamente 2. puntualmente
prone adj. postrado
—**prone to** propenso a
pronounce verb. pronunciar
pronounced adj. pronunciado
pronunciation noun. pronunciación
proof noun. prueba

prop *noun.* puntal
prop *verb.* apoyar
propaganda *noun.* propaganda
proper *adj.* 1. apropiado, adecuado 2. correcto
proper name *noun.* nombre propio
properly *adv.* 1. apropiadamente, adecuadamente 2. correctamente
property *noun.* 1. propiedad 2. accesorio
proportion *noun.* proporción
proportional *adj.* proporcional
proposal *noun.* 1. propuesta 2. proposición
propose *verb.* 1. proponer 2. presentar 3. proponer matrimonio, pedir la mano
proposition *noun.* proposición
proposition *verb.* hacer proposiciones deshonestas
proprietor *noun.* propietario
pros *noun.* pro
—**pros and cons** pros y contras
prose *noun.* prosa
prosecute *verb.* procesar, enjuiciar
prosecution *noun.* 1. proceso, juicio 2. acusación
prospect *noun.* 1. porvenir, futuro 2. perspectiva
prospect *verb.* prospectar, explorar
prosperity *noun.* prosperidad
prosperous *adj.* próspero
prostitute *noun.* prostituta
protect *verb.* proteger, amparar
protected *adj.* protegido
protection *noun.* protección
protective *adj.* protector, de protección
protein *noun.* proteína
protest *noun.* 1. protesta, queja 2. manifestación
protest *verb.* protestar
Protestant *noun. adj.* protestante
protester *noun.* manifestante
proud *adj.* 1. orgulloso, soberbio 2. magnífico, espléndido
proudly *adv.* orgullosamente
prove *verb.* 1. probar 2. resultar
proven *adj.* probado
provide *verb.* 1. proporcionar, 2. proveer, suministrar, facilitar

provided, providing *conj.* siempre que, a condición de que
province *noun.* provincia
provincial *adj.* provincial
provision *noun.* 1. provisión, abastecimiento 2. cláusula, disposición, estipulación 3. condición
provision *verb.* aprovisionar, abastecer
provisional *adj.* provisional
provoke *verb.* provocar
proximity *noun.* proximidad
prudent *adj.* prudente
prune *noun.* ciruela pasa
prune *verb.* podar
psychiatric *adj.* psiquiátrico
psychiatrist *noun.* psiquiatra
psychological *adj.* psicológico
psychologist *noun.* psicólogo
psychology *noun.* psicología
public *adj.* público
—**public relations** relaciones públicas
publication *noun.* publicación
publicity *noun.* publicidad
publicize *verb.* 1. publicar 2. anunciar
publicly *adv.* públicamente
publish *verb.* 1. publicar 2. anunciar, hacer público
publisher *noun.* 1. editor 2. editorial
publishing *noun.* edición
Puerto Rico *noun.* Puerto Rico
Puerto Rican *noun. adj.* puertorriqueño
pudding *noun.* budín
pull *noun.* 1. tirón, jalón 2. calada, chupada 3. sorbo 4. atracción 5. enchufe
pull *verb.* 1. tirar, jalar, arrastrar 2. remar 3. sacar, arrancar
—**pull at/on** chupar
pulse *noun.* pulso
pulse *verb.* latir, palpitar
pump *noun.* bomba
pump *verb.* 1. bombear 2. sonsacar, sacar información de alguien
punch *noun.* 1. perforadora, taladro 2. ponche 3. puñetazo 4. fuerza, garra
—**Punch** Polichinela
punch *verb.* 1. perforar, taladrar 2. dar un puñetazo
punish *verb.* castigar
punishment *noun.* 1. castigo 2. pena

pup, puppy *noun.* cachorro
pupil *noun.* 1. alumno 2. pupila
purchase *noun.* compra, adquisición
purchase *verb.* comprar, adquirir
purchaser *noun.* comprador
pure *adj.* puro
purely *adv.* puramente
purity *noun.* pureza
purple *noun. adj.* púrpura, morado
purpose *noun.* 1. propósito, fin 2. función, uso, utilidad 3. determinación
purse *noun.* 1. monedero 2. bolso
purse *verb.* fruncir
pursue *verb.* 1. perseguir 2. dedicarse a 3. seguir
pursuit *noun.* 1. persecución 2. desempeño, ocupación
push *noun.* 1. empujón 2. empuje, dinamismo, ímpetu
push *verb.* 1. empujar 2. apretar, pulsar 3. promover 4. pasar, traficar

put *verb.* 1. poner 2. colocar 3. presentar 4. expresar, exponer 5. escribir
—put aside 1. dejar a un lado 2. omitir, pasar por alto
—put down 1. aplastar, suprimir 2. atribuir
—put in 1. introducir 2. dedicar 3. presentar
—put off 1. desechar 2. diferir, aplazar
—put on 1. ponerse 2. encender, prender 3. afectar, adoptar
—put out 1. tender la mano 2. echar 3. apagar 4. emitir, lanzar 5. molestarse
—put up with transigir
putt *verb.* patear
puzzle *noun.* 1. enigma 2. rompecabezas
puzzle *verb.* 1. dejar perplejo, confundir 2. devanarse los sesos, romperse la cabeza
pyramid *noun.* pirámide

Q

qualification *noun.* 1. aptitud, capacidad 2. diploma, título 3. reserva, salvedad
qualified *adj.* cualificado, capacitado
qualify *verb.* 1. capacitar, reunir las condiciones 2. calificar
—qualify as obtener el título, obtener la licencia para ejercer una profesión
—qualify for clasificarse
qualifying *adj.* eliminatorio
quality *noun.* 1. calidad 2. cualidad
quantity *noun.* cantidad
quarrel *noun.* pelea, riña
quarrel *verb.* pelearse, reñir
quarry *noun.* 1. cantera 2. presa, víctima
quarry *verb.* sacar, extraer
quarter *noun.* 1. cuarto 2. veinticinco centavos 3. barrio 4. gracia 5. trimestre
—from all quarters de todas partes
quarter *verb.* 1. dividir en cuatro, cuartear 2. acuartelar, alojar

quarter-final(s) *noun.* cuartos de final
quarterly *noun.* publicación trimestral
quarterly *adj.* trimestral
quarterly *adv.* trimestralmente
quarters *noun plural.* 1. dependencias 2. cuartel
quartet *noun.* cuarteto
queen *noun.* 1. reina 2. dama 3. marica
query *noun.* 1. pregunta 2. signo de interrogación
query *verb.* 1. poner en duda, cuestionar 2. preguntar
quest *noun.* busca, búsqueda
question *noun.* 1. pregunta 2. cuestión 3. problema 4. duda 5. posibilidad
question *verb.* 1. hacer preguntas, interrogar 2. cuestionar, poner en duda
questionable *adj.* 1. cuestionable, discutible 2. dudoso
questionnaire *noun.* cuestionario
queue *noun.* fila

queue *verb.* hacer cola
quick *adj.* **1.** rápido **2.** listo, agudo **3.** ágil
quick *adv.* de prisa, rápido, rápidamente
quickly *adv.* deprisa, rápidamente
quiet *noun.* tranquilidad, calma
quiet *adj.* **1.** tranquilo **2.** silencioso **3.** suave **4.** callado **5.** relajado, calmado **6.** discreto
quiet (down) *verb.* **1.** tranquilizar, calmar **2.** tranquilizarse, calmarse

quietly *adv.* **1.** tranquilamente **2.** silenciosamente
quit *verb.* abandonar, dejar
quite *interj.* pues sí, así es
quite *adv.* **1.** totalmente **2.** bastante
quiz *noun.* **1.** concurso **2.** prueba
quota *noun.* cuota
quotation *noun.* **1.** cotización **2.** cita **3.** citación
quote *verb.* **1.** cotizar, estimar **2.** citar

R

rabbit *noun.* conejo
race *noun.* carrera
race *noun.* raza
race *verb.* **1.** correr **2.** competir en una carrera **3.** hacer una carrera
racial *adj.* racial
racism *noun.* racismo
racist *noun. adj.* racista
rack *noun.* anaquel
radar *noun.* radar
radiation *noun.* radiación
radiator *noun.* radiador
radical *noun.* radical
radical *adj.* radical, fundamental
radically *adv.* radicalmente
radio *noun.* radio
radio *verb.* **1.** radiar **2.** comunicarse por radio
radioactive *adj.* radioactivo
radius *noun.* radio
raffle *noun.* rifa
raffle *verb.* rifar
rag *noun.* trapo
rage *noun.* rabia, ira, furia
rage *verb.* **1.** estar furioso **2.** enfurecerse, rabiar **3.** bramar, embravecerse **4.** arrasar, hacer estragos
ragged *adj.* **1.** harapiento, andrajoso **2.** roto, deshilachado **3.** irregular, accidentado
raid *noun.* **1.** incursión, ataque **2.** redada
raid *verb.* **1.** asaltar, atracar **2.** invadir **3.**
hacer una redada
rail *noun.* **1.** barra, pasamanos, riel **2.** carril, raíl
rail (in/off) *verb.* cercar
railroad *noun.* **1.** ferrocarril **2.** vía férrea
rain *noun.* lluvia
rain *verb.* llover
rainbow *noun.* arco iris
raise *noun.* aumento
raise *verb.* **1.** levantar **2.** subir, aumentar **3.** cultivar **4.** criar **5.** plantear, sacar **6.** provocar, suscitar **7.** recaudar, movilizar, reunir **8.** reclutar **9.** erigir
rally *noun.* **1.** reunión, mitin **2.** rally **3.** recuperación **4.** peloteo
rally *verb.* **1.** reunir **2.** concentrar **3.** recuperarse
ram *noun.* **1.** carnero **2.** ariete, espolón, pisón
ram *verb.* **1.** apisonar, apretar **2.** chocar, embestir
random *adj.* aleatorio, al azar
range *noun.* **1.** gama, variedad, surtido **2.** alcance, autonomía **3.** escala, rango **4.** cadena, cordillera **5.** dehesa, terreno de pasto **6.** campo de tiro **7.** cocina
range *verb.* **1.** alinear **2.** ordenar, clasificar **3.** variar, fluctuar **4.** extenderse, cubrir
rank *noun.* **1.** fila, hilera **2.** rango, categoría **3.** clase
rank *verb.* **1.** clasificar **2.** ocupar un puesto

rank *adj.* **1.** absoluto, total **2.** fétido
rap *noun.* golpe seco
rap *verb.* dar un golpe seco
rape *noun.* violación
rape *verb.* violar
rapid *adj.* rápido
rapidly *adv.* rápidamente
rare *adj.* **1.** raro, poco común **2.** poco hecho
rarely *adv.* raramente
rash *noun.* erupción, sarpullido
rash *adj.* imprudente
rat *noun.* **1.** rata **2.** canalla
rat *verb.* **1.** rajarse, volverse atrás **2.** chivarse
rate *noun.* **1.** tasa, índice **2.** porcentaje **3.** velocidad, ritmo **4.** tarifa
rate *verb.* estimar, valorar, considerar
rather *adv.* **1.** bastante **2.** algo, un poco **3.** antes que, en lugar de **4.** más bien, para ser más precisos
ratify *verb.* ratificar
rating *noun.* **1.** clasificación, posición **2.** índice de audiencia
ratio *noun.* proporción
rational *adj.* racional
rationality *noun.* racionalidad
rattle *noun.* **1.** ruido, golpeteo, tintineo **2.** sonajero
rattle *verb.* **1.** hacer ruido, sonar **2.** desconcertar, confundir
rave *verb.* **1.** delirar **2.** hablar con entusiasmo
raw *adj.* **1.** crudo **2.** bruto, sin refinar, en rama **3.** en carne viva **4.** verde, inexperto
ray *noun.* **1.** rayo **2.** brizna, resquicio
Rd *abbr.* **1.** calle **2.** carretera
reach *noun.* alcance
reach *verb.* **1.** llegar (a) **2.** alcanzar **3.** alargar la mano **4.** contactar **5.** extenderse
react *verb.* reaccionar
reaction *noun.* reacción
reactor *noun.* reactor
read *noun.* lectura
read *verb.* **1.** leer **2.** adivinar, descifrar **3.** decir **4.** estar escrito **5.** indicar, marcar
reader *noun.* **1.** lector **2.** libro de lectura

readily *adv.* **1.** de buena gana **2.** fácilmente
readiness *noun.* **1.** prontitud **2.** buena disposición
reading *noun.* **1.** lectura **2.** interpretación
ready *adj.* **1.** preparado, listo **2.** dispuesto **3.** pronto **4.** a punto de
real *adj.* **1.** verdadero, real **2.** auténtico
real *adv.* muy
real estate *noun.* bienes raíces
realism *noun.* realismo
realistic *adj.* realista
reality *noun.* realidad
realization *noun.* **1.** comprensión **2.** realización
realize *verb.* **1.** comprender, darse cuenta **2.** llevar a cabo **3.** reportar
really *interj.* ¿de verdad?
really *adv.* **1.** en realidad **2.** realmente, muy
realm *noun.* **1.** reino **2.** dominio, sector
rear *noun.* **1.** parte trasera **2.** trasero
rear *verb.* **1.** criar **2.** encabritarse **3.** levantar, alzar
rear *adj.* trasero, de detrás
reason *noun.* razón
reason *verb.* razonar
reasonable *adj.* **1.** razonable **2.** sensato, juicioso
reasonably *adv.* razonablemente
reasoning *noun.* razonamiento
reassurance *noun.* tranquilidad, consuelo
reassure *verb.* tranquilizar
reassuring *adj.* tranquilizador
rebel *noun.* rebelde
rebel *verb.* rebelarse
rebellion *noun.* rebelión
recall *noun.* **1.** retirada, destitución **2.** memoria, recuerdo
recall *verb.* **1.** hacer volver **2.** recordar
receipt *noun.* **1.** recibo **2.** recepción
receive *verb.* recibir
receiver *noun.* **1.** auricular **2.** receptor **3.** síndico (de quiebras)
recent *adj.* reciente
recently *adv.* recientemente
reception *noun.* **1.** recepción **2.** acogida

recession noun. recesión
recipe noun. receta
recipient noun. receptor
reckless adj. temerario
reckon verb. 1. calcular 2. considerar 3. pensar, creer
recognition noun. reconocimiento
recognize verb. reconocer
recommend verb. recomendar
recommendation noun. recomendación
reconcile verb. 1. reconciliar 2. conciliar 3. resignarse
reconciliation noun. reconciliación
reconstruction noun. reconstrucción
record noun. 1. documento, constancia (escrita) 2. registro 3. datos 4. disco 5. récord, plusmarca 6. historial, antecedentes
record verb. 1. registrar 2. dejar constancia escrita 3. grabar 4. consignar
recorder noun. 1. flauta 2. grabadora, magnetófono
recording noun. grabación
recover verb. 1. recuperar 2. recuperarse
recovery noun. recuperación
recreation noun. recreación
recreational adj. recreativo
recruit noun. 1. recluta 2. nuevo miembro
recruit verb. 1. reclutar 2. contratar
recruitment noun. 1. reclutamiento 2. contratación
rectangular adj. rectangular
recurrence noun. recurrencia
recurrent adj. recurrente
recycle verb. reciclar
red noun. adj. 1. rojo 2. tinto 3. comunista
redemption noun. redención
reduce verb. 1. reducir 2. rebajar 3. disminuir 4. adelgazar, perder peso
reduction noun. 1. reducción 2. rebaja
reed noun. 1. junco, caña 2. lengüeta
reef noun. arrecife
reel noun. 1. carrete, bobina 2. baile escocés
reel verb. 1. tambalear 2. tambalearse
re-elect verb. reelegir

refer (to) verb. 1. referirse (a) 2. enviar, remitir 3. consultar
referee noun. árbitro
referee verb. arbitrar
reference noun. 1. referencia 2. consulta
referendum noun. referéndum
refined adj. refinado
reflect verb. 1. reflejar 2. reflexionar
reflecting adj. reflector
reflection noun. 1. reflejo 2. reflexión
reform noun. reforma
reform verb. 1. reformar 2. reformarse
reformed adj. reformado
reformer noun. reformador
refreshing adj. 1. refrescante 2. reconfortante
refrigerator noun. frigorífico, refrigeradora
refuge noun. refugio
refugee noun. refugiado
refund noun. reembolso
refund verb. reembolsar
refusal noun. negativa
refuse noun. basura, desperdicios
refuse verb. 1. negarse 2. rechazar 3. negar, denegar
regain verb. 1. recobrar, recuperar 2. volver a alcanzar
regard noun. 1. consideración 2. respeto 3. estima
regard (as) verb. 1. considerar 2. estimar 3. mirar 4. prestar atención, tener en cuenta
regarding prep. con respecto a, en cuanto a
regardless adj. adv. 1. a pesar de 2. sin hacer caso de
regards noun plural. saludos, recuerdos
regime, régime noun. régimen
regiment noun. regimiento
regiment verb. disciplinar, reglamentar
region noun. región
regional adj. regional
register noun. 1. registro 2. lista
register verb. 1. registrar 2. registrarse, inscribirse, matricularse 3. certificar 4. marcar
registered adj. certificado

registrar *noun.* registrador
registry *noun.* registro
regret *noun.* 1. pesar 2. remordimiento
regret *verb.* 1. lamentar 2. arrepentirse (de)
regular *noun.* 1. soldado profesional 2. habitual
regular *adj.* 1. regular 2. habitual 3. normal, común 4. frecuente 5. profesional
regularly *adv.* regularmente
regulate *verb.* regular
regulation *noun.* 1. regla 2. regulación
regulator *noun.* regulador
rehabilitate *verb.* rehabilitar
rehabilitation *noun.* rehabilitación
rehearsal *noun.* ensayo
reign *noun.* reinado
reign *verb.* reinar
rein *noun.* rienda
reinforce *verb.* reforzar
reject *noun.* artículo defectuoso
reject *verb.* rechazar
rejection *noun.* rechazo
relate *verb.* 1. relatar 2. relacionar, asociar —**relate to** relacionarse con
related *adj.* 1. emparentado 2. relacionado
relation *noun.* 1. relación 2. pariente
relationship *noun.* 1. relación 2. parentesco
relative *noun.* pariente
relative *adj.* relativo
relatively *adv.* relativamente
relax *verb.* 1. relajar, suavizar 2. relajarse
relaxation *noun.* 1. relajación 2. diversión
relay *noun.* retransmisión
relay *verb.* retransmitir
release *noun.* 1. liberación, puesta en libertad 2. lanzamiento, estreno 3. anuncio, comunicado
release *verb.* 1. liberar 2. soltar 3. hacer público, dar a conocer 4. sacar 5. estrenar
relegate *verb.* relegar
relegation *noun.* relegación
relentless *adj.* implacable
relevance *noun.* 1. pertinencia 2. relevancia

relevant *adj.* 1. pertinente 2. relevante
reliability *noun.* fiabilidad
reliable *adj.* fiable, de confianza
reliance *noun.* dependencia
relief *noun.* 1. alivio 2. auxilio, socorro 3. beneficencia 4. suplente 5. liberación 6. relieve
relieve *verb.* 1. aliviar 2. relevar, sustituir 3. destituir 4. librar 5. socorrer, auxiliar
religion *noun.* religión
religious *adj.* religioso
relish *noun.* 1. placer, gusto, deleite 2. condimento
relish *verb.* saborear
reluctance *noun.* renuencia
reluctant *adj.* renuente, reacio
reluctantly *adv.* de mala gana
remain *verb.* 1. quedar 2. quedarse 3. permanecer, continuar
remainder *noun.* resto
remains *noun plural.* sobras, restos
remark *noun.* observación, comentario
remark *verb.* observar, comentar, hacer comentarios
remarkable *adj.* 1. notable 2. singular
remarkably *adv.* 1. notablemente 2. singularmente
remedy *noun.* remedio
remedy *verb.* remediar
remember *verb.* 1. recordar 2. acordarse de
remind *verb.* 1. recordar a 2. recordar algo a alguien
reminder *noun.* recordatorio
remote *adj.* 1. remoto 2. lejano
removal *noun.* extirpación, eliminación
remove *verb.* 1. quitar, llevarse 2. quitarse
remuneration *noun.* remuneración
render *verb.* 1. dejar, volver 2. prestar, dar 3. interpretar
renew *verb.* renovar
renewal *noun.* renovación
renowned *adj.* renombrado, famoso
rent *noun.* 1. alquiler 2. rasgadura
rent *verb.* alquilar
rental *noun.* alquiler
reorganization *noun.* reorganización
reorganize *verb.* reorganizar

repair *noun.* **1.** reparación, arreglo **2.** estado

repair *verb.* reparar, arreglar

repay *verb.* devolver, pagar, liquidar

repayment *noun.* reembolso

repeat *noun.* **1.** repetición **2.** reposición

repeat *verb.* **1.** repetir **2.** recitar

repeated *adj.* repetido

repeatedly *adv.* repetidamente

repetition *noun.* repetición

replace *verb.* **1.** sustituir, reponer **2.** volver a colocar

replacement *noun.* sustituto

replay *noun.* partido de desempate

reply *noun.* respuesta

reply *verb.* responder

report *noun.* **1.** informe **2.** rumor **3.** detonación

report *verb.* **1.** relatar, informar, dar parte de **2.** acusar, denunciar **3.** presentar informe **4.** presentarse, personarse

reporter *noun.* reportero

represent *verb.* representar

representation *noun.* representación

representative *noun.* representante

representative *adj.* representativo

repression *noun.* represión

reproduce *verb.* **1.** reproducir **2.** reproducirse

reproduction *noun.* reproducción

reproductive *adj.* reproductor

republic *noun.* república

republican *adj.* republicano

reputation *noun.* reputación

request *noun.* petición, solicitud

request *verb.* pedir

require *verb.* **1.** necesitar, precisar **2.** exigir

requirement *noun.* **1.** necesidad **2.** requisito

rescue *noun.* rescate

rescue *verb.* rescatar, socorrer

research *noun.* investigación

research *verb.* investigar

researcher *noun.* investigador

resemblance *noun.* semejanza, parecido

resemble *verb.* parecerse (a)

resent *verb.* ofenderse, tomarse a mal

resentment *noun.* resentimiento

reservation *noun.* reserva

reserve *noun.* reserva

reserve *verb.* reservar

reserved *adj.* reservado

reservoir *noun.* embalse, depósito, represa

residence *noun.* **1.** residencia **2.** estancia

resident *noun.* habitante

resident *adj.* **1.** residente **2.** interno, que duerme en casa

residential *adj.* **1.** residencial **2.** interno

residual *adj.* residual

residue *noun.* residuo

resign *verb.* dimitir

—resign to resignarse

resignation *noun.* **1.** dimisión **2.** resignación

resigned *adj.* resignado

resist *verb.* **1.** resistir **2.** resistirse

resistance *noun.* resistencia

resistant *adj.* resistente

resolution *noun.* **1.** resolución **2.** propósito **3.** definición

resolve *noun.* resolución

resolve *verb.* resolver

resolved *adj.* resuelto, decidido

resort *noun.* centro turístico, lugar de veraneo

resort (to) *verb.* recurrir (a)

resource *noun.* **1.** recurso **2.** inventiva, ideas

respect *noun.* **1.** respeto **2.** aspecto

respect *verb.* **1.** respetar **2.** acatar

respectable *adj.* **1.** respetable **2.** adecuado, decente **3.** considerable

respective *adj.* respectivo

respectively *adv.* respectivamente

respects *noun plural.* saludos, recuerdos

respiratory *adj.* respiratorio

respond (to) *verb.* **1.** responder **2.** reaccionar

response *noun.* **1.** respuesta **2.** reacción **3.** responsorio

responsibility *noun.* responsabilidad

responsible *adj.* **1.** responsable **2.** de responsabilidad

responsive *adj.* sensible

rest *noun.* 1. descanso 2. reposo 3. apoyo, soporte 4. resto

rest *verb.* 1. descansar 2. reposar 3. apoyar, apoyarse 4. relajarse, estar tranquilo 5. depender 6. basarse

restaurant *noun.* restaurante

restless *adj.* inquieto, agitado

restoration *noun.* restauración

restore *verb.* 1. restaurar 2. restablecer 3. devolver

restrain *verb.* 1. sujetar 2. refrenar

restrained *adj.* moderado, comedido, refrenado

restrict *verb.* 1. restringir 2. limitar

restricted *adj.* 1. restringido, limitado 2. vedado, prohibido

restriction *noun.* restricción, limitación

restrictive *adj.* restrictivo

result *noun.* resultado

result *verb.* resultar

—**result in** acabar en

resume *verb.* reanudar

resurrection *noun.* resurrección

retail *verb.* vender al por menor

retail *adj.* al por menor

retailer *noun.* detallista, comerciante al por menor

retain *verb.* 1. retener 2. conservar

retaliate *verb.* desquitarse, tomar represalias

retention *noun.* retención

retire *verb.* 1. retirarse 2. jubilarse

retired *adj.* 1. retirado 2. jubilado

retirement *noun.* 1. retiro 2. jubilación

retiring *adj.* 1. saliente 2. retraído, reservado

retort *noun.* réplica

retort *verb.* replicar

retreat *noun.* 1. retirada 2. retiro

retreat *verb.* retirarse

retrieval *noun.* recuperación

retrieve *verb.* 1. recuperar, recobrar 2. reparar, subsanar

return *noun.* 1. vuelta, regreso 2. reaparición 3. devolución 4. ganancia, rendimiento

return *verb.* 1. volver, regresar 2. devolver 3. reaparecer 4. fallar, declarar

reunion *noun.* reunión

rev (up) *verb.* acelerar, girar

reveal *verb.* 1. revelar 2. poner de manifiesto

revealing *adj.* revelador

revelation *noun.* revelación

revenge *noun.* venganza

revenge (on) *verb.* vengarse (de)

revenue *noun.* ingresos

reverend *noun.* reverendo

reversal *noun.* 1. inversión 2. revocación

reverse *noun.* 1. contrario 2. revés 3. marcha atrás 4. reverso, dorso

reverse *verb.* 1. invertir, poner del revés 2. cambiar 3. dar marcha atrás 4. revocar

reverse *adj.* 1. contrario 2. inverso 3. marcha atrás

revert *verb.* volver

review *noun.* 1. examen, análisis 2. crítica 3. revista 4. revisión, repaso

review *verb.* 1. examinar, analizar 2. hacer una crítica 3. revisar, repasar

revise *verb.* revisar

revision *noun.* revisión

revival *noun.* 1. renacimiento, recuperación, vuelta 2. reestreno, reposición 3. reanimación

revive *verb.* 1. recuperar, resurgir 2. reponer 3. reanimar

revolt *noun.* rebelión

revolt *verb.* 1. rebelarse, sublevarse 2. repugnar, dar asco

revolution *noun.* 1. revolución 2. vuelta

revolutionary *noun. adj.* revolucionario

reward *noun.* recompensa

reward *verb.* recompensar

rewarding *adj.* gratificante

rhythm *noun.* ritmo

rhythmic, rhythmical *adj.* rítmico

rib *noun.* 1. costilla 2. cuaderna 3. nervadura

ribbon *noun.* cinta

rice *noun.* arroz

rich *adj.* 1. rico 2. abundante 3. fértil 4. exquisito, suculento 5. suntuoso, lujoso

rid (of) *verb.* librar (de)

—get rid of librarse de

ride *noun.* **1.** paseo, vuelta **2.** viaje

ride *verb.* **1.** montar (a/en) **2.** recorrer **3.** montar a caballo

rider *noun.* **1.** jinete **2.** ciclista, motorista **3.** viajero, pasajero

ridge *noun.* **1.** cresta **2.** cadena **3.** caballete

ridiculous *adj.* ridículo

rifle *noun.* rifle

rifle *verb.* **1.** rebuscar, revolver **2.** desvalijar

rig *noun.* **1.** torre de perforación **2.** plataforma petrolífera **3.** aparejos

rig *verb.* aparejar

right *interj.* de acuerdo, bien

right *noun.* **1.** derecho **2.** bien **3.** razón, justicia **4.** derecha

right *verb.* **1.** enderezar **2.** corregir

right *adj.* **1.** derecho **2.** correcto **3.** bien **4.** verdadero **5.** adecuado, apropiado **6.** justo **7.** recto

right *adv.* **1.** exactamente **2.** inmediatamente **3.** justo **4.** totalmente, completamente **5.** a la derecha **6.** bien, correctamente

right-hand *adj.* **1.** derecho **2.** a la derecha, a mano derecha

rightly *adv.* **1.** justificadamente **2.** debidamente **3.** con razón

rights *noun plural.* derechos

rigid *adj.* **1.** rígido **2.** estricto, severo

rigorous *adj.* riguroso

rim *noun.* **1.** llanta **2.** borde, canto

ring *noun.* **1.** anillo **2.** aro **3.** argolla **4.** círculo **5.** ring, cuadrilátero **6.** red, banda **7.** toque **8.** llamada de teléfono

ring *verb.* **1.** rodear, cercar **2.** anillar **3.** sonar **4.** llamar **5.** tintinear

—ring up llamar por teléfono

riot *noun.* disturbio, motín

riot *verb.* amotinarse

rip *noun.* rasgadura, desgarro

rip *verb.* rasgar, desgarrar

ripe *adj.* maduro

rise *noun.* **1.** ascenso, subida **2.** aumento

rise *verb.* **1.** subir **2.** aumentar **3.** elevarse **4.** levantarse **5.** sublevarse, rebe-

larse **6.** ascender **7.** nacer **8.** alzarse, erigirse **9.** resucitar

rising *noun.* **1.** sublevación, rebelión **2.** salida

rising *adj.* **1.** en aumento, en alza **2.** naciente

risk *noun.* riesgo

risk *verb.* **1.** arriesgar **2.** arriesgarse

risky *adv.* arriesgado

rite *noun.* rito

ritual *noun. adj.* ritual

rival *noun.* rival

rival *verb.* rivalizar

rivalry *noun.* rivalidad

river *noun.* río

road *noun.* **1.** camino **2.** carretera **3.** calle

roar *noun.* **1.** rugido, bramido **2.** grito **3.** carcajada **4.** estruendo, fragor

roar *verb.* **1.** rugir, bramar **2.** decir a gritos **3.** reírse a carcajadas **4.** retumbar

roast *noun. adj.* asado

roast *verb.* **1.** asar **2.** tostar

rob *verb.* robar

—rob of quitar

robbery *noun.* robo

robin *noun.* petirrojo

robust *adj.* robusto

rock *noun.* **1.** roca **2.** peñasco **3.** rock

rock *verb.* **1.** acunar, mecer **2.** balancearse **3.** sacudir

rocket *noun.* cohete

rocket *verb.* dispararse

rocky *adj.* **1.** inestable, poco firme **2.** rocoso

rod *noun.* vara, barra

role *noun.* papel

roll *noun.* **1.** rollo, fajo **2.** lista **3.** panecillo **4.** revolcón **5.** balanceo **6.** retumbo, fragor **7.** michelín **8.** redoble

roll *verb.* **1.** (hacer) rodar **2.** enrollar, liar **3.** dar(se) la vuelta **4.** moldear **5.** estirar **6.** balancearse, mecerse **7.** retumbar **8.** redoblar **9.** ondular, fluir **10.** pasar, sucederse

roller *noun.* **1.** rodillo **2.** rulo **3.** ola grande

rolling *adj.* ondulante

Roman *noun. adj.* romano

Roman Catholic *noun*. católico romano

romance *noun*. 1. romance 2. amorío, idilio 3. novela sentimental

Romania *noun*. Rumania

Romanian *noun*. *adj*. rumano

romantic *adj*. romántico

roof *noun*. techo

roof *verb*. techar

room *noun*. 1. habitación, cuarto, pieza 2. espacio, sitio
—**rooms** alojamiento, habitaciones de alquiler

root *noun*. 1. raíz 2. origen

root *verb*. 1. arraigarse, echar raíces 2. escarbar, revolver

rope *noun*. cuerda, soga

rope *verb*. amarrar, atar

rose *noun*. rosa

rot *noun*. 1. putrefacción, podredumbre 2. tonterías, bobadas

rot *verb*. pudrir, corromper, descomponer

rotate *verb*. 1. rotar, girar 2. hacer girar

rotation *noun*. rotación

rotor *noun*. rotor

rotten *adj*. 1. podrido 2. malo, vil

rough *noun*. 1. bruto, gamberro 2. rough, zona de matojos (golf)

rough *adj*. 1. áspero, basto 2. accidentado 3. rudo, bruto, violento 4. turbulento, embravecido 5. aproximado, esbozado, preliminar

roughly *adv*. 1. aproximadamente 2. bruscamente, toscamente

round *noun*. 1. círculo 2. ronda 3. recorrido 4. salva, tiro 5. cartucho 6. vuelta, asalto 7. canon

round *verb*. girar, virar

round *prep*. 1. alrededor de, en torno a 2. por

round *adj*. redondo

round *adv*. 1. en sentido contrario 2. en círculo 3. de persona en persona 4. de un sitio a otro, por ahí 5. de circunferencia 6. a casa

roundabout *adj*. indirecto

rounded *adj*. redondeado, curvado

route *noun*. camino, itinerario

route *verb*. encaminar

routine *noun*. rutina

routine *adj*. rutinario, de rutina, habitual

rover *noun*. vagabundo

row *noun*. 1. bronca, pelea 2. barullo, escándalo 3. hilera, fila 4. paseo en bote de remos

row *verb*. remar

royal *adj*. 1. real 2. espléndido, magnífico, suntuoso

royalty *noun*. 1. derechos de autor 2. realeza, miembro de la familia real

rub *noun*. friega

rub *verb*. restregar, frotar

rubber *noun*. *adj*. 1. caucho 2. goma 3. condón

rubbish *noun*. 1. basura, desperdicios 2. tonterías, chorradas

ruble *noun*. rublo

rude *adj*. 1. grosero, maleducado 2. indecente

rug *noun*. 1. tapete, alfombrilla 2. manta de viaje

rugby *noun*. rugby

ruin *noun*. 1. ruina 2. perdición

ruin *verb*. 1. arruinar 2. estropear

ruined *adj*. 1. en ruinas 2. destrozado

rule *noun*. 1. gobierno 2. norma, reglamento 3. regla

rule *verb*. 1. reinar, gobernar 2. decidir, fallar 3. trazar

ruled *adj*. pautado

ruler *noun*. 1. gobernante, dirigente 2. regla

ruling *noun*. fallo, decisión

ruling *adj*. gobernante, reinante, dirigente, en el poder

rumor *noun*. rumor

run *noun*. 1. carrera 2. viaje, excursión, paseo, vuelta 3. racha, período, etapa 4. corral

run *verb*. 1. correr 2. circular, moverse 3. funcionar, estar en marcha 4. dirigir, gobernar, organizar 5. seguir vigente, durar 6. permanecer en cartel 7. tener 8. desteñir, correrse 9. llevar 10. pasar 11. estar

rung *noun*. escalón

runner *noun*. 1. corredor 2. patín

runner-up *noun*. segundo, subcampeón

running *adj*. continuo, en directo

running *adv.* seguido, consecutivo
runway *noun.* pista de aterrizaje
rural *adj.* rural
rush *noun.* **1.** abalanzamiento, ímpetu **2.** prisa, urgencia **3.** junco

rush *verb.* **1.** precipitarse **2.** meter prisa
Russia *noun.* Rusia
Russian *noun. adj.* ruso
ruthless *adj.* despiadado, implacable
rye *noun.* centeno

S

sack *noun.* saco
sack *verb.* despedir
sacred *adj.* sagrado
sacrifice *noun.* sacrificio
sacrifice *verb.* sacrificar
sad *adj.* triste, melancólico
saddle *noun.* silla (de montar), sillín
saddle *verb.* ensillar
sadly *adv.* tristemente
sadness *noun.* tristeza, melancolía
safari *noun.* safari
safe *noun.* caja de caudales
safe *adj.* **1.** seguro **2.** digno de confianza
safeguard *noun.* salvaguardia, protección, garantía
safeguard *verb.* proteger
safely *adv.* **1.** seguramente **2.** sin percance
safety *noun.* seguridad
sail *noun.* **1.** vela **2.** paseo en barco **3.** aspa
sail *verb.* **1.** navegar **2.** pilotar **3.** zarpar
sailing *noun.* navegación a vela
sailor *noun.* marinero
saint. St. *noun.* santo/a
salad *noun.* ensalada
salary *noun.* salario
sale *noun.* **1.** venta **2.** rebaja
salesman *noun.* vendedor
sally *noun.* salida
salmon *noun.* salmón
salon *noun.* salón
saloon *noun.* taberna, bar, cantina
salt *noun.* sal
salt *verb.* salar
salt *adj.* salado
salute *noun.* **1.** saludo **2.** salva

salute *verb.* saludar
salvation *noun.* salvación
same *adj.* **1.** mismo **2.** igual
same *adv.* del mismo modo, de la misma manera
same *pron.* lo mismo
sample *noun.* muestra
sample *verb.* **1.** probar, degustar **2.** catar
sanction *noun.* **1.** sanción **2.** autorización, permiso
sanction *verb.* **1.** sancionar **2.** autorizar, permitir
sanctuary *noun.* **1.** santuario **2.** asilo **3.** reserva
sand *noun.* **1.** arena **2.** playa arenosa
sand *verb.* lijar
sandwich *noun.* bocadillo, sándwich
sandwich *verb.* **1.** encajonar, apretujar entre dos objetos **2.** intercalar
sandy *adj.* **1.** arenoso, de arena **2.** rubio oscuro
satellite *noun.* satélite
satisfaction *noun.* satisfacción
satisfactorily *adv.* satisfactoriamente
satisfactory *adj.* satisfactorio
satisfied *adj.* satisfecho
satisfy *verb.* satisfacer
satisfying *adj.* satisfactorio
Saturday *noun.* sábado
sauce *noun.* salsa
Saudi (Arabian) *noun. adj.* saudí, saudita
sausage *noun.* salchicha
savage *noun.* salvaje
savage *verb.* atacar ferozmente, embestir
savage *adj.* **1.** salvaje **2.** feroz, violento
save *prep. conj.* excepto
save *noun.* parada

save verb. **1.** salvar, rescatar **2.** ahorrar, guardar, economizar **3.** parar **4.** guardar, archivar

savings noun plural. ahorros

saw noun. sierra

saw verb. serrar

say noun. opinión, voz y voto

say verb. decir

saying noun. dicho

scale noun. **1.** escala **2.** balanza **3.** escama

scale verb. escalar

scan noun. exploración con un escáner

scan verb. **1.** escudriñar **2.** dar un vistazo, recorrer con la vista **3.** explorar **4.** escanear

scandal noun. **1.** escándalo **2.** chisme, chismorreo, habladuría

scar noun. cicatriz

scar verb. dejar una cicatriz

scarce adj. escaso

scarcely adv. apenas

scare noun. **1.** susto **2.** pánico

scare verb. asustar

scared adj. asustado, atemorizado

scarf noun. bufanda

scarlet noun. adj. escarlata

scatter verb. **1.** dispersar **2.** dispersarse **3.** esparcir, desparramar

scattered adj. disperso

scene noun. **1.** escena **2.** episodio, incidente **3.** cuadro, paisaje, panorama **4.** escenario, decorado

scenery noun. **1.** escenario, decorado **2.** paisaje

scent noun. **1.** perfume, aroma **2.** rastro, pista

scent verb. **1.** oler, olfatear **2.** olerse algo, sospechar **3.** perfumar

schedule noun. **1.** horario **2.** programa

schedule verb. programar, fijar

scheme noun. **1.** plan, programa, proyecto **2.** estratagema

scheme verb. conspirar

scholar noun. **1.** erudito **2.** becario

scholarly adj. erudito, estudioso

scholarship noun. **1.** erudición **2.** beca

school noun. **1.** escuela **2.** colegio **3.** curso **4.** facultad **5.** universidad

school verb. enseñar, educar

schoolboy, schoolgirl noun. alumno/a

science noun. ciencia

scientific adj. científico

scientist noun. científico

scissors noun plural. tijeras

scoop noun. **1.** pala, cucharón **2.** palada, cucharada **3.** primicia

scoop verb. cavar

scope noun. **1.** oportunidad **2.** alcance

score noun. **1.** tanteo, resultado, puntuación **2.** cuenta **3.** partitura **4.** veinte, veintena

score verb. **1.** marcar, hacer, meter **2.** llevar el marcador

—score off/out eliminar

scorer noun. **1.** encargado del marcador, persona que lleva el marcador **2.** goleador

Scot noun. escocés

scotch verb. poner fin

Scotch, Scots adj. escocés

Scotland noun. Escocia

Scottish adj. escocés

scramble noun. lucha, pelea, confusión, barullo

scramble verb. **1.** trepar, escalar **2.** revolver **3.** cifrar, codificar

—scramble for pelearse por

scrap noun. **1.** pedacito, retazo **2.** recorte **3.** chatarra **4.** pelea

—scraps noun plural. restos, sobras

scrap verb. desechar

scrap verb. pelear

scrape noun. **1.** rasguño, arañazo, roce **2.** chirrido **3.** lío

scrape verb. **1.** rasguñarse, arañarse **2.** raspar, rascar **3.** rozar, pasar rozando

scratch noun. **1.** arañazo, rasguño, raspadura **2.** línea de salida **3.** cero

scratch verb. **1.** arañar, rasguñar, rayar **2.** rascarse **3.** retirarse

scream noun. grito, chillido

scream verb. gritar, chillar

screen noun. **1.** biombo **2.** pantalla

screen verb. **1.** ocultar, proteger **2.** proyectar, emitir **3.** investigar **4.** examinar

screw noun. **1.** tornillo **2.** vuelta

screw verb. **1.** atornillar **2.** enroscar, apretar **3.** echar un polvo, joder, follar **4.** timar, clavar

script noun. **1.** guión **2.** escritura **3.** texto

scrub noun. fregado, lavado

scrub verb. **1.** fregar **2.** restregar **3.** cancelar

scrutiny noun. escrutinio, recuento

sculpture noun. escultura

scum noun. **1.** espuma **2.** escoria

sea noun. mar

seal noun. **1.** foça **2.** sello **3.** lacre **4.** cierre hermético

seal verb. **1.** sellar **2.** cerrar herméticamente **3.** cerrar, concluir

search noun. búsqueda, registro, cacheo

search (for) verb. **1.** buscar **2.** cachear, registrar

searching adj. penetrante

seaside noun. orilla del mar

season noun. **1.** estación **2.** temporada

season verb. sazonar, aliñar

seasonal adj. de temporada

seat noun. **1.** asiento **2.** culo, trasero **3.** plaza **4.** sede, centro

seat verb. **1.** sentar **2.** tener cabida para

second noun. segundo

second verb. apoyar, secundar

second adj. adv. segundo

secondary noun. escuela de secundaria

secondary adj. secundario

second-hand adj. de segunda mano

secondly adv. en segundo lugar

secrecy noun. secreto, reserva

secret noun. secreto

secret adj. secreto

secretary noun. **1.** secretario **2.** ministro

secretion noun. secreción

secretly adv. en secreto

section noun. sección

sector noun. sector

secular adj. secular, seglar

secure verb. **1.** proteger **2.** sujetar, atar, amarrar

secure adj. **1.** seguro **2.** firme

security noun. seguridad

sediment noun. sedimento

seduce verb. seducir

see noun. sede

see verb. **1.** ver **2.** imaginarse **3.** comprender, entender **4.** acompañar **5.** visitar

seed noun. **1.** semilla **2.** pizca, punta **3.** cabeza de serie

seed verb. **1.** sembrar **2.** granar **3.** preseleccionar

seek (for) verb. **1.** buscar **2.** tratar de, intentar **3.** pedir, solicitar

seem verb. parecer

seeming adj. aparente

seemingly adv. aparentemente

segment noun. segmento

seize verb. **1.** asir, agarrar, coger **2.** incautar, embargar

seldom adv. raramente

select verb. escoger, elegir, seleccionar

select adj. selecto, escogido

selection noun. **1.** elección **2.** selección

selective adj. selectivo

self- prefix **1.** propio, a/de/por sí mismo **2.** auto- **3.** ego-

self noun. **1.** uno mismo **2.** sí mismo

self-esteem noun. amor propio

selfish adj. egoísta

sell verb. **1.** vender **2.** venderse

semi-final noun. semifinal

senate noun. senado

senator noun. senador

send verb. enviar, mandar

senior, Sr. adj. padre

senior noun. adj. **1.** estudiante del último curso **2.** mayor

sensation noun. sensación

sense noun. **1.** sentido **2.** sensación **3.** sentido común, juicio, sensatez **4.** significado

sense verb. **1.** sentir, percibir **2.** presentir

sensible adj. **1.** sensato **2.** práctico

sensitive (about/to) adj. sensible, delicado

sensitivity noun. sensibilidad

sentence noun. **1.** frase **2.** sentencia

sentence (to) verb. condenar

sentiment noun. sentimiento

sentimental adj. sentimental

separate verb. **1.** separar **2.** separarse

separate adj. 1. separado 2. distinto, diferente
separately adv. por separado
separation noun. separación
separatist noun. separatista
September, Sept. noun. septiembre
sequence noun. serie, secuencia
sergeant, Sgt. noun. sargento
serial noun. novela por entregas, radionovela, telenovela
serial adj. 1. en serie, consecutivo 2. seriado, en capítulos
series noun. serie
serious adj. serio
seriously adv. en serio
seriousness noun. seriedad
serum noun. suero
servant noun. 1. criado, sirviente 2. funcionario
serve noun. servicio
serve verb. 1. servir 2. atender 3. cumplir 4. entregar 5. sacar
server noun. 1. servidor 2. acólito
service noun. 1. servicio 2. entrega 3. revisión, mantenimiento 4. oficio 5. misa 6. vajilla 7. servicio militar
—**services** fuerzas armadas
service verb. 1. dar servicio 2. hacer la revisión
serviceman noun. militar
serving noun. porción, ración
session noun. 1. sesión 2. período
set noun. 1. juego, colección, equipo, conjunto 2. aparato 3. grupo, pandilla 4. decorado, plató 5. set
set verb. 1. poner 2. colocar 3. fijar, acordar 4. dar, asignar 5. establecer 6. montar, engastar 7. componer, encajar 8. provocar 9. ponerse 10. endurecerse 11. cuajarse
—**set about** empezar
—**set aside** apartar, poner a un lado, desechar
—**set down** 1. depositar 2. anotar, apuntar, poner por escrito
—**set out** 1. partir, salir 2. exponer, manifestar
—**set up** 1. fijar 2. levantar, erigir 3. establecerse

set adj. 1. fijo 2. inflexible, rígido 3. resuelto, decidido 4. listo
setback noun. revés
setting noun. 1. escenario 2. montura, engaste 3. arreglo, adaptación musical
settle verb. 1. resolver, acordar, decidir, fijar 2. instalar, colocar 3. asentarse 4. calmar 5. instalarse, establecerse 6. pagar, saldar la cuenta
settlement noun. 1. acuerdo, convenio 2. liquidación 3. poblado, colonia 4. establecimiento
settler noun. colono, colonizador
set-up noun. sistema
seven noun. adj. siete
seventeen noun. adj. diecisiete
seventeenth noun. decimoséptimo
seventh noun. séptimo
seventies noun plural. 1. entre setenta y ochenta 2. los años setenta
seventieth noun. septuagésimo
seventy noun. adj. setenta
several adj. varios
several pron. varios
severe adj. 1. grave, serio 2. severo 3. austero
severely adv. severamente
severity noun. severidad
sewage noun. aguas residuales
sewing noun. costura
sex noun. sexo
sexual adj. sexual
sexually adv. sexualmente
sexy adj. seductor
shade noun. 1. sombra 2. pantalla, visera 3. tono, matiz 4. poquito, tantito
shade verb. 1. proteger, resguardar 2. sombrear
—**shade into** convertirse
shadow noun. 1. sombra 2. ojera
shadow verb. 1. hacer sombra 2. seguir la pista
shaft noun. 1. mango 2. vara 3. eje 4. hueco, pozo 5. rayo
shake noun. 1. sacudida 2. batido
shake verb. 1. agitar, sacudir 2. debilitar
shaking noun. sacudida
shall verb. 1. (se usa para expresar el futuro) 2. (se usa para expresar

obligación) **3.** (se usa para expresar el condicional)

shallow *adj.* **1.** poco profundo **2.** superficial

shame *noun.* **1.** vergüenza **2.** deshonra **3.** pena, lástima

shame *verb.* **1.** avergonzar **2.** deshonrar

shape *noun.* **1.** forma **2.** figura **3.** bulto

shape *verb.* **1.** modelar, dar forma **2.** decidir, determinar

shaped *adj.* en forma de

share *noun.* **1.** parte **2.** acción, participación

share (among/between/with) *verb.* **1.** repartir, dividir **2.** compartir

shareholder *noun.* accionista

sharp *noun.* sostenido

sharp *adj.* **1.** afilado, puntiagudo **2.** definido, nítido, marcado **3.** brusco, repentino **4.** agudo, fuerte **5.** severo **6.** agudo **7.** repentino, súbito **8.** desafinado

sharp *adv.* **1.** en punto **2.** bruscamente **3.** demasiado alto

sharply *adv.* bruscamente, repentinamente

shatter *verb.* **1.** romper, quebrantar **2.** destrozar

shattered *adj.* hecho polvo, trastornado

shave *noun.* afeitado

shave *verb.* **1.** afeitarse **2.** pasar rozando
—**shave off** cepillar

she *noun.* **1.** hembra **2.** niña

she *pron.* **1.** ella **2.** la que, aquella que

shed *noun.* cobertizo, nave

shed *verb.* **1.** arrojar **2.** mudar **3.** derramar

sheep *noun.* oveja

sheer *adj.* **1.** puro, absoluto **2.** vertical, escarpado **3.** fino, ligero

sheer *adv.* verticalmente, en picado
—**sheer off/away** desviarse

sheet *noun.* **1.** sábana **2.** hoja

shelf *noun.* **1.** estante **2.** plataforma

shell *noun.* **1.** concha, caracol **2.** armazón **3.** cartucho

shell *verb.* **1.** desvainar, quitar la concha **2.** bombardear

shelter *noun.* **1.** abrigo **2.** albergue

shelter *verb.* **1.** abrigar, proteger **2.** abrigarse, protegerse

sheltered *adj.* protegido

shepherd *noun.* pastor

shepherd *verb.* guiar, conducir

sheriff *noun.* sheriff, alguacil

sherry *noun.* jerez

shield *noun.* **1.** escudo **2.** placa

shield (from) *verb.* proteger

shift *noun.* **1.** cambio **2.** turno

shift *verb.* **1.** mover, desplazar **2.** traspasar, transferir **3.** quitar

shilling *noun.* chelín

shine *noun.* **1.** brillo **2.** lustre

shine *verb.* **1.** brillar **2.** relucir **3.** sacar brillo, limpiar
—**shine at** sobresalir, destacar

shining *adj.* brillante

shiny *adj.* brillante

ship *noun.* barco, nave, buque, navío

ship *verb.* enviar, consignar

shipment *noun.* **1.** envío, consignación **2.** embarque, transporte

shipping *noun.* flota

shirt *noun.* camisa

shiver *noun.* escalofrío, tiritón, estremecimiento

shiver *verb.* temblar, tiritar, estremecerse

shock *noun.* **1.** conmoción, golpe **2.** choque, impacto **3.** shock **4.** mata de pelo
—**electric shock** *noun.* descarga

shock *verb.* **1.** conmocionar, conmover, afectar **2.** escandalizar

shocking *adj.* **1.** terrible, espantoso **2.** escandaloso

shoe *noun.* **1.** zapato **2.** herradura

shoe *verb.* herrar

shoot *noun.* brote, retoño

shoot (at) *verb.* **1.** disparar **2.** lanzar **3.** fusilar, matar de un tiro **4.** salir disparado **5.** rodar, filmar **6.** tirar, chutar **7.** cazar

shop *noun.* **1.** tienda, comercio **2.** taller

shop *verb.* comprar, hacer compras

shopping *noun.* compra

shore *noun.* costa, playa

short *adj.* **1.** corto **2.** bajo **3.** breve **4.** de menos **5.** escaso **6.** quebradizo

short adv. bruscamente, en seco

shortage noun. falta, escasez

short-lived adj. efímero

shortly adv. dentro de poco, en breve

shorts noun plural. pantalones cortos

short-term adj. a corto plazo

shot noun. 1. tiro 2. disparo 3. jugada 4. tentativa, intento 5. bala, proyectil 6. foto, toma 7. inyección, pinchazo 8. tirador

should verb. 1. deber (expressing obligation) 2. deber de (expressing probability) 3. gustar (expressing future/conditional) 4. (expressing subjunctive)

shoulder noun. 1. hombro 2. hombrera 3. ladera, falda 4. paletilla

shoulder verb. 1. ponerse al hombro, echarse al hombro 2. cargar (con) 3. abrir paso a codazos

shout noun. grito

shout verb. gritar

shove noun. empujón

shove verb. empujar

show noun. 1. exposición, espectáculo 2. exhibición, demostración, alarde 3. ostentación, apariencia 4. actuación

show verb. 1. enseñar 2. mostrar 3. notarse, verse 4. exhibir 5. indicar 6. demostrar

  —**show (a)round** conducir, acompañar

shower noun. 1. ducha 2. chubasco, chaparrón 3. lluvia

shower verb. 1. ducharse 2. tirar, rociar

shred noun. triza, jirón

shred verb. hacer trizas, cortar en tiras

shrine noun. 1. santuario 2. relicario

shrink noun. psiquiatra, loquero

shrink verb. 1. encoger 2. retroceder, echarse atrás 3. esquivar

shrub noun. arbusto

shrug noun. encogimiento de hombros

shrug verb. encogerse de hombros

shuffle noun. baraje, barajadura

shuffle verb. 1. caminar arrastrando los pies 2. barajar

shut verb. 1. cerrar 2. cerrarse

  —**shut up** hacer callar

shut adj. cerrado

shuttle noun. 1. lanzadera 2. servicio regular

shy verb. espantarse

shy adj. 1. tímido, vergonzoso, reservado 2. asustadizo, huraño

sick adj. 1. enfermo 2. mareado 3. harto, cansado 4. morboso, de muy mal gusto

sickness noun. 1. enfermedad 2. mareo

side noun. 1. lado 2. cara 3. costado 4. ijada 5. parte 6. ladera, falda 7. aspecto, punto de vista 8. bando

side adj. lateral, secundario

sidewalk noun. calzada, pavimento

sideways adj. adv. lateral, de lado, de reojo

siege noun. asedio, cerco, sitio

sigh noun. suspiro

sigh verb. 1. suspirar 2. susurrar

sight noun. 1. vista 2. visión 3. espectáculo, atracción turística 4. figura 5. mira

sight verb. 1. observar, ver, divisar 2. apuntar

sign noun. 1. signo, símbolo 2. señal 3. panel, letrero 4. gesto, seña

sign verb. 1. firmar 2. hacer señas

signal noun. señal

signal verb. 1. indicar, señalar 2. comunicar por señas

signature noun. firma

significance noun. 1. significado 2. importancia

significant adj. 1. significativo 2. importante 3. elocuente, expresivo

significantly adv. 1. significativamente 2. considerablemente

silence interj. ¡silencio!

silence noun. silencio

silence verb. hacer callar, acallar, silenciar

silent adj. silencioso

silently adv. silenciosamente

silk noun. seda

silly adj. tonto, bobo

silver noun. plata

silver adj. de plata

similar adj. similar, semejante, parecido

similarity noun. similitud

similarly adv. 1. igualmente 2. de manera similar

simmer *verb.* hervir a fuego lento
simple *adj.* **1.** simple **2.** fácil, sencillo **3.** mero **4.** ingenuo, cándido
simplicity *noun.* sencillez
simplified *adj.* simplificado
simply *adv.* **1.** simplemente **2.** sencillamente
simulation *noun.* **1.** simulación, simulacro **2.** imitación
simultaneous *adj.* simultáneo
simultaneously *adv.* simultáneamente
sin *noun.* pecado
sin *verb.* pecar
since *conj.* **1.** desde que **2.** después que **3.** ya que, puesto que
since *prep.* desde
since *adv.* desde entonces
sincere *adj.* sincero
sincerely *adv.* sinceramente
sing *verb.* cantar
singer *noun.* cantante
singing *noun.* canto, cantar
single *noun.* **1.** (disco) sencillo, single **2.** billete/boleto de ida
  —singles individuales (sport)
single *adj.* **1.** solo, único **2.** individual **3.** soltero
singular *noun. adj.* singular
sinister *adj.* siniestro
sink *noun.* **1.** fregadero, pila **2.** lavabo
sink *verb.* **1.** hundir **2.** hundirse, irse a pique **3.** caer **4.** bajar, descender **5.** hundir, hincar **6.** perforar, excavar **7.** venirse abajo, desanimarse **8.** invertir
sip *noun.* sorbo
sip *verb.* sorber, beber a sorbos
sir *noun.* **1.** señor, caballero **2.** sir
sister *noun.* **1.** hermana **2.** monja
sister *adj.* similar, parecido
sit *verb.* **1.** estar sentado **2.** sentar **3.** sentarse **4.** posar **5.** estar, encontrarse **6.** posarse **7.** posar **8.** reunirse
  —sit on ser miembro de, formar parte de
site *noun.* **1.** sitio **2.** lugar **3.** web site
sit-in *noun.* huelga, encierro
sitting *noun.* sesión
situated *adj.* situado
situation *noun.* **1.** situación **2.** ubicación **3.** empleo, vacante

six *noun. adj.* seis
sixteen *noun. adj.* dieciséis
sixteenth *noun.* decimosexto
sixth *noun.* sexto
sixties *noun plural.* **1.** entre sesenta y setenta **2.** los años sesenta
sixtieth *noun.* **1.** sexagésima parte **2.** sexagésimo
sixty *noun. adj.* sesenta
size *noun.* **1.** tamaño, magnitud, estatura **2.** talla, número
sizeable *adj.* considerable, importante
skate *noun.* **1.** patín **2.** raya
skate *verb.* **1.** patinar **2.** deslizarse
skeleton *noun.* **1.** esqueleto **2.** armazón
skeptical *adj.* escéptico
skepticism *noun.* escepticismo
sketch *noun.* **1.** esbozo, croquis **2.** borrador, esquema **3.** sainete
sketch *verb.* **1.** dibujar **2.** esbozar
ski *noun.* esquí
ski *verb.* esquiar
skiing *noun.* esquí
skill *noun.* **1.** destreza, habilidad **2.** técnica, arte
skilled *adj.* **1.** experto, cualificado, calificado **2.** especializado
skin *noun.* **1.** piel **2.** cáscara **3.** película
skin *verb.* despellejar, desollar
skinny *adj.* flaco, enjuto
skip *noun.* salto, brinco
skip *verb.* **1.** saltar **2.** saltarse
skipper *noun.* capitán
skipper *verb.* capitanear
skirt *noun.* falda
skull *noun.* calavera
sky *noun.* cielo
slab *noun.* losa
slam *noun.* golpe, portazo
slam *verb.* **1.** cerrar de golpe **2.** estamparse
slap *noun.* palmada, cachete, bofetada, bofetón
slap *verb.* abofetear, dar una bofetada
slash *noun.* **1.** tajo, cuchillada **2.** golpe
slash *verb.* **1.** dar un tajo, rajar **2.** rebajar, reducir
  —slash at golpear

slate noun. pizarra
slate verb. criticar duramente
slaughter noun. 1. masacre 2. matanza
slaughter verb. 1. sacrificar 2. matar 3. dar una paliza
slave noun. esclavo
slave verb. trabajar como una bestia, trabajar como un negro
sleek adj. 1. liso, lustroso 2. impecable
sleep noun. sueño
sleep verb. dormir
sleeve noun. 1. manga 2. funda 3. manguito
slender adj. 1. delgado, esbelto, fino 2. escaso
slice noun. 1. porción, trozo 2. parte
slice verb. 1. cortar 2. cortar a rodajas, cortar a lonchas
sliced adj. rebanado, en rodajas
slick, oil-slick noun. marea negra
slick adj. mañoso
slide noun. 1. deslizamiento, desliz 2. tobogán 3. diapositiva 4. platina, portaobjetos 5. pasador
slide verb. 1. deslizar 2. deslizarse
slight adj. 1. pequeño, ligero 2. delicado
slightest adj. mínimo
slightly adv. 1. ligeramente 2. frágilmente
slim verb. adelgazar, hacer régimen
slim adj. 1. delgado, esbelto, fino 2. escaso
slip noun. 1. error, equivocación, desliz 2. resbalón, traspiés, tropezón 3. combinación 4. papelito, trocito de papel
slip verb. 1. resbalar, tropezar 2. deslizar 3. escabullirse, escurrirse 4. soltarse, escaparse 5. pasar
slogan noun. eslogan, lema
slope noun. 1. cuesta, pendiente 2. inclinación, vertiente
slope verb. inclinarse
slot noun. 1. ranura 2. hueco, cuña
slot (in/into) verb. insertar, introducir
slow verb. retrasar, ralentizar, retardar
slow adj. 1. lento 2. atrasado 3. torpe, estúpido

slowly adv. lentamente
slump noun. 1. bajón, bajada repentina 2. crisis económica, recesión económica
slump verb. bajar/caer en picado, caer de repente, desplomarse
smack noun. 1. palmada, bofetada 2. toque, sabor, olor
smack verb. dar una palmada
—smack of verb. presentir, oler
smack adv. de lleno, directamente
small adj. 1. pequeño 2. chico 3. poco 4. minúsculo
smart noun. dolor, resentimiento
smart verb. 1. escocer, picar, arder 2. sentirse ofendido
smart adj. 1. elegante 2. listo, despierto 3. rápido
smash noun. 1. quiebra 2. golpe 3. smash, mate
smash (up) verb. 1. romper, quebrar 2. romperse, quebrarse 3. pulverizar, hacer pedazos
smell noun. 1. olfato 2. olor
smell verb. 1. oler 2. oler, olfatear
smile noun. sonrisa
smile verb. sonreír
smiling adj. sonriente
smith noun. 1. herrero 2. orfebre, artesano
smoke noun. humo
smoke verb. 1. fumar 2. ahumar
smoked adj. ahumado
smoking noun. fumar
smooth adj. 1. liso 2. homogéneo 3. tranquilo, en calma 4. suave, parejo 5. sin problemas 6. zalamero, meloso
smooth (down/out) verb. alisar
smooth (into/over) verb. esparcir
smoothly adv. suavemente
smuggle verb. pasar de contrabando
snack noun. tentempié
snake noun. serpiente
snake verb. serpentear
snap noun. ruido seco
snap adj. precipitado, repentino
snap (at) verb. 1. partir 2. chasquear 3. regañar, hablar con brusquedad 4. intentar morder

snatch *noun*. **1.** arrebatamiento **2.** fragmento

snatch *verb*. **1.** arrebatar, arrancar, coger **2.** aprovechar

sneak *noun*. acusica, chivato, soplón

sneak *verb*. **1.** moverse sigilosamente **2.** sacar a escondidas **3.** acusar, delatar

sniff *noun*. aspiración

sniff *verb*. **1.** resollar **2.** olfatear, husmear

snooker *noun*. snooker, billar ruso

snow *noun*. nieve

snow *verb*. nevar

so *conj*. **1.** así que, por lo tanto, de manera que **2.** para

so *adv*. **1.** tan, tanto **2.** así **3.** eso **4.** también **5.** así es, en efecto

soak *verb*. **1.** remojar **2.** empaparse **3.** remojarse, empaparse
  —**soak in/into/through** penetrar
  —**soaked through** empapado, hecho una sopa

soap *noun*. jabón

soap *verb*. enjabonar

soar *verb*. remontar el vuelo, elevarse

sober *adj*. **1.** sobrio **2.** formal **3.** serio

so-called *adj*. supuesto, presunto

soccer *noun*. fútbol

social *adj*. social

socialism *noun*. socialismo

socialist *noun*. *adj*. socialista

socialize *verb*. relacionarse, mezclarse con la gente

socially *adv*. socialmente

society *noun*. **1.** sociedad **2.** asociación **3.** alta sociedad **4.** compañía

sock *noun*. **1.** calcetín, media **2.** puñetazo

sock *verb*. pegar un puñetazo

socket *noun*. enchufe

sodium *noun*. sodio

sofa *noun*. sofá

soft *adj*. **1.** blando **2.** suave **3.** no alcohólico **4.** tonto, bobo

soften *verb*. suavizar

softly *adv*. suavemente

software *noun*. software

soil *noun*. tierra, suelo

soil *verb*. ensuciar, manchar

solar *adj*. solar

soldier *noun*. soldado

sole *noun*. **1.** planta **2.** suela **3.** lenguado

sole *adj*. **1.** único **2.** exclusivo

solely *adv*. únicamente, sólo

solemn *adj*. **1.** solemne **2.** serio

solicitor *noun*. **1.** representante, agente **2.** abogado municipal

solid *noun*. sólido

solid *adj*. **1.** sólido **2.** macizo **3.** de una sola pieza **4.** seguido, ininterrumpido

solid *adv*. ininterrumpidamente

solidarity *noun*. solidaridad

solitary *adj*. **1.** solitario **2.** único

solo *noun*. solo

solo *adj*. en solitario

solution *noun*. solución

solve *verb*. resolver

solvent *noun*. *adj*. solvente

some *adj*. **1.** bastante **2.** algo de **3.** cerca de, alrededor de

some *adv*. un poco, algo

some *pron*. *adj*. **1.** algún, alguno/a, algunos/as **2.** unos/as **3.** un poco, unos pocos, unas pocas **4.** cierto

somebody *pron*. alguien

somehow *adv*. de algún modo, de alguna manera

someone *pron*. alguien

someplace *adv*. en algún lugar

something *pron*. algo

sometime *adv*. **1.** en alguna ocasión **2.** en algún momento

sometimes *adv*. a veces

somewhat *adv*. algo, un tanto

somewhere *adv*. en algún lugar

son *noun*. hijo

song *noun*. **1.** canción **2.** canto

soon *adv*. **1.** pronto, en breve, dentro de poco **2.** temprano

soothe *verb*. calmar, tranquilizar, aliviar

sophisticated *adj*. **1.** sofisticado **2.** sutil, complejo

sophistication *noun*. sofisticación

sore *noun*. llaga, herida, úlcera

sore *adj*. **1.** doloroso **2.** dolorido **3.** resentido, enojado

sorrow *noun*. pena, pesar, dolor

sorry *interj.* ¡perdón!, ¡disculpe!
sorry *adj.* **1.** lo siento **2.** triste, arrepentido, desolado **3.** lamentable
sort *noun.* clase, tipo, género
sort *verb.* clasificar
soul *noun.* **1.** alma, espíritu **2.** persona
—**soul music** música soul
sound *noun.* **1.** sonido **2.** ruido **3.** volumen
sound *verb.* **1.** tocar, hacer sonar **2.** sonar, resonar **3.** parecer **4.** pronunciarse **5.** auscultar **6.** sondear
sound *adj.* **1.** sano, sólido, firme **2.** juicioso, sensato, acertado **3.** completo, severo **4.** bueno **5.** profundo
soup *noun.* sopa
soup up *verb.* trucar
sour *verb.* **1.** agriar **2.** agriarse
sour *adj.* **1.** agrio, ácido, amargo **2.** rancio **3.** amargado, áspero
source *noun.* **1.** fuente, origen **2.** nacimiento
south *noun.* sur
south *adj.* **1.** sur, meridional **2.** del sur
south *adv.* hacia el sur
southern *adj.* **1.** sur, meridional **2.** del sur
sovereign *noun. adj.* soberano
soviet *noun. adj.* soviético
sow *noun.* puerca, marrana
sow *verb.* sembrar
space *noun.* **1.** espacio, hueco **2.** sitio, lugar
—**outer space** espacio exterior
space (out) *verb.* espaciar, separar
spacious *adj.* espacioso
Spain *noun.* España
span *noun.* **1.** luz, tramo **2.** envergadura **3.** espacio, período, lapso
span *verb.* **1.** atravesar, cruzar **2.** abarcar
Spanish *noun. adj.* español
spare *verb.* **1.** prescindir, pasar sin **2.** disponer de **3.** perdonar **4.** evitar **5.** escatimar
spare *adj.* **1.** de repuesto, **2.** de sobra **3.** libre
spark *noun.* chispa
spark *verb.* echar chispas, chispear
—**spark off** hacer estallar, provocar

sparkle *noun.* **1.** centelleo, destello **2.** viveza
sparkle *verb.* **1.** centellear, destellar **2.** brillar, lucirse
sparkling *adj.* **1.** espumoso **2.** con gas **3.** brillante, chispeante
speak *verb.* **1.** hablar **2.** conversar **3.** decir **4.** pronunciar
speaker *noun.* persona que habla, interlocutor, conferenciante
speaking *adj.* hablante, parlante
special *noun.* especial
special *adj.* **1.** especial **2.** extraordinario **3.** específico, particular
specialist *noun.* especialista
specialize (in) *verb.* especializarse
specialized *adj.* especializado
specially *adv.* **1.** especialmente **2.** particularmente
specialty *noun.* especialidad
species *noun.* especie
specific *adj.* **1.** preciso **2.** específico
specifically *adv.* específicamente
specify *verb.* **1.** especificar **2.** precisar
specimen *noun.* espécimen, muestra
spectacle *noun.* espectáculo
spectacles *noun plural.* gafas, anteojos
spectacular *adj.* **1.** espectacular **2.** impresionante
spectator *noun.* espectador
spectrum *noun.* **1.** espectro **2.** gama
speculate *verb.* especular
speculation *noun.* especulación
speech *noun.* **1.** habla **2.** palabras **3.** lenguaje, forma de hablar **4.** discurso
speed *noun.* **1.** velocidad **2.** rapidez
speed *verb.* **1.** ir corriendo, ir a toda prisa **2.** ir con exceso de velocidad
speeding *noun.* exceso de velocidad
speedy *adj.* rápido
spell *noun.* **1.** hechizo **2.** encanto **3.** turno **4.** temporada **5.** período
spell *verb.* **1.** deletrear **2.** formar **3.** escribir correctamente **4.** significar, representar
spelling *noun.* ortografía
spend *verb.* **1.** gastar **2.** pasar
spent *adj.* **1.** usado, gastado **2.** agotado
sperm *noun.* esperma

sphere *noun*. esfera
spice *noun*. 1. especia 2. salsa, sabor
spice *verb*. sazonar, condimentar
spider *noun*. araña
spike *noun*. 1. punta, pincho 2. clavo
spill *verb*. derramar, verter
spin *noun*. 1. vuelta, giro 2. paseo
spin *verb*. 1. hacer girar 2. hilar
spine *noun*. 1. columna vertebral 2. espina dorsal 3. lomo 4. espina
spiral *noun*. espiral
spiral *verb*. moverse en espiral
spiral *adj*. 1. espiral 2. en espiral
spirit *noun*. 1. espíritu 2. valor
spirits *noun plural*. 1. humor, ánimo 2. licor
spiritual *adj*. espiritual
spit, spittle *noun*. saliva
spit *noun*. asador
spit *verb*. escupir
spite *noun*. rencor
—in spite of a pesar de
spite *verb*. fastidiar
splash *noun*. 1. salpicadura 2. mancha 3. chapoteo
splash *verb*. 1. salpicar 2. esparcirse 3. chapotear
splendid *adj*. 1. maravilloso 2. espléndido
split *noun*. 1. grieta, raja 2. división
split *verb*. 1. rajar 2. dividir
spoil *verb*. 1. estropear 2. mimar
spoke *noun*. radio, rayo
spoken *adj*. hablado, oral
spokesman *noun*. portavoz
sponge *noun*. 1. esponja 2. bizcocho
sponge *verb*. 1. lavar con esponja 2. vivir de gorra
sponsor *noun*. patrocinador
sponsor *verb*. patrocinar
sponsorship *noun*. patrocinio
spontaneous *adj*. espontáneo
spoon *noun*. 1. cuchara 2. cucharada
spoon *verb*. dar de comer
sport, sports *adj*. deportivo
sport *noun*. 1. deporte 2. buena persona, buena gente 3. diversión
sport *verb*. lucir
sporting *adj*. 1. deportivo 2. caballeroso

spot *noun*. 1. mancha 2. punto 3. grano 4. sitio, lugar
—on the spot en el acto
spot *verb*. 1. ver 2. reconocer 3. darse cuenta
spotted *adj*. moteado, con puntos
spread *verb*. 1. untar 2. extenderse 3. difundirse
spring *noun*. 1. primavera 2. fuente, manantial 3. origen
spring *verb*. 1. saltar 2. accionar
—spring from surgir de
stick *noun*. 1. ramita 2. bastón 3. palo, vara
stiff *adj*. 1. rígido, tieso 2. duro 3. espeso 4. difícil 5. fuerte 6. frío, formal, estirado
still *noun*. fotograma
still *adj*. 1. quieto, inmóvil, parado 2. sin gas
still *adv*. 1. aún, todavía 2. a pesar de todo, no obstante, sin embargo
stimulate *verb*. estimular
stimulating *adj*. estimulante
stimulation *noun*. estimulación
stimulus *noun*. estímulo
sting *noun*. 1. aguijón 2. picadura
sting *verb*. 1. picar 2. escocer, arder
stink *noun*. peste, hedor
stink *verb*. apestar
stir *noun*. agitación, conmoción
stir *verb*. 1. remover, revolver 2. moverse, agitarse 3. conmover, provocar, estimular
stirring *adj*. emocionante, conmovedor
stitch *noun*. 1. puntada 2. punto 3. flato
stitch *verb*. coser, suturar
stock *noun*. 1. existencias, stock 2. reserva, provisión 3. ganado 4. caldo 5. culata
stock *verb*. 1. tener en stock, vender 2. abastecer, surtir
stock *adj*. corriente, típico
stock exchange, stock market *noun*. bolsa
stocking *noun*. media
stocks *noun plural*. 1. acciones, valores 2. cepo
stoke *verb*. atizar
stomach *noun*. 1. estómago 2. barriga

stone *noun. adj.* **1.** piedra **2.** unidad de peso que equivale a 6.4 kg **3.** cálculo

stone *verb.* apedrear, lapidar

stool *noun.* taburete

stop *noun.* **1.** parada **2.** alto, interrupción **3.** descanso, pausa **4.** punto **5.** registro, llave **6.** tope

stop *verb.* **1.** parar **2.** pararse **3.** detener **4.** suspender, cortar, interrumpir **5.** impedir, evitar **6.** tapar **7.** obstruir, atascar **8.** quedarse

stopping *noun.* empaste

storage *noun.* almacenamiento

store *noun.* **1.** provisión **2.** reserva **3.** almacén, depósito **4.** tienda

store *verb.* **1.** almacenar, guardar, acumular **2.** proveer

storm *noun.* **1.** tormenta **2.** bronca

storm *verb.* **1.** vociferar, bramar **2.** marcharse hecho una furia **3.** asaltar, tomar por asalto

story *noun.* **1.** historia **2.** cuento

stout *adj.* **1.** sólido, fuerte **2.** firme, resuelto **3.** corpulento, robusto

stove *noun.* estufa, cocina, horno

straight *noun.* heterosexual

straight *adj.* **1.** recto, liso **2.** derecho, recto **3.** honrado, directo, sincero, franco **4.** arreglado, ordenado **5.** claro **6.** consecutivo **7.** serio, dramático

straight *adv.* **1.** recto, en línea recta **2.** directamente **3.** con franqueza

straighten *verb.* **1.** enderezar, poner derecho **2.** arreglar, ordenar

straightforward *adj.* **1.** sencillo **2.** honrado, sincero

strain *noun.* **1.** tensión **2.** presión **3.** carga **4.** esfuerzo **5.** estrés **6.** torcedura, esguince **7.** raza, tipo **8.** vena **9.** son, compás

strain *verb.* **1.** estirar, tensar, forzar **2.** torcerse, hacerse un esguince, dañarse **3.** poner a prueba, abusar **4.** colar, escurrir

strained *adj.* tenso, forzado

strand *noun.* hebra, hilo

strange *adj.* extraño

strangely *adv.* extrañamente

stranger *noun.* **1.** extraño, desconocido **2.** forastero

strap *noun.* **1.** correa **2.** asa

strap *verb.* **1.** azotar a alguien con correa **2.** atar con correa

strategic *adj.* estratégico

strategy *noun.* estrategia

straw *noun. adj.* **1.** paja **2.** pajita

strawberry *noun.* fresa

stray *noun.* animal extraviado

stray *verb.* extraviarse, perderse

stray *adj.* **1.** perdido, extraviado, callejero **2.** aislado

streak *noun.* **1.** raya, veta, filón **2.** vena

streak *verb.* **1.** rayar, surcar **2.** pasar como un rayo

stream *noun.* **1.** riachuelo, arroyo **2.** flujo, chorro **3.** corriente **4.** clase, grupo, nivel

stream *verb.* **1.** manar, correr, chorrear **2.** separar por niveles

street, St. *noun.* calle

strength *noun.* **1.** fuerza **2.** intensidad **3.** número, efectivos

strengthen *verb.* **1.** fortalecer **2.** fortalecerse

stress *noun.* **1.** estrés **2.** tensión **3.** énfasis, acento

stress *verb.* enfatizar

stretch *noun.* **1.** estiramiento **2.** extensión, tramo, trecho

stretch *verb.* **1.** estirar, extender **2.** extenderse

strict *adj.* **1.** estricto, severo **2.** riguroso

strictly *adv.* rigurosamente

stride *noun.* zancada

stride *verb.* andar a zancadas

strike *noun.* **1.** huelga **2.** hallazgo, descubrimiento **3.** golpe, strike (sports)

strike *verb.* **1.** pegar, golpear **2.** atacar **3.** encender, prender **4.** hacer huelga, declararse en huelga **5.** encontrar **6.** chocar contra **7.** parecer, dar la impresión **8.** acuñar **9.** desmontar

striker *noun.* **1.** huelguista **2.** delantero

striking *adj.* **1.** llamativo **2.** impresionante, sorprendente

string *noun.* **1.** cuerda, cordel, cabuya **2.** fibra, hebra **3.** sarta, collar, ristra **4.** hilera, fila

string *verb.* **1.** ensartar **2.** encordar **3.** desfibrar, quitar la hebra **4.** colgar

stringent adj. riguroso, severo

strip noun. 1. tira, franja 2. tira cómica, historieta

strip verb. 1. quitar, despojar 2. desnudar, desnudarse

stripe noun. 1. raya, lista 2. galón

striped adj. a rayas

strive verb. esforzarse

stroke noun. 1. caricia 2. golpe 3. ocurrencia 4. campanada 5. trazo, pincelada 6. brazada 7. apoplejía

stroke verb. acariciar

stroll noun. paseo, vuelta

stroll verb. pasearse

strong adj. 1. fuerte 2. sano 3. firme 4. que cuenta con un número de

strongly adv. firmemente, rotundamente

structural adj. estructural

structure noun. 1. estructura 2. construcción

struggle noun. lucha

struggle verb. 1. luchar 2. forcejear 3. tener problemas

stubborn adj. cabezota

student noun. 1. estudiante 2. alumno

studio noun. 1. estudio 2. taller

study noun. 1. estudio 2. biblioteca, despacho

study verb. 1. estudiar 2. examinar, mirar detenidamente

stuff noun. 1. cosa, cosas 2. sustancia, materia 3. chismes, cachivaches, trastos 4. paño, tela, género

stuff verb. 1. llenar, rellenar 2. meter, atestar 3. atiborrarse 4. disecar

stumble verb. 1. tropezar 2. avanzar dando tropezones/traspiés 3. balbucir

stump noun. 1. tocón, cepa 2. palo, poste 3. muñón 4. raigón

stump verb. 1. andar pisando muy fuerte 2. dejar perplejo, desconcertar 3. eliminar, dejar fuera de juego

stun verb. 1. dejar inconsciente, aturdir 2. pasmar, asombrar

stunning adj. alucinante, estupendo, maravilloso

stupid adj. 1. estúpido 2. atontado

style noun. 1. estilo 2. moda 3. clase, elegancia

style verb. 1. marcar, peinar 2. diseñar

stylish adj. 1. con estilo, elegante 2. a la moda

sub noun. sub

subdued adj. 1. suave 2. apagado

subject noun. 1. súbdito 2. tema, asunto 3. asignatura 4. motivo 5. sujeto

subject verb. 1. dominar, subyugar 2. someter

subject adj. dominado, subyugado

—**subject to** 1. sujeto a 2. expuesto a 3. propenso a

subjective adj. subjetivo

submarine noun. adj. submarino

submission noun. sumisión

submit verb. 1. presentar 2. someter 3. someterse, rendirse

subordinate noun. adj. subordinado

subscription noun. 1. suscripción 2. abono, cuota

subsequent adj. subsiguiente, posterior

subsequently adv. posteriormente

subsidiary noun. filial

subsidiary adj. 1. secundario 2. filial

subsidize verb. subvencionar

subsidy noun. subsidio, subvención

substance noun. sustancia

substantial adj. 1. sustancial 2. importante

substantially adv. sustancialmente

substitute noun. sustituto

substitute verb. sustituir

substitution noun. sustitución

subtle adj. 1. sutil 2. agudo, perspicaz

suburb, suburbs noun plural. afueras

suburban adj. de las afueras, de cercanías

succeed verb. 1. conseguir, triunfar, tener éxito 2. suceder

success noun. éxito

successful adj. afortunado, exitoso

successfully adv. con éxito

succession noun. sucesión

successive adj. sucesivo

successor noun. sucesor

such adj. 1. tal 2. parecido, semejante 3. así 4. tan, tanto

such pron. 1. el que, la que, lo que, los que, las que 2. tal

suck *verb.* **1.** mamar, chupar **2.** sorber **3.** aspirar **4.** ser una mierda

sudden *adj.* súbito, repentino

suddenly *adv.* súbitamente, de repente, de golpe

sue *verb.* demandar
—**sue for divorce** solicitar el divorcio

suffer *verb.* **1.** sufrir, padecer **2.** soportar **3.** resentirse, verse afectado

suffering *noun.* sufrimiento

suffice *verb.* bastar, ser suficiente

sufficient *adj.* suficiente, bastante

sufficiently *adv.* suficientemente

sugar *noun.* azúcar

sugar *verb.* azucarar, endulzar

suggest *verb.* **1.** sugerir **2.** proponer **3.** insinuar

suggestion *noun.* **1.** sugerencia **2.** propuesta **3.** insinuación **4.** indicio, asomo

suicide *noun.* **1.** suicidio **2.** suicida

suit *noun.* **1.** traje **2.** pleito, juicio **3.** petición de mano, oferta de matrimonio **4.** palo

suit *verb.* **1.** convenir, venir bien **2.** quedar bien, favorecer **3.** adaptar

suitable *adj.* adecuado, conveniente, apropiado

suitably *adv.* convenientemente, adecuadamente, apropiadamente

suitcase *noun.* maleta

suite *noun.* **1.** juego **2.** suite

sulfur *noun.* azufre

sum *noun.* **1.** suma **2.** cantidad **3.** total **4.** problema de aritmética

summarize *verb.* resumir

summary *noun.* resumen

summer *noun.* verano

summit *noun.* **1.** cumbre, cima, cúspide **2.** punto álgido

summit *adj.* cumbre

summon *verb.* convocar

sun *noun.* sol

sun *verb.* tomar el sol

Sunday *noun.* domingo

sunlight *noun.* luz del sol

sunny *adj.* **1.** soleado **2.** alegre

sunset *noun.* puesta de sol, crepúsculo

sunshine *noun.* **1.** luz del sol **2.** alegría, jovialidad

super *adj.* estupendo, tremendo

superb *adj.* magnífico, excelente

superficial *adj.* superficial

superintendent *noun.* superintendente, director, inspector

superior *noun.* superior

superior *adj.* superior

superiority *noun.* superioridad

supermarket *noun.* supermercado

supervise *verb.* supervisar, controlar

supervision *noun.* supervisión

supervisor *noun.* supervisor

supper *noun.* cena

supplement *noun.* suplemento

supplement *verb.* complementar

supplementary *adj.* suplementario

supply *noun.* suministro, provisión, abastecimiento
—**supplies** *noun plural.* **1.** provisiones **2.** existencias

supply *verb.* proporcionar, abastecer

support *noun.* **1.** apoyo **2.** soporte

support *verb.* **1.** aguantar, sostener **2.** apoyar, respaldar **3.** corroborar, confirmar **4.** mantener

supporter *noun.* **1.** defensor, partidario **2.** seguidor

supporting *adj.* secundario

suppose *verb.* **1.** suponer **2.** creer
—**supposing** suponiendo que, en el caso de que

suppress *verb.* **1.** suprimir **2.** reprimir **3.** contener, sofocar **4.** censurar **5.** ocultar

suppression *noun.* **1.** supresión **2.** represión **3.** ocultación

supreme *adj.* supremo

sure *adj.* **1.** seguro **2.** cierto

sure *adv.* claro, por supuesto

surely *adv.* **1.** seguramente **2.** sin duda

surface *noun.* **1.** superficie, cara **2.** apariencia

surface *verb.* **1.** revestir, asfaltar **2.** salir, aflorar

surge *noun.* **1.** oleada, arranque **2.** oleaje, marejada

surge *verb.* levantarse, agitarse

surgeon *noun.* **1.** cirujano **2.** oficial médico

surgery *noun.* **1.** cirugía **2.** quirófano

surgical *adj.* quirúrgico
surplus *noun.* excedente
surprise *noun.* sorpresa
surprise *verb.* sorprender
surprised *adj.* sorprendido
surprising *adj.* sorprendente
surprisingly *adv.* sorprendentemente
surrender *noun.* rendición
surrender *verb.* **1.** rendirse **2.** rendir **3.** renunciar (a) **4.** devolver
surround *verb.* **1.** rodear **2.** cercar, sitiar
surrounding *adj.* circundante
surroundings *noun plural.* **1.** alrededores, cercanías **2.** entorno, ambiente
survey *noun.* **1.** examen, estudio **2.** encuesta **3.** reconocimiento, inspección **4.** medición
survey *verb.* **1.** mirar, contemplar **2.** estudiar, examinar **3.** encuestar **4.** reconocer, inspeccionar **5.** medir, levantar el plano
surveyor *noun.* **1.** agrimensor **2.** topógrafo **3.** perito
survival *noun.* supervivencia
survive *verb.* sobrevivir
surviving *adj.* superviviente
survivor *noun.* superviviente
suspect *noun.* sospechoso
suspect *verb.* **1.** sospechar **2.** desconfiar **3.** creer
suspect *adj.* **1.** sospechoso **2.** dudoso
suspend *verb.* **1.** suspender **2.** colgar, pender **3.** aplazar, posponer
suspension *noun.* suspensión
suspicion *noun.* **1.** sospecha **2.** pizca, atisbo
suspicious *adj.* **1.** desconfiado **2.** sospechoso
sustain *verb.* **1.** sostener, aguantar **2.** mantener, dar fuerzas
swallow *noun.* **1.** golondrina **2.** trago
swallow *verb.* **1.** tragar, engullir **2.** tragarse
swamp *noun.* pantano, ciénaga
swamp *verb.* empantanar, inundar, anegar
swan *noun.* cisne
sway *noun.* **1.** balanceo, bamboleo **2.** dominio, influencia

sway *verb.* **1.** balancear, mecer **2.** balancearse, mecerse **3.** influir, influenciar
swear *verb.* **1.** jurar **2.** blasfemar
sweat *noun.* sudor
sweat *verb.* **1.** sudar **2.** sudar la gota gorda, matarse a trabajar
sweater *noun.* suéter, jersey
Sweden *noun.* Suecia
Swedish *noun. adj.* sueco
sweep *noun.* **1.** barrido **2.** gesto/movimiento amplio **3.** batida, rastreo
sweep *verb.* **1.** barrer **2.** limpiar, recoger **3.** arrasar **4.** arrastrar, llevarse **5.** azotar, asolar **6.** deslizarse, pasar rápidamente **7.** extenderse, recorrer
sweeping *adj.* **1.** amplio **2.** aplastante, arrollador **3.** radical
sweet *noun.* caramelo, golosina
sweet *adj.* **1.** dulce **2.** fresco, sano **3.** melodioso **4.** encantador **5.** agradable **6.** mono, lindo
swell *noun.* marejada, oleaje
swell *verb.* **1.** hinchar **2.** hincharse **3.** aumentar
swell *adj.* estupendo, bárbaro, formidable
swift *noun.* vencejo
swift *adj.* rápido, veloz
swiftly *adv.* rápidamente
swim *noun.* baño
swim *verb.* **1.** nadar, flotar **2.** dar vueltas
swimming *noun.* natación
swimming *adj.* nadando, flotando
swing *noun.* **1.** balanceo, vaivén, oscilación **2.** swing (golf) **3.** swing (music) **4.** giro, viraje, cambio **5.** columpio
swing *verb.* **1.** balancearse, oscilar **2.** girar, doblar **3.** cambiar, decidir **4.** columpiarse
swinging *adj.* con mucha marcha
Swiss *noun. adj.* suizo
switch *noun.* **1.** interruptor, conmutador **2.** cambio, viraje **3.** vara, varilla
switch *verb.* **1.** cambiar **2.** desviar, trasladar
—switch off apagar
—switch on encender

Switzerland noun. Suiza
swollen adj. hinchado
swop, swap noun. intercambio, canje, trueque
swop, swap verb. intercambiar
sword noun. espada
sworn adj. 1. declarado 2. jurado, bajo juramento
syllable noun. sílaba
symbol noun. símbolo
symbolic adj. simbólico
symmetry noun. simetría
sympathetic adj. 1. compasivo 2. comprensivo
sympathy noun. 1. compasión, lástima

2. simpatía 3. solidaridad, comprensión
symphony noun. sinfonía
symptom noun. síntoma
syndicate noun. 1. corporación, sindicato 2. agencia de prensa
syntax noun. sintaxis
synthesis noun. síntesis
synthetic noun. adj. sintético
Syria noun. Siria
Syrian noun. adj. sirio
system noun. 1. sistema 2. organismo 3. método
systematic adj. sistemático
systematically adv. sistemáticamente

T

table noun. 1. mesa 2. tabla, cuadro
tablespoon noun. 1. cuchara sopera 2. cucharada grande
tablet noun. 1. pastilla 2. comprimido 3. lápida
tabloid noun. tabloide
tack noun. 1. tachuela 2. hilván 3. bordada, viraje 4. rumbo, dirección
tack verb. 1. clavar con tachuelas 2. dar bordadas, virar
tackle noun. 1. placaje 2. equipo, aparejos 3. jarcia, cordaje
tackle verb. 1. agarrar, asir 2. abordar 3. emprender 4. encararse con 5. entrar (a), placar
tactical adj. táctico
tactics noun plural. táctica
tag noun. 1. etiqueta, marbete 2. cita 3. cabo
tag verb. etiquetar
tail noun. 1. cola 2. cruz (coin)
tail verb. seguir de cerca
tailor noun. sastre
tailor verb. 1. confeccionar, hacer a medida 2. adaptar
take noun. 1. caja, ventas, recaudación 2. toma
take verb. 1. tomar 2. coger 3. agarrar

4. sacar 5. extraer 6. llevar 7. llevarse 8. anotar, apuntar 9. aguantar, tolerar 10. necesitar, requerir 11. tener cabida 12. aceptar 13. obtener, ganar 14. dar, estudiar 15. medir 16. asumir 17. tomar a cargo de uno, encargarse de 18. tomarse, reaccionar ante 19. robar
—**take a turn for the better/worse** mejorar or empeorar, volverse mejor or peor
—**take away** quitar, llevarse
—**take for granted** dar por supuesto, dar por sentado
—**take in** 1. engañar 2. acortar, achicar
—**take off** 1. despegar 2. quitar, quitarse 3. descontar
—**take on** 1. abordar, emprender 2. contratar 3. asumir
—**take over** tomar el poder, asumir el mando
—**take up** 1. llevar, ocupar 2. subir, levantar 3. volver, retomar
tale noun. 1. historia, relato 2. mentira, trola
talent noun. talento
talented adj. talentoso

talk *noun.* **1.** conversación, plática **2.** conferencia, charla **3.** comentario, chismorreo, cotilleo **4.** palabrería, charlatanería
—**talks** conversaciones, negociaciones
talk *verb.* **1.** hablar **2.** chismorrear
tall *adj.* alto
tan *noun.* bronceado
tan *noun. adj.* marrón claro
tan *verb.* **1.** curtir **2.** broncearse
tangible *adj.* tangible
tangle *noun.* desorden, maraña, enredo
tangle *verb.* enredar, enmarañar
tank *noun.* **1.** tanque, depósito **2.** tanque de guerra
tanker *noun.* **1.** petrolero **2.** avión cisterna
tap *noun.* **1.** golpecito, palmadita **2.** grifo
tap *verb.* **1.** explotar, utilizar **2.** pinchar, intervenir
—**tap at/on/with** *verb.* golpear ligeramente, dar una palmadita
tape *noun.* **1.** cinta **2.** cinta métrica **3.** meta
tape *verb.* **1.** grabar **2.** cerrar con una cinta, pegar con cinta adhesiva
target *noun.* blanco
tariff *noun.* **1.** lista de precios **2.** arancel
task *noun.* tarea
task force *noun.* destacamento especial
taste *noun.* **1.** gusto **2.** sabor **3.** prueba, degustación **4.** afición
taste *verb.* **1.** probar, degustar, catar **2.** saber (a) **3.** saborear **4.** experimentar, probar
tax *noun.* **1.** impuesto **2.** carga
tax *verb.* **1.** gravar, imponer contribuciones **2.** cargar, abrumar
taxation *noun.* impuestos, sistema tributario
taxi, taxi-cab *noun.* taxi
taxi *verb.* rodar por la pista
taximeter *noun.* taxímetro
taxpayer *noun.* contribuyente
tbsp *abbr.* cucharada sopera
tea *noun.* té
teacart *noun.* mesita de ruedas
teach *verb.* enseñar, dar clases

teacher *noun.* maestro, profesor
teaching *noun.* **1.** enseñanza **2.** lección **3.** doctrina
team *noun.* equipo
tear *noun.* **1.** lágrima **2.** rasgón, desgarrón, rotura
tear *verb.* **1.** romper, rasgar, despedazar **2.** romperse, rasgarse, hacerse pedazos/trizas **3.** ir/correr a toda velocidad
tease *noun.* provocador, bromista
tease *verb.* **1.** molestar, irritar **2.** provocar, picar **3.** tomar el pelo, reírse de alguien
teaspoon *noun.* **1.** cucharilla **2.** cucharadita
technical *adj.* técnico
technically *adv.* **1.** técnicamente **2.** desde el punto de vista técnico **3.** en teoría
technician *noun.* técnico
technique *noun.* técnica
technological *adj.* tecnológico
technology *noun.* tecnología
teddy (bear) *noun.* oso de peluche
tedious *adj.* tedioso, aburrido
teenage *adj.* adolescente
teenager *noun.* adolescente
tel. *abbr.* número de teléfono
telecommunications *noun plural.* telecomunicaciones
telegraph *noun.* telégrafo
telegraph *verb.* telegrafiar
telephone *noun.* teléfono
telephone *verb.* telefonear, llamar por teléfono
telescope *noun.* telescopio
telescope *verb.* encajar, meter
televise *verb.* televisar
television, TV *noun.* televisión
tell *verb.* **1.** contar **2.** decir **3.** mandar **4.** distinguir **5.** divulgar, revelar **6.** notarse, hacerse notar
telling *adj.* eficaz
temper *noun.* **1.** humor **2.** genio **3.** furia
temper *verb.* **1.** templar **2.** suavizar
temperament *noun.* temperamento
temperature *noun.* **1.** temperatura **2.** fiebre
temple *noun.* **1.** templo **2.** sien
temporarily *adv.* temporalmente

temporary *adj.* temporal
tempt *verb.* tentar
temptation *noun.* tentación
tempting *adj.* tentador
ten *noun. adj.* diez
tenant *noun.* inquilino, arrendatario
tend *verb.* 1. tender, inclinarse, tener tendencia 2. atender, cuidar
tendency *noun.* tendencia
tender *noun.* 1. guardián 2. oferta 3. gabarra
tender *adj.* 1. tierno 2. sensible, delicado 3. afectuoso
tennis *noun.* tenis
tense *noun.* tiempo
tense *verb.* tensar
tense *adj.* 1. tenso 2. tirante
tension *noun.* tensión
tent *noun.* tienda (de campaña)
tentative *adj.* 1. provisorio, de prueba, provisional 2. vacilante, tímido
tenth *noun.* décimo
term *noun.* 1. período, etapa 2. mandato 3. trimestre 4. plazo 5. término
—**terms** condiciones
term *verb.* llamar, calificar
terminal *noun. adj.* terminal
terminate *verb.* 1. terminar, concluir 2. terminarse
termination *noun.* fin, conclusión
terminology *noun.* terminología
terrace *noun.* terraza, bancal
terrible *adj.* terrible, espantoso
terribly *adv.* muy, extremadamente
terrific *adj.* 1. estupendo, fabuloso 2. tremendo, enorme
terrified *adj.* aterrorizado
terrify *verb.* aterrorizar
terrifying *adj.* aterrador, espantoso
territorial *adj.* territorial
territory *noun.* 1. territorio 2. especialidad, campo
terror *noun.* 1. terror 2. diablillo
terrorism *noun.* terrorismo
terrorist *noun.* terrorista
test *noun.* 1. examen, test 2. ensayo, prueba
test *verb.* 1. probar, examinar 2. hacer un análisis

testament *noun.* testamento
testify *verb.* 1. declarar, atestiguar 2. testificar
testimony *noun.* testimonio
text *noun.* texto
textbook *noun.* libro de texto
textile *noun.* textil
texture *noun.* textura
Thai *noun. adj.* tailandés
Thailand *noun.* Tailandia
than *conj. prep.* 1. que 2. de
thank *verb.* agradecer
thank you *interj.* ¡gracias!
thankfully *adv.* agradecidamente
thanks *interj.* ¡gracias!
thanks *noun plural.* agradecimiento
that *conj.* 1. que 2. para que 3. ¡y pensar que!, ¡ojalá!
that *relative pron.* que
that *adj.* 1. ese, esa 2. aquel, aquella
that *adv.* tan
that *pron.* 1. ése, ésa, eso 2. aquél, aquélla, aquello 3. el, la, lo
the *def. art.* el, la, los, las
—**the more the better** cuanto más mejor
theater *noun.* teatro
theatrical *adj.* 1. teatral 2. dramático
thee *pron.* 1. te 2. ti
theft *noun.* robo, hurto
their *adj.* su, sus
theirs *pron.* 1. (el) suyo, (la) suya, (los) suyos, (las) suyas 2. de ellos, de ellas
them *pron.* 1. los, las (direct object) 2. les (indirect object) 3. ellos, ellas (after prep) 4. le, la
theme *noun.* 1. tema 2. asunto
themselves *pron.* 1. se 2. sí mismos, sí mismas 3. ellos mismos, ellas mismas 4. ellos solos, ellas solas
then *conj.* entonces, en ese caso
then *adj.* entonces
then *adv.* 1. entonces 2. en aquel momento 3. luego, después 4. además
theological *adj.* teológico
theology *noun.* teología
theoretical *adj.* teórico
theoretically *adj.* teóricamente
theorist *noun.* teórico

theory *noun.* teoría
therapeutic *adj.* terapéutico
therapist *noun.* terapeuta
therapy *noun.* terapia
there *interj.* **1.** venga, bueno **2.** ¿ves?
there *adv.* **1.** allí, allá, ahí **2.** en eso, en ese punto
there *pron.* haber (there is/are)
therefore *adv.* por tanto, por consiguiente
thermal *adj.* **1.** termal **2.** térmico
these *adj.* estos, estas
these *pron.* éstos, éstas
thesis *noun.* tesis
they *pron.* ellos, ellas
thick *noun.* **1.** espesor **2.** centro
thick *adj.* **1.** grueso **2.** espeso, denso **3.** numeroso **4.** cargado
thickness *noun.* densidad, espesor
thief *noun.* ladrón
thigh *noun.* muslo
thin *verb.* **1.** disminuir **2.** disiparse **3.** diluir, aclarar
thin *adj.* **1.** fino **2.** delgado **3.** aguado, poco espeso, claro **4.** ralo, escaso **5.** poco convincente, pobre
thing *noun.* **1.** cosa **2.** asunto, cuestión **3.** criatura, ser
things *noun plural.* **1.** cosas, bártulos **2.** ropa
think *noun.* reflexión, pensamiento
think *verb.* **1.** pensar, reflexionar **2.** creer **3.** opinar **4.** imaginar **5.** esperar
third *noun.* **1.** tercio **2.** tercero **3.** tres
third *adv.* en tercer lugar
thirdly *adv.* en tercer lugar
thirsty *adj.* sediento
thirteen *noun. adj.* trece
thirteenth *noun.* **1.** decimotercera parte **2.** decimotercero
thirties *noun plural.* **1.** entre los treinta y treinta y nueve **2.** años treinta
thirtieth *noun.* trigésimo
thirty *noun. adj.* treinta
this *adj.* este, esta
this *adv.* tan, así de
this *pron.* éste, ésta, esto
thorn *noun.* espina
thorough *adj.* **1.** cuidadoso, minucioso, concienzudo **2.** completo, absoluto

thoroughly *adv.* **1.** cuidadosamente, minuciosamente, concienzudamente **2.** completamente
those *adj.* **1.** esos, esas **2.** aquellos, aquellas
those *pron.* **1.** ésos, ésas **2.** aquéllos, aquéllas **3.** los, las
thou *pron.* vos, tú
though *conj.* aunque
though *adv.* sin embargo, a pesar de todo
thought *noun.* **1.** pensamiento **2.** reflexión
thoughtful *adj.* **1.** pensativo **2.** considerado, atento
thoughtfully *adv.* **1.** pensativamente **2.** con consideración
thousand *noun. adj.* mil
thread *noun.* **1.** hilo, hebra **2.** rosca
thread *verb.* **1.** enhebrar **2.** ensartar **3.** abrirse camino
threat *noun.* amenaza
threaten *verb.* amenazar
three *noun. adj.* tres
three-dimensional, 3-D *adj.* tridimensional
threshold *noun.* **1.** umbral **2.** puertas
thrift *noun.* economía, frugalidad
thrill *noun.* emoción
thrill *verb.* emocionar, conmover
thriller *noun.* obra de suspense/o
thrive *verb.* **1.** crecer **2.** prosperar
thriving *adj.* próspero, floreciente
throat *noun.* **1.** garganta **2.** cuello
throne *noun.* trono
through *prep.* **1.** por, a través de **2.** de cabo a rabo, de principio a fin, entero **3.** a causa de
through *adj.* directo
through *adv.* **1.** directamente **2.** entero, todo **3.** de un lado a otro
throughout *prep.* **1.** por todas partes **2.** durante todo
throughout *adv.* enteramente, por completo
throw *noun.* lanzamiento, tirada
throw *verb.* **1.** lanzar, tirar, echar **2.** desarzonar, desmontar **3.** confundir, desconcertar **4.** derribar

thrust noun. 1. ataque, asalto 2. empuje 3. empujón

thrust verb. 1. acometer, atacar 2. empujar 3. meter, hincar

thumb noun. pulgar

thumb (through) verb. 1. hojear 2. manosear

thunder noun. 1. trueno 2. estruendo

thunder verb. tronar

Thursday noun. jueves

thus adv. así

tick noun. 1. garrapata 2. tictac 3. instante, segundo

tick verb. hacer tictac

ticket noun. 1. billete, boleto 2. multa 3. etiqueta 4. candidatura, planilla
—**one-way ticket** billete/boleto sencillo
—**round-trip ticket** billete/boleto de ida y vuelta

tide noun. marea

tidy verb. ordenar

tidy adj. 1. ordenado 2. considerable

tie noun. 1. corbata 2. lazo, vínculo 3. empate

tie verb. 1. amarrar, atar 2. atar, anudar 3. atarse, anudarse 4. relacionar 5. empatar

tiger noun. tigre

tight, tightly adv. 1. bien cerrado 2. apretado

tight adj. 1. apretado, estrecho 2. riguroso, estricto

tighten verb. 1. apretar, tensar 2. hacer más severo

tights noun plural. medias

tile noun. 1. teja 2. baldosa 3. azulejo

tile verb. 1. tejar 2. embaldosar 3. alicatar, revestir de azulejos

till prep. conj. hasta (que)

till noun. cajón

tilt noun. inclinación, ladeo

tilt verb. inclinar, ladear

timber noun. 1. madera de construcción 2. árboles maderables 3. viga

time noun. 1. tiempo 2. hora 3. momento 4. vez 5. época, período

time verb. 1. cronometrar 2. escoger el momento de/para 3. planear, calcular

times noun plural. 1. tiempos 2. veces

timetable noun. horario

timing noun. 1. cronometraje 2. coordinación, sentido del tiempo

tin noun. 1. estaño, hojalata 2. lata

tin adj. de lata

tiny adj. minúsculo, pequeñísimo, diminuto

tip noun. 1. consejo, sugerencia 2. propina 3. punta, cabo, extremidad

tip verb. 1. inclinar 2. ladearse, inclinarse 3. volcar 4. dar una propina

tire noun. neumático

tired adj. cansado

tissue noun. 1. tejido 2. pañuelo de papel

title noun. título

to prep. 1. a 2. hacia 3. hasta 4. según 5. en 6. contra 7. por 8. de

to adv. cerrado

toast noun. 1. brindis 2. tostada

toast verb. 1. brindar por 2. tostar

tobacco noun. tabaco

today noun. adv. hoy

toe noun. 1. dedo del pie 2. punta

together adv. 1. juntos 2. al mismo tiempo

toilet noun. lavabo, servicios

token noun. 1. señal, prueba 2. ficha

tolerance noun. tolerancia

tolerate verb. tolerar

toll noun. 1. peaje 2. número de víctimas, pérdidas

toll verb. tañer, doblar

tomato noun. 1. tomate 2. tomatera

tomb noun. tumba

tomorrow noun. adv. 1. mañana 2. futuro

ton noun. tonelada

tone noun. tono

tongue noun. 1. lengua 2. idioma

tonic noun. 1. tónico 2. tónica

tonight noun. adv. esta noche

tons noun plural. montones

too adv. 1. demasiado, muy 2. también

tool noun. instrumento

tooth noun. diente

top noun. 1. cumbre 2. cima 3. copa 4. parte superior 5. cabeza, primer lugar

6. lo alto de **7.** tapadera **8.** tapón **9.** blusa (corta), camiseta, top **10.** peonza, trompo

top *verb.* **1.** encabezar **2.** cubrir, recubrir **3.** coronar **4.** superar, sobrepasar **5.** desmochar, descabezar

top *adj.* **1.** mejor, primero **2.** superior, de arriba **3.** máximo

topic *noun.* asunto, tema

topical *adj.* **1.** actual, de actualidad **2.** local

topple *verb.* **1.** volcar **2.** volcarse **3.** derribar, derrocar

torch *noun.* **1.** linterna **2.** antorcha

torture *noun.* tortura

torture *verb.* torturar

toss *noun.* **1.** sacudida **2.** tirada, lanzamiento

toss *verb.* **1.** arrojar, tirar, lanzar **2.** sacudir **3.** echar a cara o cruz

total *noun. adj.* total

total *verb.* sumar, ascender a

totally *adv.* totalmente

touch *noun.* **1.** toque **2.** roce **3.** tacto **4.** contacto **5.** retoque **6.** sello, estilo

touch *verb.* **1.** tocar **2.** tocarse **3.** rozar **4.** conmover

touching *adj.* conmovedor

tough *noun.* chulo, matón

tough *adj.* **1.** fuerte **2.** duro **3.** resistente **4.** violento, conflictivo **5.** difícil, espinoso

tour *noun.* **1.** viaje, excursión **2.** visita **3.** gira

tour *verb.* viajar

tourism *noun.* turismo

tourist *noun.* turista

tournament *noun.* torneo

tow *noun.* remolque

tow *verb.* remolcar

toward, towards *prep.* **1.** hacia **2.** para **3.** con respecto a, para con **4.** alrededor de, sobre

towel *noun.* toalla

towel *verb.* secar con toalla

tower *noun.* torre

tower *verb.* descollar, sobresalir

town *noun.* ciudad, población

toxic *adj.* tóxico

toy *noun.* juguete

toy (with) *verb.* jugar con

trace *noun.* **1.** rastro, huella, vestigio **2.** pizca

trace *verb.* **1.** localizar, averiguar el paradero **2.** trazar **3.** calcar

track *noun.* **1.** rastro, huella **2.** camino, senda **3.** pista **4.** vía

track *verb.* seguir la pista, rastrear

tract *noun.* **1.** extensión **2.** tracto **3.** folleto

tractor *noun.* tractor

trade *noun.* **1.** comercio **2.** negocio **3.** oficio **4.** industria

trade *verb.* **1.** comerciar **2.** cambiar, intercambiar

trader *noun.* comerciante

tradition *noun.* tradición

traditional *adj.* tradicional

traditionally *adv.* tradicionalmente

traffic *noun.* tráfico

traffic *verb.* traficar

tragedy *noun.* tragedia

tragic *adj.* trágico

trail *noun.* **1.** pista, rastro **2.** camino, sendero **3.** reguero, estela

trail *verb.* **1.** arrastrar **2.** ir arrastrando los pies **3.** seguir la pista (de)

trailer *noun.* **1.** remolque **2.** caravana **3.** tráiler, avance

train *noun.* **1.** tren **2.** cola **3.** serie, sucesión **4.** séquito, comitiva **5.** recua, fila, convoy

train *verb.* **1.** formar, enseñar, instruir, entrenar, adiestrar **2.** apuntar **3.** enfocar **4.** guiar **5.** entrenarse

trained *adj.* cualificado, capacitado, educado, adiestrado

trainee *noun.* **1.** aprendiz **2.** recluta

trainer *noun.* entrenador, preparador

training *noun.* **1.** entrenamiento **2.** formación, instrucción, adiestramiento

trait *noun.* rasgo, característica

transaction *noun.* transacción

transcript *noun.* **1.** transcripción **2.** expediente

transfer *noun.* **1.** traspaso, traslado **2.** transferencia **3.** calcomanía

transfer *verb.* **1.** traspasar, trasladar **2.**

trasladarse **3.** transferir **4.** pasar **5.** transmitir

transform *verb.* transformar

transformation *noun.* transformación

transit *noun.* tránsito, paso

transition *noun.* transición

transitional *adj.* transitorio

translate *verb.* traducir

translation *noun.* traducción

translator *noun.* traductor

transmission *noun.* transmisión

transmit *verb.* transmitir

transparent *adj.* transparente

transplant *noun.* trasplante, injerto

transplant *verb.* **1.** trasplantar **2.** injertar

transport *noun.* transporte

transport *verb.* transportar

transportation *noun.* transporte

trap *noun.* trampa

trap *verb.* **1.** atrapar, cazar, agarrar **2.** tender una trampa

trash *noun.* basura

—**trash can** cubo de la basura

travel *noun.* viaje, viajar

travel *verb.* **1.** viajar **2.** ir **3.** recorrer

traveler *noun.* **1.** viajero **2.** viajante

tray *noun.* bandeja

tread *noun.* **1.** paso **2.** pisada, huella **3.** escalón **4.** llanta de neumático

tread *verb.* **1.** pisar, hollar **2.** caminar, andar

treasure *noun.* tesoro

treasure *verb.* **1.** valorar **2.** guardar, atesorar

treasurer *noun.* tesorero

treat *noun.* regalo

treat *verb.* **1.** tratar **2.** invitar, convidar

treatment *noun.* **1.** trato **2.** tratamiento

treaty *noun.* tratado

tree *noun.* árbol

trek *noun.* **1.** expedición **2.** caminata

trek *verb.* caminar

tremble *noun.* temblor

tremble *verb.* temblar

tremendous *adj.* tremendo, enorme

trench *noun.* trinchera

trend *noun.* tendencia

trial *noun.* **1.** prueba, ensayo **2.** proceso, juicio **3.** aflicción, sufrimiento, desgracia

triangle *noun.* triángulo

tribal *adj.* tribal

tribe *noun.* tribu

tribunal *noun.* tribunal

tribute *noun.* tributo, homenaje

trick *noun.* truco, trampa, engaño

trick *adj.* trucado

tricky *adj.* difícil, complicado, espinoso

trigger *noun.* **1.** gatillo **2.** disparador **3.** desencadenante

trigger (off) *verb.* **1.** desencadenar, provocar **2.** hacer estallar

trillion *noun. adj.* billón

trim *noun.* corte

trim *verb.* **1.** cortar, recortar **2.** podar **3.** adornar, decorar

trim *adj.* arreglado, aseado, cuidado

trio *noun.* trío

trip *noun.* viaje, excursión, salida

trip (over/up) *verb.* **1.** tropezar **2.** ir con paso ligero

triple *noun. adj.* triple

triple *verb.* triplicar

triumph *noun.* triunfo

triumph *verb.* triunfar

triumphant *adj.* triunfante

trivial *adj.* **1.** trivial, insignificante, banal **2.** superficial, frívolo

trolley *noun.* carrito

troop *noun.* **1.** tropa **2.** grupo

troop *verb.* ir en tropel

troops *noun plural.* tropas

trophy *noun.* trofeo

tropical *adj.* tropical

trouble *noun.* **1.** problema, apuro, dificultad **2.** disturbio, conflicto, altercado **3.** enfermedad

trouble *verb.* **1.** preocupar **2.** molestar **3.** molestarse

troubled *adj.* **1.** preocupado, inquieto **2.** conflictivo

trousers *noun plural.* pantalones

trout *noun.* trucha

truce *noun.* tregua

truck *noun.* camión

true *adj.* **1.** verdadero, verídico **2.** cierto, exacto **3.** fiel, leal **4.** auténtico, real

truly *adv.* **1.** verdaderamente, realmente **2.** de verdad

trumpet *noun.* **1.** trompeta **2.** barrito
trumpet *verb.* **1.** tocar la trompeta **2.** barritar
trunk *noun.* **1.** tronco **2.** baúl **3.** trompa **4.** maletero
trust *noun.* **1.** confianza **2.** carga, cuidado **3.** responsabilidad **4.** fundación **5.** fideicomiso **6.** fondo de inversión **7.** trust, cartel
trust *verb.* **1.** confiar **2.** esperar
trustee *noun.* **1.** fideicomisario **2.** administrador
truth *noun.* verdad
try *noun.* **1.** tentativa, intento **2.** ensayo
try *verb.* **1.** intentar **2.** probar **3.** juzgar, procesar **4.** poner a prueba
trying *adj.* **1.** difícil; molesto, latoso **2.** pesado
T-shirt, tee shirt *noun.* camiseta
tube *noun.* **1.** tubo **2.** trompa **3.** metro, ferrocarril subterráneo
tuck *noun.* pliegue
tuck *verb.* **1.** meter **2.** plegar
Tuesday *noun.* martes
tug *noun.* **1.** tirón, estirón **2.** remolcador
tug *verb.* tirar (de), dar un estirón
tumble *noun.* **1.** caída, tumbo **2.** voltereta
tumble *verb.* caerse, tropezar
tumor *noun.* tumor
tune *noun.* melodía
tune *verb.* **1.** afinar **2.** sintonizar **3.** poner a punto
Tunisian *noun. adj.* tunecino
tunnel *noun.* túnel
tunnel *verb.* excavar un túnel
turbulent *adj.* turbulento
turf *noun.* césped
Turk *noun.* turco
turkey *noun.* pavo
Turkey *noun.* Turquía
Turkish *noun. adj.* turco
turmoil *noun.* caos, confusión
turn *noun.* **1.** giro **2.** vuelta **3.** curva, recodo **4.** turno **5.** número **6.** cambio

turn *verb.* **1.** girar **2.** dar media vuelta, girarse **3.** torcer **4.** doblar **5.** dirigir **6.** volver **7.** volverse **8.** convertirse **9.** enroscar, atornillar **10.** cambiar, meterse a
—**turn down** **1.** rechazar, rehusar **2.** bajar (el volumen)
—**turn inside out** volver del revés
—**turn off** apagar
—**turn on** encender, prender
—**turn out** **1.** producir **2.** expulsar, echar **3.** resultar **4.** concurrir, presentarse
—**turn over** voltear, dar la vuelta
turnover *noun.* facturación, volumen de ventas
tutor *noun.* **1.** profesor, profesor particular **2.** método
tutor *verb.* **1.** enseñar, instruir **2.** dar clases particulares
TV *abbr.* televisión
tweed *noun. adj.* tela inglesa de lana de Escocia
twelfth *noun.* duodécimo
twelve *noun. adj.* doce
twenties *noun plural.* **1.** entre veinte y treinta **2.** los años veinte
twentieth *noun.* vigésimo
twenty *noun. adj.* veinte
twice *adv.* dos veces
twin *noun.* **1.** gemelo **2.** copia
twist *noun.* **1.** torsión, giro, vuelta **2.** trenza
twist *verb.* **1.** torcer, retorcer, dar vueltas, serpentear **2.** trenzar, entrelazar **3.** enrollar
twisted *adj.* **1.** torcido **2.** deformado, contrahecho
two *noun. adj.* dos
type *noun.* **1.** tipo **2.** carácter **3.** letra
type *verb.* mecanografiar
typical *adj.* típico
typically *adv.* típicamente
typing, typewriting *noun.* mecanografía

U

ugly *adj.* **1.** feo **2.** desagradable
ulcer *noun.* úlcera
ultimate *adj.* último, final, postrero
ultimately *adv.* al final, finalmente
umbrella *noun.* paraguas
umpire *noun.* árbitro
umpire *verb.* arbitrar
unable *adj.* incapaz
unaffected *adj.* **1.** sencillo, natural **2.** inalterado, no afectado
unanimous *adj.* unánime
unanimously *adv.* unánimemente
unaware *adj.* ignorante, inconsciente
unbelievable *adj.* increíble
uncertain *adj.* incierto
uncle *noun.* tío
uncomfortable *adj.* incómodo, molesto
uncommon *adj.* raro, poco común
unconditional *adj.* incondicional
unconscious *noun.* inconsciente
unconscious *adj.* inconsciente
uncover *verb.* descubrir
under *prep.* **1.** debajo de **2.** bajo **3.** menor de, de menos de **4.** a las órdenes de **5.** de acuerdo con, según
under *adv.* por debajo
underestimate *verb.* subestimar
undergo *verb.* sufrir, padecer, pasar por
undergraduate *noun.* estudiante universitario no licenciado
underground *noun. adj.* subterráneo
underground *adv.* **1.** bajo tierra **2.** clandestinamente
underline *verb.* **1.** subrayar **2.** destacar
undermine *verb.* minar, socavar
underneath *prep. adv.* bajo, debajo de
underneath *noun.* parte inferior
understand *verb.* **1.** comprender, entender **2.** tener entendido
understandable *adj.* comprensible
understanding *noun.* **1.** inteligencia **2.** comprensión **3.** entendimiento **4.** acuerdo
understanding *adj.* comprensivo
undertake *verb.* **1.** emprender, acometer **2.** asumir, comprometerse a

undertaking *noun.* **1.** empresa, tarea **2.** promesa, garantía
undesirable *adj.* indeseable
undoubted *adj.* indudable
undoubtedly *adv.* indudablemente
undue *adj.* **1.** indebido **2.** excesivo
unduly *adv.* **1.** indebidamente **2.** excesivamente
uneasy *adj.* **1.** inquieto **2.** molesto
unemployed *noun plural.* desempleados, parados
unemployed *adj.* desempleado, parado, en paro
unemployment *noun.* desempleo, paro
uneven *adj.* desigual, irregular
unexpected *adj.* inesperado
unfair *adj.* injusto
unfamiliar *adj.* **1.** desconocido **2.** no familiarizado
unfold *verb.* **1.** desplegar, desdoblar **2.** revelar
unfortunate *adj.* **1.** desafortunado, desgraciado, desventurado **2.** infeliz, inoportuno
unfortunately *adv.* por desgracia, desgraciadamente, desafortunadamente
unhappy *adj.* **1.** infeliz **2.** inoportuno
unidentified *adj.* no identificado
unification *noun.* unificación
uniform *noun. adj.* uniforme
unify *verb.* unificar
union *noun.* **1.** unión **2.** sindicato
unique *adj.* único
unit *noun.* unidad
unite *verb.* **1.** unir, unificar **2.** unirse
united *adj.* unido
unity *noun.* unidad
universal *adj.* universal
universally *adv.* universalmente
universe *noun.* universo
university *noun.* universidad
unknown *adj.* desconocido
unless *conj.* a menos que, excepto
unlike *prep.* a diferencia de
unlike *adj.* diferente
unlikely *adj.* **1.** improbable **2.** insólito **3.** inverosímil

unlucky adj. 1. desafortunado 2. nefasto
unnatural adj. 1. poco normal 2. anti-natural
unnecessary adj. innecesario
unpleasant adj. desagradable
unpopular adj. impopular
unprecedented adj. sin precedente
unreasonable adj. 1. irrazonable, poco razonable 2. excesivo
unrest noun. agitación
unsatisfactory adj. insatisfactorio
until prep. conj. hasta (que)
unusual adj. 1. raro, poco común, extraño 2. excepcional
unusually adv. excepcionalmente
unveil verb. descubrir, destapar
unwilling adj. reacio, reluctante
up prep. 1. arriba de, en lo alto de 2. a lo largo de 3. hacia arriba
up verb. aumentar, elevar, subir
up adv. adj. 1. arriba 2. hacia arriba, para arriba 3. de pie 4. levantado 5. erguido 6. concluido, terminado 7. agitado, sublevado
update verb. actualizar, poner al día
upgrade noun. mejora
upgrade verb. mejorar
uphold verb. 1. apoyar 2. confirmar 3. mantener
upon prep. 1. sobre 2. al
upper noun. pala
upper adj. 1. superior 2. alto
upright adj. adv. 1. derecho, vertical 2. honrado
uprising noun. sublevación
upset verb. 1. volcar 2. desbaratar, dar al traste 3. afectar, trastornar
upset adj. 1. molesto, disgustado 2. afligido

upstairs noun. piso de arriba
upstairs adv. arriba
up-to-date adj. 1. actualizado, al día 2. actual, moderno
upward adj. hacia arriba, ascendente
uranium noun. uranio
urban adj. urbano
urge noun. impulso, deseo
urge verb. 1. instar, animar 2. insistir, recomendar
urgency noun. urgencia
urgent adj. urgente
urgently adv. urgentemente
urine noun. orina
us pron. 1. nos (direct/indirect object) 2. nosotros, nosotras (after prep)
use noun. 1. uso, utilización, empleo 2. modo de empleo 3. utilidad
use verb. 1. usar, utilizar, emplear 2. consumir, gastar
used adj. 1. utilizado, gastado 2. usado, de segunda mano
useful adj. útil
usefulness noun. utilidad
useless adj. inútil
user noun. usuario
usual adj. habitual, acostumbrado, común
usually adv. por lo general, normalmente
utility noun. 1. utilidad 2. servicio público
utilize verb. utilizar
utmost adj. extremo, mayor
utter verb. pronunciar, articular
utter adj. absoluto, total
utterly adv. completamente, totalmente
U-turn noun. cambio de sentido

V

v., vs. *abbr.* contra, versus
vacancy *noun.* 1. vacante 2. vacío
vacant *adj.* 1. libre 2. vacío
vacation *noun.* vacaciones
vaccine *noun.* vacuna
vacuum *noun.* 1. vacío 2. aspiradora
vacuum *verb.* pasar la aspiradora
vague *adj.* vago
vaguely *adv.* vagamente, un poco
vain *adj.* 1. vanidoso, presumido 2. vano, inútil
vale *noun.* valle
valid *adj.* válido
valley *noun.* valle
valuable *adj.* valioso
value *noun.* 1. valor, importancia 2. precio
value *verb.* 1. valorar 2. tasar
valued *adj.* valioso, precioso
values *noun plural.* valores
valve *noun.* 1. válvula 2. lámpara
van *noun.* camioneta
vanish *verb.* desvanecerse, desaparecer
vapor *noun.* vapor
variable *noun.* variable
variable *adj.* variable, inestable
variation *noun.* variación
varied *adj.* variado
variety *noun.* 1. variedad 2. surtido 3. (espectáculo de) variedades
various *adj.* 1. diverso, vario 2. diferente
vary *verb.* variar
vase *noun.* jarrón, florero
vast *adj.* vasto, inmenso
vat *noun.* tinaja, cuba
vegetable *noun.* 1. verdura, hortaliza 2. vegetal
vegetarian *noun.* vegetariano
vegetation *noun.* vegetación
vehicle *noun.* vehículo
veil *noun.* velo
veil *verb.* velar, cubrir con un velo
vein *noun.* vena, nervio
velocity *noun.* velocidad
velvet *noun. adj.* terciopelo
vendor *noun.* vendedor, tendero

Venezuela *noun.* Venezuela
Venezuelan *noun. adj.* Venezuela
ventilation *noun.* ventilación
venture *noun.* empresa arriesgada, aventura
venture *verb.* 1. aventurar 2. atreverse 3. arriesgar
veranda(h) *noun.* porche
verb *noun.* verbo
verbal *adj.* verbal
verdict *noun.* veredicto
verge *noun.* margen, borde
verge on *verb.* rayar en
versatile *adj.* 1. versátil, polifacético 2. flexible
verse *noun.* 1. estrofa 2. versículo 3. verso
version *noun.* versión
versus *prep.* contra
vertical *adj.* vertical
very *adj.* 1. justo, mismo 2. extremo, final 3. sólo, mero
very *adv.* 1. muy 2. completamente 3. exactamente
vessel *noun.* 1. recipiente, vasija 2. nave, buque
vest *noun.* 1. camiseta 2. chaleco
veteran *noun. adj.* veterano
veterinary *adj.* veterinario
veto *noun.* veto
veto *verb.* 1. vetar 2. prohibir
via *prep.* vía, por
vicar *noun.* 1. párroco 2. vicario
vice *noun.* vicio
vicinity *noun.* vecindad, proximidad, inmediaciones
vicious *adj.* 1. vicioso 2. cruel, malintencionado
victim *noun.* víctima
victor *noun.* vencedor, ganador
Victorian *noun. adj.* victoriano
victory *noun.* victoria
video *noun.* vídeo
video *verb.* grabar en vídeo
videotape *noun.* cinta de vídeo
videotape *verb.* grabar en vídeo

view *noun.* **1.** vista **2.** opinión, parecer
view *verb.* ver, examinar
viewer *noun.* **1.** espectador **2.** visor
viewpoint *noun.* punto de vista
vigor *noun.* vigor
vigorous *adj.* vigoroso
vigorously *adv.* vigorosamente
villa *noun.* chalet, casa de campo, villa, quinta
village *noun.* pueblo
villager *noun.* habitante del pueblo, aldeano
vine *noun.* **1.** vid **2.** parra **3.** trepadora
vinegar *noun.* vinagre
vineyard *noun.* viña, viñedo
vintage *noun.* **1.** cosecha **2.** añada
violence *noun.* violencia
violent *adj.* violento
violently *adv.* violentamente
violet *noun.* violeta
violin *noun.* violín
virgin *noun.* virgen
virtual *adj.* virtual
virtually *adv.* prácticamente
virtue *noun.* virtud
virus *noun.* virus
virus *adj.* vírico
visa *noun.* visado
vise, vice *noun.* torno de banco
visibility *noun.* visibilidad
visible *adj.* visible
vision *noun.* **1.** visión **2.** visión (de futuro) **3.** vista
visit *noun.* visita
visit *verb.* visitar, ir a
visitor *noun.* **1.** visita **2.** turista, visitante
visual *adj.* visual

visually *adv.* visualmente
vital *adj.* vital
vitamin *noun.* vitamina
vivid *adj.* **1.** vivo, intenso **2.** despierto, activo
vividly *adv.* intensamente, vivamente
vocabulary *noun.* **1.** vocabulario **2.** léxico
vocal *adj.* **1.** vocal **2.** hablador, locuaz **3.** ruidoso
vogue *noun.* moda
voice *noun.* voz
voice *verb.* **1.** expresar **2.** sonorizar
voiced *adj.* sonoro
void *noun.* vacío
void *adj.* nulo, inválido
—**void of** vacío, carente
volcanic *adj.* volcánico
volcano *noun.* volcán
volt *noun.* voltio
voltage *noun.* voltaje
volume *noun.* volumen
voluntarily *adv.* voluntariamente
voluntary *adj.* **1.** voluntario **2.** benéfico
volunteer *noun.* voluntario
volunteer *verb.* **1.** ofrecerse voluntario **2.** ofrecer, expresar
vote *noun.* **1.** voto **2.** derecho de voto
vote *verb.* votar
voter *noun.* votante, elector
voucher *noun.* vale, bono
vow *noun.* voto, promesa
vow *verb.* jurar, prometer
voyage *noun.* viaje, travesía
voyage *verb.* viajar
vulnerability *noun.* vulnerabilidad
vulnerable *adj.* vulnerable

W

W *abbr.* vatio

wage *verb.* hacer, emprender, llevar a cabo

wage(s) *noun plural.* salario, sueldo

wagon *noun.* 1. carro 2. furgoneta

waist *noun.* 1. cintura, talle 2. parte estrecha

wait *noun.* espera

wait (for) *verb.* esperar, aguardar —**wait on** servir

waiter *noun.* camarero

wake *noun.* estela

wake *verb.* 1. despertar 2. despertarse

Wales *noun.* Gales

walk *noun.* 1. paseo, caminata 2. andares, modo de andar 3. itinerario, ruta

walk *verb.* 1. andar, caminar 2. pasear, sacar a paseo 3. ir a pie, ir caminando

walker *noun.* paseante, peatón, excursionista

wall *noun.* 1. pared 2. muro, tapia, muralla

wall *verb.* amurallar

wallet *noun.* cartera, billetera

wallpaper *noun.* 1. papel pintado 2. fondo de escritorio

wallpaper *verb.* empapelar

wander *noun.* paseo

wander *verb.* 1. pasear 2. errar, vagar

want *noun.* 1. deseo 2. pobreza, miseria 3. falta, ausencia, escasez

want *verb.* 1. querer 2. desear 3. necesitar, precisar, requerir 4. carecer de 5. faltar

wanted *adj.* se busca

war *noun.* guerra

war *verb.* guerrear

ward *noun.* 1. sala, pabellón 2. pupilo

warden *noun.* 1. director 2. alcaide

wardrobe *noun.* 1. guardarropa, ropero 2. vestuario

warehouse *noun.* almacén, depósito

warfare *noun.* guerra, arte militar

warm *verb.* 1. calentar 2. entusiasmarse (con)

warm *adj.* 1. caliente 2. tibio, templado, cálido 3. de abrigo, abrigado 4. simpático, afable

warmly *adv.* 1. calurosamente, efusivamente 2. acaloradamente 3. bien abrigado

warmth *noun.* calor

warn *verb.* advertir, avisar, prevenir

warning *noun.* 1. advertencia 2. aviso

warning *adj.* de aviso

warrant *noun.* orden judicial

warrant *verb.* justificar

warren *noun.* madriguera, conejera

warrior *noun.* guerrero

wartime *noun.* tiempo de guerra

wary *adj.* cauteloso, cauto, prudente

wash *noun.* 1. lavado 2. baño 3. colada, ropa sucia 4. chapoteo 5. capa 6. estela

wash *verb.* 1. lavar, fregar, bañar 2. lavarse 3. chapotear 4. arrastrar, llevarse

washing *noun.* 1. lavado 2. colada, ropa sucia

waste *noun.* 1. residuos 2. desperdicio, derroche 3. terreno baldío, yermo

waste *verb.* desperdiciar, malgastar, derrochar, perder

watch *noun.* 1. reloj (de pulsera) 2. vigilancia 3. guardia, vigía, centinela

watch *verb.* 1. mirar, ver 2. observar 3. vigilar, cuidar 4. esperar 5. acechar

water *noun.* agua

water *verb.* 1. regar 2. abrevar, dar de beber 3. hacerse la boca agua 4. llorar

waters *noun plural.* aguas

watt *noun.* vatio

wave *noun.* 1. ola 2. onda 3. gesto con la mano

wave *verb.* 1. ondear, agitar, blandir 2. saludar (con la mano)

wax *noun.* 1. cera 2. lacre

wax *verb.* 1. encerar 2. crecer (moon)

way *noun.* 1. camino 2. dirección 3. viaje, travesía 4. ruta, vía 5. distancia 6. manera, modo, forma 7. costumbre 8. sentido

—**way of life** modo de vida
way *adv.* muy, mucho
we *pron.* nosotros, nosotras
weak *adj.* 1. débil 2. endeble, frágil 3. aguado, diluido 4. pobre, poco convincente 5. sin gracia, soso
weaken *verb.* 1. debilitar 2. debilitarse 3. flaquear
weakness *noun.* debilidad
wealth *noun.* 1. fortuna, riqueza 2. abundancia
wealthy *adj.* rico
weapon *noun.* arma
wear *noun.* 1. ropa 2. uso 3. desgaste, deterioro
wear *verb.* 1. vestir 2. llevar, llevar puesto 3. tener, lucir 4. desgastarse 5. durar, aguantar
wearily *adv.* con cansancio
wearing *adj.* agotador, cansado, pesado
weary *verb.* 1. cansar 2. cansarse
weary *adj.* cansado, agotado
weather *noun.* tiempo, clima
weather *verb.* 1. erosionar, desgastar 2. resistir, aguantar, soportar
weave *verb.* 1. tejer, trenzar 2. tramar, crear, inventar 3. zigzaguear, serpentear
web *noun.* 1. tela 2. tejido 3. membrana interdigital
wed *verb.* casarse (con)
wedding *noun.* boda
wedge *noun.* 1. cuña 2. calza 3. porción, pedazo
wedge *verb.* 1. acuñar, meter cuñas 2. calzar
Wednesday *noun.* miércoles
weed *noun.* mala hierba
weed *verb.* escardar, desherbar
week *noun.* semana
weekend *noun.* fin de semana
weekly *noun.* semanario
weekly *adj.* semanal
weekly *adv.* semanalmente, cada semana
weep *verb.* llorar
weigh *verb.* 1. pesar 2. sopesar
weight *noun.* 1. peso 2. pesa

weight *verb.* cargar
weird *adj.* extraño, raro
welcome *noun.* bienvenida, acogida, recepción
welcome *verb.* dar la bienvenida, recibir con gusto
welcome *adj. interj.* bienvenido
welcoming *adj.* acogedor
welfare *noun.* 1. bienestar 2. asistencia social
well *interj.* 1. bueno 2. bien, pues 3. ¡vaya!, ¡anda!
well *noun.* 1. pozo 2. hueco
well *verb.* brotar
well *adj.* 1. bien 2. bien de salud
well *adv.* 1. bien 2. adecuadamente
—**as well** también
well-being *noun.* bienestar
well-known *adj.* conocido, famoso
Welsh *noun. adj.* galés
west *noun.* oeste
west *adj.* 1. oeste 2. del oeste
west *adv.* al oeste
West Indian *noun. adj.* antillano
western *noun.* western
western *adj.* del oeste
wet *noun.* 1. humedad 2. lluvia
wet *verb.* mojarse
wet *adj.* 1. mojado 2. lluvioso
whale *noun.* ballena
wharf *noun.* muelle
what *relative pron.* 1. lo que 2. el que, la que, los que, las que
what *pron. adj.* 1. qué 2. cuánto
whatever *relative adj. relative pron.* todo lo que
whatever *adj. pron.* 1. cualquier, cualquiera 2. cuanto
whatever *adj.* en absoluto
whatever *pron.* qué
whatsoever *adj.* en absoluto, para nada
wheat *noun.* trigo
wheel *noun.* 1. rueda 2. volante
wheel *verb.* 1. conducir 2. girar 3. revolotear
wheelchair *noun.* silla de ruedas
when *conj.* 1. cuando 2. si
when *adv.* cuando
whenever *adv. conj.* cuando, siempre que

where adv. relative pron. dónde
whereabouts noun. paradero
whereabouts adv. dónde
whereas conj. mientras
whereby relative pron. por lo cual
wherever relative pron. 1. dondequiera que 2. donde
wherever adv. donde sea
whether conj. si
which relative adj. relative pron. que
which adj. pron. cuál
whichever relative adj. relative pron. 1. cualquier 2. el que, la que
while, whilst conj. 1. mientras 2. aunque
while noun. rato, momento
whip noun. 1. látigo 2. azote
whip verb. 1. azotar, fustigar 2. batir, montar 3. moverse rápidamente
whisk noun. 1. sacudida, movimiento rápido 2. batidora
whisk verb. 1. llevar rápidamente 2. batir
whiskey noun. whisky
whisper noun. susurro
whisper verb. 1. susurrar, cuchichear, hablar en voz baja 2. murmurar
whistle noun. 1. silbido, pitido 2. silbato, pito
whistle verb. 1. silbar 2. pitar 3. pasar silbando
white noun. 1. blanco 2. clara (de huevo) 3. blanco de los ojos
white adj. 1. blanco 2. con leche
who relative pron. 1. que 2. el que, la que, los que, las que
who pron. quién, quiénes
whoever relative pron. quien, quienquiera que, el que
whoever pron. 1. quienquiera que, cualquiera que 2. quién
whole noun. 1. todo 2. totalidad
whole adj. entero, íntegro, todo
wholesale adj. adv. 1. al por mayor 2. en masa, indiscriminado
wholly adv. completamente
whom relative pron. 1. que, quien, quienes 2. a quien, a quienes 3. al que, a la que, a los que, a las que 4. de que
whom pron. a quién, a quiénes

whose relative adj. relative pron. cuyo, cuya, cuyos, cuyas
whose adj. pron. de quién, de quiénes
why adv. relative pron. por qué
wicked adj. malvado, cruel
wicket noun. 1. terreno 2. entrada, turno
wide adj. 1. ancho, grande 2. de largo 3. amplio, extenso 4. variado, diverso
wide adv. completamente
widely adv. ampliamente
widen verb. ensanchar, ampliar, extender
widespread adj. extendido, generalizado
widow noun. viuda
widow verb. enviudar
width noun. anchura
wife noun. esposa, mujer
wig noun. peluca
wild adj. 1. salvaje 2. bravío 3. agreste 4. furioso, borrascoso 5. loco, alocado 6. disparatado, descabellado, desorbitado 7. precipitado, impetuoso 8. colérico, frenético
wilderness noun. 1. desierto 2. monte 3. tierra virgen
wildlife noun. fauna
wildly adv. salvajemente, furiosamente, locamente
will noun. 1. voluntad, albedrío 2. testamento
will verb. 1. (expressing future) 2. querer, desear 3. (expressing willingness) 4. soler, acostumbrar (expressing habits)
willing adj. complaciente, dispuesto
willingness noun. buena voluntad
win noun. victoria
win verb. 1. ganar 2. ganarse
wind noun. 1. viento, aire 2. aliento 3. gases, flato
wind verb. 1. dejar sin aliento, cortar la respiración 2. enrollar 3. ovillar 4. serpentear, zigzaguear 5. dar cuerda
wind adj. de viento
winding adj. tortuoso
window noun. ventana, ventanilla
windy adj. de mucho viento, ventoso
wine noun. vino
wing noun. 1. ala 2. aleta 3. extremo, banda 4. escuadrón

winger *noun.* extremo
wings *noun plural.* bastidores
winner *noun.* ganador, vencedor
winning *adj.* **1.** ganador, vencedor, premiado **2.** encantador, cautivador, irresistible
winter *noun.* invierno
wipe *noun.* lavado, fregado
wipe *verb.* **1.** limpiar **2.** secar, enjugar
wire *noun. adj.* **1.** alambre, cable **2.** hilo **3.** telégrafo **4.** telegrama
wire *verb.* **1.** atar con alambre **2.** enviar un telegrama **3.** telegrafiar
wireless *noun.* radio
wisdom *noun.* sabiduría
wise *adj.* **1.** sabio **2.** sensato, juicioso
wish *noun.* deseo
—**wishes** *noun plural.* saludos, recuerdos
wish *verb.* **1.** desear **2.** querer
wit *noun.* **1.** agudeza, ingenio, chispa, gracia **2.** persona salada, chistoso, ingenioso **3.** juicio, inteligencia
witch *noun.* bruja
with *prep.* **1.** con **2.** junto con **3.** de **4.** a
withdraw *verb.* **1.** retirar **2.** retirarse
withdrawal *noun.* retirada
withdrawn *adj.* reservado, introvertido
withhold *verb.* negar, rehusar
within *prep.* dentro de
within *adv.* dentro, en el interior
without *prep.* sin
witness *noun.* testigo
witness *verb.* **1.** presenciar, ver **2.** firmar como testigo
witty *adj.* ingenioso, agudo, salado, gracioso
wolf *noun.* lobo
wolf *verb.* zampar
woman *noun.* mujer
wonder *noun.* **1.** admiración, asombro **2.** maravilla, milagro
wonder *verb.* **1.** sorprenderse, extrañarse **2.** preguntarse
wonderful *adj.* maravilloso
wonderfully *adv.* maravillosamente
woo *verb.* cortejar
wood *noun. adj.* **1.** madera **2.** palo de madera
wooden *adj.* de madera

woodland *noun.* bosque
woods *noun.* bosque
wool *noun. adj.* lana
woolen, woollen *adj.* de lana
word *noun.* **1.** palabra **2.** noticia
word *verb.* expresar
wording *noun.* redacción, expresión
work *noun.* **1.** trabajo **2.** obra
work *verb.* **1.** trabajar **2.** tener empleo **3.** funcionar **4.** dar resultados **5.** progresar, desarrollar **6.** volverse **7.** fabricar
worker *noun.* **1.** trabajador **2.** obrero
workforce *noun.* mano de obra
working class *noun.* proletariado
works *noun plural.* **1.** mecanismo **2.** obras, acciones **3.** fábrica
workshop *noun.* taller
world *noun.* **1.** mundo **2.** inmenso
worldwide *adj.* mundial, universal
worldwide *adv.* mundialmente, universalmente
worm *noun.* gusano, lombriz
worm *verb.* **1.** deslizarse, insinuarse **2.** sacar, sonsacar, ganarse la confianza de alguien
worn *adj.* desgastado, deteriorado
worried *adj.* preocupado
worry *noun.* preocupación
worry *verb.* **1.** preocupar **2.** preocuparse **3.** molestar, estorbar **4.** acosar, perseguir, atacar
worse *adj. adv.* peor
worse *pron.* lo peor
worsen *verb.* empeorar
worship *noun.* adoración, veneración
worship *verb.* **1.** adorar **2.** rendir culto
worst *adj. adv.* peor
worst *pron.* lo peor
worth *noun.* valor
worth *adj.* **1.** que vale, que tiene un valor de **2.** digno de, merecedor de, que merece la pena
worthwhile *adj.* que vale/merece la pena
worthy *noun.* prócer, dignitario
worthy *adj.* **1.** noble **2.** digno, merecedor
—**worthy of** merecedor/digno de
would *verb.* **1.** (past tense of will) **2.** (speaking of something that will, may or might happen) **3.** (politely expressing

an opinion) **4.** (expressing annoyance)
would-be *adj.* **1.** aspirante **2.** frustrado
wound *noun.* herida
wound *verb.* herir
wounded *noun plural.* heridos
wounded *adj.* herido
wrap *noun.* chal
wrap *verb.* **1.** enrollar **2.** envolver
wreck *noun.* **1.** restos **2.** ruina, cacharro **3.** naufragio
wreck *verb.* destruir, hacer pedazos, hundir
wretched *adj.* **1.** miserable **2.** maldito
wrist *noun.* muñeca
write *verb.* escribir

writer *noun.* escritor
writing *noun.* escritura
writings *noun plural.* escrito, obra escrita
written *adj.* escrito
wrong *noun.* mal
wrong *verb.* ser injusto con, juzgar, agraviar
wrong *adj.* **1.** equivocado, erróneo, incorrecto **2.** malo **3.** inadecuado, impropio, inoportuno **4.** que no va bien, que no funciona
wrong *adv.* mal, incorrectamente
wrongly *adv.* **1.** incorrectamente **2.** injustamente

X, Y, Z

xenophobe *noun.* xenófobo
xenophobia *noun.* xenofobia
xenophobic *adj.* xenófobo
X-ray *noun.* radiografía
X-ray *verb.* hacer una radiografía
yacht *noun.* yate
yard *noun.* **1.** yarda **2.** patio **3.** recinto
yarn *noun.* **1.** hilo **2.** cuento
year *noun.* año
yell *noun.* grito, alarido
yell *verb.* gritar, dar alaridos
yellow *verb.* amarillear
yellow *noun. adj.* amarillo
yen *noun.* yen
yes *interj.* sí
yesterday *noun. adv.* ayer
yet *conj.* pero, aunque
yet *adv.* todavía, aún
yield *noun.* cosecha, rendimiento
yield *verb.* **1.** ceder **2.** producir
you *pron.* **1.** tú, vosotros, vosotras, usted, ustedes (subject) **2.** se, uno (impersonal subject) **3.** te, ti, os (object) **4.** la, le, lo, los, las (direct object) **5.** le, les (indirect object)
young *noun plural.* crías
young *adj.* joven

youngster *noun.* joven
your *adj.* **1.** tu, tus **2.** vuestro, vuestra, vuestros, vuestras **3.** su, sus
yours *pron.* **1.** (el) tuyo, (la) tuya, (los) tuyos, (las) tuyas **2.** (el) suyo, (la) suya, (los) suyos, (las) suyas **3.** (el) vuestro, (la) vuestra, (los) vuestros, (las) vuestras
—yours faithfully/sincerely/truly le saluda atentamente (letters)
yourself *pron.* **1.** te, se **2.** tú mismo, usted mismo, tú misma, usted misma
yourselves *pron.* **1.** os, se **2.** vosotros mismos, ustedes mismos, vosotras mismas, ustedes mismas
youth *noun.* **1.** juventud **2.** joven
youthful *adj.* **1.** joven **2.** juvenil
yuan *noun.* yuan
Zambia *noun.* Zambia
zero *noun.* **1.** cero **2.** hora cero
Zimbabwe *noun.* Zimbabue
zinc *noun.* cinc
zipper *noun.* bragueta
zone *noun.* zona
zoo *noun.* zoo, parque zoológico
zoom *noun.* zumbido
zoom *verb.* pasar volando